Facing Violence

Facing Violence

The Path of Restorative Justice and Dialogue

Mark S. Umbreit
Betty Vos
Robert B. Coates
Katherine A. Brown

LYNNE
RIENNER
PUBLISHERS

BOULDER
LONDON

Published in the United States of America in 2010 by
Lynne Rienner Publishers, Inc.
1800 30th Street, Boulder, Colorado 80301
www.rienner.com

and in the United Kingdom by
Lynne Rienner Publishers, Inc.
3 Henrietta Street, Covent Garden, London WC2E 8LU

ISBN: 978-1-881798-45-3 (pb : alk. paper)
LC: 2004299900

First published in 2003 by Criminal Justice Press.
Reprinted here from the original edition.

Printed and bound in the United States of America

The paper used in this publication meets the requirements
of the American National Standard for Permanence of
Paper for Printed Library Materials Z39.48-1992.

5   4   3

CONTENTS

ABOUT THE AUTHORS

Mark S. Umbreit is a Professor and the founding Director of the Center for Restorative Justice & Peacemaking at the University of Minnesota, School of Social Work. He has authored five books and numerous articles in the fields of restorative justice, victim offender mediation, and peacemaking. Dr. Umbreit has conducted training seminars and lectures throughout the United States, Canada, and Europe, as well as in Japan and China. His research has included single- and multi-site studies of victim offender mediation, family group conferencing, and peacemaking circles in numerous communities in the United States, in Canada, and England.

Betty Vos, a social work practitioner for over 30 years, served as Assistant Professor of Social Work at Valparaiso University and the University of Utah before joining the Center for Restorative Justice & Peacemaking, where she is a part-time Senior Research Associate. Her recent research and publications have focused on restorative justice dialogue in bias-motivated crimes, victim offender dialogue in serious and violent crime, juvenile victim offender mediation, and peacemaking circles.

Robert B. Coates is currently part-time Senior Research Associate with the Center for Restorative Justice & Peacemaking. He has held positions of Associate Director, Harvard University Center for Criminal Justice; Associate Professor, University of Chicago School of Social Service Administration; and Professor of Social Work, University of Utah Graduate School of Social Work. Dr. Coates has also spent a dozen years serving churches as a pastor. He has authored numerous publications on deinstitutionalization, community-based services, system change, and restorative justice.

Katherine A. Brown has 19 years of experience in the mental health field within the context of the private sector and state government. At present she is a mental health administrator with the Ohio Department of Rehabilitation and Correction, where she coordinates reentry programs for seriously mentally ill offenders being released from prison and returning to the community. Prior work experiences include administrative duties for the Ohio Department of Mental Health, Director of Suicide Prevention Services, family therapist, and president of a for-profit business that provided psychological services to long-term facilities.

ACKNOWLEDGMENTS

The initiation and completion of this study could not have occurred without the valuable contributions of numerous individuals and agencies. A special thanks is offered to David Doerfler, Director of the Victim Offender Mediation/Dialogue Program in the Victim Services unit of the Texas Department of Criminal Justice during the period under study, and his successor, Eddie Mendoza, and to Karin Ho, Director of the Victim Offender Dialogue Program in the Office for Victim Services of the Ohio Department of Corrections and Rehabilitation. Their vision in designing and administering these programs and their commitment to the importance of program evaluation provided the foundation upon which this study was made possible. The active support of Raven Kazen, Director of Victim Services in the Texas Department of Criminal Justice, and Reggie Wilkinson, Director of the Ohio Department of Corrections and Rehabilitation, was also invaluable in providing broader administrative support for both the development of these programs and the importance of evaluating their effectiveness. A special thanks is also due to the staff of the programs in Texas and Ohio who helped in the ongoing coordination of receiving case referrals, reviewing program records and making interview arrangements with correctional institutions.

Research Associates Marilyn Peterson Armour and Chad Breckenridge provided valuable assistance in interviewing subjects in the Texas program and providing written analysis. The contributions of Vicki Griffin in manuscript preparation, as well as Heather Burns in offering editorial comments, were also greatly appreciated.

Funding and ongoing support for this project was made possible through a grant from the Center on Crime, Communities, & Culture of the Open Society Institute in New York.

INTRODUCTION

A young woman is murdered at a car wash. An entire family is killed by a drunk driver. The victim of a violent assault survives but spends years struggling to heal physically and emotionally. Offenders are apprehended, charged, tried, convicted and sentenced. But it is not enough. Driven by the need for some kind of face-to-face encounter with the person who has harmed them, victims and family members of victims begin placing calls, knocking on doors, talking to officials and making the urgency of their needs known. And gradually, in a number of jurisdictions around the United States, departments of correction and their victim services units have begun to respond (Office for Victims of Crime, 2000).

The earliest of these victims to seek meetings with their offenders were swimming against the tide. In the early 1980s, when they first made efforts to meet with the persons who had harmed them, victim offender mediation was in its infancy, and had rarely been attempted in cases of serious or violent crime. Moreover, victim services and victim organizations were often opposed to any action that might be construed as either helping offenders or as somehow "soft" on them.

But these victims persevered, so that by the time the present volume was written in 2002-2003, victim service units, correctional departments and other agencies in at least 15 states were at various levels of developing statewide protocols for allowing such an encounter between a victim/survivor of a severely violent crime and the offender who had harmed him or her (Umbreit et al., 2003). Program staff, too, persevered, charting new courses in unexplored terrain. They were resting on a solid foundation of victim offender mediation practice and research spanning two decades; but there was much to learn about the special needs of both victims and offenders in the aftermath of severe violence and trauma.

The present study has focused on pioneering efforts in two states: the Texas Victim Offender Mediation/Dialogue Program of the Victim Services Division of the Texas Department of Criminal Justice, and the Ohio Victim Offender Dialogue Program of the Office of Victim Services in the Ohio Department of Rehabilitation and Correction. The study was undertaken to document the experience of participants — victims, offenders, program staff and volunteers — in these new beginnings. With a sample size of 40 victims and 39 offenders, it is the largest study to date of the specialized application of victim offender mediation and dialogue in cases of serious and violent crime.

This book is primarily about telling the rich stories of courageous crime victims and offenders who have chosen to meet each other in the wake of horrific violence and suffering. It is more about bearing witness to their enormous strength, resilience, and even compassion than about offering highly sophisticated conceptual analysis or critiques of their experience. All of us on the research team found that we entered sacred territory as we interviewed these individuals and worked with their stories — sacred in the sense that listening deeply to their personal stories often opened windows into the core of their being, their struggle to find meaning and hope in the presence of an overwhelming sense of despair and suffering. These people were not simply research subjects. They were courageous individuals who opened their hearts and minds to share their stories with strangers, and in doing so they touched our souls. They taught the research team much about the meaning of suffering and the capacity of the human spirit to rise above the devastating impact of severe criminal violence, including murder.

As researchers committed to a more qualitative approach to this type of study, we had to be very mindful of always maintaining a balance between listening to and honoring their powerful stories, while also being able to develop a conceptual framework for understanding the phenomenon of victim offender dialogue across numerous cases of severe violence in multiple sites. This required an infrequently used, yet increasingly important, research skill, that of listening and understanding from both the head and the heart. In many respects, the findings that we share in this book are a result of our bearing witness to the touching of the soul of humanity in the presence of ultimate violence, if not evil. In the very place one would least expect to find such powerful healing, we witnessed again and again moving expressions of compassionate strength in the struggle of victims and offenders to gain meaning in their lives. In the words of Bernie Glassman (1998), we found that places of great suffering can also be places of great healing if we bear witness to the suffering.

The book is divided in three sections. First we set the stage by providing the conceptual framework from which this work evolved, the developing theory base which has begun to emerge from the practice of restorative justice through dialogue. We also provide a review of the numerous empirical studies that have examined victim offender mediation and dialogue in property crimes and minor assaults.

In section two we present the research study methods and findings. The four chapters reporting on each state include a selection of case studies from both victim and offender perspectives, program descriptions, and findings from the victim and offender interviews.

Finally, in section three, we present broader outcomes of the study, along with an analysis. A typology of victim offender dialogue emerged as the study enfolded. This came as a surprise to the research team, yet presents a helpful road map of how the process of dialogue can be adapted in different settings based on underlying goals. Specific implications for program development and public policy development are also presented.

The unique characteristics of the three capital cases which were part of the Texas research sample are explored in Appendix A. Appendix B reports the results of interviews with several practitioners of the "humanistic approach" to mediation in serious and violent crime.

SECTION I.
SETTING THE STAGE:
RESTORATIVE JUSTICE AND VICTIM
OFFENDER MEDIATION

We have used the two opening chapters to set the stage for the present study. Chapter 1 provides an overview of restorative justice and the emergence of its face-to-face dialogue formats, concluding with a brief history of the beginnings of applying dialogue methods in cases of serious and violent crime. Chapter 2 summarizes the foundations upon which these applications rest by providing a review of the victim offender mediation research over the last quarter of a century.

CHAPTER 1.
RESTORATIVE JUSTICE THROUGH DIALOGUE

RESTORATIVE JUSTICE

"Restorative Justice" has emerged around the globe over the last 25 years as a different way for communities to respond to the harm caused by crime. Although its contemporary development first arose in Canada in 1974 as an alternative and creative way to respond to the needs of two juveniles on probation, it is in many ways not new. As practitioners in the justice system and in the victim services movement began to build on the early "Victim Offender Reconciliation Program" model out of the Canadian experience, increasingly they accessed processes with a more ancient history — processes which are common today in Native American and other indigenous communities around the world (Wright, 1996). The Restorative Justice movement, then, is "different" only in the sense that it has until recently been an uncommon way of responding to crime in most of the Western world.

Defining Restorative Justice

Definitions of restorative justice abound. At the heart of most definitions is the conviction that the persons or entities most directly involved in a crime (individual victims, victimized communities, offenders, and families of all) are the ones who should be central in responding to the harm caused by the crime. The focus is more on repairing the harm caused to victims through holding offenders directly accountable for their behavior than on the law that was broken. These two characteristics, in particular, serve to differentiate "restorative justice" from what Zehr (1990) has called "retributive" justice, in which both offenders and victims are more likely to be passive or absent during the justice system proceedings and the focus is on the law rather than on the harm.

There are many additional elements common to most restorative justice approaches. Restorative processes pay attention not only to the harm inflicted on the direct victims of a crime, but also to the ways the crime has harmed the offender and the community (Braithwaite, 1989). Thus, there is a focus on victim healing, offender reintegration, and community restoration. The emphasis on victim healing has led many to consider restorative justice to be a victim-centered approach. Yet the focus on providing offenders an opportunity to make amends and increase their awareness of the personal consequences of their actions can equally lead to a perception that restorative justice is offender-focused. It is the third emphasis, community restoration, that offers a beginning solution to this tension. In some senses the most truly "restorative" outcome would be one in which the victim and the offender equally can shed the victim-offender labels and become simply members of the community in which harm has been repaired and right relationship restored.

In many instances, but certainly not always, restorative procedures include some type of face-to-face meeting between the crime victim and the offender. Often, other support persons or family members are included as well. This small-scale personal encounter further differentiates restorative processes from formal courtroom procedures. Such meetings are variously termed "victim offender mediation," "victim offender conferencing," "victim offender dialogue," "circles," or even the earlier term "victim offender reconciliation" (Coates et al., 2000). While mediation, conferencing and circles have distinctive characteristics, they share the common feature of bringing a victim and an offender together with a trained facilitator (and possibly others) to discuss the impact of the crime and work toward some kind of resolution. Conferencing was initially more likely than victim offender mediation to include family members and/or community members, but this distinction is beginning to blur in more recent practice, with the vast majority of victim offender mediation programs today including parents or other support people in the mediation session. Like conferences, circles also typically gather family and community members. They can vary from small to very large in size and are distinctive in their use of processes drawn from Native American and Canadian First Nation cultures. Often a "talking piece" is passed around the circle to designate who may speak, so that the role of anyone not holding the talking piece is to listen attentively.

In general, restorative justice programs do not replace the formal justice system, but rather work in concert with it (Umbreit and Greenwood, 1999). Restorative interventions can take place at any point in the formal justice process, including diversion, sentencing, post-adjudication, incarceration, and release of the offender back into the community. There is also much use of restorative processes in crime prevention efforts, for example through such school-based programs as the use of circles in conflict resolution, or mediation between participants in minor physical fights where formal assault charges are inappropriate (Bazemore and Umbreit, 1995).

The Impact and Scope of Restorative Justice

At the end of its first quarter-century of progress, restorative justice is having a growing impact on communities and in some instances on entire justice systems throughout North America, Europe and the South Pacific (Bazemore and Walgrave, 1999). Although in most jurisdictions it is not yet a mainstream or primary approach, it is increasingly being offered as one alternative available for crime victims, offenders and communities who are interested.

Both the United Nations and the Council of Europe have begun to address restorative justice issues. Meeting in 2000, the United Nations Congress on Crime Prevention considered restorative justice in its plenary sessions and developed a draft proposal for "UN Basic Principles on the Use of Restorative Justice Programmes in Criminal Matters" (United Nations, 2000). The proposed principles encourage the use of restorative justice programming by member states at all stages of the criminal justice process, underscore the voluntary nature of participation in restorative justice procedures, and recommend beginning to establish standards and safeguards for the practice of restorative justice. This proposal was adopted by the United Nations in 2002. The Council of Europe was more specifically focused on the restorative use of mediation procedures in criminal matters, and adopted a set of recommendations in 1999 to guide member states in using mediation in criminal cases (Council of Europe, Committee of Ministers, 1999).

The American Bar Association has also addressed restorative justice through the practice of victim offender mediation, its most widely used and validated practice. The ABA has played a leadership role over many years in promoting the use of mediation and other forms of alternative dispute resolution in civil court-related conflicts, yet for most of that time remained skeptical and often critical of mediation in criminal court settings. That changed in 1994 when, after a year-long study, the ABA fully endorsed the practice of victim offender mediation and dialogue (American Bar Association, 1994). The association recommended its use in courts throughout the country and also provided guidelines for its use and development.

VICTIM OFFENDER MEDIATION

A Canadian probation officer and his Mennonite colleague responded in 1974 to two youths who had vandalized 22 victims by proposing that the youths meet with each victim, assess the loss together and develop a means to repay those losses. There was no name for the process that emerged. But the success of this intervention in Kitchener Ontario quickly resulted in the formation of more formal programs across Canada, largely though the impetus of the Canadian Mennonite Central Committee (Peachey, 1989). The Christian underpinnings of this initial program response led the ensuing process to be conceptualized as one of "reconciliation," in which it was hoped the involved persons would reconcile and create or restore a positive or "right" relationship. Hence the early programs, in Canada and in the United States, called themselves "Victim Offender Reconciliation Programs," or VORP. As the movement grew across North America, additional terms were used and the movement came to be more commonly known as "Victim Offender Mediation," or VOM.

Neither term fully encompasses what takes place in the meeting between victims and offenders. Victims and victims' advocates especially have objected to the term "reconciliation," since in many instances victims have no prior relationship with the offender and do not wish to develop one or to become reconciled. The term "mediation" often implies some type of negotiation or "meeting in the middle" between disputing parties. Again, victims and victim services workers often object, since in criminal cases the victim typically has not shared in the responsibility for developing the problem and has not sought the harm inflicted. Moreover, the process that ensues when the parties are brought together in VOM does not resemble the more settlement-driven mediation processes that are appropriate for resolving mutually shared problems among community members. Rather, the process is primarily dialogue-driven, focused on sharing experiences and perspectives first, and only secondarily turning to whatever potential resolutions or agreements might evolve. The term "humanistic mediation" (Umbreit, 1997) has been employed by many in the field to describe this approach to mediation, with its primary emphasis on facilitating a dialogue.

"Restorative dialogue" and "restorative conferencing" are emerging as useful descriptive terms, with the focus on restoring a right condition rather than necessarily a right relationship. In a right condition, the involved persons have agreed to certain conditions about how they will treat one another regardless of whether they have any kind of "relationship." Authors of the present volume, and many of the program staff involved in the work reported here, have also used the term "victim-sensitive offender dialogue" (or VSOD) as a more accurate label, particularly in the serious crimes that are the focus of the present work.

Characteristics of Victim Offender Mediation

By whatever name, victim offender mediation remains the oldest, most widely disseminated and documented, and most empirically grounded expression of restorative justice. At present there are over 300 VOM programs in the United States, and at least an additional 1,100 worldwide throughout North America, Europe, the South Pacific, Japan, South Africa, and South America (Umbreit et al., 2003). In keeping with the initial impetus of the Kitchener experiment, in general these programs have focused more on juvenile crime than adult crime. In addition, whether handling juvenile or adult crime, VOM programs have also tended to limit themselves to less serious offenses such as property crimes or very minor assaults and personal crimes.

The process undertaken by most VOM programs is very similar. Trained mediators or facilitators, who may be paid staff members but are more often community volunteers, make contact with the offenders and victims who have been referred and invite their participation, which is always voluntary for the victim and most often voluntary for the offender. If both parties express interest in meeting, facilitators typically provide at least one "preparation" meeting for both the victim and the offender, in which they explore the participant's experience of the event, the nature of the harm caused, and potential avenues for repairing the harm. Victim and offender are then brought together in a meeting that usually opens with sharing the experience of the crime, and then turns to a discussion of restitution or other resolution. Often family members, support persons, and/or other community members may also be present. Facilitators remain "neutral" in the sense that they support both the victim and the offender in sharing their experience and working toward a resolution. Some programs remain in contact with participants afterwards to monitor compliance with any negotiated agreement; in other programs the referring jurisdiction retains this responsibility.

There is a growing body of empirical research on VOM worldwide, which will be reported more fully in chapter 2. Over the past two decades of research, both victims and offenders who have participated in VOM have consistently reported high levels of satisfaction with the process and with the outcome of their meetings. Some studies have found that victims reported reduced levels of fear as a result of their meetings with offenders. In some instances, offender participants have higher rates of restitution compliance than similar offenders whose restitution requirements were not mutually negotiated with victims. And there are encouraging reports of reduced offender recidivism among many VOM programs. It is becoming increasingly clear that the VOM process humanizes the criminal justice experience for both victim and offender, holds offenders directly accountable to the people they victimized, allows for more active involvement of crime victims and community members (as participants or as volunteer mediators) in the justice process, and can potentially suppress further criminal behaviors in offenders.

During the early 1980s, many questioned whether crime victims would even want to meet face-to-face with their offender. Today it is very clear, from empirical data and practical experience, that the majority of victims of property crimes and minor assaults presented with the opportunity of mediation choose to engage the process, with victim participation rates often ranging from about 60 to 70% in many programs. A statewide randomized public opinion survey in Minnesota found that 84% of citizens, including many who had been victimized by crime, indicated they would be likely to consider participating in victim offender mediation if they were the victim of a property crime (Pranis and Umbreit, 1992). A more recent statewide survey of victim service providers in Minnesota found that 91% felt that VOM was an important service to be made available to victims on a volunteer basis and that it should be offered in each judicial district of the state (Minnesota Department of Public Safety, 1996).

VOM AND VICTIMS OF SEVERE VIOLENCE

During the early development of VORP and VOM, no one foresaw that such processes might be appropriate in cases of severe violence such as serious felony assaults, vehicular homicide or murder. It was difficult if not impossible to envision in such situations any potential for repairing the harm that had been caused. Moreover, it was thought that victims of such great injury, or survivors of victims who had been killed, would not wish to have face-to-face meetings with the perpetrators of such serious harm.

However, unlike the initial impetus for VOM, which has been viewed as offender-driven because of its initial focus on the needs of offenders, the movement to expand VOM-type meetings into the domain of serious and violent crime has been victim-driven. Some victims who were unaware of VOM simply expressed dissatisfaction with the way in which they were separated from the offender during the formal justice procedures and "knew" that they needed to find some way to have a personal encounter. Others heard of VOM processes in less serious crimes and pushed existing programs to listen to their needs and offer the service. Thus, over the past decade an increasing number of victims of sexual assault and attempted homicide, and survivors of murder and vehicular homicide victims, have been requesting the opportunity to meet the offender to express the full impact of the crime upon their life, to get answers to many questions they have and to gain a greater sense of closure so that they can move on with their lives. Most often these requests occur many years after the crime occurred.

Gradually, in a range of disparate VOM programs across the United States, practitioners have found themselves being asked to bring together victims or survivors of victims of severe violence and the offenders who had been incarcerated for the crime, so that now a small but increasing number of programs and practitioners are offering this service. Most often, this is made available by highly experienced and trained mediators familiar with the basic victim offender mediation process in property crimes and minor assaults, but who have received intense advanced training in working with severe violence. These mediators typically work closely with victim services agencies.

Pioneering Efforts

The earliest known contemporary use of mediation and dialogue in severely violent crimes arose during the early 1980s in the pioneering work of the Genesee County Sheriff's Department in Batavia, New York. The work of Dennis Whitman, director of the program, stands alone as the earliest and most creative use of mediation and dialogue to serve the needs of highly traumatized victims and survivors as they chose to meet with the offender(s). The program in Genesee County serves many crime victims and offenders a year through such restorative justice interventions as community service and a wide range of victim services. While handling only a limited number of mediation/dialogue cases involving severe violence each year in this small upstate New York community, the work of Dennis Whitman and his colleagues in Genesee County represents some of the deepest and most well-integrated expressions of restorative justice at both an interpersonal and systemic change level known in the United States (Umbreit, 1989b).

Another early expression of the use of mediation and dialogue in crimes of severe violence is seen in its periodic use with victims of severe violence and incarcerated juvenile offenders in Anchorage, Alaska. The work of Donis Morris at the McLaughlin Youth Center in Anchorage (Flaten, 1996) is one of the only known examples of working with juvenile offenders in such severely violent cases.

In the mid-1980s, only a handful of such cases in scattered locations throughout the United States were provided with the opportunity for a mediated dialogue. At present, victim services units, correctional departments and other agencies in at least 15 states are at various levels of developing statewide protocols for allowing such an encounter between a victim/survivor of a severely violent crime and the offender. Texas became the first state in the U.S. to implement a statewide program in 1993. In the early phases of that program's development, there was a waiting list of more than 300 victims of severe violence — including many parents of murdered children — who requested a meeting with the offender through the Victim Offender Mediation/Dialogue Program of the Victim Services Unit, Texas Department of Criminal Justice. A growing number of victims of severe violence in Canada and Europe have also expressed interest in a mediated dialogue session with the offender. Since 1991, the Correctional Services of Canada has been supporting the development of these services through the pioneering work of Dave Gustafson, director of the Victim Offender Mediation Program of the Frasier Region Community Justice Initiatives in Langley, British Columbia (Umbreit, 2001).

The largest programs to date in the United States have been offered through victim services units of departments of corrections in several states. These developments, however, have not come about without controversy. The concept of restorative justice and victim offender mediation remains highly controversial to many in the victim rights movement, even though far more victim advocates and organizations have become active stakeholders in the restorative justice movement than in earlier years.

Characteristics of VOM in Severely Violent Crime

While the process of victim offender mediation in property crimes and minor assaults is well tested and empirically grounded, the basic model is not adequate for working with severely violent crimes. To follow it would be likely to re-victimize crime victims and even offenders. Far more advanced training of mediators and preparation of the parties is required in cases of severe violence such as sexual assault, attempted homicide, and murder.

The use of mediation and dialogue in cases of severely violent offenses has a number of distinguishing characteristics. These include the following: emotional intensity, an especially acute extreme need for a non-judgmental attitude among mediators, longer case preparation by mediators (6 to 18 months), multiple separate meetings prior to a joint session, multiple phone conversations, negotiation with correctional officials to secure access to inmates and to conduct mediation in prison, coaching of participants in the communication of intense feelings, and clarification of the boundary between mediation/dialogue and therapy.

Because of the intense nature of these cases, there are a number of clear implications for advanced training for any person who chooses to work in this area. The field of restorative justice and victim offender mediation is only beginning to come to grips with how the basic mediation model must be adapted to serve the more intense needs of parties involved in serious and violent criminal conflict. Far more extensive training of mediators is required, as is an entire new generation of written and audiovisual training resources. For example, mediators will need special knowledge and skills related to working with severely violent crimes, in addition to the normal mediation skills. Advanced training would not focus on the mechanics of negotiation/mediation. Instead, it would emphasize an experiential understanding of the painful journey of the participants. Such advanced training would need to focus on the process of facilitating a direct and frank dialogue between the parties related to the violent crime that occurred, the journey of grief being experienced by the victim and/or surviving family members, and the possibilities for some degree of closure and healing through a process of mutual aid.

From the victim perspective, it will be important for the mediator to exhibit: an understanding of the victimization experience/phases, including dealing with grief and loss (our own and others); an understanding of post-traumatic stress and its impact; and the ability to collaborate with psychotherapists.

From the offender perspective, mediators will need: a thorough understanding of the criminal justice and corrections system; an understanding of the offender and prisoner experience; the ability to relate to offenders convicted of heinous crimes in a non-judgmental manner; and the ability to negotiate with high-level correctional officials to gain access to the offender/inmate.

Humanistic Mediation

As will be seen in chapter 12, there is a substantial range of potential program responses and emphases in offering dialogue to victims and offenders in crimes of severe violence. However such programs typically share a core value base and approach to mediation that can be described as "humanistic" and which has been more fully developed by Umbreit (1997).

Humanistic mediation represents a "dialogue-driven" rather than "settlement-driven" approach to confronting conflict. It emphasizes the importance of the following elements: meeting with the parties individually and in person prior to the joint mediation session, in order to listen to their story, build rapport, explain the process and prepare them for engagement in a mediated dialogue; a non-directive style of mediation in which the parties are primarily speaking to each other with minimal intervention by the mediator; and a mediator attitude of unconditional positive regard and connectedness with all parties, while remaining impartial (e.g., not taking sides).

While the focus of the mediator's work is on the creation of a safe or even sacred place to foster direct dialogue among the parties about the emotional and material impact of the conflict, written settlement agreements often occur but are not central to the process. Humanistic mediation is a specific practice application of the broader theory of transformative mediation (Bush and Folger, 1994). It is grounded more in a paradigm of healing and peacemaking than problem solving and resolution. The telling and hearing of each other's stories about the conflict, the opportunity for maximum direct communication with each other, and the importance of honoring silence and the innate wisdom and strength of the participants, are all central to humanistic mediation practice. It is particularly important to use a humanistic style of mediation when working with crimes of severe violence since the primary issues typically involve exchanging information, expressing feelings, reconstructing the event, and for many, a search for meaning following such a devastating event in their lives.

Qualities of the mediator that are central to victim-sensitive offender dialogue through humanistic mediation include: being fully present and centered on the needs of the involved parties; feeling compassion and empathy for all the involved parties; being comfortable with silence, with ambiguity, and with intuition; maintaining a spirit of humility about one's own contribution to the healing process; and bearing witness to the enormous courage, strength and capacity of the parties to help each other, and honoring the meanings they place on the encounter.

RESEARCH ON DIALOGUE IN CRIMES OF SEVERE VIOLENCE

Victims and offenders often speak of their participation in a mediated dialogue as a powerful and transformative experience that helped them in their healing process. Parents of murdered children have expressed their sense of relief after meeting the offender/inmate and sharing their pain, as well as being able to reconstruct what actually happened and why. One such mother whose son was murdered stated, "I just needed to let him see the pain he has caused in my life and to find out why he pulled the trigger." A schoolteacher who was assaulted and nearly killed commented after meeting the young man in prison, "It helped me end this ordeal...for me, it has made a difference in my life, though this type of meeting is not for everyone." An offender/inmate who met with the mother of the man he killed stated, "It felt good to be able to bring her some relief and to express my remorse to her." A doctor whose sister was killed by a drunk driver and who was initially very skeptical about meeting the offender stated following his mediation session, "I couldn't begin to heal until I let go of my hatred...after the mediation I felt a great sense of relief...I was now ready to find enjoyment in life again."[1]

Only three previous studies of victim offender mediation in crimes of severe violence are known to have been conducted in North America. Two of these were small exploratory initiatives that each examined four case studies in the U.S. The third reported on 22 offenders and 24 victims who participated in mediation in Canada.

The first study (Umbreit, 1989b) found that offering a mediated dialogue session in four very violent cases — including a sniper shooting case — was very beneficial to the victims, offenders and community members or family members who were involved in the process. Three of these four cases (all adult offenders) were handled by a police department in upstate New York (Genesee County) that operates a comprehensive restorative justice program. The second study (Flaten, 1996) involving four cases of severely violent crime committed by juvenile offenders found very high levels of satisfaction with the process and outcomes, from both victims and offenders. The offenders were inmates in a juvenile correctional facility in Alaska.

The third study, completed in Canada (Roberts, 1995), examined the Victim Offender Mediation Project in Langley, British Columbia. This community-based Canadian program, after having pioneered the early development of victim offender mediation and reconciliation with property offenses and minor assaults many years ago, initiated in 1991 a new project to apply the mediation process in crimes of severe violence involving incarcerated inmates. Prior to initiating this project, a small study (Gustafson and Smidstra, 1989) had been conducted by the program to assess whether victims and offenders involved in severely violent crime would be interested in meeting with each other in a safe and structured manner, after intensive preparation, if such a service were available. A very high level of interest in such meetings was found.

In the study conducted by Roberts (1995), virtually all of the 22 offenders and 24 victims who participated indicated support for the program. This support was reflected in their belief that they found considerable specific and overall value in the program, felt it was ethically and professionally run, and would not hesitate to recommend it to others. The overall effects of the mediation session expressed by victims included: they had finally been heard; the offender now no longer exercised control over them; they could see the offender as a person rather than a monster; they felt more trusting in their relationships with others; they felt less fear; they weren't preoccupied with the offender any more; they felt peace; they would not feel suicidal again; and they had no more anger.

For offenders, the overall effects of a mediated dialogue with the victim included: discovering emotions; feelings of empathy; increasing awareness of the impacts of their acts; increasing self-awareness; opening their eyes to the outside world, rather than to closed institutional thinking; feeling good about having tried the process; and achieving peace of mind in knowing one has helped a former victim.

SUMMARY

The present study has arisen out of the gradual development of restorative justice in general, of victim offender mediation in particular, and of the beginning efforts to provide mediated dialogue for victims in violent crime who wish to meet with the offender who has harmed them. The following chapter provides more detailed background on what is known about victim offender mediation through the extensive research that has been conducted over the last quarter of a century.

Notes

1. Quotations are taken from cases in which the first author served as either mediator or consultant (see Umbreit, 1992).

CHAPTER 2.
VICTIM OFFENDER MEDIATION:
WHAT THE RESEARCH TELLS US

Bringing victims of serious and violent crime together with their offenders in facilitated dialogue is a process that differs in many ways from the more traditional approaches to victim offender mediation developed and utilized in less serious crime over the last 25 years. Nevertheless, the evolution of current dialogue approaches in cases of violent crime rests upon the foundation of this earlier work. And in many instances the push toward expanding VOM processes into this new domain took place because, in the face of victim requests for such services, mediators already had a strong positive base on which to build.

The present chapter serves to set the context for the work which follows by highlighting what is already known about victim offender mediation. Considerable empirical work has been done over the past 25 years or so to document the impact of victim offender mediation programs. Here, we take a look at how well this ongoing experiment with restorative justice is succeeding. We will consider characteristics of VOM, participant characteristics, participant satisfaction, fairness, restitution, diversion, recidivism and cost. A total of 50 studies of victim offender mediation in five countries were reviewed for the present chapter. An earlier version of the present summary was reported in Umbreit, Coates and Vos (2002).

CHARACTERISTICS OF VICTIM OFFENDER MEDIATION

A national survey of VOM programs in the United States (Umbreit and Greenwood, 1999) provided an overview of the types of cases typically brought to mediation. Juvenile offenders were more likely to be the primary focus of U.S. VOM programs, with 45% of programs offering services solely to juveniles, and an additional 46% serving both juveniles and adults. Only 9% of VOM programs nationwide were focused on adults alone. Among the reports reviewed for the present chapter, 49%

studied only juvenile programs, 29% studied programs serving both age groups, and 22% studied programs serving only adults.

VOM programs across the United States were most often offered by private, not-for-profit community-based agencies (43% of programs). Various elements of the justice system were responsible for another 33% of VOM programs, including probation (16%), correctional facilities (8%), prosecuting attorney's offices (4%), victims' services (3%), and police departments (2%). The remaining 23% are offered by churches or church-related agencies (Umbreit and Greenwood, 1999).

In the U.S. survey, fully two-thirds of the cases referred to VOM were misdemeanors; the remaining third were felony cases. The four most common offenses referred, in order of frequency, were vandalism, minor assaults, theft, and burglary. Together these four offenses accounted for the vast majority of referrals. The primary referral sources were probation officers, judges, and prosecutors (Umbreit and Greenwood, 1999).

Not surprisingly, the participating programs reported a wide range of points in the justice system process at which VOM occurs. Slightly over a third (34%) represent true diversion from the justice system, occurring after an offender had been apprehended but prior to any formal finding of guilt. Just under a third (28% each) occurred after adjudication but before disposition, and after disposition. A small number of programs (7%) reported that their mediations could occur at any point in the process, and the remaining 3% reported working with cases prior to any court involvement.

All of the programs in the 1999 survey (Umbreit and Greenwood, 1999) reported that participation was completely voluntary for crime victims. Voluntary offender participation was reported by 79% of the surveyed programs. Not all victims, however, have felt they had a choice. A 1996 study of VOM programs in England (Umbreit and Roberts, 1996) found that victims who participated in face-to-face mediation were more likely than victims who participated in a form of "shuttle" mediation (in which the mediator carried information back and forth between participants) to feel that they participated voluntarily. In studying juvenile VOM programs in six Oregon counties, Umbreit et al. (2001) found that 91% of the victims experienced their participation as voluntary. Offenders were even more likely than victims to report that they did not see their participation as voluntary. In the same Oregon study, nearly half of the juvenile offenders felt they had no choice.

Careful preparation of participants has been one of the hallmarks of the VOM movement. In the national survey (Umbreit and Greenwood, 1999), 78% of the programs reported that participants received at least one preparation meeting. In general, preparation "meetings" are understood to consist of personal, face-to-face contact with the participants, either by the actual mediator or by some other worker from the VOM program. In fact, such meetings sometimes are carried out via telephone. In some programs, the offenders are more likely than the victims to have received their preparation in face-to-face meetings (Umbreit et al., 2001).

In spite of such variation, preparation usually gets high marks from both offenders and victims in those studies that have evaluated participant satisfaction with their preparation. Across six empirical studies reporting percentages (Collins, 1984; Fercello and Umbreit, 1999; Roberts, 1998; Strode, 1997; Umbreit, 1995; and Umbreit et al., 2001), the proportion of victims feeling adequately prepared to meet the offender ranged from 68% to 98%. Only three studies reported offender opinions of their preparation for mediation (Fercello and Umbreit, 1999; Roberts, 1998; and Umbreit et al., 2001). Offender satisfaction with preparation ranged from 89% to 93%.

An additional study (Roberts, 1995) reported on a Canadian program working with violent crimes. This program developed an unusual and more intensive preparation component: offenders and victims were videotaped in conversation about the offense with program staff, and these videos were then shared with the other participants in the mediation. Though no percentages were given, the study reported that "both parties expressed strong satisfaction for the manner in which they were prepared." Similarly, in his exploratory study of seven violent cases that came to mediation, Flaten (1996) noted that preparation was cited as the single most important factor contributing to the success of mediation.

Who Participates and Why

Across a range of programs, participation rates by victims who have been referred to victim offender mediation vary from about 40% to 60%. A few studies have addressed the characteristics that are predictive of referred cases coming to mediation. Three studies in the U.S. (Coates et al., 2002; Gehm, 1990; and Wyrick and Costanzo, 1999) found that individuals representing a business or an institution that had been victimized by a crime were more likely to participate in VOM than individuals who were simply personally victimized; a British study (Marshall, 1990), however, found the opposite.

Two studies in the U.S. examined offender race/ethnicity as a potential factor in the likelihood of a case coming to mediation. Gehm (1990), in a study of programs in Indiana, Wisconsin and Oregon, found that victims were more likely to mediate if the offender was white. Wyrick and Costanzo (1999), however, found in California that white offenders were no more likely to reach mediation than Hispanic offenders, although they were significantly more likely to do so than offenders of other minority groups.

Seriousness of offense has yet to demonstrate any consistent pattern as a predictor of participation rates. Its impact may vary greatly by program type and focus. Gehm (1990) found that victims were more likely to participate if the offense was a misdemeanor rather than a felony. In their California sample, Wyrick and Costanzo found that property offense cases were significantly more likely to be mediated than personal offense cases. They also found that the time lapse between the crime and the referral was correlated differently with participation rates by type of offense. Specifically, longer time lapses for property cases resulted in fewer mediations, while longer time lapses in personal offenses resulted in more mediations. A recent Minnesota study found that the seriousness of the crime was positively related to the likelihood that the victim would elect to come to mediation (Coates et al., 2002).

Several studies have noted that victim willingness to participate was driven by a desire to receive restitution, to hold the offender accountable, to learn more about the "why" of the crime and to share their pain with the offender, to avoid court processing, to help the offender change behavior, or to see that the offender was adequately punished (Coates and Gehm, 1985; Perry et al., 1987; Umbreit, 1989a; Roberts, 1995; Umbreit, 1995; Niemeyer and Shichor, 1996; Strode, 1997; and Umbreit et al., 2001). In two of these studies (Coates et al., 2002; Umbreit et al., 2001), the top ranking victim reason for choosing to participate was to help the offender. Offenders choosing to participate often wanted to take direct responsibility for their own actions, to pay back the victim, to apologize for the harm they caused, and to get the whole experience behind them.

Less is known about why some persons who are referred to VOM elect not to participate. Only a handful of studies have interviewed such persons to examine their reasons for choosing not to participate. Among victims, refusals typically come from persons who (1) believed the crime to be too trivial to merit the time required, (2) feared meeting the offender, (3) wanted the offender to have a harsher punishment, or (4) felt there had been too much time delay (Coates and Gehm, 1985; Umbreit, 1995). Additional concerns expressed by occasional victims in a recent Minnesota study (Coates et al., 2002) included feeling the meeting wouldn't be safe, pressure from family or friends not to participate, and not wanting to help the offender. A mitigating factor in some programs is that restitution may already be established by a judge before a referral is made to mediation; thus, victims may perceive they have less to gain in such situations.

Even less attention has been given to offender reasons for non-participation. In one study, offenders reported that they were sometimes advised by lawyers not to participate (Schneider, 1986). And some simply didn't want "to be bothered" (Coates and Gehm, 1985).

Participant Satisfaction

Victim offender mediation proponents often speak of their efforts as ways of humanizing the justice system. Traditionally, victims were left out of the justice process. Neither victims nor offenders had opportunities to tell their stories and to be heard. The state somehow stood in for the victim, and the offender seldom noticed that his or her actions impacted real, live people. In addition, victims, too, were left with stereotypes to fill their thoughts about offenders. VOM, reformers believed, offered opportunities for both parties to come together in a controlled setting to share the pain of being victimized and to answer questions of why and how. This personalizing the consequences of crime, it was thought, would enhance satisfaction levels with the entire justice process.

The vast majority of studies reviewed for this chapter reported in some way on satisfaction of victims and offenders with victim offender mediation and its outcomes. Across program sites, types of offenders, types of victims, and cultures, high levels of participant satisfaction were found.

Before exploring the nature of this satisfaction further, it must be remembered that 40 to 60% of persons offered the opportunity to participate in VOM refused. Therefore, the voluntary nature of participating in VOM is a self-selection factor overlaying the findings reported here. Thus, the high levels of satisfaction may have something to do with the opportunity to choose. Perhaps those who are able to choose among justice options are more satisfied with their experiences.

Expression of satisfaction with VOM is consistently high for both victims and offenders across sites, cultures, and seriousness of offenses. Typically, eight or nine of ten participants report being satisfied with the process and with the resulting agreement (Davis, 1980; Coates and Gehm, 1985; Perry et al., 1987; Marshall, 1990; Umbreit, 1991; Umbreit and Coates, 1992; Warner, 1992; Roberts, 1995; Carr, 1998; Roberts, 1998; Evje and Cushman, 2000; Umbreit et al., 2001).

Even in an England-based study (Umbreit and Roberts, 1996), which yielded some of the lowest satisfaction scores among the studies reviewed, 84% of those victims engaged in face-to-face mediation were satisfied with the mediation outcome. For those individuals involved with indirect mediation, depending on shuttle mediation between parties instead of face-to-face meetings, 74% were satisfied with their experience. These findings were consistent with an earlier study based in Kettering, UK: in a small subsample of participants, 62% of individual victims and 71% of corporate victims were satisfied (Dignan, 1990). About half of the Kettering offenders responding reported being satisfied. Participants involved in face-to-face mediation were more satisfied than those who worked with a go-between.

Victims have often reported being satisfied with the opportunity to share their stories and their pain resulting from the crime event. For example, one victim stated she had wanted to "let the kid know he hurt me personally, not just the money...I felt raped" (Umbreit, 1989a). Some victims have pointed to their role in the process with satisfaction. One victim said: "we were both allowed to speak...he (mediator) didn't put words into anybody's mouth" (Umbreit, 1988). Another female victim indicated, "I felt a little better that I've a stake in punishment" (Coates and Gehm, 1985). Another indicated that "it was important to find out what happened, to hear his story, and why he did it and how" (Umbreit and Coates, 1992). Numerous victims have reported being motivated by the need for closure. Thus, one victim of violent crime indicated that prior to mediation, "I was consumed with hate and rage and was worried what I would do when he got out" (Flaten, 1996).

Of course, not all victims have been so enamored with the process. A male victim complained: "It's like being hit by a car and having to get out and help the other driver when all you were doing was minding your own business" (Coates and Gehm, 1985). A Canadian stated: "Mediation process was not satisfactory, especially the outcome. I was not repaid for damages or given compensation one year later. Offender has not been adequately dealt with. I don't feel I was properly compensated" (Umbreit, 1995).

Offenders have generally reported surprise about having positive experiences. As one youth said, "He understood the mistake I made, and I really did appreciate him for it" (Umbreit, 1991). Some reported changes: "After meeting the victim I now realize that I hurt them a lot...to understand how the victim feels makes me different" (Umbreit and Coates, 1992). One Canadian offender stated his pleasure quite succinctly: "Without mediation I would have been convicted" (Umbreit, 1995).

The following comment reflects the feelings of some offenders that victims have occasionally abused the process: "We didn't take half the stuff she said we did; she either didn't have the stuff or someone else broke in too" (Coates and Gehm, 1995).

Secondary analysis of satisfaction data from a U.S. study and a Canadian study yielded remarkably similar results (Bradshaw and Umbreit, 1998; Umbreit and Bradshaw, 1999). Using step-wise multiple regression procedures to determine those variables most associated with victim satisfaction, the authors discovered that three variables emerged to explain over 40% of the variance. In each study, the key variables associated with victim satisfaction were: (1) the victim felt good about the mediator; (2) the victim perceived the resulting restitution agreement as fair; and (3) the victim, for whatever reason, had a strong initial desire to meet the offender. The latter variable supports the notion that self-selection and choice are involved in longer-run satisfaction. These findings also underscore the important role of the mediator, and, of course, the actual outcome or agreement resulting from mediation.

These high levels of satisfaction with victim offender mediation have also translated into relatively high levels of satisfaction with the criminal justice system. Where comparison groups were studied, those victims and offenders going through mediation indicated being significantly more satisfied with the criminal justice system than those going through traditional court prosecution (Davis, 1980; Umbreit and Coates, 1992; Umbreit, 1995).

Fairness

Related to satisfaction is the question of fairness. Many studies of victim offender mediation asked participants about the fairness of the mediation process and of the resulting agreement (Davis, 1980; Collins, 1984; Coates and Gehm, 1985; Strode, 1997 Umbreit, 1988, 1989, 1991, 1995; Coates and Umbreit, 1992; Umbreit and Roberts, 1996; Evje and Cushman, 2000; Umbreit et al., 2001).

Not surprisingly, given the high levels of satisfaction, the vast majority of VOM participants (typically over 80%) across setting, cultures, and types of offenses reported believing that the process was fair to both sides and that the resulting agreement was fair. Again, these experiences led to feelings that the overall criminal justice system was fair. Where comparison groups were employed, those individuals exposed to mediation came away more likely to feel that they had been treated fairly than those going through the traditional court proceedings. For example, in a study of burglary victims in Minneapolis, Umbreit found that 80% who went through VOM indicated that they experienced the criminal justice system as fair compared with only 37% of burglary victims who did not participate in VOM (Umbreit, 1989a).

These positive satisfaction and fairness experiences have generated support for VOM as a criminal justice option. When asked, typically nine of ten participants said they would recommend a VOM program to others (Coates and Gehm, 1985; Umbreit, 1991; Evje and Cushman, 2000; Umbreit et al., 2001).

Restitution

Early on, restitution was regarded by many VOM program advocates as an important byproduct of bringing offender and victim together in a face-to-face meeting. Restitution was considered somewhat secondary to the actual meeting, in which each party had the opportunity to talk about what happened. The form of restitution or what is called reparation in some jurisdictions is quite varied, including direct compensation to the victim, offender community service or work for the victim, and sometimes unusual paybacks devised between victim and offender. Today, some jurisdictions see VOM as a promising major vehicle for achieving restitution for the victim. In this approach, the VOM meeting is necessary to establish appropriate restitution amounts and garner the commitment of the offender to honor a contract. Victims have frequently reported that while restitution was the primary motivator for them to participate in VOM, what they appreciated most about the program was the opportunity to talk with the offender (Coates and Gehm, 1985; Umbreit and Coates, 1992).

In many settings, restitution is inextricably linked with victim offender mediation. About half the studies under review looked at restitution as an outcome of mediation (e.g., Collins, 1984; Coates and Gehm, 1985, Perry et al., 1987; Umbreit, 1988; Galaway 1989; Umbreit, 1991; Umbreit and Coates, 1992; Warner, 1992; Roy, 1993; Evje and Cushman, 2000; Umbreit et al., 2001). Of those cases that reached a meeting, typically 90% or more generated agreements. Restitution of one form or another (monetary, community service, or direct service to the victim) was part of the vast majority of these contractual agreements. Looking across the studies reviewed here, it appears that approximately 80 to 90% of the contracts were reported as completed. (In some instances, the length of the contract exceeded the length of the study.)

One study was able to compare restitution completion between youth participating in VOM with a matched group who did not (Umbreit and Coates, 1992.) In that instance, 81% of participating youth completed their restitution agreements, contrasted with 57% of those not in the VOM program, a finding that was statistically significant. But in another study, comparing an Indiana county whose restitution was integrated into victim offender mediation with a Michigan county with court-imposed restitution, no difference in completion rates was found (Roy, 1993). Each was just shy of 80% completion.

A study of juvenile VORP in six California counties showed a staggering increase in the average amount of obligated restitution that was paid. In comparison to restitution paid by youths who did not participate in VOM, the increases ranged from +95% in Sonoma to +1000% in Los Angeles County (Evje and Cushman, 2000).

Diversion

Many VOM programs are nominally established to divert offenders into less costly, less time consuming, and often what are intended to be less severe sentencing options. Even though diversion is a goal lauded by many, others have expressed concern about the unintended consequence of "widening the net": that is, ushering in youth and adults to experience a sanction more severe than they would have if VOM did not exist (Coates et al., 1978; Austin and Krisberg, 1981; Binder and Geis, 1984). While much talk continues on this topic, there is a dearth of study devoted to it. Only a handful of the studies reviewed here have addressed this question.

One of the broadest studies considering the diversion question was conducted over a three-year period in Kettering, Northamptonshire, England (Dignan, 1990). Offenders participating in the VOM program were matched with similar non-participating offenders from a neighboring jurisdiction. Dignan concluded that at least 60% of the offenders participating in the Kettering program were true diversions from court prosecution. Jurisdictional comparisons also led him to conclude that there was a 13% widening the net effect — much less than local observers would have predicted.

In a Glasgow, Scotland-based agency where numbers were sufficiently large to allow random assignment of individuals between the VOM program and a comparison group going through the traditional process, it was discovered that 43% of the latter group were not prosecuted (Warner, 1992). However, most of these pled guilty and were fined. This would suggest that VOM in this instance was a more severe sanction and indeed widened the net of government control.

In a very large three-county study of mediation in North Carolina, results on diversion were mixed (Clarke et al., 1992). In two counties, mediation had no impact on diverting offenders from court. In the third county, however, the results were quite dramatic. The authors concluded: "The Henderson program's effect on trials was impressive; it may have reduced trials by as much as two-thirds."

Mediation's impact on incarceration was explored in an Indiana-Ohio study by comparing consequences for 73 youth and adults going through VOM programs and a matched sample of individuals who were processed in the traditional manner (Coates and Gehm, 1985). VOM offenders spent less time incarcerated than did their counterparts. And when incarcerated, they served county jail time rather than state time.

Recidivism

While recidivism may be best regarded as an indicator of society's overall response to juvenile and adult offenders, it is often also a traditional measure used to evaluate the long-term impact of justice programs. Accordingly, a number of studies designed to assess VOM have incorporated measures of recidivism.

Some simply report rearrest or reconviction rates for offenders going through the VOM program under study (Carr, 1998; Roberts, 1998). Since no comparison group or before/after outcomes are reported, these recidivism reports have local value, but offer very little meaning for readers unfamiliar with typical rates for that particular region.

One of the first comparative studies to report recidivism on VOM was part of a much larger research project on restitution programs (Schneider, 1986). Youth randomly assigned to a Washington, DC VOM program were less likely to have subsequent offenses resulting in referral to a juvenile or adult court (53%) than youth in a comparison probation group (63%). These youth were tracked for over 30 months. The results were statistically significant. A third group, those referred to mediation, but who refused to participate, also did better than the probation group. This group's recidivism prevalence was 55%.

The study based in Kettering, England (Dignan, 1990) compared recidivism data on the VOM offenders who went through face-to-face mediation with those who were exposed only to "shuttle mediation." The former group did somewhat better than the latter: 15.4% recidivated compared to 21.6%. As with satisfaction measures reported earlier, face-to-face mediation seems to generate better results both in the short run and in the longer run than the less personal indirect mediation.

In a study of youth participating in VOM programs in four states, youth in mediation had lower recidivism rates after a year than did a matched comparison group of youth who did not go through mediation

(Umbreit and Coates, 1992). Over all, across sites, 18% of the program youth reoffended within a one year period compared to 27% for the comparison youth, a statistically significant finding. Program youth also tended to reappear in court for less serious charges than did their comparison counterparts.

In contrast, the Elkhart and Kalamazoo county study (Roy, 1993) found little difference in recidivism between youth going through the VOM program and the court-imposed restitution program. VOM youth recidivated at a slightly higher rate, 29% to 27%. The author noted, however, that the VOM cohort included more felons than did the court imposed restitution cohort.

A study of 125 youth in a Tennessee VOM program (Nugent and Paddock, 1995) reported that these youth were significantly less likely to reoffend than a randomly selected comparison group: 19.8% to 33.1%. The VOM youth who did reoffend did so with less serious charges than their comparison counterparts.

A sizeable cohort of nearly 800 youth going through mediation in Cobb County Georgia between 1993 and 1996 was followed along with a comparison group from an earlier time period (Stone et al., 1998). No significant difference in recidivism rates was found: 34.2% was the rate among the mediated versus 36.7% among the non-mediated. The cases with the worst rates of returning to court were those where an agreement was reached but the youth violated the agreement (70%), and those where the mediation reached an impasse and the case was returned to court for a formal hearing (63%).

Wynne and Brown (1998) reported on a longstanding study of the Leeds (UK) Victim Offender Unit, which began in 1985. Of the 90 offenders who met in face-to-face mediation from 1985 to 1987, 87% had had previous convictions before mediation, but 68% had no convictions during a two year follow-up after mediation.

In another study, focused on seven varying restorative justice schemes across England, Miers et al. (2001) contended that "the only scheme that routinely involved victims (West Yorkshire) was for the most part both lower cost and more effective than the other schemes." And this same program had a "significant impact on reoffending, both in terms of the offence frequency and offence seriousness."

Stone (2000) compared youth going through Resolutions Northwest's Victim Offender Mediation Program in Multnomah County Oregon with a comparison group. Eighty percent of the youth processed through VOM did not recidivate during a one year follow-up period, while 58% of the comparison group did not reoffend during a year of follow-up.

In a Lane County, Oregon study, Nelson (2000) took a different tack. One hundred and fifty youth referred to VOM from July of 1996 to November 1998 in that county were also followed for a year after referral. Comparing their referral frequencies in the year prior to the referral to VOM with the year after, all referred youth had 65% fewer referrals to the system in the subsequent year. Juvenile referred to VOM but refusing to participate had 32% fewer referrals; youth who met with their victims had 81% fewer referrals that the preceding year; and juveniles who fully completed their agreements had 76% fewer referrals compared with 54% fewer referrals for those youth who did not complete any part of the agreement.

Recidivism data were gathered on VOM programs in two additional Oregon counties in the study conducted by Umbreit et al. (2001). These data reflect comparisons of the numbers of offenses one year before intervention with one year after. For the youth in the Deschutes County program there was a 77% overall reduction in reoffending. Similarly, for the group of juveniles going through the victim offender program in Jackson County, there was an overall 68% reduction in recidivism.

In a six-county VORP study in California conducted by Evje and Cushman (2000), one of the VORPs experienced a 46% higher rate of recidivism than its comparison group. In the other five counties, the VORP groups had from 21% to 105% less recidivism than their comparison groups.

Nugent et al. (1999) conducted a rigorous reanalysis of recidivism data reported in four studies involving 488 VOM youth and 527 non-VOM youth. Using ordinal logistical regression procedures, the authors determined that VOM youth, recidivated at a statistically significant lower rate than non-VOM youth and when the former did reoffend they did so for less serious offenses than the non-VOM youth.

Costs

The relative costs of correctional programs are difficult to assess. Several studies reviewed here addressed the issue of costs. The cost per case is obviously influenced by the number of cases handled and the amount of time devoted to each case.

The results of a detailed cost analysis in a Scottish study were mixed (Warner, 1992). In some instances, mediation was less costly than other options and in others more. Warner noted that given the "marginal scope" of these programs it remains difficult to evaluate what their cost would be if implemented on a scale large enough to impact overall program administration.

An evaluation of a large-scale VOM program in California led to the conclusions that the cost per case was reduced dramatically as the program went from being a start-up program to a viable option (Niemeyer and Shichor, 1996). The cost per case was $250.

An alternative way of considering the cost impact of VOM is to consider broader system impact. Reduction of incarceration time such as that found by Coates and Gehm (1985) can yield considerable savings to a state or county. And, reduction in the number of trials — such as in Henderson County, North Carolina, where trials were reduced by two-thirds — would have tremendous impact at the county level (Clarke et al., 1992). Further, researchers evaluating a VOM program in Cobb County, Georgia pointed out that while they did not do a cost analysis per se, time is money (Stone et al., 1998). The time required to process mediated cases was only a third of that needed for non-mediated cases.

The potential cost savings of VOM programs when they are truly employed as alternatives rather than as showcase add-ons is significant. Yet a cautionary note must continue to be heard. Like any other program option, these programs can be swamped with cases to the point that quality is compromised. And in the quest for savings there is the temptation to expand the eligibility criteria to include individuals who would not otherwise penetrate the justice system or to take on serious cases that the particular program staff are ill equipped to manage. Staff and administrators must be prepared to ask, "Cost savings at what cost?"

META-ANALYSIS

Increasingly, the field of social science is witnessing the emergence of meta-analyses. These are methods of research synthesis across a set of empirical studies. Meta-analysis will typically involve reviewing the relevant literature, including published journal articles, books and perhaps less well known research monographs. Data are extracted from these studies and are aggregated for further statistical analysis. Three such meta-analyses are reported on here.

Nugent et al. (2001) conducted a rigorous reanalysis of recidivism data reported in four previous studies involving a total sample of 1,298 juvenile offenders, 619 of whom participated in VOM and 679 who did not. Using ordinal logistical regression procedures, the authors determined that VOM youth recidivated at a statistically significant 32% lower rate than non-VOM youth, and when they did reoffend they did so for less serious offenses than the non-VOM youth.

In a forthcoming work, Nugent et al. have expanded their effort to include 14 studies to compare the prevalence rate of subsequent delinquent behavior of VOM participants with that of adolescent offenders who did not participate in VOM. This meta-analysis relied on a combined sample of 9,037 juveniles. The results "suggested that VOM participants tended to commit fewer reoffenses ... (and) tended to commit less serious reoffenses" (Nugent et al., forthcoming).

In another large meta-analysis conducted by the Canadian government, Latimer et al. (2001) reviewed studies on eight conferencing and 27 victim offender mediation programs. In order to qualify for inclusion in this analysis the study had to have: (1) evaluated a restorative justice program, defined as follows: "restorative justice is a voluntary, community-based response to criminal behavior that attempts to bring together the victim, the offender and the community in an effort to address the harm caused by the criminal behavior"; (2) used a control group or comparison group that did not participate in the restorative justice program; (3) reported on at least one of the following four outcomes — victim satisfaction, offender satisfaction, restitution compliance, and/or recidivism; and (4) provided sufficient statistical information to calculate an effect size.

Some of the major results of this analysis are:

- *Victim Satisfaction.* In all but one of the 13 restorative programs studied, victims were more satisfied than those in traditional approaches. The authors indicate that "VOM models tended to yield higher levels of victim satisfaction rates than conferencing models when compared to the non-restorative approaches." They suggest this difference may arise because conferences typically have many more participants than VOM, possibly making it more difficult for everyone to be satisfied.

- *Offender Satisfaction.* Initial analysis showed "no discernible impact" on offender satisfaction. However when an outlier program was removed, "moderate to weak positive impact on offender satisfaction" was noted.

- *Restitution.* "Offenders who participated in restorative justice programs tended to have substantially higher compliance rates than offenders exposed to other arrangements."

- *Recidivism.* "Restorative justice programs, on average, yielded reductions in recidivism compared to non-restorative approaches to criminal behavior."

The authors note that McCold and Wachtel (1998) attributed apparent differences in recidivism to the effect of self-selection bias. Latimer et al. (2001) conclude: "Notwithstanding the issue of self-selection bias, the results of this meta-analysis, at present, represent the best indicator of the effectiveness of restorative justice practices, i.e. those individuals who choose to participate in restorative justice programs find the process satisfying, tend to display lower recidivism rates and are more likely to adhere to restitution agreements."

SUMMARY

Just as interest in victim offender mediation is growing within the justice arena, so is the body of empirical knowledge collected to evaluate, shape and refine it. Involving victims, offenders and community members in sorting out possible solutions to conflicts is yielding, for the most part, positive responses from participants. The vast majority of participants find the experience satisfactory, fair and helpful. In a number of jurisdictions, rates of restitution completion have climbed. And offenders going through mediation approaches often have lower levels of offending than they did before or than compared with a similar group of offenders who did not meet with their victims.

Studies reviewed here range in rigor from exploratory to experimental random assignment designs. More questions need to be pursued and broadened, but given the empirical evidence generated over the past 25 years or so and across many countries, it seems reasonable to conclude that victim offender mediation does contribute to increased victim involvement, to offenders taking responsibility for their behaviors, and to community members participating in shaping a just response to law violation.

SECTION II.
THE RESEARCH STUDY: METHOD
AND FINDINGS

The eight chapters in Section II form the core of our report. Here we present the experience and perceptions of the victims, offenders, staff and volunteers who shared their stories with us. Chapters 3 through 6 focus on the Texas Victim Offender Mediation/Dialogue Program. In chapter 3 we offer several Texas case studies drawn from both victim and offender interviews. These are followed by a description of the Texas program in chapter 4, and the findings from the victim and offender interviews in chapters 5 and 6, respectively. Chapters 7 through 10 are devoted to the Ohio Victim Offender Dialogue Program, following a parallel format.

RESEARCH METHODOLOGY

Because of both the exploratory nature of this study and the very sensitive and emotionally intense experience of the participants in victim offender dialogue, the primary method used was qualitative. In both data collection and data analysis, special attention was given to understanding subjects in their life context and framework of meaning, rather than applying external conceptual frameworks upon them and placing them in pre-set categories.

Some quantitative data were collected as well. In addition to characteristics of cases and participants, these included the use of Likert scales to measure participants' overall satisfaction and assessment of the impact of the program. Likert scales are questions with a set of fixed responses designed to tap the respondent's level of agreement with a series of statements (Babbie, 2001).

Research Questions

The study was guided by the following research questions:

(1) Who participates in the mediation/dialogue process and why?

(2) What is involved in the actual process of victim offender mediation/dialogue?

(3) How satisfied are victims/offenders with their experience and with mediation/dialogue?

(4) What are the outcomes of mediation/dialogue for victims and offenders?

(5) What are the benefits and risks of mediation/dialogue for victims and offenders?

(6) How were the programs developed and what are the critical issues for their replication in other areas?

(7) What are the implications for restorative justice theory, based on the findings that emerged from this study?

(8) What are the implications for training and practice, based on the findings that emerged from this study?

(9) What are the policy implications for other jurisdictions considering a similar initiative?

These are significant research questions for several reasons. First, while there is increasing interest in the application of victim offender mediation to severely violent cases, there is little existing empirical research regarding the use of mediation/dialogue in these offenses. Second, while Texas and Ohio have launched the first statewide initiatives to offer mediation/dialogue to victims of severe violence, numerous other states are now beginning similar initiatives. Therefore, program evaluation of this pioneering effort is critical, particularly during its formative years. Third, examination of these research questions can lead to a greater understanding of the mediation/dialogue process and the benefits and risks for those participating in mediation of severely violent cases. Fourth, results of this study can significantly enhance the training of mediators for violent offenses and provide an empirical basis for replication of victim offender dialogue of violent offenses through other victim services units within correctional agencies and related agencies.

Sample

All victims and offenders in homicide and severely violent cases who participated in the two programs from their inception through the year

2000 were given the opportunity to be included in the study. Approximately 290 cases had been referred to the Texas program and 36 to the Ohio program at the time the study was initiated, although the number of cases resulting in a face-to-face mediation/dialogue session had been fewer than 15 at each site as of May, 1998.

The sample for this study consisted of a total of 79 interviews with victims and offenders who participated in the dialogue programs in Texas and Ohio. The Texas subsample included 20 victims/survivors and 19 adult offenders/inmates. Of the cases examined in Texas, 67% involved homicide (capital murder, murder/manslaughter, and vehicular homicide). The Ohio subsample included 20 victims/survivors and 20 adult offenders/inmates. Of the cases studied in Ohio, 57% involved homicide (murder, manslaughter, vehicular homicide). Specific characteristics of crimes and participants are detailed in each of the following chapters that address Texas victim findings, Texas offender findings, Ohio victim findings, and Ohio offender findings.

DATA COLLECTION PROCEDURES

Post-mediation interviews consisting of an interview schedule with primarily open-ended questions with minimal probes were conducted with a sample of victims (N=40) and offenders (N=39), approximately half from each site, who participated in the victim offender mediation/dialogue programs. An extensive amount of preparation is carried out individually with both victim and offender in the two programs, often over a 6-12 month period. Therefore, the post-mediation interviews of this study often occurred more than a year after subjects had entered the program and usually many years after the actual crime occurred. Given the exploratory nature of the study and the small number of cases going through the dialogue process, no comparison groups were used. Program policies, procedures, and case records were also reviewed.

Qualitative data were obtained primarily from in-person interviews with victims, offenders and mediators, and from intensive case study analysis, including some observations of videotaped mediation/dialogue sessions. Quantitative survey data were also obtained from victims, offenders, and mediators. This triangulation of types and sources of data was essential in strengthening the validity and reliability of research results in this exploratory study.

Instruments

This study employed three data collection instruments in addition to review of program documents. The post-mediation interview schedule for victims and offenders was based on instruments used in previous research regarding victim offender mediation programs (Umbreit, 1996, 1994), which were adapted to the unique characteristics and issues involved in victim offender mediation of severely violent crimes, including homicide. To establish their face validity, the instruments used in the current study were reviewed by a panel of three persons who have mediated homicides and by a parent of a murdered child who participated in mediation. The instruments were pre-tested on a small sample of participants. (Copies of the interview schedules for victim interviews and offender interviews are available on the website of the Center for Restorative Justice and Peacemaking, http://ssw.che.umn.edu/rjp.)

The in-depth qualitative interviews with victims and offenders were conversational in nature. They explored the issues raised in the research questions such as: why did you participate in mediation? how satisfied are you with the mediation experience? and what were the outcomes of the mediation and what benefits and costs did you experience from the mediation? The interviews allowed for more in-depth discussion of issues, follow-up probes and exploration of the experience and impact of a mediated dialogue of the effects of the offense. In addition, the interviews allowed the participants to tell their story in their own words. Several quantitative questions, utilizing Likert scales, were asked at the end of the interview. These questions addressed interviewees' overall assessment of the impact of their participation in the victim offender dialogue program.

Sixteen volunteer mediators and five program staff members across the two participating programs were interviewed. The mediator interviews examined the mediators' perceptions of critical issues in mediation of violent offenses including: criteria assessing the appropriateness of clients for mediation; critical issues, risks and benefits; mediator roles and interventions; and training and support needed by the mediator.

Policies, procedures, training and resource handbooks and other program documents were reviewed to gain information on the development and operation of the program. A particular emphasis was placed on examining and documenting the extensive and distinct preparation processes used with the victim and offender prior to bringing them together.

OPERATIONALIZATION OF RESEARCH QUESTIONS

Research questions were operationalized in the following manner:

(1) Who participates in mediation of violent offenses? This is defined by demographic information such as age, gender, race, and length of time from offence to mediation. Why a person chooses to participate in mediation is defined by the needs, motivations and expectations of the participants.

(2) What is involved in the actual process of victim offender mediation/dialogue? This includes description of the frequency and type of contact with participants, and identification of tasks, issues, and interventions involved in the process of mediation during the preparation, mediation and follow-up phases.

(3) How satisfied are victims and offenders with their experience with mediation/dialogue? This includes identification and evaluation of the components in the preparation and mediation process, as well as overall satisfaction with mediation.

(4) What are the outcomes of mediation/dialogue for victims and offenders? Outcomes are defined as changes in the subjective experience of the participants: e.g., less anger and grief, greater sense of closure, increased sense of accountability, and changes in attitude toward one another.

(5) What are the benefits and risks of mediation/dialogue for victims and offenders? Subject responses to these questions were coded and analyzed.

(6) What are the issues and guidelines in the development of a Victim Services Mediation/Dialogue Program? These include information about policy, procedures, and issues in development, training and implementation of the program.

The implications for restorative justice, training and practice in offering victim offender dialogue in crimes of severe violence were developed based on the research results from the programs in Texas and Ohio.

Scheduling of Data Collection

Program operation data and policies were collected and reviewed during the first three to six months of the project, along with periodic review of any subsequent policy or practice changes. Review of a number of videotapes of mediation sessions began during the fourth month of the study. Separate post-mediation interviews with victims and offenders were typically conducted by the principal investigator, senior research associate, or other research staff within six to twelve months after the mediation session.

Data Analysis

Qualitative data were obtained from interviews with victims, offenders and mediators and from intensive case study analysis including observations of several videotaped mediation/dialogue sessions. Quantitative survey data were also obtained from victims, offenders, and mediators. The data were analyzed in two ways:

(1) Descriptive statistics were applied to demographic and survey data.

(2) Qualitative summaries were prepared of themes and issues emerging in the interviews with victims, offenders and mediators.

Taken together, data obtained from these approaches allowed for cross-validation of both qualitative and quantitative data obtained from multiple sources. Confidence in the validity of the findings in this exploratory study was strengthened where similar findings emerged from different data sources.

CHAPTER 3.
TEXAS CASE STUDIES

The stories of six of the study's Texas participants are presented in five case studies in the following pages involving three participating victims and three participating offenders. In Case Study One, the perspectives of both the family member and the offender have been combined to tell the story of a murder and the subsequent dialogue. Victim perspectives of the dialogue following a vehicular homicide and a sexual assault are offered in Case Studies Two and Three. The remaining two case studies — dialogues following a rape and following another murder — are told from the offender perspective.

These five cases were selected to give an overview of the range of types of cases and experiences with mediation handled in the Texas Victim Offender Mediation/Dialogue Program. In all five case studies, names, identifying information, and some details have been changed to protect the privacy of the participants. The information presented in these case studies was obtained from interviews with the victims and the offenders.

CASE STUDY ONE: MURDER — VICTIM AND OFFENDER PERSPECTIVES

The Experience of the Event

Billie Lee Blair, divorced mother of an only child, was awakened by a phone call at 1:00 a.m. The male voice on the other end of the line opened with "Do you know a Bryan Blair?" When she responded with "yes, he's my son," the voice went on: "Somebody shot him a couple of hours ago. You'll need to come to San Antonio to pick up the body." Billie Lee lived alone in a small town some 200 miles from her son's college town. She called her best friend, who drove 50 miles and arrived by 4:00 a.m. Together they made the drive to San Antonio, and began making funeral arrangements.

Billie Lee stood up for herself at the funeral home and insisted on an uninterrupted time alone with her son's body. "It's very important, I feel, that a crime victim get that private time. I personally needed that time with Bryan, that was our time to say goodbye." Her loss was devastating, and there were times she felt suicidal. She had always taken care of Bryan and done what she was supposed to as a mother; now there was nothing more she could do for him.

But there were important things she could do for herself. So many things went wrong at the trial of her son's murderer that Billie Lee became an advocate and got involved in victim organizations. She was concerned when she heard that a mediation program for victims of violent crime was being considered. "What if you go talk to that murderer and they tell you, 'Yes, I held that gun on your son, and yes, he was afraid?' And that crime victim that's so alone can't deal with it and they go commit suicide? What if the offender goes back and hangs himself in his cell?"

And, she focused on keeping the offender, James, in prison. Every six months she was at the parole board to make sure he wouldn't be released. James was often moved from one institution to another because of his unruly behavior. Billie Lee wanted to know why they couldn't put him in a more violent prison, where somebody might kill him. She even said they could fix prison overcrowding by just giving them all a loaded gun, locking the door and letting them see who survived.

The offender, James Lewis, who was 17 at the time, tells his experience of that night's events: "I was selling drugs and had two warrants out against me...I knew right then they were lookin' for me." So he decided, "I'm gonna try and leave now, I'm not gonna stay and let the law catch me." His plan: to steal a car and flee Texas. He cruised a video arcade; upon seeing Bryan engrossed in a game, he approached him with "say, man, can I get a ride from you?" and told him his mother was sick. Bryan said yes but wanted to finish his game. While Bryan wasn't looking, James pulled his gun out, put three shells in it, and put it back under his shirt. They left together.

As James's directions began getting more and more complicated, Bryan finally protested and pulled the car to a stop, asking James to get out. "I tried to convince him to cut the engine, but he wouldn't. So I guess I was gonna try to wrestle him out of the car, but he reached up like he was gonna get a knife or a pistol or something, and I just blacked out and I turned around and pulled the trigger twice." The car, still running and in gear, crashed into a brick wall. When James regained consciousness he fled the scene, quickly wrapping the pistol in his jacket and stuffing both down a nearby sewer.

James ran home to his mother's house. "She knew I had a burglary warrant but I wasn't man enough to tell her that I just shot somebody." Within three days, police came to the home while he was still sleeping. "I woke up and rolled over and there was two detectives...they asked me my name, gave me my rights and told me to get my clothes on." They didn't tell his mother what they were taking him to jail for. At the jail, officers presented him with his pistol and his jacket, both with his fingerprints on them.

James had no idea what he was in for. He heard his victim's mother was trying to get him sentenced to death, but stated he knew she couldn't do it, "because I didn't take nothing from him." He thought he might get 10 years or 15 at the most. He was shocked when his lawyer told him the best he could get was a plea bargain for 40 years, but he took it. And he added, "I don't blame her. Somebody kills my child, I wouldn't feel too much different. In my situation, justice was served."

Introduction to Mediation and Reasons for Participating

For a long time Billie Lee was adamantly against meeting with James. She watched videos of other mediations but felt if she were to meet with James, "nothing's gonna change and I'm not gonna know any more when I leave than when I started." But as her own healing progressed, her anger abated and she began to have reasons to meet with him. She wanted him to know how she felt about her son, and she wanted to make a change in his life. As she put it, "I wanted to make such an impression on him that his life would never, ever be the same. Mine's not, Bryan's isn't, and I told him, 'When you asked Bryan for a ride, our three lives were cemented together for eternity.'"

James was approached by a mediator from the Texas Victim Offender Mediation/Dialogue Program and invited to participate in dialogue with his victim's mother. The mediator was able to bring him a videotape of Billie Lee talking about her experience: "She just explained how she felt, she is real emotional — it's not real easy." It took him a long time to decide he would be willing to meet with her, but he began the preparation process with the mediator and felt this was what changed his mind.

He didn't really think there would be any benefits for himself. He felt the only thing he could give his victim's mother was "answers to why her son was murdered," and to let her know that when he got out he wasn't going to stalk her. He wasn't even sure that telling her he was sorry would make any difference: "That's gonna change what happened to her child? That ain't gonna change nothin'."

Preparation

The preparation phase in this case lasted for over two years, largely because James was continually in trouble in the prison, was frequently in lock-down, and often had to be moved from one prison to another.

As part of her preparation, Billie Lee studied James's life in detail. She learned where he grew up, read books on the slums he had come out of, and garnered tidbits of information from every source she could find. She came to understand that he had grown up in anger and violence and had never known the kinds of things she had so carefully taught her own son. She learned that as a very young boy he had seen his older brother kill a man. And she felt that his excessive infraction record in the institution was a result of having no life skills, no way of handling any feelings. Out of all this material she carefully drafted an opening statement that she hoped would cause James to *feel* the pain he had created.

Billie Lee found the process of her preparation to be very helpful and deeply appreciated the support of her mediator throughout. She rated her evaluation of the preparation as "somewhat satisfied" because she wished she had been given more detail about the physical setting. She was shocked to discover how tiny the table was separating herself from James in the conference room – it placed her much too close to him for comfort, and she had nowhere to set all the things she had brought with her to share. She recommended that victims be given a chance to see the meeting set-up ahead of time, get a feel for it, and have the opportunity to make changes if possible.

James and the mediator met sporadically over the two-year stretch of the preparation phase. Interruptions were frequent due to his being in lock-down, but at other times they met as often as twice a month. Over time James came to trust the mediator and the process. "He told me, 'I've been doing this quite a while, and so far we never had no one attack their offender.'"

For James, the preparation process was "a healing process, it's like a therapy." He felt preparation was as good as it could have been, though he still was unprepared for how emotional both he and Billie Lee became. The most helpful thing the mediator did was bringing videos of other mediations. "I seen from my own eyes that he's not new at this, he's pretty professional."

The Mediation/Dialogue Session

The session lasted for eight hours, with small breaks and a break for lunch. Present were only Billie Lee, James, the mediator, and the camera crew.

According to Billie Lee, James had brought no opening statement. She began with hers, and shared Bryan's baby book and a large photograph of him. "I asked him if he remembered what Bryan looked like and he said, 'No.' How can you kill somebody that you don't even know?" Fairly quickly she knew she had him where she wanted him. He hung his head and began to cry — and, to her own surprise, she reached for a tissue and wiped his eyes. "I felt compassion for him — my child had those skills, my child was nurtured, this young man had no life skills at all. He was lost." Later in the interview Billie Lee described an even more surprising moment: she herself was crying, and James reached over with a tissue and wiped her tears.

Billie Lee reported that at one point in the mediation James said, "But I don't have anything to give you," and she responded, "Yes you do. You can change. You can be different. I know what your I.Q. is, you're capable of learning." And she gave him a book she had found written by someone else who had grown up in the same ghetto and succeeded. She described his response: "He just cradled the book in his arms, and he said, 'I ain't never had no book come to me before. You can get 'em, but I ain't never had no book.'"

Billie Lee received a lot of information from James and found it very helpful. He told her how the events of the crime unfolded and he shared Bryan's last words. And she came to understand that he didn't set out to commit murder. "He really didn't want to kill him. He got scared, he panicked. And you can't say it was an accident, because he did have a loaded gun. But I think he thought he'd just shoot Bryan in the arm."

James was surprised that Billie Lee looked almost exactly as he had remembered her from the courtroom many years earlier. He said Billie Lee explained to him all the things she'd been through: her own experience with a violent husband and then raising Bryan without a father, Bryan's life and hopes and dreams, his photograph, and all his baby pictures. When James was asked how this affected him, he responded, "There's no way I can sit here and try to describe the feeling, it was so emotional, I looked into her eyes and I couldn't say nothing, for about ten minutes."

James reported that when he told Billie Lee that his own mother had advised him against doing the mediation, she was concerned that he had gone against what his mother said. He responded, "My mother got five kids, all her boys in prison. You only had one son, he's gone forever. She'll probably never know how you feel. That's why I disregarded what she said."

James described how Billie Lee confronted him about his prison behavior. "She said, 'You got a hundred cases, why do you have all these cases?' I explained how when I came to prison I just didn't care. But now I care." And, he told her about his own childhood, about moving from a small town to an urban ghetto as a 10 year old and getting hooked on drugs. He was stunned when she pulled out a book by someone from his own neighborhood: "She found out how it is livin' in the ghetto and livin' on the streets, 80% of the black families they don't have no father — she gave me this big twenty-one dollar book." She told him she wanted to help him, that she wanted him to get back in the class and get his G.E.D. And when she left, "She smiled, she laughed, and she said, 'James, I could go off filled with hatred —I just don't hate you no more.'"

Outcome and Evaluation

Billie Lee accomplished what she set out to do. James felt the pain she wanted him to feel — perhaps, she thinks, for the first time in his life. She was able to bring him what she had given her own son, and what she felt no one in his life had been able to do for him. And she got a commitment out of him to change. At the time of the interview, she reported James's prison infractions had completely ceased. She worried that he wasn't going as deep as he needed to but was very glad for his behavior change.

When asked to evaluate the impact of the mediation on her outlook on life, Billie Lee rated her outlook as only "somewhat" changed, because of the changes she had already undergone. In particular she felt her spiritual journey had both helped her heal and helped prepare her for her meeting with James. "I just inhale books...I began learning tolerance, not so much for Bryan's murder, as for other people. We are all the children of the world, and my spiritual belief is that the power that created us all has put us here to learn lessons."

Billie Lee was extremely pleased with her mediator's role during the session. She knew there were times when he might have wanted to jump in and was impressed that he held back and let her and James handle the process in their own way. She did report that she found it difficult to bring the session to an end, and rated her satisfaction level as "somewhat satisfied." This led her to recommend that preparation could also include thinking about a closing statement: "What would be the last words the victim would want to leave in the offender's ears?" She also found it somewhat unfair that for the preparation phase, mediators can travel to where the offenders are located to meet with them, but victims have to travel to where the mediators are. "It's not balanced."

James could hardly find words for how impactful the meeting has been in his life. "And wow, you know, wow, if I ever get my class back, I'll be helpin' a bunch of kids, so they don't follow in my footprints...she's always wanting me to help change other people's lives." Later he added, "I made a commitment. I'm not gonna mess up, I'm gonna do what she told me."

James was deeply impressed with Billie Lee: "She's the strongest woman I ever met." He has seen a video of Billie Lee's de-briefing and was very moved: "She was concerned about me, she asked the mediator, 'do you think he'll be all right?' just like I was her child." In fact, he felt she was more concerned about him than his own mother, who had made no contact for two years. "She calls up here every week."

Advice to Others

Billie Lee's words: "I'd encourage anybody to do it if it's appropriate, but not with somebody that's still going to be angry." She felt anyone who decides to meet their offender should get as fully informed about the person and the crime as possible, much in the way she did. She also encouraged participants to ask for a picture of the offender so they won't be surprised at the beginning of the session.

James thought perhaps it might depend on the crime, but in general felt offenders should participate in mediation if their victim wants to, because they never know what they can accomplish. "If you don't try to change your life in here, you're just wasting your time, and when you get out you're gonna come right back. So if you got somebody out there trying to help you, you'd be a fool not to take up on it."

CASE STUDY TWO: SEXUAL ABUSE OF A MINOR — VICTIM PERSPECTIVE

The Experience of the Event

Betsy Rodgers's seven year old daughter Cindy approached a school counselor after a presentation on "good touch/bad touch" and told the counselor that her stepfather was doing this touching to her. Police immediately contacted Betsy, who had been worried for some time about her alcoholic boyfriend Thomas's behavior in the home. Betsy was relieved to have outside support and cooperated fully, helping to arrange for Thomas to be arrested when he returned to town. When it appeared that her daughter would be required to testify in Thomas's trial, Betsy wrote Thomas a forceful letter insisting that he accept a plea bargain and spare her daughter this agony. He entered a guilty plea at the last possible moment before the trial date.

Betsy was quick to point out that her experience of the crime did not begin with her daughter's report but had been going on for some time with Thomas's active alcoholism and physical abuse toward her. "The crime was really what was happening in the months before Cindy's outcry, when I felt trapped and a shadow of what I was."

Introduction to Mediation and Reasons for Participating

Betsy participated in a number of groups for her own healing. In one of these, a panel of sex offenders met with a group of victims and family members of victims unrelated to their own crimes, and the leader of the group offered the potential for family members to meet with their own perpetrators. Her initial response was negative, but over time she came to feel two things: one, that there were some concessions she still wanted Thomas to make, and two, that she had some questions she wanted answered. She knew she could seek legal recourse for the concessions, but felt a personal process might be more fruitful. And she wanted to know how long the abuse had been going on, she wanted to hear Thomas take direct responsibility for what he had done rather than hide behind his plea bargain, and she wanted him to own the consequences of his actions.

Preparation

Betsy's preparation lasted nearly two years, in part because Thomas was moved from one prison to another and arrangements for meeting in the prison had to be started over. She found this delay to be frustrating, yet thinks the added time may have ultimately been helpful for both her and Thomas, allowing more time for feelings to be dealt with before meeting. She described her preparation process as "exceptional" and commented that it would have helped with her healing even if it had never led to an actual meeting. What she found most helpful was that "the process helped me see what I was guilty of and what I wasn't guilty of. I still feel guilty, because I knew, and I didn't know what to do. But before, I felt guilty for the *whole* thing, and now I feel guilty for the omission of what *I* didn't do, but not for what *he* did."

Betsy toured the prison the evening before her mediation and found this extremely helpful. It gave her a much more realistic picture of what prison life was like, and helped decrease her nervousness; and she felt protected and safe. She was grateful that on the day of the mediation she didn't also have to be dealing with having just walked into a prison for the first time. Safety and control were especially important for her because of her own history as a victim of Thomas's violence.

The Mediation/Dialogue Session

The dialogue meeting between Betsy and Thomas lasted about five hours. Those present included only Betsy, Thomas, the mediator, and the camera crew. Betsy was pleased about the way the room was set up. She was escorted to the room first and was already sitting at the table when Thomas was brought in, so she didn't feel anything was being "sprung" on her.

Being able to tell Thomas face to face what the impact of his actions had been was empowering for Betsy, and she felt that doing so restored some balance to the history of power and control difficulties between them. She described Thomas's initial responses as defensive and intellectualized, and reported that both she and the mediator were able to challenge him successfully at these points. Thomas's account was especially powerful because Betsy received considerable new information. The abuse had been going on much longer and was far more frequent than she had ever known. She found it very difficult to listen to these details but she was grateful for herself and for Thomas that he was honest and direct about it. Some of the concessions she had originally sought from Thomas had already been negotiated during their preparation process; the remainder were part of their affirmation agreement during the mediation and she was thankful that he agreed to all her requests.

Outcome and Evaluation

Betsy left the session with a mixture of exhaustion and relief. "I felt really validated and positive, and I felt like he took a lot more responsibility than I expected. He was more willing to work on things than I expected." She recognized that in some ways, he was working as hard on trying to heal from his problems as she had been, only with fewer resources. They were able to talk about the cycle of abuse that had existed between them, and to do so calmly, without blame or flaring tempers.

Betsy reported that her gains were both in her own healing process, and in the impact on Thomas. For herself, the meeting improved her self-awareness, particularly about how her experience with Thomas was affecting her. "You can never take all of it away, but if you're aware of it, then you can use it." She felt the impact on Thomas would ultimately contribute not only to his growth, but also to her own safety. "There's always the chance he could get out. The more help he gets towards recovery, the safer the world is. And this was a way for that."

Betsy was very satisfied with her mediator's role during the session. Mostly he was fairly quiet and left the flow of the session up to Betsy and Thomas. When he did speak, it was very helpful. He was instrumental in reaching behind Thomas's posturing to the feelings underneath. He was supportive to both of them, which she felt is what made it possible for the mediation to happen. Her only suggestion for any change in the process would be possibly to have taken more breaks in the lengthy session

Advice to Others

Betsy seemed surprised that the practice of having victims of physical abuse meet with their perpetrators could be controversial. She strongly advocated that this be an option and stressed that it can bring great benefit. "I don't feel like I was harmed at all...I think there has to be a lot of processing ahead of time, but doing it through mediation may be the exact thing that a battered woman needs to be able to feel empowered."

Betsy was quite clear that several conditions must be met for such a mediation to result in healing as opposed to revictimization. Preparation is crucial, and it must involve self-awareness, awareness of the cycle of abuse, and possibly, as in her case, experience confronting offenders other than one's own. Support and safety are equally critical. Control is essential, and arises in part out of the self-awareness. "I'm not gonna say there was not any fright in there, but I felt protected....I had control over what happened to me, and he had control over what happened to him. He could have gotten up and left. That was real important in making a closure."

It happened that one of the camerapersons filming the session was a friend of Betsy's. She found it especially helpful afterward to be able to process her reactions not only with the mediator, but also with this friend who was there and witnessed it with her. She would advise that others consider bringing support persons along; at the same time, she felt any support person either she or Thomas might have intentionally chosen would likely have been someone already heavily involved in their lives. She conjectured that each of them would have rejected outright any support person the other might have requested to have present.

CASE STUDY THREE: VEHICULAR HOMICIDE — VICTIM PERSPECTIVE

The Experience of the Event

Ramona Dominguez and her husband were accustomed to being protective of their youngest child, 15-year-old Melinda, but in their quiet neighborhood they felt comfortable giving her permission to walk two blocks to the convenience store for a candy bar in the early evening. The last time she did this, she never returned. The next morning, after the couple had turned in pictures of their missing daughter to the police station, five officers and a priest arrived to bring them the news: "A young lady last night had been struck here on our street. We both asked, 'did she make it?' And they just hung their heads and shook their heads no."

The day after the funeral Ramona and her husband went to ask the detectives "if we could set up our own search for the man that had struck and killed our daughter." The detectives shared what clues they had, and the couple went into high gear. They concluded that it was likely the driver lived nearby, since few outsiders drove the neighborhood streets. From car parts found at the scene, the make and year of the car had been identified. Ramona and her husband made the rounds of area repair shops pretending they had the same type of car and asking for quotations on the part that had been damaged in the accident. With incredible luck, a repairman said he had a quote already prepared because he had just done one.

The couple turned all their information over to the detectives, and within a matter of days the car and driver had been identified and the man had been charged. But what they hoped would provide closure instead began a new nightmare: evidence was so slim that the driver ultimately pled to "failure to render aid" and was given only a five-year sentence. As Ramona pointed out, "Now I had the pain of finding out that the judicial system truly is made for the protection of the criminal."

Ramona reported that her daughter's death had far reaching impact on other family members. Melinda's brother, 17 at the time, had been very close to his sister and became so suicidal that for the next two years either Ramona or her husband stayed home with him to keep watch. Ramona also felt that Melinda's death hastened her husband's death, putting excessive stress on a heart already compromised with congestive heart failure. He died three years after Melinda.

Introduction to Mediation and Reasons for Participating

From the beginning, Ramona wanted to meet with the driver who had struck her daughter, but her husband was opposed. Together they became active in M.A.D.D. and through this group they learned of the Texas Victim Offender Mediation/Dialogue Program. After her husband's death she felt free "to go ahead and get this done," so she contacted the program and began working with a mediator. She had two reasons for wanting to meet with the offender: to tell him she had forgiven him, and to hear him tell her he was sorry. She was sorely disappointed when it turned out the offender was unwilling to meet with her, stating he couldn't remember and was unable to place himself at the scene of the incident.

Ramona was surprised when her mediator suggested the possibility of meeting with a different offender convicted of another vehicular homicide. Yet after thinking it over she felt it might contribute to her own healing, and she also hoped it would help the offender, who she thought had a great deal of courage to face a mother he hadn't met.

Preparation

Ramona's preparation involved several two-to-three-hour meetings with her mediator over a period of nine months. She began working through the paperwork even before she learned that her actual offender would not be meeting with her. While she found the preparation to be very helpful, she rated herself as "somewhat satisfied." Her main critique was that having to write about the incident and its consequences was "extremely heavy" for victims, "because we've already gone through all the torture of the pain of the loss of a life, and of going through the judicial system." However she felt the psychological questions were very helpful because they improved self-awareness and helped bring about healing. She worked with two different mediators during the preparation phase and felt strongly supported by both of them.

The Mediation/Dialogue Session

Ramona's session with her surrogate offender lasted eight hours, with a break for lunch. Those present included two mediators, the offender, herself, and one guard. She had made a decision not to have the session videotaped, though she later wished she had a record of it.

Ramona opened with her story, and then she wanted to hear from the offender. "When he spoke, his eyes would tear up right away. He was shaken by what he had done." She asked him why he wanted to meet with her, and he told her when he heard about the program he felt in his heart that he wanted to do this, and he signed up for it. She reported that he is still hopeful he can meet with the family he had harmed, and she wished she could contact them and tell them about him and about the program.

Ramona was quite moved by the offender's grief, his remorse, his openness, and his willingness to try to do something positive. She asked him to write to his hometown newspaper to tell his story and urge other young people not to drink and drive, and to continue his education while incarcerated. She also asked him to meet with other prisoners and encourage them to meet with the persons they have harmed.

Outcome and Evaluation

"I have finally started to heal," Ramona said. Coming a number of years after her daughter's death and after meeting with an offender not at all involved in her own loss, these are powerful words. Ramona reported that the experience was life-changing: "Now I can see my future. I had no future — I wanted to die. I am starting to live my new life and my healing has been very powerful through the mediation."

She attributed her healing both to the power of sharing her story with someone who was responsible for a similar harm, and to the good she felt the session accomplished for the offender. "I could see that this young man was a true heart, so that he was going to do a lot of good in his life." At the time of the interview, she was in contact with the surrogate offender by letter. He reported to her that the female guard who was present at the mediation told him she was very impressed, and had kept in touch with him and become another support person for him.

The two mediators stayed fairly much in the background most of the day. They took notes, helped introduce questions from time to time, and "kept us in line...because in my case, I can rattle on for days and days." She felt the process and their role all went very smoothly. She rated her overall satisfaction with her participation in the program as "somewhat satisfied" and added that she will be fully satisfied when she has the opportunity to meet with her actual offender.

Advice to Others

Ramona did not have specific advice for other victims in similar situations, although she is active through M.A.D.D. and other organizations in promoting mediation/dialogue for crime victims. Her major advice was directed at the program itself: "I still believe the Mediation Program needs to have a little stronger hand. The victim should have stronger power in their rights. If I want to speak to my actual offender, I don't care if he doesn't want to look at me."

CASE STUDY FOUR: SEXUAL ASSAULT — OFFENDER PERSPECTIVE

The Experience of the Event

Carl Miller was "kinda into the party scene" at the age of 18, "experimenting with dope, drinking a lot, and kinda being a crazy kid." He had no sense of direction, didn't know how to keep a steady job, and was just living "from day to day." He does not have a clear memory of the event that changed his life and landed him in prison. "I was messed up drunk." But he can describe the bare bones of what happened that night: "I was out at the bar and ended up meeting this girl that had asked me to take her friend home, and we were drinking, and one thing led to another, and I ended up sexually assaulting her."

When police came to question him the next day, he wasn't even sure whom they were referring to, because he had been with more than one girl the previous evening. So he stonewalled them and told them nothing. But even then he was scared. "I knew I had done wrong, I knew that I might not be comin' home." Ultimately the process of finally being arrested, coming to trial, and beginning his sentence took two years. Looking back on that period of his life, during the interview he commented, "I had always tried to run from my emotions...since I was 15, I pretty well stayed drunk up until when I went to jail."

Introduction to Mediation and Reasons for Participating

Carl was nearly halfway through his 10-year sentence when a mediator from the Texas Victim Offender Mediation/Dialogue Program contacted him in the prison, told him about the program and said that his victim's mother had expressed a wish to meet with him. "I had no idea that they did anything like this. Most of the guys back there don't know they do anything like this." From the beginning he felt that it would be a good idea. Mostly he wanted to try to "make things right the best I could." He felt his victim's mother had received some misinformation about what happened, and he wanted to set her straight. And, he wanted to let her see him as person "and not some kind of monster, let her know I'm somebody who made a mistake, not Jeffrey Dahmer or somebody like that."

Preparation

Preparation in Carl's case stretched out over a total of three years, largely because of contingencies in the participating family member's situation. In addition to frequent meetings with the mediator, Carl and his victim's mother did a lot of writing that they shared back and forth. He felt having a chance to read her journals was one of the most helpful components of his preparation. Over all he was very pleased and satisfied with his preparation, which he described as "great," and he had no difficulty with the length of time it took.

The Mediation/Dialogue Session

Carl's meeting with his victim's mother lasted for about seven hours, with one lunch break and two additional breaks. The only persons present were himself, the victim's mother, the mediator, and the two camera personnel. He was nervous ahead of time and felt it was kind of like going through the trial all over again, but felt the mediator had prepared him well and had taken care of any potential risks. Carl reported that at the beginning of the session he was very conscious of the cameras in the room, but once the conversation got going he forgot the camera and crew were even there. He felt the camera staff was very professional.

He had never previously met his victim's mother; if she was at the trial, he couldn't remember. Part of what he wanted to convey to her was the impact of the crime on himself and his family, that being in prison wasn't "a cake walk." But mostly he wanted to hear what she had to say, and to learn more about who his victim was. It helped that her mother brought a photograph of her, told him about her life, and shared with him about some of the things she liked. He discovered they had more in common than he would have thought.

Outcome and Evaluation

"By the time it was through, I was able to personalize my victim, identify with her more than before and see more of the impact that my crime had on her life and her family, and to me, that's probably one of the most therapeutic aspects of it. It wasn't like 'I did this and it's over with.'" He had never been aware how great the impact was, and felt that it "hit home."

Carl reported that the meeting had a major impact on his outlook on life and will help him greatly in his goal of not reoffending. Until the meeting he had been in the habit of minimalizing his crime as "good old boy drunk behavior." He felt he received far more out of the meeting than he could ever have anticipated.

Carl felt the mediator "did a really good job." In particular, if the conversation hit a "dead spot," the mediator would help by introducing a question that Carl had wanted to ask but hadn't quite known how to say. Carl could think of nothing he would change.

Advice to Others

Carl stressed that it's really up to each individual, particularly since participation won't help with parole. "Where it helps is in the inside. A person's gonna get out of it what they put into it." But he strongly recommended it for other offenders, and suggested that they at least go through the preparation, even if they don't get to meet with their victims.

CASE STUDY FIVE: MURDER — OFFENDER PERSPECTIVE

The Experience of the Event

Nick Krueger was in his mid-30s with a vagabond lifestyle and a criminal history, including a previous conviction for murder. In his own words, "Me and two brothers were out drinking and we went broke...we were looking for a house to burglarize over in a rich neighborhood. And after two or three houses that had those alarms, I said, we'll just go up and ring the doorbell, and take their money and tie them up." They chose a house where they had just seen a car pull out, but all did not go as planned. "When I said this is a robbery, the man jumped on top of me and I shot him. I turned to run and he jumped on my back and I shot him again. I took off running and got almost to the car and looked around and he was still coming and I fired one more shot, and that is the one that killed him."

He left his two friends and skipped town but got caught trying to steal a car. While he was in jail the other two participants were arrested and gave statements implicating him in the murder. There was a series of trials; ultimately he was found guilty of murder and sentenced to life in prison. He was aware that his previous record hurt him. "In the trial they used that first murder case against me. Well, you couldn't hardly make me look any worse than I already was, I don't guess."

Introduction to Mediation and Reasons for Participating

Nick reported that he had learned about victim offender mediation through a presentation at the facility where he was incarcerated, and had kept the presenter's card and written him to say he wanted to meet his victim's family member. But the mediator wrote him back to say the victim had to initiate it and there was nothing Nick could do but wait. Eventually he was contacted by another mediator from the Texas Victim Offender Mediation/Dialogue Program to ask if he would be willing to meet with Amy Wilkins, his victim's daughter.

Nick had two major reasons for wanting to meet with Amy. He had heard that it would help her, and he wanted her to see him "as I am to-day...I think I have a lot more sense than I had back then." He also reported that she had been "real vocal" protesting any potential for his parole, but that he didn't have any problem with her protest because he would have done the same thing in her situation. "For all she knew, I was waiting to get out of here and hurt her or her family."

The only risk he reported fearing was "her walking in and shooting me." But otherwise he felt there were no dangers for him. "When you admit that you did something wrong, it's kinda hard to get tripped up on it when you tell the truth."

Preparation

Nick reported that his preparation consisted of three or four meetings over just a few months. He thought most preparations were longer but understood that Amy was anxious to have the meeting take place. Nick felt well prepared for his meeting, though he was quick to point out that "none of this was fun for me." The mediator gave him a general idea what it was all about and how the session would go. And the mediator brought information back and forth between him and Amy. In particular, the mediator suggested that Nick plan to shake hands at the beginning of the session, and Nick told him, "No. This lady hates my guts. There's no point embarrassing her." The mediator spoke with Amy and she concurred that they not shake hands.

Nick spent several fitful nights prior to the mediation going over everything in his mind. He dreamt about it and made notes to himself about what he wanted to say.

The Mediation/Dialogue Session

Nick's session lasted about seven hours. Present at the session were Nick, Amy, Amy's husband, the mediator, and two camera personnel. Nick reported that Amy's husband sat in the background and did not participate in the meeting.

After the mediator introduced them, "We sat down and she looked me in the eye and she said, 'Nick, many years ago you left some trash on my front porch and I am here to give it all back to you.'" Then for the next two hours she proceeded to tell him how his actions affected every member of her family. "It is not something someone wants to sit around and hear, but I listened to it. I was feeling pretty low. I didn't even know she had three brothers." He was especially struck by the impact on her youngest brother – the teenager leaving for a date whose car he and his friends had seen leaving. "He felt for years that if he had come back home, he could have prevented it."

When it came his turn to tell his story, he tried to convey to her that he never went there to hurt anybody. "It was just one of those things, when you're drinking, in ten seconds it wrecks your whole life." For him there was an important difference between someone who would just "lay somebody down on the floor and shoot them in the back of the head" and the crime he had committed. He knew that she thought he was a "killer" just waiting to get out and kill again, and he wanted her to know that wasn't true. At the same time he did not duck responsibility for what he had done. "I got myself into this mess. I can't blame anybody for being here but myself." He stated, "I know she is always going to hate me," but still he hoped that if he ever did make parole, she would decide he had done enough time and not fight it.

The biggest surprise for him came at the end of the meeting, when Amy reached over, shook his hand and said, "Nick, I forgive you for killing my father." He was stunned and quite moved.

Nick described his mediator's role as fairly much in the background. He was especially grateful that the mediator brought fresh fruit and cookies and set the room up comfortably. He felt the mediator did exactly what was needed and there was nothing he would change.

Outcome and Evaluation

When the meeting was over Nick felt relieved, and had the first good night's sleep in several nights. He reported that his expectations were "more than met" because he never expected her to forgive him. The most important thing he gained was a far deeper understanding of the powerful impact his actions had on Amy's entire family.

Nick did not feel the mediation itself had any life-changing impact. He reported that for him, the life changes had started several years before, when he got off death row and his first grandchild was born. He had been in lockup for bad behavior, and he determined that he didn't want his grandchild to know him as "just an old sorry SOB." In fact, he said TDCJ did him a favor when they locked him up. "It kinda got my attention." He felt it was these changes that led him to want to meet with family members of his victim.

At the time of the interview, Nick was still waiting for a chance to see the videotape of his mediation and de-brief with the mediator. He also reported that his mother was anxious to see the tape.

Advice to Others

Nick felt that, as a rule, offenders have nothing to hide and should be willing to meet their victims. He felt probably victims would get more out of the meeting in general than offenders, but thought that's the way it should be. He hoped however offenders would only meet if they had changed their attitude and were truly sorry.

CHAPTER 4.
TEXAS VICTIM OFFENDER MEDIATION/DIALOGUE PROGRAM: A STAFF AND VOLUNTEER PERSPECTIVE

The Texas Victim Offender Mediation/Dialogue Program operates as part of the Victim Services Division of the Texas Department of Criminal Justice (TDCJ). This department oversees the world's largest prison system, in addition to having responsibility for parole, probation, state jails and victim services. In the corrections world, Texas is more likely to be singled out for its use of capital punishment than for its restorative justice programming. Yet embedded in this mammoth system is a program that not only brings restorative justice services to victims across the state, but also reaches out especially to victims and survivors of violent crime by providing them the opportunity to meet directly with the offender who has harmed them within the safety of a mediated dialogue.

The history of the TDCJ Victim Offender Mediation/Dialogue Program for violent crime begins with the stories of crime victims. Three especially stand out: Nell Myers, Ellen Halbert, and Cathy Phillips. Prior to their involvement and advocacy, Texas provided virtually no state-level services to victims and accorded them no special rights.

Nell Myers's 20-year-old daughter was raped and murdered in 1979. In the aftermath of this terrible loss, she found that every place she turned for support and assistance led nowhere. Finally, in desperation she founded her own advocacy group, People Against Violent Crime, and began reaching out to other victims. Out of this work she developed the first draft of the Texas Crime Victims' Bill of Rights, a process she once described as follows: "I didn't set out to write a bill of rights. I simply took a piece of paper, drew a line down the middle, and listed the rights of victims on one side and the rights of the accused on the other. I couldn't find any rights the victim had other than to be in the place they were when victimized" (TDCJ Newsletter, April, 2000). In 1985, as a result of her activism and that of others, the Texas Crime Victims' Bill of Rights was passed into law by the Texas Legislature, and in 1991 it was incorporated into the Texas Constitution.

Among the rights newly accorded victims in the legislation were the rights to: be present at court proceedings with the judge's consent, provide a Victim Impact Statement, receive notification of court proceedings, be protected from further harm, and receive information about parole proceedings. Along with those rights came the need to provide services to victims and to fund these services.

In 1989, as part of an effort to respond to this need, the state parole board created the first Office of Victim Services and appointed Raven Kazen as its first director. As a parole and probation officer, Kazen had worked with victims seeking monetary restitution in primarily non-violent crimes. In this new position, her first duties were to work with victims whose offenders were about to be paroled. Kazen began her work in a tiny office with a single part-time assistant; her job quickly expanded as victims learned of the service and phone calls mushroomed.

The following year Texas Governor Ann Richards consolidated the parole board into the Texas Department of Criminal Justice (TDCJ) and appointed Ellen Halbert to the Board of Criminal Justice overseeing the state system. Halbert was the first crime victim ever appointed to the board. In 1986, she had been raped, beaten, repeatedly stabbed and left for dead; it took 600 stitches to repair her physical wounds. She, too, turned her horrific experience into tireless advocacy for victims' needs. Halbert's advocacy was instrumental in increasing the commitment made by the TDCJ to victims' needs.

Cathy Phillips's 21-year-old daughter was murdered in 1989; the offender was apprehended and convicted, but Cathy knew before the trial was over that she needed to speak with him face-to-face. She wanted answers that only he could supply, and she wanted him to know how special her daughter was. For two years she pursued every available avenue; finally her call reached Raven Kazen. There was no program to provide such a service and no protocols, but with Halbert's support on the TDCJ governing board, Kazen was able to bring in a trained mediator. As a result, in 1991 Cathy Phillips met with her daughter's killer for the first facilitated dialogue for a victim of a violent crime in Texas.

Within a year, Kazen had drawn up a proposal to create a statewide service offering mediated dialogue in cases of violent crime, to become known as the Victim Offender Mediation Dialogue Program, or VOM/D.

Recruitment began for a director to establish the new program, and David Doerfler was hired in December of 1993. An ordained Lutheran minister who had once been a prison guard, Doerfler had worked extensively with sex offender groups in the prison system, bringing together offenders, victims and community members within the institutions and in aftercare settings. He, too, began as a solo staff member in a small office. The first year was spent studying other jurisdictions where dialogue had been utilized in violent crimes, developing the program philosophy and protocols, and beginning the process of preparation for the first victims and offenders. Doerfler had witnessed the power of personal encounter in his previous work and was committed to the value of offering an opportunity for healing to victim and offender alike.

The new VOM/D program facilitated its first mediation in March of 1995. By November of 1996, there were 200 mediation requests from victims on file, and it was clear the program needed more mediators. In Doerfler's words, "the long waiting period was beginning to re-victimize the victims." As the sole mediator, Doerfler had the potential for facilitating at most 20 or 21 cases a year. So he quickly developed a budget proposal to expand the office staff and to begin training volunteers to facilitate mediations.

The decision to opt for volunteer mediators instead of paid professionals as the main way to deliver the service was quite purposeful on Doerfler's part. He had worked with volunteers in his previous work with sex offender groups in prisons and had respect for their potential. The core qualities essential for being a good mediator, Doerfler believed, lay more in the person's heart than in their credentials. And he had witnessed how inspiring it was for both victims and offenders that community members cared enough to volunteer their personal time as a way of reaching out. "Even if they'd given us a blank check to hire staff, I would still have gone with volunteers."

The training program was approved in the following year's budgeting process, but approval was later reversed because the TDCJ had no policy or protocols for utilizing volunteers. So the first group of volunteers did not receive training until late in 1997, made possible in part through federal funds received through VOCA (Victims of Crime Act). In August 1999, several volunteers had been assigned cases and were in the preparation phase, and the first mediations facilitated by volunteers took place later that same year.

Doerfler remained in place as director of the VOM/D program throughout the data collection phase of the present project, and all cases reported on in the present work were mediated while he was director. The program description that follows, therefore, reflects the procedures and policies in place during his tenure.

The remainder of the present chapter provides an overview of the philosophy and practices of the Texas VOM/D program. We will consider the philosophical principles that shaped the program, the selection and training of volunteers, the preparation, meeting, and follow-up phases of the work, supervision and accountability, waiting list issues, forgiveness, and self-care.

The program description information presented here was gathered through review of program documents and extensive in-person interviews with staff and volunteers during a site visit in August, 1999. Follow up telephone interviews with Doerfler and with the present director, Eddie Mendoza, were conducted in December, 2002, to gather additional information on early program history and on developments since the time of the site visit.

Given that we are exploring a human endeavor, it should not be surprising that complete agreement regarding philosophy and implementation was not always reflected in what staff and volunteers believe and feel. In some instances, tension among personnel was reflected. Yet there remained a strong commitment to the program, to each other, and to the victims and offenders whom staff and volunteers serve.

PHILOSOPHY AND PURPOSE

Philosophical principles, and even the purpose of the Texas Victim Offender Mediation/Dialogue program, are grounded in experience and sound theory and continue to evolve. There are principles regarding hoped for outcomes and there are principles that guide how staff and volunteers are to work with victims and offenders. These principles, to a very large extent, were embodied in the thinking and being of the program's first director, David Doerfler. While others certainly brought their own experiences and perspectives to the program, there is little doubt that the director was the "intellectual/inspirational glue" that defined and held the program together during the period under study.

"The purpose of the process is healing," said Doerfler. "While it is not therapy, it's very therapeutic." In his view, victims will continue to grieve the often vicious death of a loved one, may be suffering from self-worth issues, may be consumed by rage and anger, or may be dealing with a myriad of pains and problems resulting from being a victim or survivor of violent crime. Inmates, on the other hand, are also suffering. They, too, may be struggling with feelings of guilt, rage, self-worth, hopelessness, and so on.

Ideally the program "creates an opportunity for healing as it is defined by those parties participating." Staff and volunteers hope to see movement in the participant's own grieving and an indication of personal growth. The process begins with getting a handle on a participant's self-awareness; it encourages participants to take time to work on themselves; and it ends with self-awareness. As we will see, self-awareness is a key also in the selection and training of volunteers. It is an objective of the preparation phase as participants are exposed to a number of detailed questionnaires and are encouraged to keep a journal about their personal issues and experiences.

An important aspect of getting people to look at themselves — their strengths and their fears, their good and their shadow, their joy and their pain — is freeing them up to tell their own stories. Victims may feel too blocked to share rage, to express depth of pain, to recognize any part of themselves in the offender. Inmates, while acknowledging that they committed the crime, may be unable to share the story of the event which the victim desperately wants to hear, or may be unable to touch their own feelings of rage at prior abuse, or unable to put into words their own emotions regarding the pain and loss brought about by their own hands. A significant part of the work with participants is enabling, helping them free themselves so they can share their own stories, in their own words. The stories may not be beautiful, may not be what the other party wants to hear, but according to those present in the mediation the stories invariably are powerful.

A volunteer staff person stated, "This is a process in which people find their own ways and solutions to healing...We can't dictate when these things are going to happen to the people we work with, or even how they're going to happen. We can give them lots of tools, but they are really the architects of their own healing."

Doerfler commented, "We're trying to provide you the structure for you to clarify your issues, to understand your motivations, to dig as deep as you possibly can."

The emphasis upon healing and the emphasis upon participants' control over their own healing are sometimes in tension with each other. That tension is often expressed by a difference of opinion regarding empowerment. The notion of empowerment is very dear to those who have emerged through the victims' movement. As we will see when we take up the Ohio program in chapter 8, empowerment is the cornerstone of the philosophy that undergirds that effort. There, empowerment means accepting the victim and offender where they are and letting them define the purpose of the meeting. If the victim simply wants to know why his daughter was selected from the half dozen single women at the party and the inmate is willing to address the question, then that may be the focus — the beginning and the end of any meeting.

In Texas, empowerment means something rather different. "We're not just facilitators — it's much more a therapeutic model. There is no doubt about that, but I think we're empowering people that much more," claimed Doerfler. And here resides one of the tensions, likely a healthy one, among competing purposes. Does empowerment mean giving someone an opportunity for their voice to be heard, or does it mean helping the person shape that voice so it more accurately reflects who that person really is? Strong advocates for each position exist. It is probably more difficult to fully reflect the former position in a model that has healing as its focus. Healing takes time and work, time and work that a victim or an inmate may not want to take or invest.

Part of empowerment and healing is giving participants something tangible to work on, to show them that they can change, can grow, can move from their current state of being stuck. This change, growth, or movement may involve eliciting victim/offender stories. For example, a victim who wants to stay stuck in her anger at the system may be asked what the payoff is for her staying angry at the system. Pondering an answer to that question may alter her thinking. A seed will have been planted.

We will see this tension between healing and empowerment play out in a number of ways when we look more closely at the practice of preparing participants for mediation. Who decides when a victim or inmate is ready to meet? How much time is enough, or is too much?

Intertwined with these philosophies regarding purpose and outcome are those that underpin the nature of the ongoing work with victim and offender. "Process, process, process. I cannot think of a more important word, other than self-awareness, that describes what we're about," Doerfler acknowledged. And the word "process" was sprinkled freely in his conversation as well as in those conversations with other staff and volunteers. Process connotes letting things find their natural course. Staff and volunteers plant seeds, offer tools such as inventories, lend an empathic ear to victim and inmate and encourage them to take the necessary time to wend along on their own "healing journeys." No two will be alike. Each will require patience and hard work as participants face and confront the demons that continue to hold sway.

Doerfler and others chuckled as they quickly pointed out that the process that they value so much is non-linear. For example, just as no two victims or offenders are alike, neither will two training sessions be alike. Each trainer has evolved since the last session. The trainees are a different collection of persons, perhaps necessitating different emphases. Some curriculum may be tossed out and new pieces developed to reflect the dynamics and needs of a particular group.

Being flexible to adapt to a fluid process is a characteristic that staff look for in potential volunteers. Over and over in interviews with staff and volunteers one heard the phrase "trust the process."

There is no doubt that trusting the process is at the heart of how the program functions, whether the task is training a mediator, preparing a victim or offender, or mediating a face-to-face encounter. Yet it is process that Doerfler energetically taught — not so much by traditional pedagogical methods, but by doing and being. It is not so much "look at me. I'm going to demonstrate how to do..." It is much more simply a way of administering, supervising, and working cases. There is a nearly continuous mirroring or modeling of what it means to trust the process as one works with victims and offenders. The learning is as much by feel as it is by intellect. In fact, this has become a dictum of training: "we need to get them out of their heads and into their feelings." Whether one is a staff person, volunteer, victim or offender, participation means immediately becoming immersed in an all-encompassing process that will tug, sometimes gently and sometimes not so gently, at one's self-awareness.

This notion of process should become clearer as we describe the functioning of the program, but it should be noted that the research team is keenly aware that it must attempt to place a kind of linearity on the program which staff and volunteers often resisted.

Ironically, the need to describe the program, to insure that certain practice parameters are being meet by staff and volunteers, and to document outcomes, creates an internal tension within the program and among staff and volunteers. Even given the rather dynamic approach to training, the actual working of a case after training is governed by a vast array of steps and checkpoints. At times these are referred to as "options for the volunteers," but they are also clearly being used to supervise and hold the volunteer accountable to practice the principles that undergird the program. We will describe this tension more fully when we discuss supervision and accountability below.

Again, we expect that the paradoxical tension between process and structure, between linearity and non-linearity, is a healthy one that fuels the very creative nature of this program. Doerfler alluded to the magic qualities of process, that the process is bigger than any of us or all of us, that in some ways what we all have to offer other more than anything else is, simply and profoundly, presence. And yet that presence doesn't just happen. It is also shaped. As Doerfler stated, "I push feelings more than anything in all the world , and yet underneath I'm one hell of an analytical person." His self-effacing laughter following that comment likely best captures that kind of genuine presence of which he spoke and which others reported they consciously try to emulate.

SELECTION OF VOLUNTEERS

Staff persons involved in selection of volunteers agreed that it is more important to identify the right person than to pay attention to professional credentials. The volunteer needs to be someone who has handled grieving in a healthy manner, is comfortable to work with, and is empathic. Staff and volunteers often comment that while volunteers, like everyone else, have their own personal issues to work out, only one person at a time can have a crisis; volunteers cannot work their problems out at the expense of the victim or offender. Mediators ought to be able to function at a feeling level and be aware of their own capacity for being a victim or an offender.

As one staff member put it, "we are looking for people who think outside the box and who want to help people heal." These are folks who "want to make a difference and want to be on the cutting edge."

It is estimated that some two-thirds of the people who express an interest in volunteering screen themselves out. Program staff do not weed volunteers out. Volunteers often self-select. Only a few persons start the training without finishing. A few who then finish drop out because of other changes in their lives: moving to another location, taking on more job responsibilities, personal crises. Again, staff deliberately do not seek to screen out potential mediators. They would rather trust the process, letting people sort themselves out during the intense training process.

If there are questions regarding the readiness of a volunteer to work a case, there may be a much longer delay between completion of training and referral. Initially, trained volunteers waited a long time to receive a case. By the time of our site visit, this referral process was happening more quickly, most likely resulting in fewer dropping out from the trained volunteer ranks.

From a staff point of view, "people drop out because they're not ready. As long as somebody is working on his stuff, we're going to work with them. They may not be ready to take a case yet ... but we'll help them work through it."

Training

The training of volunteers takes place in two phases. The first is an intense 72 hours when a group of some 12 volunteers come together for their initial training. Evening in-service training continues after this initial time period. Twice-a-month training opportunities are offered. These will also be times for presentation and feedback on cases the volunteers are working on. Volunteers are required to attend at least six of these sessions a year.

The initial training is described by volunteers as "intense," "soul wrenching," and "a great experience." The focus of the training is helping potential volunteers deal with their own self-awareness issues. As one staff member puts it, "while there is time for in depth processing of the victim and offender experiences, we force them to look at themselves." Another says, "We require them to do the grief inventory (we use) for the victim and the offender."

Those volunteers selected must make a two-year commitment to the program in order to have time to work a case from start to finish. At least six months elapse between selection and initial training. Doerfler explained, "We want...each mediator to go through the preparation work as if a victim or an offender...they need to know up front about the extreme demands that will be put on (when working a case)." Each volunteer goes through two pre-interviews before training begins. Prior to the first session, volunteers prepare a theme on their own issues. They "will write their own life story and discuss what motivates them, what gives them strength, and where their spirituality lies." There are suggested readings before that first training session. Volunteers are encouraged to do all the assignments, such as the grief inventory, that victims and offenders are encouraged to do.

During the intensive training, volunteer mediators will often be divided into groups. Sometimes they are asked to experience things as if they were offenders. At other times, they may be asked to experience things as a victim. Each group might, for instance, be asked, "What do you need to share your deepest shame?" Participants must then talk about what it feels like from each perspective. Videos of actual mediations are presented and processed. Victims of violent crime talk with the group. Usually, the group will travel to a prison to talk with offenders. The focus of discussions afterward is on what was felt. There is a constant push to get people out of their heads, that they might "know how to go from your head to your heart and stay there."

As one staff member pointed out, "when we process, the question isn't what did you think about the trip we took to Huntsville? It's more geared to how did you feel standing in the death chamber? Or how did your stomach feel?" When the group is sitting in a circle a "sacred talking feather" may be passed from person to person, giving each participant the chance to speak without interruption. Listening to others in the circle encourages each to speak "from the gut."

In addition to the "training" of mediators, this time of sharing intensive personal experiences serves to bond the group together. "They become a support system for themselves and each other." This sense of a significant shared experience will continue to be important as mediators move from training to handling cases. Being part of a supportive group is part of self-care, which is also a topic of training.

One participant explained her experience in this way: "It's like a little miracle, you know, when you establish the safe place components and all of that. Sharing — just to see the difference in how you come in saying, 'I'm not going to share a thing. I'm just going to sit over here.' And when you finish your sharing, you just feel like one big family. I thought that was great."

While three staff persons shared training responsibilities, for the most part, it was David Doerfler leading, guiding, infusing a spirit that permeated the training experience and models, consciously or unconsciously.

Volunteer mediators who were interviewed praised highly the quality of training that they received. One expressed an interest in more role-playing.

Others wanted more time for training, but realized that with such busy schedules that wasn't very realistic. Most were surprised by the depth and intensity. While some felt inadequate going into the training, those fears were greatly reduced by what they experienced. Most noted how unlike typical training programs this one was. As one volunteer put it, "(it wasn't) just okay now you go do this with the victim and that with the offender, it's as if we were the person that David was working with at the time."

The videotapes of actual mediations were regarded by all as very worthwhile. Those who had worked with victims were particularly pleased to have had some access to offenders; the reverse was true for those who had little experience with victims. One individual reflected what others also reported as she pointed out that the most important aspect of the training was "helping us work through our own baggage; I thought that was incredibly important and helpful." Another put it this way: "A great experience for me. And I think that's the key point first. And I think that's what the training centered around — getting your thing, or your issues somewhat in place, you know, so to make sure that you don't project those. That it's not about you. It's about the victim and the offender."

In short, the volunteers not only reflected in their interviews a very positive attitude toward the training; for the most part, they also mirrored the guiding principles of victim mediation dialogue. As Doerfler proclaimed regarding training: "The process is more important than any final goal."

Surely, the following mediator comment underscores the point: "The way this training is, at least the way I received it, there was a 'day one,' but there hasn't been a last day yet."

Preparation

In order to understand and appreciate victim offender-sensitive dialogue as practiced in Texas, one must have a grasp of how staff and volunteers see the mediation meeting. The entire process from the point of being assigned a case all the way through to post-mediation follow-up (which has no definitive end point) is referred to as a "continuum of care." Mediation is one point along that continuum. Although it certainly is an important juncture, "it is not necessarily the apex of the process."

According to Doerfler, and certainly documented by our own interviews with victims and offenders who have gone through the process, "a number of victims and offenders say that preparation was as important as the mediation itself...If you go in and you start asking questions, not giving them the answers, but eliciting their stories, their feelings…they walk away and say, 'gol, this the best thing that ever happened.' And it seems to me that's very significant."

During the period under study, this preparation phase was largely open-ended, depending upon the movement of the victim and offender. Determining readiness for mediation appeared to be a tricky balance between the victim's and the offender's sense of readiness and the assessment of the mediator.

Initially, a case is assigned to a volunteer mediator, preferably someone within a month or so of training. With the most recent cohort of mediators at the time of the site visit, this time frame seemed to be working better than with the first cohort. Mediators were assigned cases by the staff person in charge of case coordination. She may have presented a number of cases to the volunteer, and then the two of them worked together to come up with the best case for that volunteer.

Volunteers expressed some anxiety awaiting their first case, underscoring the importance of timely assignment and the involvement of the mediator in case selection. One volunteer put it this way: "Well actually before yesterday, I have to say, I was at times a little anxious about it (the case), waiting. Because it's been about a month since I went through the training. And I was thinking, 'Oh, I'm going to forget everything. I need to get started on this.' But I think that was just anxiety on my part. But as of yesterday, I was given some cases to look at. So with looking at them, it's real. And I'm excited."

After the case is assigned, the mediator and a staff person will go together for the first face-to-face visit with the victim and with the offender. This permits staff to know the cases much more intimately, to serve as a more informed resource for the mediator, and to be in a better position to supervise the management of the case.

Perhaps surprising to some observers, given the appearance of a laissez-faire approach and given the rhetoric of "trust the process," there are some very clearly specified steps and parameters to be followed throughout the mediation process: preparation, meeting, and follow-up. Volunteers have in their hands a "case development time line" that lays out step-by-step procedures and expectations for the first three months of contact with victim and offender. Obviously, these do not comprise some sort of lock-step procedure, since individual schedules and temperaments differ. Yet they do represent expectations of the program and the case coordinator.

In addition to the "time line," each mediator has a 114-page packet of materials available for possible use with victims and a 156-page packet of similar materials for use with offenders. These packets include inventories on grief and core beliefs, materials on thinking errors, an adaptation of the "twelve steps," drawn from addiction recovery programs, exercises for exploring feelings, opportunities for journaling (for sharing their story in various ways), readings on forgiveness, and so on.

Doerfler described these packets as toolboxes that mediators may dip into as they work with victims and offenders. The mediators will have done many of the exercises contained in the packet during their own training. "When you look at all the mountains of information that we provide for them, it's centered in the fact that we are trying to provide the ability for people to be in power, to have tools available for their personal goals, for processing their own healing."

The mediator offers a structured, safe environment, tools that may help a victim or an offender move in terms of personal growth, and a presence of support and trust. Even with all that the program provides the mediator, and all the mediator provides the victim and offender, Doerfler was certain that "if they (mediators) would spend 95% of their time building rapport, trust, safety with the victim and offender, you got it made — because it's always going to be the victim's or the offender's work."

While at the time of our interviewing the only cases that had actually reached mediation were those handled by the director, other staff and volunteers were working cases and had experience in this preparation phase. One individual reported that the "very specific parameters, very specific protocols and very specific directed interaction by the volunteer coordinator and director was a very important balance" for individual volunteer mediators, who otherwise worked quite "autonomously."

Another mediator described the early stage of preparation: "I thought, oh my God, I've got a live body. I'm trying to remember everything; they put together some fabulous resources for us. I mean that are absolutely incredible. I mean, honest to God, a step-by-step. Of course, you can step outside of that and use other resources, but you've got the basics."

The instructions at the three month point on the program time lines at the time of our site visit read, "Case Proceeds Through Prep Work As Long As Needed By Individual Victim and Offender." It was at this point, perhaps, where the tension between principles of healing and those of empowerment became most in play. "When are participants adequately prepared to meet?" or, "How do you know a victim or an offender is ready to meet?" were the most difficult questions for staff and volunteers to answer. Clearly, time was not a factor. There seemed to be a clear expectation that the minimum preparatory period would be six months, a year was more likely, and considerably more would be required in dicey cases.

"The process is to keep moving them (victim and offender); giving them more opportunity to move," Doerfler explained. "(Furthermore) one of the reasons you elongate the process (for them) is to know it is not a game." Doerfler believed that it takes time to sort out the motivations of each party and that sorting is part of what is done to assure a safe environment for the mediation. He pointed out that "there's all sorts of wonderful built in safeguards that you have if the victim says, 'I don't want to spend any more time preparing.' Our immediate answer is, which is a real one, 'the offender is not ready.'"

One staff person noted that victims "definitely want to move the process along faster." Sometimes volunteers do too. And there is at least some wondering about whether some victims simply want questions answered and others are more interested in the intense healing work.

One mediator explained readiness by describing a sense that "we're not going to get any farther. I'm getting into a place where I feel like this one is getting ripe."

Perhaps a more detailed description of a case will help bring to light some of the tension involved in these cases regarding readiness and time. The following statements were made by a mediator who had met with the offender twice and the victim three times. "I've met with her (victim) three times. It's proceeding extremely well. She wants to just get going. I've told her at this point that my current assessment, and I have to be real cautious because if you make a statement like, well, could be this fall, then well on September 22 (she'll expect to meet). I've told her at this point that I would think that if things continue to progress and in some ways my schedule being able to travel back and forth affects that, I would expect by spring, which would mean about nine or ten months which is on the low end of the amount of time. My goal for her right now is that she just wants to express to him how her son was hurt by this and she's not really...she has not really expressed a whole lot of anger and during our last meeting I sort of broached the topic. But my expectation is that we process things to the point where she is comfortable enough to express what has to be."

No doubt different answers to the question of participants' readiness to meet will be offered by different mediators, or even by the same mediator in different cases. But it does seem that while the above examples are consistent from certain healing approaches, they do draw into question empowerment issues, that is, at what point do mediators make decisions on behalf of and in the "best interests" of the participants? Clearly, these lines are gray and blurry.

MEETING

A fair number of cases drop out before reaching an actual face-to-face meeting, giving staff and mediators pause to reflect upon the importance of what they are doing and where the mediation session fits into the overall scheme of things.

The following are a series of comments regarding the meeting and its place in the overall process: "You got to come up with some words to capture the continuum of care that's going on here; it's more than a mediation meeting." "I want to find new words, new jargon, new terminology to move away from the face-to-face (meeting) being the end or be all." "So, a case resolved is a positive thing to me whether it's resolved with face-to-face mediation or whether the offender has just said, no way I'm ever going to look at that person. But they've been exposed to the material and victim has been exposed to the material and is able to start working through the healing." "I don't think the focus is on the mediation. I think the focus is entirely on working with the people, helping them work through what's happened. And if the mediation happens, that's wonderful. That's an incredible, wonderful by-product."

Volunteers were asked how they would feel if after months of work with the victim and offender one or both chose not to proceed. Some said they would be frustrated and disappointed. Others thought if that's the way it worked out then that simply was what was meant to be, and they would be okay with that.

One volunteer expressed these concerns in the following manner: "I realize that obviously I'd be very disappointed (if the meeting did not take place). But that would be kind of a selfish disappointment. I think it's important that we understand that we are a tool. If it's decided the mediation is not going to occur I can be grateful for the process that led them to that (decision) because the mediation is not the point. Over all, hopefully there was some growth, you know, that occurred for both parties and that the process helps." These statements reflect the healing perspective which undergirds and permeates the process. Doerfler commented that two people will be different even after spending two minutes together.

Although not all cases will reach mediation for any number of reasons, this movement toward overcoming one's fear, one's grief, one's demons reflects, nonetheless, significant steps in an individual's life. Each new question asked, each new fear named, each new step taken "moves them to another level. So no matter what level they are, the process is to keep moving them, giving them opportunities to move wherever it is! And that goes back to that understanding of healing. That you're not trying to lock them in." Clearly, to Doerfler and other staff, this movement that they call a "healing journey" does not end, with or without a mediation meeting. Tools provided and seeds planted may come to fruition tomorrow or a long way down the road.

In those cases where victim and offender had met face-to-face, the length of the mediation varied from three and one-half hours to eight hours, with eight being the norm. Doerfler believed that the length of the meetings reflects all of the work by victims and offenders on preparation. The depth and intensity of preparation contributes to the feeling of safety and comfort with the issues to be brought up. The emphasis upon self-awareness empowers the participants to be available to each other and essentially conduct their own meeting. While each participant knows the ground rules for the meeting and is quite versed on what topics are expected to be addressed, there remains a power, a sacredness which is nearly impossible to describe.

From Doerfler's perspective, his role in the actual mediation session was quite minimal. The dialogue was to be between the victim and the offender. He was there to make sure things proceed in a balanced way, to possibly remind someone of a topic they had wanted to talk about, and to thank both for having worked so hard and for being willing to take the risks inherent in facing one another. But if the preparation work had been done well, if the individuals involved had dared to look into their souls, to deal with fear, to grapple with grief, then the mediation meeting, while tremendously important to each party, would be entirely within their grasp, within their power to manage, to get out of it what they need.

That's the result of preparation. "We're going to wherever they are," Doerfler explained. "We're going to provide at least the opportunity for them to see something else, in a supportive, loving caring way."

The packet of materials for mediators contains a "mediation checklist" that highlights in considerable detail the tasks of the mediator and the process of mediation. Those tasks include, on the day before the mediation, meeting with victim and offender separately, arranging for the victim to see the mediation room and prison, and setting up the room. On the day of the mediation, the mediator finishes setting up the room and meets briefly with each participant separately, as well as signing forms regarding liability and confidentiality.

The checklist for the actual mediation includes the following:

- Mediator reviews ground rules/establishes purpose.
- Victim makes opening statement (brief preview of expectations).
- Offender makes opening statement (brief preview of expectations).
- Victim begins dialogue.
- Victim and offender continue interaction.
- Lunch break.
- Mediation resumes.
- Mediation clarifies/summarizes.
- Victim and offender continue interaction.
- Mediator reviews Affirmation Agreement process, if applicable (see next paragraph).
- Mediator facilitates brainstorming/consensus/signing of Affirmation Agreement.
- Victim and offender make closing statements.
- Mediator concludes mediation.
- Mediator interviews and debriefs offender/victim separately.

The affirmation agreement provides a structure toward the close of the mediation/dialogue session for the victim and offender to concretize particular requests of the victim which the offender agrees to. Seldom is any financial restitution a part of such agreements in the VOM/D program. More often, victims may request that the offender become involved in prevention efforts, or complete some educational program, or commit to changes in their in-prison behavior, for example. Affirmation agreements are not required but are offered as one option available to participants.

A unique feature of the VOM/D program since its inception has been the routine videotaping of the actual meeting between the victim and the offender. Videotaping is only done if both parties consent, and there have been rare instances where someone has refused, but the bulk of mediation/dialogue sessions that have been facilitated in the Texas VOM/D program have been recorded on videotape. Participants have a range of options for how the tape may be used. It is routinely used with each participant in a debriefing meeting, usually within a month or two of the dialogue session. With permission, it may also be used in training, or it may be shown to other potential participants as a way of demonstrating what can be possible in such a meeting.

When asked about the presence of support persons in the meeting, Doerfler indicated that on three or four occasions support persons were present. He noted, however, that "the more people you have in there the more complicated it gets." It was his desire to create an optimum environment in order to meet the needs of victims and offenders and thus he shied away from adding persons to the session.

Other chapters in this book report on the victim and offender perspectives and reactions to mediation. It is enough to say here that from a staff/volunteer perspective, while the mediation meeting neither defines their work nor is the end-all of what they do, they each view that mediation meeting as a sacred ground. One could feel the awe of the power, of the magic, of the spirit in their voices as they described meetings and as they anticipated doing mediation.

Follow-up

While follow-up is immensely important, Doerfler admitted that this is an area that staff were still struggling to define. Is it aftercare? Does it have an end? How would they know?

Typically, the victim and offender are seen in-person a month after the mediation. A number of phone calls may have taken place in between. By this point the video of the mediation will have been processed. From the director's perspective, taping the mediation is incredibly important for the participants during the follow-up phase. In the intensity of the moment, participants may forget that entire topic areas were discussed. While the mediator may be able to help jog an individual's memory, the video tells it just as it happened. This record of what happened can be critical as victims, for example, begin to second-guess their own experiences. Many of them have had little family support for meeting the offender, and some have been chastised for doing so. Thus, there are pressures to mistrust their own feelings; the video serves to validate what they went through.

The healing journey does not end with mediation. Victims and offenders will continue to ask questions of themselves, and will often continue seeking help and support from the mediator, who has traveled with them along a most wrenching, life altering journey. Such is to be expected. A special circumstance arises for those victims whose offender is on death row and is executed. Doerfler had three occasions when he was invited by the inmate or the victim to be present for the execution. He had met with inmates just prior to their deaths. He had met with victims to help them understand what would happen and express their own often conflicting feelings. And he would often meet after the execution with victims, who were struggling to integrate the death of the offender who had taken the life of their loved one. The offender would no longer be remembered simply as faceless demon; the offender was remembered as a person with a face, with a voice, with a presence — with whom the victim had shared much intensity and often intimacy.

Doerfler readily admitted, "We don't know how to close a case yet." Some of the inmates were on parole and needed support. And as indicated above, the victim may need continued care or support even if the offender is executed. A volunteer who was working a case reflected on the intensity of her involvement with the victim: "the commitment to it (mediation) is so intense and you have a tie with this person forever." As another staff member said, "Closed isn't a word we know!"

Staff were struggling with ways of defining their work. They need to be able to close cases to a certain extent in order to better satisfy reporting requirements within the large agency. Staff were wondering about some kind of graded system reflecting a continuum of care. While they may be able to convince themselves that a case is "closed" at some point, it will always be clear that the case can be reopened at any moment if requested by victim or offender.

While acknowledging the importance of documenting the program's "numbers," a staff person underscored a philosophical and practical difficulty facing the program as follows: "What's important is the soul and the spirit and keeping the tension between the desire to see the numbers and the knowledge that the spirit can't be counted."

Related to closing a case is the definition of "successful or unsuccessful closure." Clearly, the program was having "success" with a number of individuals who never reached mediation. So what is successful or unsuccessful? From Doerfler's perspective, any case where an individual experiences some movement reflects some measure of success: "Any point of movement is resolution within a process." An unsuccessful case would arise when the individual experienced no change or remained stuck. When this happens, it is often due to a victim being re-victimized by the system or influenced by friends, family, the general public, or the media; or it may occur if victims leave unexamined certain attitudes or fears, resulting in a person feeling trapped by events and feelings beyond their control.

SUPERVISION AND ACCOUNTABILITY

Perhaps it is paradoxical in a program that honors flexibility and process with such passion to find a rigorous set of parameters for doing preparation, mediation and follow-up, as well as established points for monitoring the progress of a case. But such certainly is present in this program.

In addition to the case preparation protocols referred to earlier, there are check-in points where staff are in a position to monitor the movement within a case. A staff person will go along on the initial mediator visits to the victim and to the offender. It is expected that mediators will check in through the in-service training meetings. If they are not heard from in a reasonable amount of time, they are called by staff. It is expected that the mediator will present the case being worked on twice before volunteers and staff — one of these will be toward the beginning of the case and one toward the mediation point. They then must "present" again to staff to justify that the case is ready for mediation. Staff may ask them to go deeper, or may ask for an additional visit. While this had not yet been requested, as the director noted, "it's certainly within our procedure to do that."

Volunteer mediators seemed appreciative for the protocols, for the in-service opportunities, and for the open access they have with the staff. If anything, some were likely to be unaware that these are also mechanisms for monitoring and controlling the process.

Waiting List

At the time of the site visit, over 300 victims had expressed an interest in participating in the program since its inception. Clearly, staff felt badly about their inability to respond to all the requests for help in a timely fashion. Doerfler explained: "Actually, I don't think we handle it well. I don't have an answer to that except that we know we have re-victimized people and starting now with additional staff we are trying to reconnect with those people."

Some of those who had made the requests were simply lost track of. Some had moved and had not informed the staff of their whereabouts. Others may have changed their minds or simply lost interest. There was also the difficulty of the distance separating victims from prisons and from mediators. As the mediator pool continued to increase, it was hoped that more victims would have access to mediation opportunities.

In the effort to reestablish contact with victims on the waiting list, it was estimated that the active waiting list was composed of about 100 people. With 60 new requests coming in annually, these numbers continued to be staggering. It was noted that those victims who are good advocates, "squeaky wheels" if you will, may move up the waiting list. And those who have inmates on death row are likely to be processed first. In those cases, there is the external pressure of a possible execution which pushes, some-times, for a faster process than that with which staff are comfortable.

The extensive waiting list, on the one hand, underscored the program's need for more resources, and, on the other, raised a discussion that is often distasteful to participants committed to a healing approach. As one staff person suggested, maybe some victims simply come to get their questions answered. Is it enough for them and for the program to simply do that in a safe environment? The argument goes that some persons may not want or need the extensive and intensive work which now characterizes the program. Those victims could get their questions answered in a responsible manner, while reducing the numbers on the waiting list and increasing the number of closed cases. At the time of the site visit, the waiting list posed a monumental problem to be solved for the longevity and integrity of the program.

As we have clarified elsewhere in this chapter, all of the cases studied in the present work completed their mediation/dialogue meetings while the program functioned as described in the present chapter. However, it should be noted that between the time of the site visit and the preparation of the present document, the Texas VOM/D program undertook a number of changes under the guidance of Eddie Mendoza, who succeeded Doerfler as director in late 2001. By late 2002, the program had succeeded in eliminating the waiting list. Among those changes were further increases in the number of trained volunteers, reorganization of the existing preparation protocols, and shortening of the average length of time spent in preparation to six months.

Mendoza was quick to point out that in making these changes, none of the preparation components were dropped or altered. In his view, commitment to participant healing remains the central guiding principle of the VOM/D program; delivering service in a more structured and efficient manner has been incorporated as a crucial component of the healing process which is offered by VOM/D.

Forgiveness

There is probably no question or issue more overburdened with emotion than whether to expect victims involved in mediation to forgive the offender for violent actions against themselves or their loved one. This is one of the great fears often voiced by critics of any form of victim offender mediation. And it causes shivers to shoot up the spines of many who wonder if such dialogue between victims of violent crime and offenders is not some kind of vehicle for the offender to feel forgiven.

Ironically, some victims enter the process feeling that for their own religious reasons they must forgive. Program staff are quick to point out that they in no way want to build up the expectation that forgiveness is possible or desirable. They are willing to talk about it if the victim brings it up. They might ask questions to help the victims flesh out their own understanding of forgiveness. For example, Doerfler might ask, "Is it really forgiveness if you have to?"

Other staff members are quite adamant about not imposing views of forgiveness on the victim. "Victims have their own ideas of what forgiveness is and specifically don't want you to tell them what forgiveness is." "I have no idea what forgiveness is…I'll know it when I get there, maybe."

The director did want to bring in more training materials on the subject of forgiveness so mediators would be in a better position to develop their own understandings and be sensitive to the needs of victims and offenders around that issue. A number of the volunteers did note the importance of materials about spiritual issues, specifically about forgiveness.

Mediator Self-Care

Given the intense nature of this work — being exposed to deep pain, hearing the accounts of often brutal murders, remaining non-judgmental in contexts where judgment is the norm — there exists substantial concern for the welfare of the mediator. When we asked what mediators are told about self-care and when we asked volunteers how they take care of themselves a number of helpful suggestions arose.

From day one in training, mediators, through discussion and experiential learning, are taught about the tension between needing to detach while being totally personally present for another. They are also told that to avoid burnout they must embrace the pain, welcome it, and see the beauty of others overcoming the paralyzing grip of pain. "Close out your neutrality, but hold onto your impartiality," advised Doerfler. And, "Don't lose yourself, but do commit yourself." This experiencing of the pain is part of the sacred quality which many refer to. It is also part of that dictum, "trust the process and things will be okay."

Debriefings of mediators are built-in throughout the process of working with a specific victim and offender. Volunteers are debriefed at the beginning of the case, after mediation and at points along the way as needed. Staff try to stay on the alert for mediators exhibiting signs of excessive strain. Mediators also point to those contacts as important in their self-care, as well as to the group of volunteers with whom they were trained. This group functions like a support group, and the twice-monthly meeting reinforces that response. Many of the volunteers talk to one another in unstructured times. Volunteers also point to "significant others" and families as being very supportive.

CONCLUSION

The Texas Victim Offender Mediation/Dialogue Program is an intense effort to affect the lives of victims of violent crime and their offenders by providing opportunities for each to heal the deep wounds and pains of violence. It is a labor-intensive program. Its staff and volunteers are profoundly committed to the hope and belief that people can change, can grow if given the tools and the encouragement to do so. Tensions exist at times within the program's philosophy, competing interests, and practices. Yet one has the sense that it is that tension which also fuels new ideas and new visions.

We evaluators have had the difficult task of placing a kind of linearity on what staff genuinely belief to be a non-linear process — such is the task of researchers. We hope we have struck a balance that honors the integrity of the process while remaining committed to provide adequate description so that others might learn from the Texas experience.

We leave the last words on staff/volunteer perspective to David Doerfler:

> What happened to Pilgrim, the horse, and Grace, the young girl, in *The Horse Whisperer* — when Tom forces the horse to lie on his side on the ground and then makes Grace walk across the terrorized animal — is at the nub of what happens in healing. Each, the horse and the girl, had a choice to go on fighting life or to accept it. Victims often choose to remain victims, as that pain or rage serves their needs. Offenders often choose not to face the reality of what they have done. Like Pilgrim, once the layers of fear and non-reality are pared away, once victims and offenders walk to the brink and look beyond, they are freed to accept things as they are and then to move on. We help people face their darkest hour and prepare for the dawn.

CHAPTER 5.
TEXAS VICTIMS: EXPERIENCE AND IMPACT

This chapter and the next present results from 39 interviews with persons who participated in 22 violent crime mediation/dialogue sessions facilitated by the Texas Victim Offender Mediation/Dialogue Program. Twenty victims or victim family members and 19 convicted offenders were located and agreed to be interviewed for the participant component of the Texas Study. Interviewers from the Center for Restorative Justice and Peacemaking conducted 21 in-person interviews between February 1997 and December 1998, and 18 telephone interviews between July, 1999 and January, 2001. The interview schedules consisted of primarily open-ended questions designed to tap participants' experience, perceptions and recommendations. These were followed by several closed-ended Likert-Scale items assessing participants' evaluation of various components of the mediation/dialogue program, and more. All interviews were audio-recorded; the first five family member interviews were also videotaped.

As is so often the case in exploratory field research, the specific questions that were asked during the interviews developed and changed somewhat over the four-year course of data collection. In reporting results in these two chapters, every effort has been made to clarify whether participants are making spontaneous comments or responding to specific questions, and in the latter case, to make clear how many participants were asked the question.

TEXAS RESEARCH SAMPLE DESCRIPTION

The present chapter opens with introductory information about all participants and crimes in the 22 mediation/dialogue sessions under study. The remainder of this chapter focuses on the experiences and perspectives of the 20 victim/family member participants who were interviewed. Offender accounts will be taken up in chapter 6.

Descriptive information for the cases covered in these mediation/dialogue sessions is provided in Tables 5.1 and 5.2 below. The 22 sessions involved 21 offenders and 24 victims or family members who met in dialogue regarding 22 separate crimes. To minimize confusion, the material has been organized into "cases," with each "case" comprising the crimes of a single offender who participated in mediation/dialogue, regardless of whether or not the offender was interviewed. This has resulted in a total of 21 cases: 12 murder cases (including three cases of capital murder), 2 vehicular homicides, 1 vehicular assault, 5 sexual assaults, and 1 burglary.

Two of the 21 offenders and two of the 24 victims/family members could not be reached for research interviews. One additional family member declined to be interviewed. The fourth victim/family member was the victim of a vehicular assault by a drunk driver and had been severely brain damaged from the accident. Though she was present for the dialogue, her husband was the primary participant. Her husband was also the primary respondent during the research interview. Therefore this case has been counted as a single participant for the purposes of this report, resulting in the total of 20 victim/family member participant interviews.

Table 5.1: Texas Research Sample — Summary by Crime Type

Dialogue Sessions, by crime	Research Interviews			
	Both Victim and Offender	Victim only	Offender only	Total
Capital murder	3			3
Murder/manslaughter	9		1	10
Vehicular homicide/failure to render aid	1		1	2
Assault		1		1
Sexual assault	3	1	1	5
Burglary	1			1
Total number of dialogue sessions	17	2	3	22

In 19 of the 21 cases, the participating victims or family members were able to meet in dialogue with their actual offender. In two cases (one sexual assault case and one vehicular homicide), the actual offender was unwilling to meet, but a surrogate offender was found who had been convicted of a similar offense and who volunteered to meet with the participating victim or family member. In both of these cases, the participating surrogate offender was interviewed for the research project.

Twenty of the 22 mediation/dialogue sessions were held in the prison facility where the offender was serving his or her sentence. In one case, the offender had been released on parole after serving two years of a five-year sentence; the mediation/dialogue session was conducted four months after his release and was held at the home of the brain-damaged victim and her husband, at their request. In another, the surrogate offender was also not in prison, and the session was held in a church at a location convenient to both the offender and the victim.

CHARACTERISTICS OF VICTIMS/FAMILY MEMBERS AND CRIMES

The remainder of the present chapter presents information gleaned from the 20 interviews with participating victims/family members. Two of the interview participants were the direct victims of the crime that came to mediation; these included one burglary victim and one victim of childhood sexual abuse. The remaining 18 interview participants were family members of the actual crime victim. These included 11 mothers, 1 father, 1 sister, 1 brother, 1 wife, 1 husband, 1 daughter and 1 granddaughter. The 20 victim participants included 4 men and 16 women.

All 20 victim/family member participants were Caucasian, including 3 who were Hispanic. At the time of the dialogues, participants ranged in age from 27 to 61, with an average age of 43. For 15 of the participants, including one of the actual victims, it was the first time they had been victimized by a crime. Victims of the crimes ranged in age from 7 to 72 at the time of the crime, with an average age of 27; 11 were 21 or under.

Table 5.2: Texas Research Sample — All Victims and Offenders

Case	Crime	Victim Died in Crime	Relationship of Dialogue Participant to Victim	Research Interviews[a]	
				O	V
1	Aggravated sexual assault	N	Mother	1	1
2	Aggravated sexual assault (V suicide)	N	Mother	1	1
3	Driving while intoxicated, involuntary manslaughter	N	Husband	--	1
4	Solicitation capital murder	Y	Brother	1	1
5	Murder; aggravated robbery; abduction; aggravated sexual assault	Y	Mother	1	1
6	2nd degree murder (two separate dialogue sessions)	Y	Father		1
			Mother	1	1
7	Capital murder	Y	Mother	1	1
8	Intentional murder w/ deadly weapon	Y	Mother	1	1
9	Capital murder (2 crimes in single dialogue session)	Y	Granddaughter and Sister	1	2
10	Capital murder	Y	Mother	1	1
11	Capital murder	Y	Mother	1	1
12	Burglary	N	Victim	1	1
13	Murder	Y	Wife	1	1
14	Indecency with a child	N	Mother	1	--
15	Failure to render aid	Y	Mother (surrogate O)	1	1
16	Murder	Y	Mother	1	1

Case	Crime	Victim Died in Crime	Relationship of Dialogue Participant to Victim	Research Interviews[a]	
				O	V
17	Murder	Y	Daughter	1	1
18	Child sexual abuse	N	Victim (surrogate O)	1	1
19	Aggravated intoxication and manslaughter	Y	Father	1	--
20	Murder	Y	Sister	1	--
21	Aggravated sexual assault against a child	N	Mother	--	1
	Total			19	20

a) O=offender; V=victim or victim's family member.

The mediation/dialogue sessions in which the interviewees participated were held between March of 1995 and December of 2000. The average length of time from the commission of the crime to the mediation/dialogue session was 9.45, years with a range of 2.33 years to 26.8 years. Crimes in which the victim was murdered took longer on average to come to mediation (11.15 years) than other crimes (5.78 years). The interviews with victims and family members were conducted an average of 11.1 months after the mediation/dialogue sessions, with a range of two weeks to three years.

In 12 of these 19 crimes, the 13 direct victims were not previously acquainted with the offender. Of the remaining seven, five crimes were intrafamilial, including the three incest cases, the burglary of a stepfather by his stepson, and a murder solicited by the victim's wife, although the actual killer in that case was not known to the victim. The two remaining crimes in which the victim and offender were acquainted were murders. The offender and his murder victim in one case were friends; the offender, under the influence of drugs and alcohol, had approached his friend for a place to stay and became enraged and violent when she turned him down. The drug dealer in another case was acquainted with his female murder victim's fiancé, whom he also murdered, but had only briefly met the young woman herself.

In three additional cases, although the actual killer was not known to the victim, the killer arrived on the scene in the company of someone known to the victim. These included an ex-girlfriend in two cases and a daughter's ex-boyfriend in the third.

Of the 18 family member participants, only three were previously acquainted with the offender with whom they met. In all three instances, the family member was related to the participating offender, including two ex-spouses and a brother-in-law.

Four of the participating family members met with death row offenders who were subsequently executed. The special nature of these situations will be further explored in Appendix A.

EXPERIENCE OF THE CRIME

Both the family members and the victims described their experience of the crime, including, for family members, how they first learned about it, and for all interviewees, their experience with the justice system.

Learning of the Event

In the burglary case and one sexual assault case, the interviewees were themselves the direct victims of the crime and had no need to be informed that it had occurred. In addition, the wife of one murder victim was present when the offenders entered the home and was with her husband when he died shortly thereafter. The daughter of a second murder victim received a call from her mother when her father had been shot and arrived in time to be present when he died at the scene. One mother of an incest victim was informed by her child of the abuse shortly after the couple had separated for other reasons.

Of the remaining 15 interviewees, 10 were initially informed by other relatives who had taken the call from officials. In some instances, not all information was revealed, so that they learned first that there had been a mishap or accident and then were told the full extent of the loss when they arrived to join the rest of the family.

The remaining five interviewees were informed of the crime by officials. In two of the sexual assault cases, police contacted the mothers when the daughters reported the incident. Both of these mothers had positive feelings about the efforts of these officials to help their daughters. The mother in a vehicular homicide case also reported strong support from the five officials who arrived to let the family know their missing daughter's body had been found.

Very different scenarios unfolded in the two murder cases in which the family member learned of the event from justice system officials, although family members in both cases experienced similar insensitivity. The ordeal faced by the victim's mother in the first cases is reported in chapter 3. In the second case, the family became caught up in the efforts of police to locate their daughter before it was even clear a crime had been committed. After a customer found the convenience store where their daughter worked to be empty and the till open, a dispatcher called the family's home at 10:00 p.m. without identifying herself and began to ask increasingly pointed and detailed questions about their daughter's whereabouts and habits. Not until the mother challenged the caller did the dispatcher identify herself and explain that the store was empty and their daughter was missing. Once the body was located, however, the department immediately sent a pair of officers to the home to inform the parents in person.

Six family members of murder victims reported fairly intense initial denial experiences, ranging from "this isn't happening" to a numbness the family member compared to out-of-body experiences she had heard about. One mother whose daughter was assaulted and four family members of murder victims reported a premonition of or intuition about the crime before officially learning about it. Two of these mothers woke up spontaneously from sleep at about the time of their daughters' deaths and knew something was terribly wrong. One of these mothers reported that she is extremely grateful for this awareness because she felt it helped her face reality and avert denial. Only one of the family members with a premonition experienced any level of denial reaction, simply reporting that the first two days were "unreal."

Experience with the Justice System

There was one case with no justice system involvement; the actual offender in this case had never admitted to or been prosecuted for the crime and the participant met with a surrogate. For an additional five interviewees, no information was available about participants' reactions to the way the justice system responded to their situation. Of the remaining 14, five were essentially positive. These participants felt supported by the system, felt they had been kept adequately informed, and felt that they had a voice in what happened. They reported such experiences as having a role in the pre-trial process, attending the trial, and helping to prevent the offender's release.

The remaining nine interviewees reported mixed or negative justice system experiences. Problems they perceived included the insensitive initial contacts about the crime (described above), receiving incomplete or misleading details about the crime, feeling that the system didn't sufficiently investigate the crime, being excluded from hearings or trials, being instructed to curtail their behavior in the courtroom, not being informed about changes in trial dates and procedures, not receiving information about victims services, being frustrated that laws seemed to protect offenders more than victims, and being upset with the way the system separates the offender from the impact of his or her actions.

> We got a lot of abuse from the system. The first attorney told my mother that this case is not hers, it belongs to the state of Texas, and

he would call her if he needed her. And he would do whatever he damn well pleased, essentially.

INTRODUCTION TO MEDIATION AND FIRST REACTIONS

Nine of the 20 interviewees became actively involved in victims services and/or victims' organizations following the crime, and first learned about the potential for meeting with their offender through these connections. Five of them immediately knew this was something they wanted to do.

I went to a Parents of Murdered Children meeting one night and one of my friends told me he had signed up to do this program. And when he told me about it, I said, well, I've got to do this.

Four of them, however, reported that their first reaction upon hearing of the idea was strongly negative. "I just right then said 'no.' I don't want to meet somebody that killed my daughter and put me in ten years of misery." Their reasons for changing their minds varied. Two of them watched videos of other mediations and were moved by the healing they saw happening, in spite of the fact that not everything could be resolved. One mother realized that there were still some concessions she wanted from the offender, and that she might be more likely to obtain them if she met with him in mediation than if she pursued them through additional court proceedings. The mother of a murdered daughter was intensely opposed to the idea until she witnessed how healing the mediation experience was for her ex-husband.

Nine participants, including one who was active in victim organizations, reported that they sought to meet with their offenders on their own before learning about the program. Many had wished to meet directly with their offender since very early in the process, in some instances dating from the trial. For some of these persons the process of finding out about the program was almost haphazard, and included following up after an HBO television special on more general victim offender mediation, talking with judges and parole boards, and ultimately, connecting with the Victim Service Division. They never imagined there was actually a program designed to deliver what they sought.

The remaining two interviewees had more idiosyncratic introductions to mediation. The husband of the brain-injured victim, who was contacted by the victim services office, initially rejected the idea. He changed his mind when he decided that meeting with the offender might be able to help his wife clarify her memories of the incident. And the burglary victim received a Twelve-Step Program "amends" letter from the offender (his own step-son) and sought to meet with him as a result of that contact.

REASONS FOR PARTICIPATING IN MEDIATION/DIALOGUE

The reasons interviewees gave for initially seeking mediation fall into the following categories: to seek information (13 of 20); to show offenders the impact of what they have done (11 of 20); to have a human, face-to-face encounter with the offender (8 of 20); to hold the offender accountable (6 of 20); to advance their own healing in other ways (6 of 20); to share forgiveness with the offender (5 of 20); to help prevent further crime (3 of 20); because it seemed right (2 of 20); to obtain specific restitution (1 of 20); to hear an "amends" step (1 of 20); and to be reunited (1 of 20).

Thirteen of the 20 interviewees hoped to receive additional information of some kind. For two of these, this was minimal or circumscribed. The husband of the brain-damaged DWI victim hoped information obtained from the offender would help restore his wife's memory of the incident, and another participant had only minor questions and didn't really think he would receive any useful information.

The remaining 11 participants hoped for details about exactly what had happened (10 of 11) and why it had happened (6 of 11). A mother of a murdered son stated: "Because I had no answers I made up a lot of things in my brain, and all of it was just something I had just assumed that that is the way that it had happened....I needed to know the answers." A victim who chose to meet with a surrogate felt "he just may say some things that will help me clear up in my head things that are going on, questions that I've already had."

Four parents of murdered daughters had questions about whether their daughters had done anything to invite the attack or were in any way to blame. Three of these further explained that at some level their own parenting was at stake: in raising their daughters, had they taught them something that placed them at risk?

Seven interviewees did not mention obtaining information as a reason for seeking to meet. Three of these, a direct victim and two family members, were themselves present at the crime. As a wife put it, "I wasn't in there trying to find answers, because the answer was that (my husband) was gone." The fourth explained, "We'll never know why they killed them. That's something I don't think even the killers can really tell us." The remaining three did not comment on why they didn't seek information.

Eleven of the interviewees — including nine relatives of murder victims, the mother of a molested child, and the husband of the DWI victim — sought to convey to the offenders the impact of what they had done. One was quite explicit about this component: "The way our justice system works…he's very much isolated from the impact of his crimes," so she wanted him to know "how far reaching the impact is, and how time consuming, and how long it lasts and what it does." The mother of a murder victim stated: "If he could feel the pain in my heart, if he could feel the hole that he left in my life, then that would be justice." For four of these family members, a specific component of showing the impact was teaching the offender about the life of the person who had been murdered. They wanted the offender to know that the person was "real."

Eight of the participants used combinations of words describing human encounters in reporting why they sought to meet: to sit "face to face" or "eye to eye," to "look him in the eyes," to "sit down and talk with him." In seven of these cases, the victim had died; six had been murdered, and the seventh was a young woman who committed suicide after the offender had been tried and convicted for her rape. In addition, these seven included all four of the family members whose offenders were sentenced to execution. The eighth was the stepfather seeking a meeting with his stepson.

Six participants sought to hold the offender accountable in some way. Mostly this involved hearing the offender take ownership of the crime. In two of these cases, the offender had accepted a plea bargain without formally admitting guilt, and the family members wanted to hear the admission directly. In the remaining two cases, the offender had stood trial and was sentenced to execution. As the sister of a murder victim put it, "I wanted him to look me in the face and tell me that he did kill my sister." One family member who did not list this as a reason explained that she had agreed to the plea bargain on the condition that the offender would take the stand and acknowledge what he had done, so she felt he had already been held accountable in that way.

Six participants more explicitly named their own healing as a major reason for seeking to meet. Three were relatives of murder victims. A father had adamantly opposed the notion of mediation until he watched videos of other mediations. He specifically changed his mind because, in his words,

"I could see this guy healing ... I knew I could go into a meeting with (the offender) and if it was bad I wouldn't be any worse off, and if it was good, I would be so much better off." A mother had come to feel that sharing her forgiveness with the offender was the most important next step in her own healing, and a daughter hoped that the opportunity to meet would decrease her nightmares. A victim of sexual abuse stated, "I've never had anywhere to go with all this stuff that goes along with it." The mother in another sexual abuse case wanted her power back: "It was that power of somebody being able to strip your whole world of everything. And I needed that back."

Five participants wished to share directly with their offenders the fact that they had forgiven them. Three of these were relatives of murder victims. Two mothers, both of whose offenders were sentenced to execution, reported that as part of their own healing process and personal faith, they had come to forgive their offenders. Sharing this forgiveness before the offenders were executed became a crucial central reason for seeking to meet. The wife of a murder victim spoke of having watched a news report of a violent crime with her husband before his death, in which he supported forgiving the offender as the right thing to do. She added, "I wanted (the offender) to know I was forgiving him because I knew that it was something my husband expected me to do."

The two remaining interviewees who spoke of sharing forgiveness with the offender included the stepfather who hoped to tell his stepson he was forgiven, and the mother of a vehicular homicide victim, who stated: "I wanted to tell him I forgave him from the first week that we went back to church." Ultimately, she was unable to convey her forgiveness because the offender declined to meet with her, and she met with a surrogate.

Three family members included rehabilitation/prevention themes among their reasons for seeking to meet. In two of these cases, the offender was either already out on parole or soon would be. For example, the husband of the brain-injured victim wanted to help rehabilitate the offender "so he will never get behind the wheel of a car after a beer" again. The third offender had served 15 years and was expected to be released in an additional three years. The mother of his murder victim reported deciding, "I'm gonna go talk to that guy and I'm gonna make a change in his life."

Two participants, both mothers of murder victims, felt a general sense of mission or purpose rather than a specific reason; it was something they needed to do, something that felt "right."

In contrast to what is so often the case in the mediation of non-violent offenses, only one of the 20 participants named seeking specific restitution as a part of the reason for deciding to participate in mediation. This one respondent was the mother of an incest victim, who sought explicit concessions from the offender. The last two reasons for participating — to hear an amends and be reunited — were the major reasons the stepfather sought to meet with the stepson who had burgled his home.

Interviewees weren't routinely asked whether they had consulted anyone else in reaching their decision to seek to meet. However eight participants spontaneously mentioned discussing it with others, including three who had sought the counsel of relatives, three who discussed it with friends, and two who did both. Only one of the eight reported receiving support for the idea from her ex-husband, who had already participated. The remaining seven experienced more negative reactions. One said that her husband had reservations and didn't want her hurt, and another reported that her friends thought it was too risky and that she shouldn't re-hash the crime.

Risks Considered

Six of the participants were not asked if they considered any risks in making their decision to meet and did not mention any. Of the remaining 14, nine felt there weren't any risks, though four of these reported that others were worried that such a meeting would be risky for them. Comments included: "I never thought about it, it was just something I wanted to do for so long." "To me, there were no risks, there was only going to be the possibility of some answers." The only specific warning anyone reported from others came from a participant in a "Parents of Murdered Children" group, who said the group was afraid anyone who met with their child's murderer would "start to have feelings for the monster."

Five victims/family members did think there would be some risk, but chose to go ahead and meet anyway. Three worried about a possible negative impact on themselves including: the potential for making things worse by getting so close to the emotional wound, fear of being revictimized either by the offender or by the bureaucracy, or fear of experiencing rageful feelings that hadn't previously surfaced. One worried that such a meeting might reduce the offender's sentence. And one was concerned for the offender, fearing the confrontation might make him suicidal.

PREPARATION FOR THE MEDIATION/DIALOGUE SESSIONS

The Texas program provided both the victims/family members and the offenders with careful, extensive preparation prior to bringing them together for the mediation/dialogue session. These procedures have been described in more detail in chapter 4. Preparation for all 20 interviewees included a series of meetings with the mediator and a number of paper and pencil questionnaires exploring the details of the crime, their reactions, and their hopes and fears about the dialogue session.

The length of preparation for the 20 interviewees averaged 15 months, with a range of 2 months to 35 months. Three of the four participants whose offenders were executed received unusually brief preparation (average four months) because of the short time until the date of the offender's execution. The next shortest preparation length was nine months. There were no other differences in preparation length by type of crime. In some of the more lengthy instances, preparation extended beyond the "readiness" of participants for outside reasons, such as a change in prisons or other administrative difficulties in scheduling the meeting.

Victim/Family Member Evaluation of the Preparation Process

Participants were asked to rate their evaluation of the preparation on a Likert scale; these results are reported in Table 5.3 below. In addition, they were asked about their reactions to the length of the preparation. Seventeen of the 20 participants were satisfied with the length of the preparation process they went through. Some commented that it felt long at the time, but that it paid off. "After time went on, it was probably really best, now that I look back on it, to do it after that long of a wait...I think there needs to be a certain point of healing time there." Only three of the 20 interviewees felt the preparation length was too long. In one instance, the mediator had become ill, but the participant received no communication for three months to explain the delay. As she commented, "I don't think the victim should be the one picking up the phone to find out the mediator had pneumonia." The remaining two felt the preparation requirements were much too lengthy for the simple goals they had in coming to dialogue.

Table 5.3: Victim/Family Member Satisfaction with Preparation for Mediation/Dialogue

Very satisfied	17	(85%)
Somewhat satisfied	2	(10%)
Somewhat dissatisfied	1	(5%)
Very dissatisfied		
Total	20	(100%)

Elements of the preparation that were spontaneously mentioned as especially helpful included the written questionnaires (14 of 20), uncovering feelings they hadn't been aware of (10 of 20), the mediator's ability to relay information between the offender and the participant during preparation (7 of 20), advancing their healing process (6 of 20), the mediator's personal encouragement and relationship (6 of 20), envisioning potential risks of mediation (5 of 20), planning what to say (2 of 20), watching videos of other mediations (1 of 20), the impact of the preparation materials on other family members (1 of 20), and providing specific information about sexual perpetrators (1 of 20) . Two participants stated that they felt the preparation alone had helped them heal even if it had never resulted in a mediation.

Positive comments included the following:

> I mean, there is stacks of paperwork that you have to go through and when you first look at it you think oh, this is ridiculous, some of the questions that they ask, but really and truly, I wouldn't change a thing ... I really believe it works. You would have to put your anger, your fear, your hostility — you put it on paper.

> There were so many things that we had to go through – preparation, meetings, the worksheet. It was things I never thought I could do, but I did. The preparations were so helpful but they were emotionally draining, too ... It was painful, but it helped, you know, to do that, it helped.

> One of us would have blown up if there hadn't been preparation.

Suggestions for Changes in the Preparation Process

Recommendations for helpful changes in the preparation procedures came both from some who reported themselves to be "very satisfied" with preparation and from the three who were only "somewhat satisfied" or "somewhat dissatisfied." The most common suggestion, raised by five of the 20 participants, was to reduce the amount and complexity of the written questionnaires and worksheets. Two reasons lay behind this suggestion. For the burglary victim and the husband of the DWI victim, the requirements seemed top heavy. "You can't take the same set of floor plans and build six different houses with it...It seemed to me like I had the same program if I was meeting somebody who killed my Mama." They both felt the program should be more flexible. The mother of a sex abuse victim concurred: "You might want to cut back on that. A lot of the questions in the beginning didn't pertain to me, it was more on crime in general."

The other two felt the written materials were too detailed and intimate, regardless of the reason for meeting. One commented that the questionnaires were "extremely hard for the victim." Closely related was the suggestion to decrease the length of time it took for preparation, raised by three participants. "It was frustrating to drag it out for the sake of the program, this is the way the rules are written and this is what we have to do."

The remaining direct suggestions were made by one participant each. One family member who had reported herself "very satisfied" with the preparation, in fact had complied with none of the protocols or written work. This mother of a murder victim had already met with her daughter's killer in a previous mediation session with a minimum of preparation. She felt that anyone who has already survived the murder of an offspring is capable of coping with meeting with the offender and capable of assessing his or her own readiness to do so.

A respondent who identified herself as "mostly satisfied" with the preparation had several specific recommendations. She took with her to the mediation a number of large items, such as books and photo albums, she wished to share with the offender, and was disappointed that actual setting of the mediation provided no table space for her to place these things: "I would have, on this side of the victim, some place to put stuff so the offender didn't see it until it was the appropriate moment to do that." She also felt she had not been prepared for how to bring the session to a close:

"I didn't know how to stop it; he (the offender) was just draining me." In addition, while she understood the financial constraints of the Texas program, she felt there was an unfair burden on victims and family members who had to travel on their own time and at their own expense to all the preparation meetings with the mediator, while the mediator traveled to the offenders and held preparation sessions with them wherever they were located.

One of the open-ended interview questions asked whether participants had been surprised by anything. Two responses to that question, both from persons "very satisfied" with their preparation, have implications for ways it could be improved. The family member in one of the earliest mediations was shocked when she walked into the mediation room by how the offender looked. Offering to provide recent photographs (with permission of participants) could avert this problem, and was in fact carried out in many subsequent mediations. Another family member never made a list of the things she wanted to say or the questions she wanted to ask because she ordinarily has such a reliable memory. Not only did her memory falter at the moment of the actual meeting, she also developed a migraine, but had brought no medication with her. Both these problems likely derive from the intense emotionality of the mediation experience, and perhaps participants should be encouraged to make lists and prepare for possible recurrence of stress-related health problems they have previously experienced.

One component of the preparation phase that is usually offered to participants is the opportunity to tour the prison facility where the mediation will be held prior to the session. Ten of the 18 participants whose dialogue sessions were held in a prison reported that they had elected to take the tour, and they found it extremely helpful for a variety of reasons. For those who had never been in a prison before, it was helpful to adjust to the starkness of the setting before meeting with their offender. "It was much worse than I had imagined." One family member who was a parole officer and had often been in such facilities was still moved by how the experience helped him envision the daily life of the offender. Another family member commented, "You want the man that killed your daughter to not be comfortable, to be in a punishment situation. Believe me, (the offender) has been in a punishment situation."

One respondent was taken aback by some unexpected information she received during the prison tour. After the door had shut behind her and the mediator, the guard informed her that in hostage situations, they do not negotiate. She wished she had known this earlier.

Feelings Immediately Before Mediation/Dialogue

Some degree of pre-session nervousness was reported by 12 of the 20 interviewees. As one parent of a murdered child put it, "You will never, ever be prepared; you just won't." This ranged from a very minimal level of anxiety that quickly faded, to the following statement by the mother of a murdered daughter: "I was scared to death!...It was a long walk, believe me. You talk about that movie, *Dead Man Walking* — there was a dead mother going!" Not all of them named specific fears, but for those who did, they included: fear of setting the offender off (3), concern about how they themselves would behave (2), worry over how the person would look (2), and nervousness over what feelings they might experience (2). As one participant put it, "I was terrified sitting down and looking at that and talking about that and being that close to that wound. It was just a terrifying thought."

THE MEDIATION/DIALOGUE SESSIONS

The 19 mediation/dialogue sessions in which these 20 interviewees participated averaged five and a half hours in length, with a range of three hours to eight and a half hours. There were no differences in dialogue length by type of crime. Excluding camera personnel, most sessions involved only the victim/family member, the offender, and a single mediator. Support persons for victims/family members were present in the mediation in four sessions; in one additional session, the support person was waiting in another room outside.

In the Texas program there is a general format for beginning the mediation/dialogue sessions; typically the mediator begins with a brief opening statement that serves as a check-in and reminder about the purpose and the ground rules of the meeting. Usually both the victims/family members and the offenders have been encouraged to prepare statements or outlines of what they wish to say. Sometimes these are quite extensive. Typically the victims/family members describe their experience of the crime, talk about its impact, and, in cases where the victim has died, share detailed information about the life of the person who has been killed. In most instances, the victim or family member leads with these remarks, followed later by the offender. However, this depends on the preference of the victim or family member; three participating family members reported that, in fact, they preferred to have the offender go first, and this wish was honored.

Aside from this basic structure, conversations simply flowed back and forth for the duration of the session, proceeding much like any exchange of information between two adults. There was a minimum of interrupting, participants quietly waited for one another to finish a train of thought, voices in general tended not to be raised, and there were many periods of silence. The respectful, quiet character of the dialogue process seemed to be largely taken for granted by these participants. The pervasiveness of these qualities was underscored by participants' comments on their surprise over the rare exceptions.

Opening Moments

Only a few participants described the opening moments of their sessions, and these descriptions reflected the pre-session anxiety levels reported above. Three family members described somewhat lengthy initial silences during which, eventually, they and the offender finally made eye contact. Sample descriptions included the following: "We sat down at the table across from each other. I knew when he was looking at me and I wouldn't look at him, and he knew when I was looking at him and he wouldn't look at me. And that went on for maybe five minutes. And then finally we looked each other in the eye;" and, "Before he even sat in the chair in front of me, our eyes locked. And it was just like our eyes were like magnets. I mean, he looked at me and I looked at him and I could not say a word. And we must have held that stare for three or four minutes without saying a word." A fourth participant, the husband of the DWI victim, said that it took the offender an extremely long time to look directly at the woman he had injured.

Victim/Family Member Participation

The following section lists those aspects of their participation in the mediation sessions that interviewees described as significant to them. Participants reported that they told the offender their own experience of the crime (16 of 20), talked about its effect on the victim (14 of 20, including one direct victim), described its impact on themselves (13 of the 18 family members), asked specific questions (9 of 20), shared information about the victim (9 of 20), and gave the offender instructions or made specific requests (8 of 20).

For the 16 participants who reported telling offenders what they had experienced, details typically included how they found out about the crime, what kinds of information and misinformation they were given, the waiting they went through, and what their immediate reactions were. As much as possible, they appear to have placed the offender in their shoes and simply told their story.

Fourteen participants, including 13 family members and one direct victim, spent time telling offenders how the offenders' actions had affected the victim. The brother of a murder victim let the offender talk at some length about being separated from family and missing them, and finally interrupted with: "Look, this is what I can't have, what you took from my brother." The mother of a murdered daughter stated: "When I told him about my daughter's appearance and what she looked like and how we couldn't open her casket, the physical changes that he had caused, he put his elbows on the table and his face in his hands, and then he sat back and said 'Nobody ever told me that.'" Thirteen family members specifically described how the crime had affected them personally over time.

> I think I told him pretty well right off the bat that he has wrecked my life and that I hate his guts.

> I was glad I was able to really finally get to tell him, 'this is what you did to me.'

> I really had to let him know that he was responsible for a lot of sadness and devastation and destructive behavior and all of the things that go along with a crime like this because it was so brutal and it was so devastating.

One of these, the mother of a murder victim, was concerned that the offender thought his actions had affected only her. She invited affected friends and family members to write letters about the impact of the murder on themselves and brought eight of these letters with her to the mediation. At the suggestion of the mediator, she read them out loud as part of the mediation process.

Nine interviewees described the kinds of questions they asked; all nine had many questions about the actual crime. "I brought ten pages of questions. I knew what I needed to know." "I want you to tell me the facts:

what did you do, and when did you do it?" Four of these also sought some information about the offender's life leading up to the crime, and one asked the offender to describe how he had met her daughter and what their relationship had been. An additional five participants reported asking questions, but gave no further details. The remaining six did not report asking questions in the dialogue sessions.

Eight of the interviewees reported making explicit requests of their offenders. Four of these involved something specific for the victim/family member and/or for others directly affected by the crime. At the family member's request, the offender in a sexual abuse case agreed to relinquish parental rights and to stop writing letters to the victim's mother. Another sexual abuse offender agreed to write a letter of apology to his victim that the victim's mother would hold until an appropriate time. The daughter of a murder victim carefully described to her offender each of the victim's children, children-in-law, and grandchildren, and then asked him to write a letter of apology to each. "And it cannot be the same letter. He has to approach them from the way that I perceived that it affected them. And this is an extremely intelligent human being, he won't have any problem doing this." She, also, will hold the letters, and let family members know they are available if they wish them. And the offender who had permanently injured his victim in a drunken driving incident agreed to keep in touch and to send her a dollar every month to put toward whatever charity she chose. At the time of the research interviews, three years after their mediation, the letters and dollar bills were still coming regularly, and he had maintained his sobriety.

The remaining four requests were directed at others. Two had to do with helping to prevent further crime. The mother of another murder victim obtained an agreement from her offender, who was only 19 at the time of the crime, that he would specifically work with and speak to juveniles to prevent similar crimes. The mother of a vehicular homicide victim reported that she told her surrogate offender, "I want you to write to your hometown, I want you to write to your newspapers to the young teenagers, your friends who are still out there racing and running recklessly and driving recklessly." The brother of a murder victim told his offender, "Every once in a while, when you do get out, go find you a tree and sit underneath it and just think about what you did to my brother, what you did to your family, what you did to your self...and just sit there and think about it and cry. Cry for my brother."

Nine participants, including eight family members and one direct victim, shared information about the victim, including details about the victim's life (7 of 9), emphasizing that the victim was real (6 of 9), and bringing photographs (7 of 9). Six of the participants who gave details about the victims were relatives of victims who had died. The seventh was a sexual abuse victim, who gave details about how the abuse had affected her entire life.

Seven, all of them family members of murder victims, brought photographs, including in three instances photo albums documenting the life of the victim. As one mother explained, "I took my son's baby book. I wanted (the offender) to know him, that he was real, that he was not just a body he left sitting in the car, that my son had hopes and dreams and goals and plans, and those were never realized because of (the offender's) choice." Another mother wore a large button pin with her daughter's picture. She reported that the offender didn't even remember what her daughter looked like, but that he said, "I see her, I see your picture, and I won't forget what she looks like again." The wife of a murder victim brought not only photographs of her deceased husband, but also photographs of the family members whose lives had been affected.

Six of family members of deceased victims spoke of showing the offenders that the victim who had died was "real." "He understood that my daughter was real, she used to be ten years old." "My daughter was not something that wasn't real. She was a real live person. You took her future and my future."

Offender Participation

Nineteen of the 20 interviewees commented in some detail about how the offender responded during the mediation. Domains that they mentioned included accepting responsibility (15 of 19), answering questions (14 of 19), showing or demonstrating remorse (9 of 19), and becoming tearful (8 of 19).

Fifteen reported that the offender accepted responsibility for his or her actions. Sample descriptions included:

> He took a lot more responsibility than I expected him to. He admitted to things that I didn't even know about.

> She really apologized to me for what she did.

He said "I killed your daughter." That wasn't second or third hand, that was him saying that, and that just meant a lot.

I had heard that he had confessed...it was gratifying to hear it out of his mouth and not out of a reporter's mouth.

Fourteen participants reported that the offender answered questions, although one person qualified this by adding "as best he could." Several participants received new information. Two parents obtained information that confirmed that their daughters had not provoked their attackers in any way. One mother in a sexual abuse case received far more details about the abuser's actions than she had been aware of. A mother of a murder victim asked for, and received, a detailed description of her son's last moments. The exchange that followed was notable for its intense emotionality: "I found that I had some anger left inside of me that I didn't realize was there. And I lashed out at him. I raised my voice to him, I began to cry, I was pretty much sobbing." The sexual abuse victim who met with a surrogate was particularly struck by the information he was able to give her: "There were some real 'aha' moments. Things that he said that I went, 'I never thought about that.'"

Nine participants stated that the offender showed or demonstrated remorse, and one gave a mixed report, "Both yes and no." Even though he believed that the offender "really knew she hurt me," he felt she hadn't changed.

Eight participants reported that the offender became tearful or cried during the session. For some, this happened near the beginning of the session. The husband of the DWI victim described the scene: "I said, 'Honey, this is the guy that hit you.' And she went over to him and gave him a big hug. And he cried and the tears just poured down his face for a good twenty to thirty minutes." The mother of a murder victim described the moment of first eye contact with her offender: "I believe he first showed emotion when he saw the pain in my eyes...he put his head down and a tear just started rolling down his nose." In other cases it occurred at particularly emotion-filled moments during the course of the session. One mother of a murder victim reported that "he started crying when he looked through the picture album. He said later he did not think of (the victim) as being real until he looked at this album."

Victim/Family Member Evaluation of Offender Participation

Nineteen participants shared their assessment of the offender's sincerity; 16 felt the offender was sincere. The remaining three reported they felt there was some degree of sincerity, but with qualifications. For example, one mother felt the offender was probably sincere at the time but later fell into old patterns of thinking.

Seventeen interviewees commented on the extent to which they believed the information shared by the offender. Thirteen believed what the offender shared, two did not believe the offender, and two were mixed, one believing "60 to 80%" and the other "mostly." A parent of a murder victim explained it this way: "It's well known I hate his guts…And he's going to tell me what happened? No. He's going to clean it up to where he don't look quite so bad."

Victim/Family Member Surprises

Questions about surprises were not a routine part of the first several interviews. In all, six participants were not asked whether they had any surprises and did not comment on any. An additional five who were asked reported no surprises. Nine, however, did find themselves surprised by something during the mediation. Six of these, some of whose feedback has already been discussed under recommended preparation changes, focused on some aspect of the offender's appearance or behavior. One was surprised by her own behavior, finding herself getting up and shaking hands with the offender at the beginning of the session when she hadn't planned to. One was surprised that at the last minute the offender refused to allow her husband to participate. The remaining surprise was reported by the woman who was asked by the mediator to read the letters she had brought out loud.

Mediator Role and Evaluation

All 20 participants had very similar descriptions of the mediator's role: after introductory remarks setting the stage, mediators were relatively silent, and simply let the sessions flow freely. "He had tutored us both well and he really didn't have to (talk) very much;" "He let it flow, let it happen;" "He let us talk;" and "He didn't interfere." For seven of them, these same themes were echoed when they talked about the mediator's most helpful contribution: "The most helpful thing was just sitting there and allowing it to happen. He had prepared us to a point where it was almost like we didn't need him there." "I think that was one of the best things, just to let the victim and defendant really kind of carry our own ball." Two participants offered further explanations of why this mattered: "I like that because I didn't want it to seem like he was trying to control what I was saying, and I didn't want the mediator to pull things out of her that she didn't want to say or that she didn't want to admit." "Talking more is leading and inter-fering...I think that your feelings just come and go so quickly and your emotions are just so tied into that, that I know for myself I would have been angry had anybody tried to channel my energy into another way."

A theme that underlies all these comments is that the thorough prepara-tion seems to have contributed in several ways to the smoothness of the mediation process that participants experienced. Because of the many hours spent with both the victim/family member and the offender, mediators know the issues, are able to help the flow when things stall, and able to confront when offenders become evasive. And because of the extensive exploration ahead of time, participants are able to conduct the bulk of the session largely unaided.

The participants described the mediators' few interventions in similar terms. They occasionally re-focused the conversation, reminded partici-pants of something they had wanted to say or ask, challenged evasiveness, reached for the feelings behind what was being said, and, in one instance, helped a family member stay in touch with intense feelings. For example, "There were a couple of times when (the offender) was intellectualizing, getting off on tangents, philosophy kind of things instead of the real, over-analyzing, and the mediator was able to bring it back to 'this is what we're talking about.'" When mediators did suggest to participants that they might wish to introduce something they had discussed during the preparation phase, they always did so in a way that did not specifically name what they were referring to, so that the participant was left with the choice about whether or not to open up the topic area.

Eight of the participants felt the mediators' most helpful contributions were in these action domains. These included three who named re-focusing, two each who listed reminding them and encouraging feelings, and one who named challenging the offender's avoidance. One commented, "He helped us not sidestep or squirrel our way out of a question." The mother who had become so enraged upon hearing the description of her son's murder stated: "He encouraged me...so that I could vent every bit of that anger. I believe that was really beneficial." The daughter of a murder victim had brought photos anticipating she would show them at some point, but her mediator spread them out on the table so they were visible throughout the session; she named this as the most helpful mediator action.

The participants commented on the mediators' sense of balance and their capacity to be present for both themselves and the offenders, a process they presumed was very difficult. "It's hard to be fair in something like this…It would be hard, I think, to be fair to a murderer." The granddaughter felt that without the mediator's intense preparation and capacity to be present in his relationship with the offender, the offender who killed her grandmother would never have participated so openly. "He had probably opened up more to (the mediator) than he had anyone else, probably ever, about these crimes and about his life. I felt like he probably saw him not just as a friend, but as someone he could go to and lean on a little."

Feelings Immediately Afterwards

First reactions at the conclusion of the session can be summed up in two words: relief and exhaustion. Four participants did not comment on their immediate reactions. Of the remaining 16, six reported both relief and exhaustion, seven reported relief only, and three reported exhaustion only. Typical comments included:

> When I walked out it was like this load, the part of you that holds on to all the unknowns, to all the anger, to all the frustration, to all the pain, .. .some type of negative energy kind of was lifted out of me, and I was also exhausted.

> I had a fifty ton weight lifted off my back.

> Happiness, release of tensions, drained because of the tension.

> It was like my body had worked so hard to empty out so much dead weight that I was absolutely weak.

> I was completely numb. I really felt like I was in the twilight zone.

SHORT-TERM ACHIEVEMENTS

All 20 participants described important achievements they felt they had accomplished during the mediation/dialogue sessions. Although these themes echo the range of reasons initially given for their decisions to participate, there are some differences. Most obtained results they had not anticipated or sought, and not everyone received the specific hoped-for outcome that had led them to make the decision.

Some of the achievements they named were actions they themselves took, some were actions taken by the offender, and some were interactive, involving both parties' actions. The achievements included receiving admissions of responsibility (12 of 20), having a human, face-to-face encounter (10 of 20), receiving answers to questions (10 of 20), asking the questions that mattered (8 of 20), holding the offender accountable (7 of 20), having an impact on the offender (7 of 20), sharing forgiveness with the offender (5 of 20), and receiving apologies (4 of 20).

Twelve of the 15 participants who reported that their offenders accepted responsibility described the experience as highly impactful, even though only six reported that they had initially sought such a response. One mother commented: "I think in a lot of ways this is probably the hardest thing the offender ever did, was to sit in front of me and accept responsibility." Another stated: "He was extremely accountable for everything he did. He wanted me to understand that he was totally responsible for the murder of my son."

A major common theme was the human nature of the encounter, named by 10 participants. "One thing that I did get accomplished was I did see him face-to-face." "Just being able to look at somebody and see that they smile with their eyes." "Just getting to sit across from him and seeing him in the eye, looking him in the eyes." The mother of another murder victim was moved by the parallel feelings and actions she shared with the offender: when the offender began to cry early in the session, she reached over with a tissue to wipe his tears. But later in the session as she herself began to cry, "He took tissue and he wiped the tears from my face. I would hope that when we put together the video of this, that part's included, not only that I comforted him."

Ten participants stressed the importance of the answers or information they received from the offenders. This included the parents of murdered daughters described above who had feared their own parenting might have contributed to their daughters' deaths. Three others were grateful for additional details about the actual events of the crime. These were the mother of an incest victim, the mother of a murdered son who learned what his last words were, and the mother described above who became enraged upon hearing the details. In spite of the shock this caused, the third mother felt the process had been extremely crucial in enabling her to work through her rage. The husband of the DWI victim was grateful that the offender was so willing to describe the incident. Two additional participants commented how helpful it was to hear more information about the life experiences of their offenders.

Eight participants said a major accomplishment was getting to ask the questions they wanted to ask. All eight felt this was beneficial, even though only six felt they had really received the answers they sought. The two who did not receive full answers commented: "It's funny how when you go through a process like that, the unknowns become much less important," and, "I know I didn't really get any of the questions answered really, but I felt a sense of relief."

Seven participants spoke of the accomplishment of simply being able to confront the offenders, to hold them accountable, to make them face what they had done. In the words of one mother of a murdered daughter, "You can tell the police officers, you can tell your friend, you can tell other people that have lost somebody, you can tell your therapist, this is how I feel and this is what he's done to me, but there's no describing that feeling when you finally get to look at him eye to eye and say 'this is what you've done, she was a real person.'" Another commented: "it was just the biggest relief…just being able to say I'm gonna confront you and you're gonna listen to what I have to say."

Having some kind of impact on the offender was named by seven participants as an important outcome. This accomplishment is highly interactive in nature, being based both on what the victim/family member has done and on how the offender has responded. Six participants described their impact as something they hoped would change the offender's future behavior. One of these met with an offender who had already been released, and the remaining five met with offenders nearing their release dates. None of the family members who met with a death row offender named having such an impact as an important outcome.

Comments included: "I think he got healing from it. That I think is not a very measurable benefit, but a benefit. I know what a dangerous person he was when he was miserable ... the more healing he can get, the safer I am," and "I know it benefited her...I think she thinks about it now." The mother who had set out to change the life of the offender learned that he had accumulated 148 disciplinary actions between his initial incarceration and the time of their mediation. At the time of the research interview some six months later, she commented, "He's not in trouble any more," even though she felt he was still just skimming the surface.

The seventh participant who named an impact on the offender as important was less concerned about affecting future behavior; she simply wanted the offender to feel what she'd been through: "I felt like I had accomplished what I went in there to do, which was essentially give him back all the pain and anguish he'd caused."

Five participants, including four relatives of murder victims and the burglary victim, spoke of the importance of sharing their forgiveness with the offender. All but one of these had already come to the point of forgiveness prior to the meeting. The fourth, the mother of a murder victim, had not anticipated forgiveness but was moved to do so during the session. "For me truly, truly to forgive him, then I felt like in my heart I did what God wanted me to. And I felt a relief...I hadn't slept in years good at night – and I slept all night long when I got home."

Four family members reported being especially affected by the apologies they received from their offenders. Two of these were parents of murdered children. One, who was moved by the effort the offender was making to turn his life around, commented: "he made the statement that he was really sorry my daughter had to forfeit her life for him to have another chance at life." The other is the mother who became overwhelmed with feelings when the offender described what he had done. "I was crying pretty hard. And he just sat there and he just said over and over and over again, 'yes ma'am, I know, yes ma'am, I'm so sorry.'" The other two were the stepfather whose home was burgled by his stepson, and the mother of a vehicular homicide victim who met with a surrogate.

LONGER-TERM OUTCOMES

Eighteen of the 20 participants spoke of major positive life changes, which they attributed to their participation in the mediation/dialogue sessions, including changes in their general outlook on life (11), changes in their view of the offender for the better (13), personal growth and healing

(14), and a positive impact on their spirituality (9). Participants also spoke of understanding why the event took place (4), forgiveness, (11) and issues of future contact with the offender (7).

Overall Outlook on Life

Fifteen of the participants were asked in a structured question whether their overall outlook on life had changed since meeting with the offender; the results are summarized in Table 5.4. In addition to the 11 who responded positively on the structured scale, two additional participants who were not asked the structured question reported spontaneously that their outlook on life had changed, for a total of 13. A wife responded to the question with, "Are you kidding? I mean, it totally changed my life." Another participant stated she could "start living now...I feel human for the first time in years." Another added, "I don't know if it's to the degree that other people have noticed it or not, but it's my inner feelings and I feel much more able to cope." The two who spontaneously described such a change included one who felt she had gained "self awareness" and another who commented that prior to the mediation, "My life was damn near over at that point."

Changes in View of Offender

Thirteen participants reported that their view of the offender changed as a result of the meeting, all for the better. Seven felt that the offender became more human to them as a result of the meeting. "I believe he has a decent heart," "He's not a Charles Manson," "He's just another person, just another human being." Five felt they understood the offender better, and five felt more compassion.

The experiences of four of these family members are especially noteworthy for their complete about-face in attitude. The granddaughter commented, "For a very long time, I would have put the needle in his arm. Before that, I would have shot him; before that, I would have tortured him." A mother reported that before deciding to meet her daughter's killer, she would come into the parole board office at each hearing saying, "Is he dead yet? Does he have AIDS? Has somebody killed him? Well, this is a violent prison, why can't we put him there?" The mother of another murder victim commented, "I don't think I have ever hated three people more in all my life. But now I pity him."

Table 5.4: Has Your Overall Outlook on Life Changed Since Meeting the Offender?*

No	4	26.7%
Yes	11	73.3%
Of those who answered yes:		
a. Definitely more positive and at peace with the circumstances I am faced with.	11	(73.3%)
b. Somewhat more positive and able to cope with my life.	0	
c. Somewhat more negative and less able to cope with my life.	0	
d. Definitely more negative and angry about the circumstances I am faced with.	0	
e. Other.	0	
None of the above.	0	

* Fifteen participants were asked this question.

A father initially had wished for the death penalty for his offender: "There's nothing more insulting than, you're a citizen, somebody's killed your daughter, he's admitted to it, and you find out they can't even ask the death penalty." He had even come to feel death would not be sufficient punishment because it was too quick, and it would be better for the offender to rot in prison for the rest of his life. Yet both this father and the burglary victim sought to help their offenders obtain parole as a result of their experiences during the dialogue.

Three family members, all of them relatives of murder victims, did not change their opinions. For two, this meant they retained their negative opinions. "I will always think he's an animal...he had time, he did not have to kill my daughter"; and "I think it's something the offender would do again." The third, when asked if her opinion had changed, simply said, "No, I have never harbored hate."

And there were four participants for whom there is no information about their opinion of the offender. Two were simply not asked the question. The remaining two met with surrogates and had no prior experience with the offender with whom they met. One of them, however, commented, "I already knew he was sincere. God bless him for having the courage to come out and face someone, a mother, that he doesn't know."

Personal Growth and Healing

Among the 13 who reported a changed outlook on the closed-ended question, eight participants mentioned spontaneously in the research interview that they felt more at peace. Comments included: "I didn't have any peace. I do now. I was able to release all that stuff and give it all back to the offender — I left it there," and, "I'm much more at peace with myself and with the offender and with the way my grandmother died."

One participant who met with a surrogate offender reported that an important component of personal growth for her was that the dialogue session validated her experience. She added, "My whole life has been about finding the part of my soul that's missing."

Twelve family members whose relative had died, including all four whose offenders were sentenced to execution, reported that their negative feelings had greatly diminished since the meetings. Not everyone spontaneously named the feelings that had changed, but of those who did, specific feelings mentioned included anger (7), sadness or depression (3) and fear and bitterness (1). Two participants reported sleeping better and one described leaving bad feelings behind when leaving the mediation/dialogue session. One participant reported that this change primarily took place during her preparation, in which she explored residual rage at her father's early death. She commented that the preparation alone helped her heal, even if she had never gotten to meet with the offender. Typical comments included:

My daughter's dead ... But I know I'm better, I can sleep at night, I know it's a good feeling not to hate some monster.

I went there with all this baggage and bad feelings ... When I left, I left something with (the offender).

My feelings were using up a lot of energy.

I had no future. I wanted to die. I have my future again.

There is a syndrome called P.L.O.M. syndrome, "poor little old me," and I don't have to suffer that anymore.

Impact on Spiritual Outlook

Fifteen of the participants were asked in a structured question whether their participation in the mediation/dialogue program had an impact on their spirituality. The results are summarized in Table 5.5 below. The participant who reported "none of the above" clarified, "It didn't change it, it impacted one particular part."

Table 5.5: Effect on Victim/Family Member Religious or Spiritual Life*

Did the process of preparing to meet the victim and the actual meeting have any effect on your religious or spiritual life?		
No	**6**	**40%**
Yes	**9**	**60%**
Of those who answered yes:		
a. Greatly enriched my religious/spiritual perspective.	7	(46.7%)
b. Contributed to a deeper religious/spiritual perspective.	1	(6.7%)
c. Contributed to a weakening of my religious/spiritual perspective.		
d. Greatly weakened my religious/spiritual perspective.		
None of the above.	1	(6.7%)

* Fifteen participants were asked this question.

Five of the seven further commented that they very much felt the presence of God supporting them through the mediation. One prayed before going in, "Please, just help me hear God to keep me focused," and commented afterwards, "I couldn't do today without God." Another mother commented, "I had prayed very, very hard for God to work on my heart...to be able to go in and say and do the right things and behave in a way that would be prideful to my daughter." She added that during the session, "I just felt God's protection all over me...my faith has only increased...because I haven't made God responsible for the bad things that have happened in my life." And the mother of another murder victim said, "I've taken the power of what happened to me and I've gone into the prisons and empowered them to change their lives and I wouldn't have been able to do that if (my son) hadn't been murdered." She added, "I very consciously everyday work at doing what I can to change this planet to a more peaceful, loving, gentle caring place, and I'm only one person — but I'm pretty powerful."

Five of those who reported that their spirituality didn't change as a result of the meeting had more to say about why that was the case. For all of them, other events in their lives had more profoundly affected their spirituality than the dialogue session. One participant felt the direction of the change was the other way around; the changes in her spirituality led her to seek the mediation. The mother of a murder victim commented, "I think losing my son had more affect on my spiritual life than the meeting."

Forgiveness Issues

A total of 11 participants mentioned forgiveness at some point in their interview. Of these, six had come to forgive the offender, and all six shared this forgiveness with the offender during the mediation/dialogue session. Of the five who reported that they had not forgiven, three felt they had moved closer to forgiveness and might some day do so. "I don't know if I've forgiven him. Sometimes I think I have, and then he gets a stay of execution! But I would say I have more days where I'm feeling forgiveness towards him than otherwise. Whereas before I had more days where I would die before I forgave him." "There's no way I can go to heaven if I don't attempt to forgive. If I'm ever gonna make it to heaven, I can't do it by hating somebody. I've tried; I may not be all right with (the offender), but I'm all right with God 'cause I've tried." The remaining two participants felt they could not forgive. In one instance, the offender raised the issue in the meeting: "He just about asked me. He said, 'I wish you could forgive me, I shouldn't expect you to.' It was a lead-in. I said, 'I'm human. I don't have it in me. Forgiveness means it is all right what you did to me.'" Another parent of a murder victim commented, "God gave me two precious gifts and he took one of them away. That I can never forgive him for."

Understanding Why the Event Took Place

Three of the four family members who reported that understanding why the event took place was an important outcome were parents of murdered daughters. For all three, the dialogues set to rest their fears that their parenting had in any way contributed to their daughters' deaths. Both were vastly relieved to hear from the offenders that nothing their daughters had done in any way invited or caused their deaths. The fourth, the wife of a murder victim, commented as follows:

> I think that is probably the greatest gift that it gave me. I mean, I didn't like why. I don't drink, and a lot of it has to do with (the crime) because I see the end result of what it will do. But finally, I could find out why. I really didn't care what the answer was, I just wanted the answer.

Further Contact with Offenders

Nine participants are not in any type of continued contact with the offenders and have no wish to do so. For an additional four participants, the offender was subsequently executed. Of the remaining seven, six are already in contact with the offender with whom they met. This includes one family member who met with a surrogate. This last participant, and the other who met with a surrogate, also clarified that they hope eventually to be able to have such a meeting with their actual offender.

Victims/family members who maintain contact chiefly do so through letters. As already noted, one offender sends monthly updates and includes a dollar each month for the charity of the victim's choice. Family members in two additional cases are exchanging letters periodically as a way of supporting the offender's goals and rehabilitation. Three family members became involved in supporting the offender in obtaining parole or being moved to a prison closer to home.

VICTIM/FAMILY MEMBER EVALUATION OF THE EXPERIENCE

All participants were asked to rate their satisfaction with their involvement in the program, and 15 were additionally asked to rate the helpfulness of the meeting. These results are summarized in Table 5.6 and 5.7 below. The single interviewee who selected "somewhat satisfied" was the mother of a vehicular homicide victim. She had met with a surrogate offender, and she clarified that her reasons for selecting this response was that she still hopes to be able to meet with the actual offender in her case.

For many participants, the simple selection of set responses on an evaluation scale was not sufficient to convey some of their feelings, and they commented as follows:

On a scale of one to ten, it's a hundred.

There aren't any words that would adequately express what I feel, I just feel good.

I think it is the best thing I have ever done for myself.

It was worth every moment of preparation, every second of the process, to just have that information.

Five commented on what they found most helpful or beneficial in their meeting. The wide variety across these five responses underscores the great range both of motivation for participating in dialogue with the offender and of specific outcomes experienced by victims of violent crimes. In their own words:

Probably the self awareness.

I know my daughter didn't give him any reason to kill her.

I finally got to tell him what I wanted to.

I did have him look me straight in the face and tell me he killed her.

The most important thing was that I could tell him I had forgiven him.

Table 5.6: Victim/Family Member Overall Satisfaction with Involvement in Victim Offender Mediation and Dialogue Program

Very satisfied	19	(95%)
Somewhat satisfied	1	(5%)
Somewhat dissatisfied	0	
Very dissatisfied	0	
Total	20	(100%)

Table 5.7: Victim/Family Member Rating of the Helpfulness of the Meeting*

Very helpful	15	(100%)
Somewhat helpful	0	
Not at all helpful	0	
Total	15	(100%)

*Fifteen participants were asked this question.

Recommendations for Other Victims and Family Members

Eleven interviewees were asked whether they would recommend participation and all stated they would do so, though they were quick to add that it needed to be completely up to the individual. As one put it, "yes, if their intent and purpose is the same." Four further commented that they already are active in strongly recommending participation to friends who have been victimized and/or speaking to groups. And four underscored that it's "not for everyone."

Fifteen of the participants commented on what they would advise others in similar circumstances. This included the 11 who recommended mediation/dialogue for other victims of violent crime. Five felt strongly that meeting with the offender should be made routinely available as an option for victims of violent crime. One expressed hope that the present study would help make mediation more obtainable for others. One encouraged victims to assess their own readiness to meet rather than rely on program staff to determine when they are ready. And one felt the state should reach out more than it does to make sure victims know the opportunity is available.

The reasons participants suggested others strongly look into meeting with their offender echoed the reasons they themselves chose to meet: for healing, to express feelings, to obtain answers, to make the offenders face what they have done, and to help with rehabilitation. Comments included the following:

> How could you be any worse off?

> Only one person deserves your anger.

> There's only one person who can answer all your questions.

> I think it is one of the most cleansing things that you can do.

> I believe that every inmate that comes in here that has done a violent assault ought to have to face what he's done. He ought to have to admit what he's done and say how he's gonna correct what he's done, he's gonna have to show corrections that he's making within himself and within the system.

Other advice included a strong recommendation to bring photos, though the participant also cautioned, "I recommend that you do not take treasured family photos, what I did was scan them in a copy machine and mount them on white card stock. I wrote on it who it was." From the same participant came advice about the opening statement: "I would recommend to anyone that they really work on that first section of what you have to say. First of all, they can get up and walk out at any time."

Changes Recommended by Victims/Family Members

When asked whether there was anything the mediator could have done differently or better, 14 of the 20 participants could think of nothing. The seven suggestions of the remaining six interviewees have more to do with preparation, structure, and other needs than with mediator activity during the session.

In terms of preparation, one expressed surprise at how differently the mediator behaved in the session from her behavior during the preparation. She was pleased with her mediator's laid back role during the meeting, but wished she had realized there would be a difference. One, mentioned earlier, wished there had been more attention given to the physical arrangement of the room so she would have had space for the items she had brought with her. One whose meeting was held in the community was distressed that she had to drive to a second location and sign papers with a notary public, the offender and the mediator before beginning the dialogue. One commented she wished in retrospect they had taken more breaks.

Two who commented raised post-dialogue issues. One who had evidently resisted de-briefing urged that the mediator insist on it and in fact push for it: "Don't allow us to dictate when debriefing comes. We can put debriefing off forever and we need it." Another who had requested her offender to write her now felt the relationship was becoming too intense and wished for support and assistance to back off without harming the offender: "I don't want to hurt his feelings, but I do want him to go on even without me."

One who met with a surrogate offender had a strong recommendation that the program put more pressure on offenders to meet if a victim wishes to do so. "When a man has been found guilty of a crime and is now convicted, the power and rights should be stronger on the victim's side."

CONCLUSION

All 20 of these participating victims and family members had powerful, positive experiences in meeting with offenders who had caused them harm or, in two instances, surrogate offenders who had caused others similar harm. Their reasons for seeking to do so were divergent, their experiences within the mediation dialogue sessions varied, and not all of their objectives were met. But they concurred that they were glad they took the opportunity, they believed it had helped them, and they were satisfied with the experience they had had. In the words of a mother of a murder victim, "If everybody in the country would do it we'd have a better world because I know it makes you a better person and it makes them a better person."

CHAPTER 6.
TEXAS OFFENDERS: EXPERIENCE AND IMPACT

Descriptive information on the research design and the entire set of Texas program research participants has been provided in chapter 5. The present chapter reports on 19 offenders who were interviewed in the research project between October 1998 and January 2001. Nine were interviewed in person, and 10 were interviewed by telephone. All interviews were tape recorded and transcribed. Parts of three interview audiotapes were lost, but most data were still available through the interviewer's notes and summary narrative.

CHARACTERISTICS OF OFFENDERS AND CRIMES

The 19 offenders included 17 men and two women. There were 17 Caucasians, including two Hispanics, and two African Americans. At the time of the crime, the age of the 18 offenders for whom data were available averaged 25 and ranged from 17 to 48; six were 21 or under. Twelve of the 18 who were asked said they had never previously been convicted of a violent crime. The 20 crimes committed by the 19 offenders are summarized in Table 6.1 below; one offender committed two separate murders, each of which was the focus of a combined mediation session.

An average of 9.4 years elapsed between the time of the crime and the date of the mediation/dialogue session, with a range from three years to 27 years. The murders took considerably longer than other crimes to come to mediation, averaging 11.3 years. The average for all the other crimes was 5.3 years.

In 12 of the 20 crimes (committed by 11 offenders) — including one sexual assault, two vehicular homicides, and 9 murders — the actual crime victim was not previously acquainted with the offender. However, in one of these murder cases the offender's co-defendant knew the victim and thereby gained entry to the house. In another, the offender had been friends with the victim's daughter, but had never met the victim.

Table 6.1: Crimes of the Texas Offenders

Crime	N	(%)
Murder/manslaughter	13	(65%)
Vehicular homicide	2	(10%)
Sexual assault	4	(20%)
Theft/burglary	1	(5%)
Total	20	(100%)

In the remaining eight crimes, there was some degree of acquaintance between the offender and the crime victim. These victims included an acquaintance, a friend, and two spouses who were murdered, two daughters and the child of a friend who were victims of sexual assault, and a former stepfather who was a burglary victim. Because the Texas program is focused on serious and violent crime, it should perhaps be noted at this point that the offender who met with his stepfather reported that there had been physical threat in their relationship, although the burglary itself was not a violent crime.

Three of the offenders, who participated in mediation/dialogue with a total of four family members, had been sentenced to execution for their murders and were on death row at the time of the mediation dialogue sessions. All three have since been executed. More detailed coverage of the special issues involved in these three cases is provided in Appendix A. In the present chapter, material on these cases is simply integrated with that of the rest of the offenders.

The 19 offenders participated in a total of 20 facilitated dialogue sessions between May 1995 and December 2000. They met with 21 persons directly affected by their crimes: 2 actual victims, and 19 family members of their victims, including 11 mothers, 2 fathers, 1 wife, 2 sisters, 1 brother, 1 daughter and 1 granddaughter. These figures include data on two offenders who participated in dialogue as surrogate offenders with victim/family members of a similar crime; they met with an actual victim and a mother of a victim.

Offender Descriptions of the Crime Events and Reactions

Offenders were asked to describe in their own words what happened at the time of the crime. One offender declined to answer this question. Of the remaining 18, 11 described what they had done in clear, direct language and took ownership of it: "I walked into a store, took the money, took the girl, took her to my house, raped her, killed her, then I went and dumped her off." "I was involved in a car race...I hit somebody and then noticed the victim from behind. And I had a shock, and to rationalize the situation I took off." "I had been drinking. I was driving home. I hit another car head on. Both people in the other car died instantly." "I molested my daughter. It went on, for her I'm sure it was like a lifetime, but my crime spread out over about three months."

The remaining seven minimized their offense or used vague or passive language to describe what they had done. One offender convicted of murder described his crime as follows: "I think it was just more of a pure opportunity that came up. I'd be passing by that area and the opportunity would present itself, and that's when I committed the crimes." Similarly, one sex abuser condensed several months of repeated abuse into the following sentence: "I was intoxicated and molested a (young) girl."

Nine offenders reported some extent of blackout or memory loss at the time of the crime itself. For two of these, the memories became clear at a later point: "In between, I didn't remember, but I finally sliced back on it, so that's when I turned myself in." The remaining seven reported in the research interviews that they still didn't remember parts of the events; six of these were among the offenders noted above who gave vague or minimizing accounts of their actions. "'I didn't even know I had done it the next day"; "I don't remember how I actually got the knife, don't remember actually stabbing her"; "I have a problem with the chronological sequence. I remember incidents or parts randomly."

Offenders were not routinely asked whether or not they were using drugs or alcohol at the time of the crime. Five made no mention of alcohol or drug use, and three volunteered that they were not on any drugs or alcohol at the time of their crime: "I told him I ain't on drugs, never have." "No, they kinda produce anxiety and paranoia, I didn't like it so I just never messed with drugs."

The remaining 11 offenders reported either drug or alcohol use or both: "I was constantly putting a needle in my arm every day." "I was experimenting with dope, drinking a lot, being a crazy kid." "It looked like a good idea. When you are filled up drinking, anything seemed like a good idea." Five of these were among the offenders who gave vague descriptions of their actions and who reported memory loss about details of their crime.

Nine of the offenders referred to events in their earlier life as part of their descriptions of their crimes. For four, the threads went back to their childhood: "When I was a kid growing up, Daddy wouldn't let me fight. One day in seventh grade, from that day forward, I wasn't taking it no more." Two reported they had been victims of childhood sexual abuse, and one reported a long-standing emotional problem: "any kind of emotion or feeling, I would literally bury them." The remaining five traced the important patterns to their teenage years. "From the time I was about 13 or 14 is when it all started, small stuff, stealing bikes and stuff like that."

Offenders were asked to describe the initial impact of the crime and how they felt about it. Seven did not comment on specific feelings, and four of these gave no further detail, simply describing events rather than feelings or reactions. Of the remaining three, one referred to frustration later on that the parole board gave him more prison time than others whose release was not opposed by their victims; one commented that "there was always the chance I still coulda got away," and one simply said "I wasn't thinking straight, I was thinking everybody but me sent me to prison."

Of the remaining 12, one reported not having feelings, three reported a mix of both negative and positive feelings, and eight reported only negative feelings. The one who denied having feelings reported, "I can't really say that I had any feelings about it, it was like I blocked everything out. I never allowed myself to deal with the pain."

Negative feelings included fear or worry (6), loneliness and loss (3), guilt (2), suicidal feelings (2), sadness (1), and feeling numb and shut down (1). "Scared for sure. I knew I had done wrong, I didn't know what was gonna happen." "Just a fear, Oh my God, I couldn't have done this." "I was gonna commit suicide." "I couldn't release all the guilt. I couldn't eat, I couldn't sleep for days, at work they had this article about this girl that had died in a car race and I knew it was my fault." "The confusion and shock, realizing my life had changed forever, a numb feeling, kinda shut down."

Of three who reported mixed reactions, one expressed concern for others rather than himself: "I guess I was very relaxed…at the time I was not worrying about myself, I was more worried for my brother, I was trying to get them out of trouble for something I had done." The other two found something positive that emerged from the crime in addition to strong negative feelings reported above: "But one thing that did transpire at the time of the murder is I never used drugs again." "But what it did do is start me in therapy recovering, recognition of my own childhood trauma."

Five of the 19 offenders reported that they turned themselves in. Two took this action immediately following the crime: "I called the police and told them what had happened, no sirens, to not wake the kids." Two others left the scene at the time of the crime but turned themselves in later, one (quoted earlier) when he finally remembered it, and one after attempting suicide and finding he couldn't do it. "I knew what I had to do was turn myself in, I was really scared. Not running, that was basically the first good decision I'd made in a long time." And one voluntarily turned himself in after the sex abuse investigation had been completed.

Thirteen of the remaining 14 left the scene and/or attempted to avoid arrest. Three of these reported denying what they had done even after being arrested: "I wasn't even sure which one they was talking about, and they wouldn't give any names, so I stonewalled them." "They wanted to ask me if I did it, I had to make a decision, to build a wall, because I didn't want people, especially my family, to be hurt." One offender had no opportunity to leave the scene; he was hospitalized for serious injury in the vehicular accident caused by his drunken driving, and was transferred to a prison hospital within a day of the accident.

Only four of the 19 offenders, including three who personally knew their victim and had turned themselves in, spontaneously reported any degree of feeling or empathy for their victim at the time of the crime. "When I looked at her, that she was in trouble, that she wasn't here no more, I told her I was sorry,…I just kept thinking about what the funeral was like and how hard her family and friends was probably grieving." "As egotistical and cocky as I was, I understood that…these lives were important. If I had pled not guilty, then I was somehow denouncing the importance of those lives. I didn't want to put them or their family members or anybody else through that."

INTRODUCTION TO MEDIATION AND FIRST REACTIONS

Prior to being invited to participate in mediation/dialogue, eight of the 19 offenders were previously aware of the mediation program and/or had initiated efforts to contact their victims/family members. One of these had participated in a mediation arranged by a cable television program; he had told his victim's mother at that time, if she wanted to meet again, "you know where I am, you know where I'm gonna be." Two had written "amends" letters to their victims/family members through their participation in twelve-step programs. Though they had at that time been unaware of the mediation/dialogue program, they were grateful to have the chance to further carry out their amends in person. And one was in touch with the victim's family through a mutual friend, who told the offender the victim's mother wished to meet; both the offender and the mother then initiated contact with program staff.

The remaining four had learned about the program through Victim Services and had made efforts themselves to initiate mediation through the program. This included the two surrogate offenders. In one of these cases, the offender was told he could not meet with his victim/family member unless that person initiated contact. "The mediator asked me if I'd like to meet with somebody else, another victim. I said it can't hurt." The other surrogate offender, not incarcerated, was a frequent speaker at sex abuse victim panels. "A victim at such a panel had questions that she needed to ask, and felt like out of my honesty and openness and not trying to cover up with any minimization, that she could do some recovery by mediating with me." The remaining two had contacted Victim Services to indicate their willingness to participate, and were left to wait until the victim made contact. One of them commented, "Of all the people in the program at that time, we were the only two that had written in to see each other."

Eleven of the 19 offenders had been unaware of any program for meeting with their victim/family members when they were contacted by program staff. Three offenders, all of them on death row for murder, reported that they had always hoped to be able to meet. "In my own soul searching, I had gotten to the point where I wished I could in some way contact the victims families, just to nothing more than be able to say that I'm sorry and ask for forgiveness." "I've always wanted to tell this woman and her family that I was sorry for what I done. I just didn't have the avenue for doing it."

Of the remaining eight, the initial reactions on learning about the program were positive for three, negative for three, and mixed for two. "When he asked me I already knew I was gonna say 'yeah.'" "I said, well, I have to do it." "I had heard so many things and rumors and death threats on me, at first I declined, I was just scared." "I didn't know why he wanted to talk to me." "I was still angry all the time, just wanted to go home." This last offender reported that he changed his mind after he watched videos of other mediations, which led him to trust the mediator.

For the two whose initial reaction was mixed, the issue was timing. One had heard about the program and decided to postpone initiating contact because it was too soon, but was pleased when the family member initiated mediation six months later. And the second reported that the family member had sought mediation a few months after the accident. "They diagnosed me with post traumatic shock, I was in no shape to mediate." But when he was ready, he got in touch with the program and asked if they could proceed.

REASONS FOR PARTICIPATING IN MEDIATION/DIALOGUE

In describing why they chose or sought to participate in mediation/dialogue, offenders reported general reasons (5 offenders), benefits to the victim/family member (17 offenders), and benefits to themselves (16 offenders). All offenders listed at least one reason, for a total of 70 responses. It should be noted that many reasons could conceivably benefit both the victim/family member and offender; great care was exercised in categorizing the data to reflect the intent of the interviewee.

General reasons included: to try to make something good come out of something bad (2), because it was the right thing to do (2), and because the mediator was warm and made the offender feel comfortable (1). "Maybe take a chance and make something good come out of it." "To take whatever darkness I could out of this world." "Just to try to make things right, the best I could." "To give something back because I took a lot."

Seventeen of the 19 offenders listed a total of 35 responses naming benefits to the victim or family member as among the reasons they chose to participate. These included apologizing (7 offenders), helping the victim/family member heal in general (7 offenders), answering questions (5 offenders), taking responsibility (4 offenders), helping them release their anger (3 offenders), listening to whatever they needed to say (3 offenders), allaying the victims'/family members' fears (3 offenders) and because they owed it to them (2 offenders).

The seven who listed apology offered little further comment about it; the wish to apologize typically was embedded in a list of reasons focused on accountability and healing for the victim/family member. The seven who listed supporting the healing of their victim/family members in a general way had such comments as: "I wanted to do something that would help the families to live on," and "I wanted to do basically anything I could to help them deal with what had happened."

Five focused on answering questions. "For me to answer any questions that he had, to help him work through it." "The only thing I could give that woman is answers to why her son was murdered, there's a lot of questions, mysteries that was haunting her all these years." One surrogate stated: "to help her be able to ask some questions of a perpetrator, not her own, some of those burning questions that she never got to ask." The notion of answering questions proved a turning point for one offender who had initially decided not to participate: "I looked at it like, if that lady dies in her sleep tonight, she would benefit from this here, all these questions, answers."

Taking responsibility can easily be for both the offender's and victim/family member's benefit. The four who cited a desire for accountability named some way they felt it would help their victim/family members. "For the victim's recovery,...to let the victim know that I was aware of my abusive behavior, to be accountable for those type of things." "I want them both to know that I am taking responsibility and I don't take any of this lightly." "To let him know it's not your fault."

Listening to whatever the victim/family member needed to say and helping the victim/family member release anger are closely related, and were each listed by three offenders. "To give her the chance to say whatever she wanted to." "To allow them to tell me whatever it is they felt they had to tell me, regardless it was good or bad, I just felt that I had to listen." "To help her to give release to her anger." "Because of my childhood, I understood that hate was a cancer. What I hoped for is if they were able to identify and release some of the anger and frustration and pain, then perhaps that would allow them to grow."

Three spoke of allaying victim/family member fears. For one, this had to do with rumors that the murder he committed had been a hate crime. He wanted his victim's mother to know "he was never singled out, he just pulled up at the wrong place at the wrong time." This same offender and two more also sought to assure their victim's family member that there was nothing to fear in the future. "I figured she thought since I was ready to go home, I was gonna stalk her."

And two simply felt they owed it to their victim/family member, with little further comment.

During the research interviews, offenders were asked whether or not as part of deciding to participate they considered any potential benefits to themselves. Three offenders took pains to make it clear they expected nothing for themselves. "There's really no benefits. I didn't feel it was me, I hurt her just as much as I hurt myself." "I didn't expect anything" "I can't stress enough that I wasn't motivated for myself."

The remaining 16 offenders offered a total of 30 responses that included some type of benefit to themselves as part of their reason for choosing to participate in mediation/dialogue. These included for their own general healing or rehabilitation (7 offenders), being accountable as it related to their own healing (4 offenders), to lift a burden or clear their conscience (4 offenders), to seek forgiveness (4 offenders), to change the victim/family member's view of the offender (3 offenders), to change the victim/family member's view of what happened (3 offenders), to learn who the victim was and get the other side of the story (3 offenders), and to obtain information for their own healing (2 offenders).

The seven descriptions of general healing were sometimes vague or cryptic and sometimes elaborate: "For recovery." "To be able to go on." "To bring more clarity and healing on my side." "I would feel better if she could unload on me." "It was important for me to be able to begin picking up the pieces."

Four named being accountable or facing what they'd done as something that would support their own healing. "I wanna face my fears, the only way I'm going to be able to survive the rest of my life." "So instead of putting the blame on everybody else, I finally took full responsibility for everything I had done in my life."

Four wanted to clear their conscience or relieve a burden. Two did not further elaborate. A third commented "it would help me by knowing they were all right." The fourth stated he would feel better if the victim's mother could "get her hands on me and just literally unload on me."

Four spoke of wishing to ask the family member for forgiveness or hoping to be forgiven. One of these was a surrogate offender, and he clarified that he hoped his actual victim could forgive him; he did not seek forgiveness from the surrogate victim with whom he met. Two specifically named "asking for forgiveness" as one of their reasons for deciding to meet. A third commented, "I had hoped to find a forgiveness. You know, that was kind of the selfish part of it; I wanted to be forgiven."

Four offenders wished to change victim's or family members' perceptions of themselves and/or of the crime. "To let her see me as a person and not a monster, that I'm somebody who made a mistake." "To let them know I'm not this monster they had imagined in their minds." Both of these offenders also wished their family member to know what really happened: "The (family member) wasn't too informed with what had happened, she had been spreading some rumors that weren't true." "To look these people in the eye and tell them I never meant to do it on purpose." One additional offender wanted the family member to see him differently. Another wanted to let the family member know what really happened "because it was never discussed, because I denied it all the way to the very end."

Three wanted to learn more about the victim. "That I would get to know who my victims were. That was important to me." "To actually see who she really was, see the effects of what happened." "I felt I needed to see the other side of the story,…this would help me stop thinking just about myself." This last offender further added: "A lot of prisoners don't think about what they did, and that is the reason for the high turnaround rate."

And two sought information that would help them with their own healing. "To be able to get the full impact from their perspective of just where I was at that time in my life." One of these was a surrogate offender whose main reason for meeting with someone not his own victim was to help the victim; however, he also felt he would benefit because she had a lot of the same questions he had.

Six offenders mentioned some kind of spiritual component in listing their reasons to meet. Two reported spending time praying in reaching their decision; another felt the contact from his victim's mother requesting to meet was "an answer to a prayer." One of these, and one additional offender, reported that they had given their lives to Christ, and the decision to mediate was an inevitable next step. And two spoke of God "putting it in my mind" or "putting it down into my heart to reach out."

Fourteen offenders made no mention of whether they had consulted anyone else in the process of deciding to participate in mediation. One additional offender clarified quite explicitly that he had not consulted anyone else: "The family that I left, they're out there, they have nothing to do with what I do in here. This is another life. I don't tell them much. I pretty much just keep it separate."

The remaining four offenders reported talking it over with either friends, family members, or both. The three who spoke with friends reported finding them supportive. One of these had made contact with the victim's family through this mutual friend. Another reported his friend's advice before going in to the mediation: "He was telling me, you're gonna feel like crap, whatever you do, don't go off on her. He was reminding me, don't do nothing crazy." A death row offender who spoke with his "Christian brothers" on death row also reported that talking with his family about the mediation led to "more open conversation, they were pretty supportive, I think it helped open up some doors, more heartfelt discussions." He added that it had helped them face his upcoming execution.

Only one offender reported a negative reaction from his family. His mother was "one hundred percent against it, she thought (the victim's mother) would come down here and hurt me."

Risks Considered

Eighteen offenders were asked whether they considered any risks or fears in making their decision. Four felt there was no risk; one elaborated, "The mediator had earned my trust, he told me it'd be a safe setting, so I really wasn't afraid of anything." The remaining 14 offenders gave a total of 16 risks or fears they had considered.

The most frequently named fear was what the victim/family member or family member might do, reported by 12 offenders. Seven of these reported fearing physical harm at some level. Two had received or heard of threats from the family member they were to meet with. One commented, "I always have feared my life, even when tours come through." The other had heard "that he would gladly take my life to get this few minutes back with his daughter." Another offender, whose victim's mother had actively protested his parole, was worried the victim would walk in and shoot him. A fourth offender thought "she might take this video to anyone, people might want to kill me." Other fears were that the family member might "take it out on my family" or "spit on the glass, try to hit me."

The remaining five were also focused on the rage or anger that the victim or family member might feel toward them, but did not anticipate physical actions: "I expected to be yelled at and cussed at and everything else" "I thought he'd come tell me I was wrong." "Somebody getting on their soapbox, throwing slurs, calling names, getting angry."

The four remaining risks were named by one offender each. One feared a negative impact on his appeals or parole, but added, "I got to the point where I didn't really care about that part of it, even if down the road it could be used against me, well, big deal. This is what I need." One feared "a sense of confidentiality and protection, this type of thing becoming sensationalized." One was simply scared of facing the family member: "It's very fearful having to sit in front of somebody, I mean, what do you say? I killed your daughter: What else goes with that?" The fourth reported being most worried about not saying anything that would hurt the victim.

PREPARATION FOR THE MEDIATION/DIALOGUE SESSIONS

Information for this section is taken both from Texas program records and from the research interviews with the offenders. According to program records, the offenders' preparation averaged 17 months, and ranged from 4 months to 25 months. In an open-ended question inviting descriptions of the preparation, only eight offenders commented on the length and structure; their estimates of the length corresponded with the data reported by the program. Only four had comments about the reasons for the length. One received a shorter than usual preparation because "this lady was anxious to get this over with." One ascribed the 18-month length to his own behavior because he had gotten into a fight on the unit. One experienced a delay due to video recording issues; the mediation was postponed until the program successfully negotiated permission to record the session. And one simply reported sometimes the meetings were "a few months apart" depending on the mediator's schedule.

In describing the preparation they received, the offenders focused on being told what would happen (13), working through the packet of readings and questionnaires (10), having the mediator bring information back and forth from the victim/family member (4), the mediator's efforts to put them at ease (4), the process of facing their actions and their feelings (4), and the videotapes, role plays and coaching (1 each).

Comments included the following:

> He laid it out on the line so I could understand what was gonna happen.

> Saying so far we never had no one attack their offender, even if she does go off, it won't be nothing violent...she's got to go through a preparation just like you do.

> A few packets to work on about my emotions, what I was going through at the time, not dealing with thoughts, emphasize it wasn't an accident, it was my choice, consequences.

> It was a lot of questions about putting yourself in the victim's place, what kind of position did you put the victim in.

> Relaying anything I wanted to share with them, things to let them know I care, or let me know this is what they were thinking.

> She came in one day and plopped down a 150-something page packet and she said "here, I'll see you in a month." And I guess she knew the best way to handle me, cause I started to read it. That prep packet is the single most important thing I've ever done to understand myself.

She pointed out stuff I've never really thought of, like my people, I destroyed their lives, too, like my Mom. Cause I don't think she ever knew she would raise a murderer.

She really checked me on a lot of things I didn't realize I did, the way I speak, helped me clarify how I feel without coming out all wrong.

Offender Evaluation of the Preparation Process

Offenders were asked to rate their satisfaction with their preparation. Their responses are reported in Table 6.2.

Table 6.2: Offender Satisfaction with Preparation for Mediation/Dialogue

Very satisfied	19	(100%)
Somewhat satisfied		
Somewhat dissatisfied		
Very dissatisfied		
Total	19	(100%)

Additionally, all 18 who were asked in an open-ended question whether they felt adequately prepared gave a positive response. "Absolutely." "Yes, once they had met me, it was absolutely great." "I think I was well prepared. Nothing occurred that I didn't have somebody prepare."

Five of these further clarified that, in the end, nothing can fully prepare a person for what they were to experience. "How could anybody prepare you for meeting somebody that you ripped her heart apart?" "I don't think anything would have gotten me ready to sit down in front of a man, taking his daughter's life, and I am to meet with him? There is nothing that really can."

Offenders described which preparation components were helpful in response to two separate questions in the interview. Ten offenders spontaneously named 17 preparation components in describing why they felt adequately prepared. In addition, a follow-up question asked offenders what they had found most helpful; 18 offenders named an additional 25 items in response.

The program paperwork topped the list of helpful component, mentioned a total of 14 times by 10 offenders. Two who felt it was helpful gave no further detail about how it helped. Of the remaining eight offenders, six focused on how the paperwork helped them face the details of what they'd done and felt, even though, for some, it was quite painful. "I believe the homework helped a lot. My main question coming into everything was to understand why this happened and help me see some things that had been going on with me." "Everything that I was feeling got out on paper one way or another at some point in that packet." "It brought it back out. It had been ten years. I just wrote how it was. It disrupted how I did my daily activity. I couldn't concentrate. It was painful to a point, but I didn't never resent it, God was telling me it's time to face your fears."

The paperwork focusing on the twelve-step approach, and the components emphasizing the offense cycle, were named as helpful by three offenders each. "He gave me a book that I read, I was able to actually in a way turn it into my own little twelve steps, it was a very insightful period." "Within that packet were the real keys to getting to know myself, the twelve steps, the cycle of re-offense, it helped me understand why I'd been doing the same things over and over in my head."

The next element most frequently named as helpful consisted of mediator-related factors, including both relationship qualities and specific actions. These were named 12 times by 11 offenders. Three actions were named by one person each: that the mediator was uncompromising and held the offender accountable, that the mediator listened and talked with the offender, and that the mediator shared the offender's faith. The remaining eight offenders named nine mediator personality qualities that they found helpful, including being gentle, patient, not fake, open, sharing, encouraging, enthusiastic, comfortable, and knowing how to deal with people.

Bringing information back and forth was the next most frequent response, named by five offenders. "The victim's mom would do a lot of journal writing, and sharing those writings with me, and just discussing it, I felt that was pretty good." One surrogate offender especially appreciated this aspect: "Background on who you were going to mediate with, just having something to familiarize yourself with."

Watching videos of other mediations and role-play or exercises were each mentioned by three offenders. "I was totally prepared for it from watching the videos of other people." "A lot of little skits, the very last time he played as if he was the victim who died...it brought me to tears, it was a really good skit." "There were a lot of exercises, they could tell, as a teen I was real bottled up inside, and it really helped me to process the emotions I tried to cover up." This last offender further commented that the preparation "really helped me, even if I didn't meet with the victim."

Explaining the mediation process, coaching, and counseling about feelings were each named by two offenders. "The preparation was covered in how to talk to somebody you wronged. It helped me to know how to talk to her without bringing more pain. I think I'd have botched it for sure if I'd a just went in there blindly." "He can read emotions and he focuses on them a lot,...so I wouldn't hold it in during the meeting."

Suggestions for Changes in the Preparation Process

Two questions attempted to elicit offender suggestions for changes. Offenders were asked whether there was anything they wished had been done differently, and they were asked more explicitly whether they would recommend any changes. Most could think of nothing they would change. "If there is something that he could have done, I wouldn't know what it is." "For myself, I can't think of anything different." One commented that when he got into the mediation room, all the lights and cameras made him nervous, but added "I knew it was going to be there, it was just walking in and seeing it."

Only seven had any suggestions. Two of the earlier participants wished they could have seen photographs of the person they would be meeting with; this option was later incorporated into preparation procedures.

Two additional offenders had specific changes to recommend. One felt he should have received more information about the purpose: "I would have been better prepared in my understanding of human nature and the sense that this is primarily for the victim, and you are merely a tool for the victim." The other had comments about some of the paperwork: "There was a few days in there I didn't particularly care for, repetitive questions, I felt like the re-offense cycle needed to be explained a lot better."

Two offenders responded by mentioning something they hadn't liked at the time, but qualified their comments by saying it had turned out for the best. For one it was the frequency of the meetings: "In a way, I wished he could have met with me more often, but I think it helped make me stronger." "There were some times I felt rushed. They thought I was ready to go ahead with it. I didn't have much confidence, but it just worked out. They were right, I was prepared." And one was unhappy with the length of time required, but quickly added that this was "out of their control. Everybody was waiting to see if we could do this and record it."

Feelings Immediately Before the Mediation/Dialogue

Sixteen of the 19 offenders reported feeling nervous or scared, ranging from "butterflies" to "very scared." Eight did not offer further detail about the source of their nervousness: "I was a nervous wreck"; "Nervous and scared until I sat down and talked with him"; "It's very nerve wracking." Two feared actions or reactions by the family member. For one, this simply consisted of potential verbal anger: "I expected a lot of rage, I was preparing myself, this is something I could not blame them for if this was to happen." For the other the fear extended to safety issues: "Wondering if they were coming to get me, I know by being in here, if you want to bring something in, you can bring it in,...scared because I didn't know if they had a gun or not." This last offender reported being quite surprised immediately before the session to discover the family member's brother was also present in the visiting room, though it turned out he did not attend the session.

Two reported being fearful of their own potential behavior. "Not knowing if I was going to function correctly." "What would I say, what would I do." One of these reported how the mediator tried to help him deal with this: "The night before, the mediator had come out and told me to breathe. I said, yeah, I am not going to forget to breathe, right? I walked in the chapel and I couldn't breathe, I teared up, I couldn't look at the victim, I couldn't do anything."

Four other sources of fear or nervousness were named by one offender each. One feared retraumatization. " I really started the program initially to get emotional stability and help from it myself, I did not want to go in here and be traumatized or emotionally scarred worse than before going in." One whose meeting had previously been postponed was fearful that the family member would cancel. One reported shame as the source: "I was pretty nervous, not because I was not prepared, but a lot of shame. I've been living with shame my whole life." And one felt scared of potential judgment: "I was scared. Felt like I was fixing to meet the most awful judgment ever, I was devastated to have to face this woman."

Two who were nervous also reported loss of sleep. One who worked the night shift found that he was "up all day, what would I say, what would I do." The other commented, "for weeks I would wake up at night, I'd be dreaming and wake up thinking about the thing, having a conversation with her in my mind."

Five who were nervous or scared also reported a range of positive feelings simultaneously. "At the same time I wanted to be accountable and responsible." "Nervous, but I felt comfortable and felt like it was the right thing to do, at peace." "Not a bad stress, more like being pulled to do something that I know is right, that I needed to do for myself, too." One surrogate offender added, "Kind of in an excited way, not only is someone facing the possibility of letting go of some stuff, so am I."

Two offenders reported that they didn't have any feelings and that they purposely tried not to. "I tried not to feel, the most important thing to do was spend that day in prayer, try and empty myself, for God to fill me with whatever he wanted out of this." "The best thing was just not to show nothing." This latter offender reported that he spent the day going over clippings and trying to think "what I'd be able to tell her."

And one reported that at the last minute he tried to back out. "I told the mediator I ain't gonna do it. It messed him up, he begged me like an hour straight. He said, just do it for her." This offender did not specify what the reason was for his abortive effort to cancel, but earlier in the research interview he had made clear a major reason he chose to participate was to answer his family member's questions and clear up mysteries she had.

THE MEDIATION/DIALOGUE SESSIONS

According to program records, the 20 mediation/dialogue sessions in which these offenders participated ranged from three to nine hours in length and averaged six hours. Of the 16 offenders who gave information on the length of their session, 12 agreed with the figures reported by the program. Three thought their three or four hour sessions had been longer by one to two hours, and one thought his six hour session had lasted for only three hours. Only one offered evaluative comments on the length: "It seemed longer. Matter of fact, I cut it short, it was about all that I could stand."

There were no differences in the length of the session by type of crime. As reported by offenders, the number of persons present at the mediations, excluding camera personnel, ranged from three to eight and averaged 3.6. By far the most frequent number present was three: 12 of the 20 sessions consisted of simply a single mediator, a single victim or family member, and a single offender.

All but one of the 20 mediation/dialogue sessions were held in the facility where the offender was incarcerated. The remaining session, a meeting with a surrogate offender not incarcerated, was held in a church at a mutually agreeable location.

The presence of security personnel was only rarely mentioned; three offenders reported that security was outside the door, and three reported security was present in the room. One felt fortunate that the female sergeant who was present was someone he worked with and liked to talk with; he experienced her presence as support more than as surveillance. Another, whose guard was posted outside the door, added "that was part of it, as far as being in safety." And the only offender who reported the presence of two security officers in the room commented, "The one thing I was happy about is they didn't have ten guards circling around us. It wasn't a threatening, hostile environment."

Only six victims/family members were reported to have brought support persons along. One of these remained outside the mediation room; the remaining five were present in the room but sat either to the back or to one side and did not participate during the mediation. Not a single offender brought a support person to be present at the meeting. One offender, however, had arranged for a friend to be waiting afterwards, "for moral support."

The Texas program routinely makes videotapes of its mediations, used both for debriefing afterwards with the victim/family member and the offender, and (with permission) for training mediators and as part of the preparation for prospective participants. Eighteen of these 20 mediations were videotaped. In one instance, the justice system denied permission to videotape a session with a death row inmate. In the other, the participating offender declined permission.

Opening Moments

No information is available on the opening moments for seven of the 20 mediation/dialogue sessions. Ten offenders had comments on their nervousness at the beginning of their sessions, and these as well as two additional offenders described the initial encounter with their victim/family member.

The ten offenders who commented on the emotional atmosphere were describing 11 sessions. Seven sessions were described as comfortable, two as somewhat nervous, and two as a combination. "They did their best to try to put me at ease." "(The mediator) brought me in and set everything up, making me feel relaxed, just like a final go through." "I was nervous because of my bond with my mom, and when I saw (the victim's mom) she was already red eyed from tears." "Scared, couldn't believe how grown up he was, tried to make him feel comfortable."

Two who said the opening moments were comfortable reported a hug at the beginning of the session: "It was the biggest surprise. I walked into the room, I wasn't expecting anything, and (the victim) got up out of his chair and came over and hugged me." "I believe when I walked in, I believe we hugged, and that was really emotional." A surrogate offender described a shared response to the mediator's opening: "one of the first things, what would you desire to have happen in this meeting. Both of us just broke down."

Mediation/dialogue sessions in the Texas program always begin with an introduction by the mediator, outlining the purpose of the meeting and the ground rules. Only four offenders commented on this component of the opening phase. "Then we sat down and the mediator gave her part, what we could and couldn't do, what we were there for." "When it first started, the mediator said no cussing and all that, do not cross the table." "(The mediator) introduced it, he was more or less in charge."

After this introduction, usually victims and family members are offered the opportunity to speak first if they so wish. Of the eight offenders who had comments on who spoke first, seven indicated that the victim/family member led off. "She got a chance to say her say first, it was her time." "We both said hello but she spoke first. I wanted to let her say what she needed to say first. I didn't want to set the tempo. This was her show to begin with." The one offender who indicated he spoke first said he did so in response to family member wishes: "Their first thing was they wanted to know about me and my life." No information on who spoke first was available from the other 11 offenders.

Both victims/family members and offenders in the Texas program are encouraged to prepare "statements," which may be written or not, covering the information they hope to convey during their session. The sessions typically begin with the sharing of these statements. Fairly quickly, though, the process becomes one of open exchange and resembles a conversation more than a series of statements.

In the discussion that follows, the elements of the conversation as reported by the offenders have been organized into four components: offender description of victim/family member participation, offender responses to victim/family member statements, offender descriptions of their own participation, and victim/family member response to offender account. It should be remembered, however, that participants report a free flowing process, and these four sections summarize information that was likely scattered across the lengthy mediation/dialogue sessions.

Great precaution should be exercised in the interpretation of this data. What is being reported is what offenders commented on. The fact that a given offender didn't mention something does not mean it didn't occur, but simply that, for whatever reason, the offender didn't mention it. The following material is offered not as a picture of what happened in the mediation sessions, but as a compendium of what offenders described about their sessions.

Offender Description of Victim/Family Member Participation

Five offenders gave no details about the contents of their partici-pant's statements, although their later descriptions of their own reac-tions make clear that their victim's family members spoke about the crime and its impact. The remaining 14 offenders named a total of 16 items that their participating victims or family members talked about. These included discussing the impact of the crime on themselves and others (7 offenders), giving information about the victim (7 offenders), and talking about the offender (2 offenders).

For the seven offenders whose participants spoke about the impact of the crime on themselves, the information chiefly focused on pain and loss. "She sat there and told me how this affected her family, told me for about two hours how I affected each one of them." "She was more hurt than angry. The loss is more painful than any anger." One family mem-ber of a murder victim brought photographs of additional family mem-bers who were affected.

Seven offenders spoke of learning about the victim of the crime; in five instances participating family members shared this information, and in one surrogate meeting the actual victim did so. "She wanted me to know the victim." "Her child when he was born and brought up, being brought up without a father" "I enjoyed learning who the victim was as a person." "She talked about her trauma." Three offenders reported that the family members brought photographs of the victim who had died. "The photo album was really key, made it really, really real."

Two offenders reported that the victim or family member shared in-formation about the offender. For one, a relative of the victim who met with him, this was the entire focus of the victim's statement. "He talked about me, about how he saw me, how strung out on drugs I used to be. He didn't talk about the crime. He just wanted to make things better." The other was impressed with what the mother of his victim had learned about him. "This lady knew everything about me. She had kept close tabs on me all the time I had been down here. She knew my history and how I came to be on her front porch."

A total of 10 offenders reported that their participants had asked questions. Four gave no further information about the content of the questions. Of the remaining six, five were focused on specific details about the crime. "He wanted to know how long it took for her to die. I can't remember." "She wanted to know the truth, why was her son killed, how was he killed, what was he doing at the time of the killing." "She just really wanted to know what happened." The sixth offender reported that his victim "had questions about me, and now."

Offender Responses to Victim/Family Member Statements

Offenders were asked in the research interviews to describe their reactions to hearing the victim or family member talk about the crime and its impact. This section explores the reactions shared by the 18 offenders who clearly reported that their participating victims or family members spoke about the crime and its impact. Offenders reported experiencing difficult emotions (16 offenders), expanding their awareness of the impact of their crime (14 offenders), feeling something positive (7 offenders), experiencing some degree of empathy for victim pain (4 offenders), and feeling remorse or self-judgment (3 offenders).

All but two of the 18 offenders who listened to the impact of their crime described how difficult it was hearing the participants' accounts of their experience. Emotional terms included "it hit me hard," "hurt," "sad," "painful," "disturbing" "very emotional" "feeling pretty low" and "it floored me." One added, "it was so emotional, I damned near thought of committing suicide." Some gave more detail: "...you would have seen me sitting there speechless; it was really hard for me to make words." "There's no way I can describe it. I looked into her eyes and I couldn't say nothing, dropped my head. The mediator said 'it's gonna be all right.'" "I was sobbing as hard as any person could possibly sob. I couldn't hold all those feelings any more. It just opened everything up like a clogged drain."

Of the two who did not report difficult emotions, one reported trying very hard not to show any feelings on purpose. "I sat back and tried to look very stoic. I didn't wanna move, be expressive with my hands or body movements or even facial expressions. In no way did I want the victim to even remotely assume I would try to take charge of this." The other simply reported his thoughts about what the family member shared, without naming any feelings.

Fourteen described how much they learned about the effect of their crime. Three of these reported that they had already thought about it a great deal but were still surprised to learn how far it went. "I had reflected on what we termed the 'ripple effect' of this." "It helped me realize, as an offender, I assumed a lot of things." "It made me look at things that I hadn't looked at before in my crime."

The remaining 11 offenders expressed more shock at the extent of their impact. "I was so out of touch with myself that I really had no idea of the magnitude of that." "Really I didn't think that it would affect a lot of people like that. And I started thinking about it." "To hear how far that went. The realization of how much farther that goes, and it is just an ongoing thing. It is something that never really ends."

Seven offenders felt something positive in the midst of their difficult experience listening to the participant accounts. Two of these were participating as surrogates: "...it seemed like that was all right, just to hear her out was what she needed from me." Three meeting with family members of victims had similar responses: "There was also an air that it was a positive thing." "It was something I was willing to hear." And two spoke more explicitly about trying to give something back: "It felt good to mend that broken spot in her life, though she can't ever replace what was lost, but she can express something." "I drew a picture for her (of the daughter he murdered). It's no substitute for her daughter, but I tried to do my best."

Four spoke of feeling the family member's pain, at least to some degree. Two of these, both of whom were shortly to be executed, felt they couldn't experience the depth of the pain: "I wanted to say I could feel her pain, but I've never been there, never lost any family members." "I could not feel the depth of those feelings,...I had already understood on a very superficial level." The other two identified more directly; both of these had known their murder victim personally. "I allowed myself to feel his pain, the way he expressed it." "Just knowing the pain she had gone through, I could relate to it, I've got a daughter...you could not only see it, you could feel it."

Three spoke of feelings of remorse or self-judgment. "You just feel so small and humiliated. My life's been nothing, and I had it easy, I had been humbled already." "It left me thinking, what kind of monster would do this to someone, and to think that was me that did it."

Offender Descriptions of Their Own Participation

Eighteen of the 19 offenders described some aspect of the statements they gave, for a total of 29 items. The one exception was the offender reported above who attempted to remain stoic; he stated that he wished to just "absorb whatever the victim offered me." In addition, six offenders commented on the process of sharing their statement or information.

Offenders reported that they gave information about the crime (11 offenders), gave information about themselves (7 offenders), took ownership and were accountable (6 offenders), reported specific feelings they had shared with the family members (3 offenders), assured the family member's safety (1 offender), and apologized (1 offender).

Eleven offenders reported giving information about their crime, including both specific events (9 offenders) and their motivation (2 offenders). "I just started telling what actually happened from my side." "I explained to her what happened, how we got there, how everything came about, how we ran." "She had been told we were planning to kill one victim for two weeks ahead of time, she went all those years with that in her mind." "I hope I got through to her that I never went there to hurt anybody."

Seven offenders reported sharing information about themselves. For five, this included history about their life prior to the crime. "All the problems I had created in my life by not being with God and turning to alcohol and drugs and blaming other people for my failures." "We talked a lot about each of our backgrounds, how we grew up."

For the remaining two, the information focused on their lives since the crime. One spoke about prison life: "I was able to express that this is not just some cake walk down here, it's not golf courses and all that." The other reported an extensive exchange with his victim's mother about his infractions since being incarcerated. "She said why do you have all these cases? I just explained over and over again, I didn't care, when I came to prison I didn't care about dying, it didn't matter to me."

Six offenders spoke about taking ownership, being accountable, and being honest in the process of sharing their information. "The one thing I've been trying to stress, I'm gonna be honest with her." "There was some admission that I had finally made that some things that I buried within myself, that I'd never admit to anyone else before, they were the second people I actually ever admitted to." "I was making sure she knew this was my fault, not her daughter's."

Three reported that they shared specific feelings with the family members. "When it was all over, I told her I didn't say nothing here tonight to add to your pain." "I told her I don't have any problem with the protest that you've done to me all these years, because I've got a stepdad out there that if someone had killed him like I had killed your father, I would be doing the same thing." In a surrogate situation, the offender explained: "I started opening up, telling her how I felt about her losing her daughter, and how I felt about my own victim, and that kinda helped her."

One offender reassured his victim's mother of her safety: "I needed her to know that she was safe from me, because I thought maybe she had some fear of that." And only one offender directly mentioned apologizing.

Of the six offenders who commented on the process of sharing their statements, five indicated how difficult this was, and one spoke of how what he had learned made it easier. "I had wrote down a little paragraph just to try to keep my thoughts in order. I tried to remember everything I wanted to say. I pretty much read it. It was pretty hard to look up." "Basically just getting it out in the open, accepting the fact that I caused this, I did this, it was like walking through a fire." "I'm sure I was trying to hide my feelings. A couple of times tears ran down my face."

Victim/Family Member Response to Offender Account

Only eight offenders commented on their participants' response to their statements. Two felt the participant believed them, and two had more questions. Four reported the participants' emotional reactions, and one reported that when he tried to describe what he'd done, his victim focused on the future instead. Comments included:

> He said, I don't think you'd be here right now if you'd done it on purpose.

> I don't believe it was a moving experience for him like it was for me. I don't think he believed the sincerity that I was talking.

I could see the ripping inside of her from talking about it...I could see how it just devastated her.

I'd apologize for something, and he'd say, that's gone, that's over, that's in the past, we have to look forward now.

Offender Surprises

Eighteen offenders were asked if anything in the mediation/dialogue session surprised them. Three reported no surprises. "How would I be surprised? What would surprise me?" "No, the mediator told me exactly what it would be like."

The remaining 15 offenders named a total of 17 surprises, including the victim or family member's compassion and forgiveness (5 offenders), the extent of the impact of their crime (4 offenders), how well the meeting went (3 offenders), that the participant made physical contact (2 offenders), and three surprises named by just one offender each: that the offender didn't fall apart, that the participant showed as much anger, and that the participant laughed.

Comments on compassion and forgiveness included: "I was gonna fall out of the chair when we got to the end of the meeting. (The family member) reached over and shook my hand and said, 'I forgive you for killing my father.' I wasn't expecting that." "Her compassion. Her deep feeling for me. I met another face of God that night, and the face God wore that night was hers." "She said, I wanna help you. I want you to get the G.E.D. She's trying to lead me from this side to that side. After it was all over, she said I just don't hate you no more. She wants to help, make sure I stay outta trouble."

Four commented on their surprise over how far-reaching their crime was. "Really I didn't think it would affect a lot of people like that, and I started thinking about it. Yeah, it affected a lot of people's lives." "The photo album had a real strong effect on me. You live all these years knowing what you did and going through life trying to close it off."

Three were surprised how well it went: "There was not a real anger or outpouring of anger. They were very understanding of our lives, which makes it kinda surprising."

Two were surprised that the participant reached out to touch them. One was the handshake, reported above by the offender who was surprised at his participant's forgiveness. The other was the hug at the beginning of the session reported by the offender who met with his stepfather.

Nonverbal Communication

In describing the content and process of their mediation experience, 16 of the 19 offenders mentioned a range of nonverbal communication. These references are scattered throughout this report; the present section summarizes all of them. Offenders referred to eye contact (8 offenders), physical touch (7 offenders), crying (6 offenders), and laughter (4 offenders).

Eye contact was a crucial component remarked on both for its presence and for its absence or difficulty. Three offenders spoke of how difficult it was to meet their participant's eyes. One of these described an extensive exchange about whether or not he was speaking the truth. "She said sometimes I would hesitate and I wouldn't look at her. Well, I told her, how can you look at somebody you know you killed their son? How can you look at the mother?"

For the remaining five offenders, eye contact was simply very important. It helped ease the opening moments for one. Another who made frequent mention of it commented, "Never look away is what I basically kept telling myself. He deserves to be looked in the eye, that's just the way your parents teach you."

Seven offenders mentioned a total of eight items involving some form of physical touch. For the five whose participants reached out and touched them (three hugs and two handshakes), the moment was highly charged and very moving. These moments have already been described above. Two offenders spoke of how much they wished they could hug the family member. One of these was moved to learn the family member had also wished to hug him; they were separated by a glass. The only reported instance of an offender reaching out to touch a participant was an offender who reached out with a Kleenex and wiped the tears from the face of the family member who was crying.

Six mentioned tears or crying. Four reported that both they and their participant cried at some point in the session, sometimes together. "There were a lot of tears between both of us." One, quoted above for wiping his family member's tears, mentioned only the participant's crying, and one offender mentioned only her own crying, "a couple times tears ran down my face."

Four offenders spoke of sharing laughter with the participant. "Basically as a whole we laughed and cried together." "We were able to laugh and share little jokes, like, I told her she had a captive audience."

Reactions to Video

Apart from describing whether or not there were camera personnel present in the mediation room, only six offenders had comments on the experience of having their sessions videotaped. Three reported feeling totally comfortable. "They weren't even in it, they say 'we're not here' and that's pretty much what happened, we pretended they weren't there." Two were nervous at first but then got comfortable. "Once everything got going, you didn't even know they were there. The staff that did the filming, they were very professional." Only one reported a discomfort that lasted for the duration of the session: With me as paranoid as I am, I never ceased to acknowledge their presence, it all added to my sense of exploitation. Microphones, lights, you couldn't really get used to that at all."

Affirmations

As described in chapter 4, a customary component of the facilitated dialogue program in Texas is the working out of some kind of agreement toward the end of the session, termed the "Affirmation." Offenders were not routinely asked whether or not they worked out an affirmation or what its components might have been, but follow-up questions were used to elicit more information if they mentioned it.

Six offenders mentioned some aspect of their affirmation. Three spoke only in positive terms. Two of these named some of their components, including pursuing more education, staying in treatment, adding value to those around me, being the best person I can be. One of these also reported asked something of the family member in the affirmation: "...that the victim agrees to get mad at me and not at God regarding the crash and the loss of his daughter, and that, with their approval, the video be used as a learning tool." Another spoke of how he relied on his affirmation: "It's been real helpful to know that I have to do that because sometimes I don't want to do that. I keep this thing pretty handy because I've had to read it over a few times. It's set in granite that I won't quit."

The three who reported negative feelings about their affirmations were all sex offenders. One simply stated, "It was hard to agree to some things." Two reported feeling they had agreed to things they might not be able to fulfill. One felt in the emotionality of the situation that "I agreed to something that I should have thought more about. The victim wanted financial restitution — I ain't got no viable income. It sounds good at that point, you just about agree to anything." Both this offender and the other who worried about being able to carry out the agreement also spoke of needing to move on at some point and not have their lives be so focused on a single event.

Mediator Role and Evaluation

Fourteen offenders had comments describing the mediator's general role and activity during the sessions. Overwhelmingly, they reported that mediators remained largely quiet through most of the session. Thirteen offenders offered a total of 24 items describing what mediators did do on those rare occasions when they intervened. These included helping if it lagged or got silent (4 offenders), helping out in stuck spots (4 offenders), reminding participants about topics they had wished to bring up (4 offenders), introducing topics (5 offenders), asking questions (2 offenders), helping with the affirmation (2 offenders), and three items mentioned by only one offender each: helping a family member calm down, rephrasing offender questions, and coaching a family member through an intense emotional experience.

Eighteen of the offenders were asked what they found most helpful about the mediator's role during the session. A total of 35 mediator actions were named, including various active interventions (13 offenders, 21 items), remaining quiet (8 offenders), and simply being supportive (6 offenders).

The active interventions named as most helpful included helping if the meeting lagged (5 offenders), supporting feelings (4 offenders), asking questions (3 offenders), helping in stuck spots (2 offenders), reminding (2 offenders), confronting offender avoidance (2 offenders), helping with the affirmation (1 offender), calming the family member down (1 offender), and breaking the ice (1 offender).

Comments included:

> Moments of silence were very precious at times because it was just a time to sit back and reflect momentarily on what was said.

> She allowed us to be our self. Not trying to guide us in what we ought to ask or what we ought to say.

> If I didn't quite explain it and he knows where I'm capable, he would re-ask the question.

> She was having one emotion where she was very angry, and it turned into rage, and then it turned into a void. And he walked her through it. So he really guided her and me through the process.

> When we'd get stuck and didn't know what to say, we'd look at her, and she'd help us gear into a clearer direction.

> I didn't know if I could bring anything written down or not, sometimes they don't let you do that, so I didn't bring anything with me, but I had already given the mediator a list of everything I wanted to cover, so she helped me remember it.

An additional question designed to elicit evaluation of the mediator was what the offender found least helpful about the mediator's role during the session. Of the 16 offenders who were asked, 15 could not think of anything, and the sixteenth responded with a comment on the preparation phase rather than the mediation itself. "I can't even imagine doing anything different. It worked so well for me, so I don't see anything negative or anything that I could change." "I think everything she did was excellent." One offender concluded his response to this line of questioning by offering, "Is there any way we could get the mediators like a promotion or something?"

Feelings Immediately Afterwards

Eighteen offenders were asked to describe how they felt immediately upon completing the mediation/dialogue sessions. The great majority reported positive feelings, either wholly (8 offenders) or in part (8 offenders). Only two offenders reported solely negative feelings immediately afterwards.

A total of 26 positive reactions were named by 16 offenders, including happiness (5 offenders), relief or release (4 offenders), feeling a weight or burden had lifted (4 offenders), feeling glad it was over (4 offenders), sleeping well (3 offenders), feeling at peace (2 offenders), feeling proud (2 offenders), and general positive feelings (2 offenders). Typical comments included: "Kinda like a weight had been lifted off my shoulders, I felt better, I felt that I had gotten to have my say, and also listen to her side." "I would say probably a combination of relief and accomplishment. You take a step, and when you put your foot out there, you really see nothing, and after it's over with, you find out it's all right, I can bring up my other foot." "I just really felt at peace for the first time in a long time, and I slept real good that night, I remember that." "Very much at peace. I felt cleansed, washed, freshed, a great burden had been lifted off my shoulders, I felt joy."

Eight of the above offenders also made clear what a difficult process it had been in spite of their positive feelings. Five spoke of what an emotional ordeal the meeting was, and four of them reported tiredness. "I was kinda tired, for one thing. It was pretty stressful, emotionally, when we got through I was just drained." "I think that is the tiredest I've been in years, emotionally chaosed. It was like having a personal open heart surgery." "It drained me of all my energy. I was exhausted when it was ended, enormous migraine headache." One of the eight was the only offender to report being "scared" immediately afterwards. This offender worried about being unable to measure up to the affirmation agreement workout out with the participating family member.

Only two offenders had nothing positive to say about their immediate reactions. Both of them reported feeling tired as well as drained, and did not list any other feelings. It should be noted that two of the offenders who reported being "glad it was over" (listed as a positive feeling above) had no additional positive feelings to offer, suggesting that feeling released from something difficult was the extent of their positive response immediately afterwards.

OUTCOMES

Offenders were asked a number of open-ended questions to elicit their perceptions of the results of their mediation dialogue sessions. In addition, there were several closed-ended questions with Likert scale response options.

Overall Outlook on Life

Offenders were asked both a closed-ended question (18 offenders) and several open-ended questions (19 offenders) about whether their participation in the program affected their outlook on life. Responses to the closed-ended question are presented in Table 6.3.

Table 6.3: Has Your Overall Outlook on Life Changed Since Meeting the Victim/Family Member?

No	5	27.8%
Yes	13	72.2%
Of those who answered yes:		
a. Definitely more positive and at peace with the circumstances I am faced with.	11	(61.1%)
b. Somewhat more positive and able to cope with my life.	1	(5.6%)
c. Somewhat more negative and less able to cope with my life.		
d. Definitely more negative and angry about the circumstances I am faced with.		
e. Other.	1	(5.6%)

Of the five offenders who responded in the negative, two spoke of how their outlook had already changed before the mediation, and indicated that their participation had merely reaffirmed the direction they were going. A third gave an opposite response in the open-ended questions, describing important changes in his life outlook. Only two of these 18 consistently reported no change in their outlook whatever. One perceived himself as still not a very nice person and elsewhere said, "I'm always gonna be that way." The other simply never mentioned any effort to change his behavior or any impact on his outlook

In responding to the open-ended questions, 15 offenders reported that their participation had a major impact on their personal growth and rehabilitation. In addition to the 13 who responded "yes" on the closed-ended question, this included the offender mentioned above who responded "no," and the offender who was not asked the closed-ended question.

Comments included: "That made all the difference in my life." "For me it was a life changing event. I can't see how anybody could go through that program and not be a changed person." "If I didn't do this, I think there would be a good chance of me coming back. I don't want that to happen. I've got something planned for my future." "Meeting her has helped put a period at the end of that cycle, where it won't start again."

Some offenders offered further explanations about why their participation had such an impact. Four spoke of increased accountability: "It made me accountable for the type of person I was, and to understand the things that I must do to change those things." "The program allowed me to be accountable, don't blame other people for my actions, those are the tools they gave me. Before, I didn't have that." "It's a growing process to be able to admit you're wrong, meeting people you done wrong."

Three offenders each spoke of feeling more open, being more at peace, and having more incentive. "I'm at peace, my outlook is just a lot better, more open for everybody, not just me." "(The victim) is closer to what I believe in, being in AA, he's helped me, gives me an incentive to do well." Another reported an even stronger incentive: "I've made it through the wall, I wanna live." Impressively, a death row inmate commented, "I've learned to flow with feelings, … I'm free to actually open up and live my life the way I've always wanted to."

Two offenders spoke strongly about the impact of personalizing their victim. "Just being able to identify with the victim, on a personal level, that helped me to not so much minimize my crime, because a lot of times I've just sat there and said, good old boy drunk behavior." "Now that I have seen the other side, it's just really helped me focus on the more important things in life. The little quick pleasures are just not worth it."

Changes in Offender View of the Victim/Family Member

Offenders were asked whether their feelings for the victim changed. All offenders at first interpreted this question to mean the person with whom they had met; follow-up questions with six offenders elicited in addition whether or not their feelings about their actual victim had changed.

Of the 17 offenders who met with family members, 12 reported that their feelings had changed for the better. "Before it all happened, I didn't even know who she was… She's a hell of a woman, a lot stronger than I woulda been." "Greatly, by the end I realized, here's two very special people." "I felt like we created a very close friendship type bond, from not knowing to friendship." This included one offender in a surrogate situation: "getting to know her, I had a different perception, like you can never judge a book by its cover."

Four of the five offenders who reported no change clarified they had never felt badly toward their victim's family member: "No, I never had any bad feelings about her at all, I understood why she protested me." "No, cause I still respect her stance as far as being a mother and being a victim." The remaining offender reported that while his attitude and feelings did not change, "I think I was a bit more understanding of her perspective. After the mediation, I knew exactly how she felt and what she felt."

Two offenders who met with actual victims and four who met with family members commented on whether or not their feelings for their victim changed. One of these was a surrogate situation, and this offender clarified that while his feelings for the victim he met with didn't change, his feelings for his own victim changed deeply because of "the reality of what a victim was feeling." The other offender who met with an actual victim reported a dramatic positive change: "Yes, definitely, one hundred percent. I care for him like he's my Dad." Of the remaining four, three reported positive changes in their feelings for their actual victim: "Yes,…It really brought her to life." "I was able to see her more as a person, as somebody I had harmed." The one who said his feelings did not change clarified "I've always thought about her in the highest regard because she gave me my life back."

Six offenders were uncertain whether or not their participant's feelings towards them had changed. Four simply couldn't tell, and two reported evidence both ways. Twelve offenders who participated in 13 mediations reported that they strongly felt participant feelings toward them had changed. "Yes, I do, in a loving, understanding kind or way." "I think she realizes that, regardless, I am still human." "The Dad told me his image of me just changed so much, he looked at me and said, I know now why my daughter liked you." "They showed me a little of her video, she was concerned about me like her child and asked, 'do you think he'll be all right?'" One offender in a murder case offered the following: "I think (my victim) would be real proud of who I am now, because I'm the guy that she liked as a friend now, not the guy on drugs."

Offenders were also asked if they saw themselves as similar to or different from the victim/family member. Thirteen offenders responded to this question in relation to the person they had met with, and two of these plus four additional offenders also described similarities and differences they saw between themselves and their actual victim. No information is available for two offenders.

Eight offenders saw themselves as similar. "They're two very special people that have gone through some of the same things I have dealt with. I would say we're fairly similar in a lot of ways. We want to turn this into a positive thing instead of a negative thing." "I'm not any different from this person, I just made a tragic mistake."

Three felt there were both similarities and differences. One reported, "we're on different pages" but felt their previous addictive coping patterns had been similar. The other two who reported a mix both focused on how their family member had reacted to the crime: "I see myself as unlike her in not feeling a need for revenge, I think if I was in her position I would feel a sense of revenge, where she doesn't. That's how we're different." "He has forgiven me for something that I don't know how I would react should I be in his shoes."

Two felt they were simply quite different from the family member. One did not elaborate; the other also focused on the family member's reaction to the crime: "If it had been my daughter, I know what I'd a done, I'd done everything possible to get rid of me one way or the other, and I think that's the difference between me being what I am and her being who she is." These were the same two offenders who consistently reported no change in their outlook either before or after their participation in the program.

Of the six who compared themselves to their actual victim, three reported being more alike, one was mixed, and two were more different. "It's kind of odd, a lot of the things she liked were the same things I like, gave kind of a connection there." "I know in my heart that had I met him, as a stranger, I would have wanted to be his friend." The one who reported mixed feelings opened with: "The only thing that's different between me and that guy is he's white, not black," but went on to name several other differences. The two who felt only different both focused on life goals: "different life style, goals, she was gonna be somebody, she was trying to make something of herself. I wasn't, and I didn't." "She was a girl who was trying to live her life and be happy, I was kinda the opposite."

Closely related to the issue of their similarity or difference from the victim/family member is the overarching theme of shared humanity: offenders wish to be seen as human beings. When offender responses are summarized across the entirety of the research interviews, a total of nine offenders named this theme. Six of these have already been described in the forgoing material.

Three additional offenders also named this theme in comments not reported elsewhere. One raised it in responding to the final interview question, "Do you have any other comments you would like to make." His response: "Yes. I want the program to make people understand that we're not just animals, to show people the human side of the whole thing. They say, 'well, how could somebody that took a life say that? He had no respect for the life,' and I want them to understand that I do." Another reported, "She looked at me like I was just a demon, but she found out that I do got a heart, I'm not just a cold blooded killer."

The extensive comments of the third are presented here for their comprehensive perspective on this issue:

> I'm very proud of society, working to help people come to an even keel, where we can all see each other as human being, not infallible, by no means, but have hope. I've been told so many times sex offenders are not recoverable, they ought to be shot,

skin them. When I see things like this, a survivor or victim sit with a perpetrator and share the same emotions in recovery and support each other in recovery, then I am inspired and exhilarated, because I just know that people are recoverable.

Changes in Offender Understanding of How the Crime Impacted Others

Eighteen of the offenders were asked whether the meeting changed their understanding of how the crime affected others. These results are reported in Table 6.4.

Table 6.4: Extent to which the Meeting Changed Offender Understanding of How the Crime Impacted Others

A great deal	17	(94%)
Somewhat	1	(6%)
Not at all	0	
Total	18	(100%)

Five offenders who reported that their understanding changed offered no further detail. The remaining 12 spoke about the pain, the magnitude of the impact of what they'd done, and the personal connection. "It helped me to see and feel how much I had hurt him." "Not just the victim, or him, but a whole slew of cousins, friends, neighbors, and a community. I got to see the full impact of everything." From a surrogate offender: "To hear a survivor, the impact was tremendous. The total feeling of what trauma my crime caused another human being." One who had reacted to a photo album added, "It's like this detachment happened, it's like watching a movie, not feeling anything, not associate any kind of feeling with what I did, and this here is what brought that wall down and made everything open up for me." The offender who reported changing only "somewhat" clarified, "because I already had a lot of that feeling and knowing it before."

Impact on Spiritual Outlook

Offenders were given both an open-ended and a closed question to tap the impact of their mediation experience on their religious or spiritual life. Responses to the five point Likert Scale question are reported in Table 6.5 below.

Table 6.5: Effect on Offender Religious or Spiritual Life

Did the process of preparing to meet the victim and the actual meeting have any effect on your religious or spiritual life?	
No	7
Yes	12
Of those who answered yes:	
a. Greatly enriched my religious/spiritual perspective.	10
b. Contributed to a deeper religious/spiritual perspective.	1
c. Contributed to a weakening of my religious/spiritual perspective.	
d. Greatly weakened my religious/spiritual perspective.	
None of the above.	1

Of the seven who reported no impact on their spiritual life, three clarified that such impact had already happened before the mediation; for two, their spirituality contributed to their decision to participate. "After being locked up I found out I wasn't in as much control over things as I thought, so I kinda put my trust in God. I think my spiritual life had more of an effect on my going into the mediation." Another commented, "No, it was more in the same direction I was already going." Three of the remaining offenders who reported no impact simply said they didn't have a spiritual life. "I don't have any spiritual outlook, so I guess I'm a heathen." "I don't believe in no religion or no God or none of that." The seventh offender, who responded in the negative on the Likert Scale, actually reported more of a mix in the open-ended section. "They tried to encourage me. My spiritual walk since I've been locked up has really gone down hill. I know I've betrayed Him, yet I feel betrayed on the same side."

Of the 12 offenders who responded in the affirmative on the Likert scale, seven spoke of ways in which the mediation affirmed a spiritual path they were already on and deepened their spirituality. "I know that God forgave me of my sin, but the victim had never met me before last night, it helped me grow." "Well, that had already started happening a couple years ago. As far as what the Bible teaches, I think a lot of people get bogged down in doctrine and start chasing other things. But basically the whole book is about love. And that is the main message, and it just confirmed it for me." Another offender spoke of being given a Bible in prison, reading it, and "seeing all my life in the Bible, all the mistakes I'd made, like a book about me."

The remaining five described a more life-changing spiritual impact. "Most definitely. It just shows me that God is real"; "God must have sent the mediator to me, otherwise why now am I allowing myself to grow? It must be God talking"; "That's something that it's opened up a whole lot for me. It was a big effect, felt like it was God speaking to me." And the offender described earlier who reported not caring if he lived or died and getting into extensive trouble in the institution stated, "Since that incident happened with the victim's mom, I turned my life around, I don't fight no more, I'm not perfect but I pray to God in heaven because he's the one who blessed me."

Forgiveness Issues

Seeking or receiving forgiveness is not a goal of the Texas program, and there was no routine question in the interview schedule inquiring about forgiveness issues. However, a total of 13 offenders spontaneously mentioned forgiveness. Three, covered in the section on reasons for seeking to mediate, hoped that they would receive forgiveness from their victim's family members. A fourth, meeting in a surrogate situation, hoped his actual victim's family could forgive him.

Seven offenders in six murder cases and one vehicular homicide reported that they received forgiveness from the family members who met with them. As described elsewhere, these encounters were extremely moving and impactful. "If you murder somebody's child, and they forgive you, if she can forgive me, I can forgive." "She told me she forgave me. There's no way to measure the value of that. There is nothing greater than that, a person couldn't ask for more than that."

Three offenders stated that they didn't expect to receive forgiveness. "I told her, I'm not asking you for forgiveness. I don't even forgive myself, I don't expect anyone else to." "I never really expected her to forgive me, just her decision, whatever called her to come see me, was enough alone." In contrast to the one who couldn't forgive himself, another spoke of struggling to do so: "I realized I still had this stuff inside, it hurts inside, it was hard for me to forgive myself."

Comparisons between the Program and Other Consequences of Their Crime

There were no routine questions inviting offenders to compare the mediation process with other consequences of their crime, but eight of the 19 offenders volunteered comments on the difference. Four elements of how the program is different from prison were present in these comments: letting emotions flow (4 offenders), accountability (3 offenders), rehabilitation (3 offenders), and personalizing the impact of the crime (2 offenders). Not every offender listed every element, but the substance of what they all were saying could be summed up in the following way: Accountability, to a person rather than a system, coupled with open-flowing emotions, helps prevent reoffending.

Comments included: "In an institution like this you have the tendency to desensitize your emotions." "I felt like maybe if I was the first to open up my feelings and let some of the other convicts watch the tape, maybe they would be able to come forward with their feelings, too, and not be so bottled up." "I had to face what I'd done, not by doing prison, but by facing the victim's mom." "The main reason a lot of guys come back is because they are not held accountable to their people, they are held accountable to a machine, or the system, or the institution, and there is a lot of animosity towards that."

Further Contact with Victims/Family Members

Fourteen offenders were asked if they would like to have another meeting with their victim/family member. Six commented on whether or not they would like to meet with their victim/family member again, one of these and three more spoke of already being in contact with their co-participant, and five responded by saying they would like to meet with other persons affected by their crime.

Three responded that they would like to meet with their victim/family member again, two had mixed feelings, and one did not think more meetings would accomplish anything. "I want to see her just as much as she wants to see me, it seemed like a dream in a way." "I would love to do more."

Four (including one who wanted to meet again) spoke of already being in contact with their co-participant, usually through the mediator. "She wrote me back, and she feels a lot better." "We decided to write each other. She seems like a second mother to me." "Now we write each other, and he (the victim/family member) faxes it to the mediator." This offender also reported that the victim made successful efforts to have him transferred to a prison closer to his home, so his mother could see him more often.

And five, including the two surrogates, spoke instead of hoping to meet with additional persons who had suffered from their crime. "I wish I could talk to him face to face and just apologize to him, and that day may come. I want him to hear from my lips that it was not his fault. I know his family can see that, but I want him to understand that I see that also." One was already in preparation to meet with the spouse of the family member he had met with and added, "I've re-done the packet. Some things have changed. I've grown a lot, it's kind of like a little mile marker."

OFFENDER EVALUATION OF THE EXPERIENCE

A number of open-ended and closed-ended questions attempted to tap offenders' evaluation of the program and its impact on them. Tables 6.6 and 6.7 below report the responses of the 18 offenders who were asked the two fixed-response questions.

Table 6.6: Offender Overall Satisfaction with Involvement in the Victim Offender Mediation and Dialogue Program

Very satisfied	18	(100%)
Somewhat satisfied	0	
Somewhat dissatisfied	0	
Very dissatisfied	0	
Total	18	(100%)

Table 6.7: Offender Rating of the Helpfulness of the Meeting

Very helpful	18	(100%)
Somewhat helpful	0	
Not at all helpful	0	
Total	18	(100%)

Nine offenders had additional comments about the level of their satisfaction. "Tremendously satisfied. You don't have enough levels there." "I'm telling you it was a day I'll never forget." "I think it was the greatest thing in the world, a blessing, a unique opportunity." "It's a wonderful program. If it helps one out of a hundred, it's done something."

Three offenders indicated some ambivalence despite the high Likert Scale rankings. "It depends on the day. Some days I'm glad I did it, some days I wish I hadn't because there is a part of me that worries that I can't fulfill everything." "I had some private expectation that I would get more out of it, when all the time the mediator had informed me and I was well aware that the program was constructed and designed for the victim, not the offender, so I felt a little disappointed that I was in the seat of the offender more than the recovering one as well." "I still say it helps her more than it helps me."

All 15 of the offenders who were directly asked whether or not their expectations were met responded in the affirmative, and 10 further indicated that their expectations had been exceeded. "Yes, Ma'am, a hundred and ten percent. I hadn't expected it to be that in depth, they far surpassed anything I had expected. I learned more and gained more and received more than I could have imagined." "Oh, more than met. I didn't expect her to forgive me." One joked, "No, initial expectations were to get cussed out and ragged on" but added, "yes, much more positive, I went in there expecting nothing positive in the sense of what I would receive from the victim, because I don't know if I could have given that."

Toward the end of the interview, all 19 offenders were asked if they had "any regrets." All 19 said that they had no regrets about participating in the program. Nine, however, listed other things about which they did feel some regret. One wished it had happened sooner, so he would have had more time in the new relationship with his victim (who was terminally ill).

Five spoke of something they wished had happened differently within the mediation session. Two wished the meeting had gone on longer. "The only regret I have out of the whole thing is an impossibility, really. I would have liked to have done this for 72 hours, because I felt like there was more the victim needed to say, and a lot more that I wanted to share with her." One regretted he couldn't give his family member a hug. One wished he had agreed to videotape the session. And one felt regret that he had slipped into a self-centered mode during the meeting. "I got the most time I could get for my crime, he mentioned that he wanted to help me, it kind of turned the tables toward me, and I kinda feel a little bit selfish, I wish I would have held to the fact that we were there for him and told him, hold off to another time."

Two spoke of worry, rather than regret, about what would happen next. One simply felt he had a long way to go in his healing. The other had concerns about laws to be followed after release, in addition to concerns about being able to fulfill the affirmation.

One reported a breach of his confidentiality about which he had regret. The family member who met with him had participated in a conference and spoke about her mediation. "And a newspaper person was doing a story, and they used my name in it, six or seven years after the crime, for the first time something hits the newspaper about it." Even so, he had no regrets about participating and reaffirmed that he "would do it again."

RECOMMENDATIONS FOR OTHERS

Seventeen offenders were explicitly asked whether or not they would recommend mediation/dialogue to others. All said they would definitely recommend it, although five qualified their recommendations with some conditions they felt would make it advisable. One additional offender who was not asked later volunteered that he was hoping his co-defendants could also meet with his victim's family member, bringing the total who would or do recommend it to 18. Five spoke of recommending it for both victims/family members and offenders; 11 recommended participation just for offenders, and two just for victim/family members. It should be noted that follow-up questions in this section of the interview typically probed how the offender might talk about mediation to others, likely biasing the response toward recommending it for offenders.

The conditions recommended by four offenders focused on motivation. Two spoke of both victim/family member and offender motivation: "It's very important that both people are doing it for the same reason." "If their hearts are in the right place, that it's not a thing for revenge." Two focused on offender motivation: "It's not for everybody, if you think it's gonna look good on your parole or help you get out, don't do it." "If a person isn't ready to accept their responsibility, they are not even going to consider it." And one offered a reason for a family member to decline: "...(not) if the offender is really kinda a real mean person, as far as the way they treated the victim before they killed him."

Four specifically named advantages for victim/family members: two focused on victims being able to have their say, and two on the healing or closure victims could obtain. Thirteen offenders named a total of 18 advantages for offenders, including to change their lives (4 offenders), for emotional and spiritual recovery (3 offenders), to release a burden (3 offenders), for general healing (2 offenders), to prevent reoffending (2 offenders), to break down barriers (2 offenders), and to be accountable (2 offenders).

Most of these reasons have already been amplified elsewhere in this report. The barriers named by two offenders had to do with what separates them from other human beings. "I'd like to stress that they do have that wall around them and they need to find out what's on the other side, and this program is the way to do that." "You can overcome that barrier that separates yourself from the world, that makes you feel you are not part of the world, like everybody despises you."

Five offered specific advice to offenders who might decide to participate: don't lie (2 offenders), at least go through the preparation phase (2 offenders), and "you'll get out of it what you put into it" (1 offender).

Four reported that they were already talking with other inmates to recommend participating. "I even talk to other inmates that wanted what I had now, and it used to be me, wanting what they had." "They bring it up to me, and I tell them to write Victim Services, and the mediator will send them the paper work, it's real inspirational itself, it's one of the biggest parts of the program."

Changes Recommended by Offenders

Eighteen offenders were asked whether they would recommend any changes in the program. Fourteen could think of nothing they would change. Three of the remaining four had specific suggestions to offer to the program. One wished there were some way to let victim/family members know that their offender wishes to meet without revicitimizing or creating the expectation that they ought to meet. One spoke extensively about the need for the program to be more balanced: "Even the most subtle program organization and opening statement and how it's viewed, us versus them instead of a common unity, the dividing line was obvious, and I thought in mediation there was more middle ground." And one suggested that offenders be allowed to bring a support person: "You have all the Victim Services people there and the victim and the victim support person. It would have been really encouraging to have someone there that knew me and that I could talk to. When it was over I felt kinda left high and dry a little bit."

The final suggestion related to something that was probably out of program control. One offender reported that during his participant's prison tour, he was required to stay in his cell, but wasn't told why, and the officers treated him as if he'd done something wrong, "threatening me a lot."

CONCLUSION

These 19 offenders have provided an in-depth window into their experience of their own crime, their reasons for participating in mediation, their experience in the mediation/dialogue program, their perceptions about its impact, and their evaluation of it. All were very satisfied, all found it very helpful, and none had regrets about their participation, even though at many points in the process they found the going difficult and did not always agree with program staff or with their participants. Perhaps the most appropriate way to close the present chapter is in the words of another offender who had comments when asked if there was anything else he wished to say: "It's a great opportunity. It's something, no matter how, you can't put it in a bottle, you're never going to be able to describe it for what it is."

CHAPTER 7.
OHIO CASE STUDIES

The stories of six Ohio study participants are presented in five case studies involving three victims and three offenders. In Case Study One, a violent assault and the subsequent mediation/dialogue are told from both the victim and offender perspective. Case Studies Two and Three offer the victims' perspectives on the events and dialogue following a murder and a vehicular homicide, respectively. Case Studies Four and Five present offender perspectives, respectively, on an assault/kidnapping case and an incest case and the subsequent dialogues.

In all five case studies, names, identifying information and some details about the events have been changed to protect the privacy of the participants. The cases were selected to provide an overview of the range of types of cases and dialogues handled by the Ohio Victim Offender Dialogue Program. Information for these case studies was obtained from interviews with program participants.

CASE STUDY ONE: ASSAULT — VICTIM AND OFFENDER PERSPECTIVES

The Experience of the Event

At the end of a long day, Sondra Perls was in her car waiting in line at the Wendy's restaurant drive-through trying to pick up a quick supper before her evening meetings. She had her window down and was just starting to place her order when an intruder put a gun to her head through the open window and motioned her to keep quiet. Accustomed to making quick decisions, she handed him her purse, but he dropped it. Then she saw he had an accomplice on the other side of her car. She decided, "I wasn't gonna be driven away and terrorized and have my body found somewhere in the woods — if they were gonna do anything to me, they were gonna have to do it right there in the Wendy's parking lot." So she stepped on the gas pedal. The intruder's gun went off, sending a bullet through her head. She ran into the restaurant, afraid she was going to bleed to death, and frantically pulled one of the workers back toward her car; he drove her to the nearest hospital.

Sondra recounted a list of all the reasons she is lucky. She received immediate medical attention, due to her own quick action. She didn't have "much damage," although she did incur some permanent damage to her speech. And witnesses saw what car the offenders escaped in and police apprehended them with two hours. Still, the impact on her life was major. In addition to surgery on the night of the attack, she had four subsequent surgeries and considerable rehabilitation. She was off work for nearly two years and ultimately changed careers. But she maintained a positive attitude: "I wake up every day and look outside and see the blue sky and think, wow, it's nice to be alive."

The offender, David Greene and his buddy, both in their late teens, had spent the day at David's house smoking marijuana. "We ran outta weed and stuff, ran outta money, so we had to go make some money." They drove to a nearby strip mall, went looking for a likely target, and selected a woman in the drive-up lane at Wendy's. "All I wanted to do was slide over so I could take her to the ATM and get some money, then she can go on her way home and I'll go on my way. That's how we was gonna do it."

David's account of what happened next closely matched Sondra's: "She threw her purse at me and took off, and my hand jerked and off went the gun." He clarified that he didn't intend to shoot her: "Reflex action, I mean, you got a gun in your hand and you got your hand on the trigger, the slightest little hit is gonna make the gun go off."

As soon as the gun discharged, David and his friend ran off. Both of them were still "pretty buzzed," so he didn't know he had actually shot the occupant of the car until police caught up with him at his home two hours later and told him she had been shot. His first reaction was to be "really scared – that maybe she died, or maybe she's gonna die, or that I was about to get put on death row. Once I found out she got shot I started crying."

The major consequences in David's life were his 10-year prison term and the resulting loss of family: "I lost my fiancée, I lost ten years of my daughter's life because I was locked up." In fact, his girlfriend did bring their daughter for a visit, but the child was so distressed when it came time to say goodbye that his girlfriend decided she wouldn't come see him any more. And for most of his prison term he was too far away for his parents to visit; his father died while he was in prison.

Introduction to Dialogue and Reasons for Participating

Despite her positive attitude, for a long time Sondra harbored hatred for the two offenders who had so severely harmed her. Even when she woke from her initial surgery she kept her mental image of David's face firmly cemented in her memory so she could identify him if need be. Eventually she found that when she visualized him, she saw a bull's-eye on his face. She didn't own a gun (and added that she never will) but felt enraged enough to want to shoot him.

Sondra's change of heart began when she saw the movie *Dead Man Walking* and couldn't stop crying when it was over. "There was a father who was saying he was so full of hate — I realized my hate was my way of not being a victim. And I didn't want to live like that any more." She began speaking to victim groups, but only on the condition that she not be called a victim. "I never, ever called myself a victim. I saw myself as a person who was shot."

She had decided not to interfere in either direction with David's parole process. But one day not long before he was due to be released, she "just woke up and had this thought in mind that I needed to go and talk to David in prison." To her surprise, she wasn't angry any more; she just wanted "to look him right in the eye and have a conversation, find out what he was like as a person, what he thought about the shooting, what had it been like in prison for him." She summed her reasons up in one word: to "demystify" him.

Sondra knew nothing about the Office of Victim Services or its programs, but her phone calls were eventually routed there and she reached a facilitator. She wanted someone to check on David in prison and make sure he wasn't "just some ranting angry person" so she'd know what she was getting into. Otherwise, she didn't envision any potential risks for herself.

David was working at his prison job, shortly before he was due to be released on parole, when his case manager came to ask if he was interested in seeing the victim. "The first thing that popped into my mind – they're about to mess with my parole." But the case manager assured him it wouldn't affect his parole, and David agreed to meet once those terms were put in writing.

His major reason: "to give her closure." He went on, "I had done what society had supposedly wanted me to do, so my closure was done. But for her to get on with her life, if she needed to see me and talk to me to get closure in her life, why not?" When he was asked if there were any benefits for himself, he added, "to help me, I wanted to let her know I was sorry, and that I didn't want to rape her...I'm not saying I'm a good person, but I'm no rapist."

Preparation

By the time Sondra's case was actually assigned to a facilitator, David's pending release date was less than one month away. There was little time for formal preparation meetings, but Sondra had several long phone conversations with her facilitator and finally did have a one-hour meeting over lunch just before the afternoon mediation/dialogue session with David. The most helpful component of her preparation was the facilitator's suggestion in their phone conversations that she write out how she had been harmed by David. Sondra hadn't given much thought to what she would want to say to David, since her focus had been more on simply engaging him as a person. And with her optimistic outlook on life, she was unaccustomed to focusing on the ways she had been injured. But she found that simply writing how his actions had affected her helped prepare her for meeting him.

David had one two-hour meeting with his facilitator in preparation for his meeting with Sondra. He felt adequately prepared and said the facilitator told him "everything I needed to know." In addition to explaining how the meeting would be run, the facilitator let him know some of the kinds of things Sondra might ask about, and told him he could also say what he wanted and ask any questions he might have. She asked him how he felt about what he had done. He told her "I wasn't raised like that, but I'm not gonna cop out and say the drugs did it. I did it, and I paid for it." The facilitator also let him know she would let Sondra speak first. His only fear was that Sondra might get angry and "jump across the table at me," but the facilitator assured him that wasn't going to happen. David also reported that when he talked with other inmates about his plan to meet with his victim, they told him he was stupid and would lose his parole, but he told them, "they promised me, I got it all on paper."

The Mediation/Dialogue Session

Up until the last minute, Sondra remained uncertain that the meeting would actually be able to take place. Ultimately, it was scheduled a mere three days before David's release, so she worried that if anything went wrong, she wouldn't have another chance. The schedule was so tight that she didn't have an opportunity to visit the prison ahead of time. Walking in was unsettling: "Suddenly there I am in this prison and I'm thinking, oh my Gosh! What have I done?"

The meeting was held in a small conference room at the prison and lasted for about two hours. Present were Sondra, a friend she had brought for support, a deputy warden, the facilitator, and David. Sondra reported an awkward beginning. "Here I've been obsessing about getting to this point for five months, and the facilitator's looking at me, and I have to start." So she simply told David she just wanted to meet with him to talk about himself, his life in prison, and his views of the shooting. And, she reported that his first words were that he was sorry.

Several minutes into the conversation, Sondra told David that she had written down how being shot had affected her life, and asked if he would be interested in hearing that. He said yes, so she read what she had written. Perhaps because she was so focused on what she was saying, or perhaps because David was skilled in hiding feelings, Sondra was unaware how deeply her story was affecting him. But the facilitator picked up on David's distress, asked him how he was feeling, and accompanied him to a side room for several minutes so he could get his composure back.

Sondra reported becoming confrontational only once, when David told her he didn't mean to shoot her. "I said, 'Yes, David, but you did put a loaded gun to my head, didn't you?' But I didn't say it in an angry way." The biggest surprise for Sondra occurred near the end of the session, when she realized she was feeling forgiving toward David. She had never intended to forgive him, or to tell him he was forgiven, but found herself thinking that if it was what she felt, she should let him know. Even so, she found it hard to get the words out, but is glad that she did.

David said he was "scared" when he was waiting in his dormitory for the warden to come get him for the session. Later he elaborated, "in prison, if I did something, I knew the consequences, but I didn't know what she was gonna do or what the consequences were gonna be." But he reported that he relaxed fairly quickly once the session began. He said the facilitator opened by thanking him for agreeing to meet and then invited Sondra to begin.

For David there were two surprises in the meeting. The most important one was that Sondra forgave him. This had been his deepest hope, but he never really expected it would happen. The second was that he himself cried. "I was the one who started crying, because she told me about everything she went through, and I felt bad." He had often thought about her during his prison term and hoped she was all right, but he had never really been confronted with the impact of his actions. And, he had worked hard to hide his feelings the entire time he was in prison. "I didn't let my emotions show to any of these guys the way I really felt about it." Toward the end of his research interview, David commented that he also cried when Sondra shook his hand and told him she forgave him; this time, apparently, he didn't have to hide his tears from her.

Outcome and Evaluation

Sondra was "euphoric" and "energized" when she left the meeting. She felt that she got a glimpse of David as a person, "a person that I liked." She felt extremely lucky that David is "the person that he is," that he was willing to meet, expressed regret, and showed some insight into what he had done. She was surprised that she came to care about what would happen to him on the outside: "What are people gonna think when this huge guy applies for a job and they find out he was in prison for shooting somebody?" Her expectations were "so exceeded" that she reported "a lightness of my whole soul. It was transforming." Since then, she has noticed that not only is her anger at David gone; she is less prone to becoming angry at other negative events in life and feels she has "a more generous spirit" than before.

Sondra could think of nothing the facilitator could have done differently. "She just has a gentle way about her, so she sets a nice tone for things." The most helpful thing the facilitator did was to stay out of the way, and to be tuned in to David's feelings and provide what he needed.

David felt "a lot of relief" when the session was over. "I got more than what I wanted – I was forgiven." A major impact for David was the change in his awareness of the harm he had caused to Sondra. He felt doubly bad – both because of how much he had hurt her, and because of what a special person he came to feel she was. "It was like I hurt a friend." This, along with being forgiven, changed his outlook. "I've been hurtin' people all my life. But since I been out, I just gotta walk away. Back then, I wouldn't walk away."

For David, the most helpful thing the facilitator did was let him leave when he started to cry. Otherwise, he too was glad the facilitator didn't talk much and just left the process up to him and Sondra.

David had told no one in his family about his plan to meet, but afterwards he told his mother: "She was proud of me for doing it."

Following David's release, Sondra stayed in contact with David's parole officer to keep tabs on how he was doing. She had wanted to help him find a job, but the parole officer said it would be better for him to do this on his own, and was later able to report that he had been successful. Shortly before he was to end his parole Sondra sought another meeting, and David agreed, even bringing his new fiancé to the meeting. Sondra was pleased with this meeting, and concluded, "I feel like I want David to have a good life." David also was happy for a second chance to meet with her. "It was nice seeing her – I introduced her to my new fiancé. If she ever wanted to see me again, I have no problem with it."

Advice to Others

Sondra felt the biggest potential benefit for others who might consider such a meeting would be "facing up to the anger." She was still somewhat baffled about her own process: "I don't know how one gets rid of anger, but I think that it's not going to go away on its own." So she felt other people who have been harmed by crime should explore "how to be strong and not be angry."

David thought all offenders would benefit from a meeting like his. "There's a lot of guys in there who hurt somebody and don't care. But if you show them what they went through because somebody hurt them, it might change their way of thinking."

CASE STUDY TWO: MURDER — VICTIM PERSPECTIVE

The Experience of the Event

Bobbie Crawford was worried about her brother, Patrick Nelson, and his girlfriend, Annie Dixon. She felt Annie's family was nothing but trouble, spreading rumors and making threats. Annie's sister's husband, Charlie Fisher, "used to call me at one, two o'clock in the morning, all piled up drunk, saying 'your brother's a rapist, your brother's dead.'" The morning Patrick disappeared, Bobbie spoke with Annie on the phone and told her, "There's something going on. Patrick would have been home or he would have called you or mom or me by now." Still, when police came to notify her three days later that they had found Patrick's body in the river, Bobbie was disbelieving. She rushed to the hospital to identify the body, and was furious that she was not allowed to see him because Annie had already identified him. She never did get to see his body to say goodbye. He had been in the water so long that they kept the casket closed at the funeral.

Initially the coroner ruled the death an accidental drowning, but over the next two years Annie's brother, Bill Dixon, and Annie's sister's husband, Charlie Fisher, were charged, tried and convicted for the murder. Charlie was sentenced for 20 years to life. Bobbie did not offer many details about how the pair came to be implicated, but did describe some of her own involvement in the process. As suspicions grew, "the cops couldn't find the car. So I found the car at a junkyard and they told me to go look through it to see if there was any mud or blood, and if there was, they would go and check the car. So me and my mom went to the junkyard, found the car, and the windshield and dash were all kicked outward."

Bobbie felt that Patrick's death robbed her of the only family she had that was worth anything. "I watched my mom die every day because of Patrick." Both her parents died not long after the trial. "I feel the Lord took the three main people away from me, and left me with the assholes down here, on crack, cocaine and heroin. When my dad died, I had to settle the estate – all their money went for drugs."

Introduction to Dialogue and Reasons for Participating

Bobbie spent a lot of time over the next few years trying to envision exactly how her brother had died. She felt she had pieced the story together fairly well but still had questions that were unanswered. She was visiting a mutual friend whose son was also in prison when the son's weekly telephone call came through. The son had been in touch with Charlie and asked to speak with Bobbie when he learned she was there. "He said, 'Bobbie, Charlie wants to talk to you.' I said 'No, I owe him nothing.' He said, 'No, he wants to tell you the truth.'" After thinking it over, she decided that if he wanted to talk with her, she should go, so she got in touch with the Ohio Victim Offender Dialogue Program.

Preparation

Bobbie's preparation for dialogue included two face-to-face meetings of about two hours each and several telephone calls over a five-month period. She found the preparation very helpful and was very satisfied with it. The facilitator helped her think through whether or not she really wanted to go through with the meeting, and assured her she could back out at any time if she changed her mind. Her work with the facilitator also helped her clarify her reasons for meeting: she came to feel it might help her answer some of her nagging questions about her brother's last night.

Bobbie's friends were against the meeting and told her they thought the facilitator was just trying to help Charlie reduce his sentence or be released on parole. But she came to trust the facilitator and became convinced the facilitator was truly trying to help her. "She let me know that this is not for Charlie, it's for me." Bobbie had several conditions under which she would be willing to meet, and the facilitator succeeded in negotiating for all of those conditions to be met, including that Charlie not be notified that she was there until she was already settled in the meeting room. She also obtained an agreement from Charlie that he wasn't to tell anyone in his family that they had met, and she told no one in her family what she was planning to do.

The Mediation/Dialogue Session

Bobbie reported that she was quite frightened on the day of the meeting. She thought Charlie might wait till the last minute and start a riot, or that Bill and Annie Dixon's family might somehow attack her. But once she was settled into the meeting room her fears subsided and she felt ready for the meeting. She had chosen not to take a support person because she didn't need one: "I can live with this every day."

Present at the meeting were two facilitators, the prison chaplain, Charlie, and Bobbie. The meeting lasted for about three hours. During the meeting, Bobbie told Charlie exactly how his crime had affected her and how she felt. "I said, 'Charlie, I live in hell every day. When I get up in the morning, who do I think of? My brother." She also learned that Charlie was planning to petition for clemency. This angered her a great deal and made her think he had probably only asked to meet with her to get her to support his petition, not to really give her "the truth." She remained very angry at him and felt she retained some power over him by holding onto her cup of coffee: "Every time I picked my cup up to take a drink, I know in his heart he thought I was gonna throw it. So that was good to let him think." But she hastened to add that she would never have thrown it. She had promised the facilitator "no cussing, hitting, spitting or anything like that" and anyway, "I wouldn't waste a good cup of coffee on him."

Outcome and Evaluation

Bobbie was relieved when the meeting was over. "I knew nobody was going to get me, no one was starting a prison riot." And she had left a burden behind. "By just getting it off my chest, letting Charlie Fisher know how I felt, after nine years holding that in. I told the mediator I feel like a lot has come off my shoulders." Later she added, "It just made me feel better, getting to actually sit down and look at the man who murdered my brother, to let him know, Bobbie hasn't forgotten Patrick."

Bobbie did not change her opinion of Charlie, or her opposition to his release. At the end she told Charlie, "Do your clemency thing, do whatever you want to, but I am going to fight you." She did not feel he had told her the whole truth and she still suspected he was more responsible for her brother's death than he was letting on. In spite of these reservations, she felt she did get some questions answered and knew more about her brother's last moments, and for that she was grateful.

When Bobbie got home from her meeting she called Annie because she had finally decided she wanted to start seeing her brother's children. She was greatly upset when Annie said "I thought you were calling to tell me about your meeting," making it clear Charlie had already called the family and let them know. This made her all the more distrustful of the information Charlie had shared with her: "He got on the phone and he called his mom after promising not to — and I'm supposed to believe everything he's telling me now?"

In spite of these shortcomings, Bobbie had no regrets about her meeting and was very satisfied with her participation in the program. She felt her facilitators did a "great" job. They let her know it was her day, and they stayed out of the way and let her run the meeting her way.

Advice to Others

Even though she felt that she herself did not receive the truth, Bobbie felt other victims could benefit by meeting with their offenders because the potential for learning the truth was always a possibility.

CASE STUDY THREE: VEHICULAR HOMICIDE — VICTIM PERSPECTIVE

The Experience of the Event

Danny Boswell, his wife, and another couple were driving home from dinner at a restaurant to celebrate his friend's new job; his friend was at the wheel. Danny was fiddling with the van radio when he heard his wife scream from the back seat, "Oh my God, he's out of control!" He looked up in time to see a heavy equipment truck coming right at them. "We couldn't get away from the truck. It hit us right in the driver's side. The van flipped over...and it was just like slow motion. Then I saw what was around me — something I will never forget." His wife, his friend and his friend's wife all died in the accident. "Later, I found out I had survivor's guilt, because three people lost their lives, and all I had was bruises from the seat belt."

The loss was devastating for Danny and his two sons, ages nine and twelve. "It was just total. My life was just turned upside down." He didn't know how to handle his own grief and stay available for his sons. When his older son Ricky saw him crying, Ricky began trying to do the things his mom would have done, so his dad wouldn't miss her so much. "But later I'd hear the boys crying in the privacy of their room, and I couldn't find words to console them." Ronnie, the younger boy, agreed to go to counseling, but Ricky refused. "If I had it to do over again, I would have taken him, kicking and screaming, because I think he really did need it. But I didn't know." Eventually Ricky turned to drugs and moved out.

At the trial, Danny learned that the offender, Fred Lincoln, had three previous drunk driving (DWI) convictions, and that his blood-alcohol at the time of the accident was .225 (more than double the Ohio limit of .10). Fred was convicted of three counts of aggravated vehicular manslaughter, with three to ten years for each count, to be served consecutively.

Introduction to Dialogue and Reasons for Participating

Danny wanted a chance to speak with Fred fairly soon after the accident. He contacted the prison where Fred was incarcerated but learned that it "wasn't policy" to permit such contact. It was some years later that Fred sought to meet and began inquiries through the prison system, and word reached the Ohio Victim Offender Dialogue Program, where Danny's request had ultimately lodged. "The facilitator contacted me and asked if I was still interested, and I said, 'yes, I am.'"

When Danny initially sought to meet Fred, his reasons focused on getting his questions answered. But by the time the meeting became a possibility, that urgency had diminished. "Time heals, and you learn to deal with your emotions, so my frame of mind had changed…The thing that I most wanted to do was to cleanse my heart and forgive." He had also learned through his lawyer that Fred was "very self incriminating, blaming himself," and he wanted to meet for Fred's benefit as well as for his own.

The equipment truck Fred was driving belonged to the company Fred worked for. He had been attending a company picnic, where he had been drinking all day, and his supervisor had given him the keys and asked him to drive the truck back to the company garage. Danny felt the supervisor was the one really at fault, but he had no interest in meeting with him: "He's in a state of denial. It's hard to forgive someone who doesn't feel they did anything wrong."

Preparation

To prepare for his meeting with Fred, Danny had one two hour face-to-face meeting and three half-hour phone calls with the facilitator over a 15-month period. He felt well prepared. "I think some of the preparation is getting you tuned into what it is going to be like in there. I was in law enforcement, but I had never sat down in a prison before, so it's good preparation." He found it especially helpful that his facilitator provided details about what the session would be like. He also thought probably they had to check him out, "to make sure I wasn't an axe murderer, or something like that."

The Mediation/Dialogue Session

Danny was "a little nervous" before the meeting but felt he knew what the outcome would be. He wished the meeting didn't have to take place inside the prison. "Even if they had a place on the grounds where they could bring the prisoner, and you weren't exposed to going though all this stuff, emptying your pockets — they even took my candy. It's not a comfortable atmosphere." The meeting room was tiny, with a small table. Present were the facilitator and another program staff person, Danny, Fred, and the unit manager. The session lasted about an hour and a half.

Danny described the opening moments as "Uncomfortable: No eye contact, probably for the first couple of minutes. But then we made eye contact and things progressed from there." Danny told Fred that why he had come was "to forgive him." Danny's biggest surprise was that Fred told Danny he'd "given his heart to the Lord" and that he knew God had forgiven him.

As he listened to Fred describe the impact of the crime on his own life, Danny experienced a mix of feelings. "It bothers me that his two children are deprived of having him home, going to see their school projects, things like that." He reported that he used to feel angry that at least Fred's children still had a father, while his own children had lost their mother. But by the time of the dialogue he was more bothered that other people — including his own son — were still engaged in the behaviors that killed his wife and put Fred in prison.

Outcome and Evaluation

Danny's feelings when the session was over were intense: "Total elation. Freedom. I was released from prison, my own prison, that day." He felt the meeting with Fred especially impacted his spiritual life and advanced his healing. "When you find it in your heart to forgive, you are so clean and released. I think I have developed more of a sense of wanting to help others." He also felt that while prison doesn't usually help offenders change for the better, Fred had made efforts to change his life. "I think being in there he fully appreciates his family and has a different outlook on life."

Danny was very satisfied with the facilitator's role. "She kept the dialogue going...if there was a stumbling block or a hesitation or a loss for words, she kept the communication open." She also was able to remind both participants of questions or topics they had wanted to bring up.

Advice to Others

Danny wished his own children and the other couple's children would take the opportunity to meet with Fred. He thinks for all victims, "questions do get answered and the healing process can start." Having been present at the scene himself, he was aware how much it helped his friend's sister just to know what happened inside the van at the end, and he felt the potential for similar details could go a long way toward helping victims heal in other situations.

CASE STUDY FOUR: KIDNAPPING AND FELONIOUS ASSAULT — OFFENDER PERSPECTIVE

The Experience of the Event

Mike Sherman, in his early twenties, was feeling desperate about the problems in his relationship with his girlfriend, Melissa Harris. They worked together and had lived together for nearly a year, but had been fighting and she had finally moved out. He took a pistol to work thinking, "If I could just show it to her, I could get her to listen to me." But nothing went as planned. "Next thing I knew, she was shot, and I panicked." At gunpoint, he forced her to come with him to his car, and began driving aimlessly, trying the whole time to talk with her. "I knew she was hurt, but it was hard for anything to sink in, the seriousness of it." Several hours later they passed a hospital, and she told him she would marry him if he'd take her in for medical care. Once in the emergency room, she told the staff what had happened, and he was arrested in the waiting room.

From that point on Mike had no direct contact with Melissa. He knew he had shot her in the thigh but had no idea how serious her injury might be or how she was recovering. He also reported that for a long time he blamed her for the entire incident, taking no responsibility upon himself. "I thought she made me do it — if she'd just done this or that differently, it would never have happened."

Mike pled guilty to the charges of kidnapping and felonious assault. But he reported that reality didn't sink in until he was moved from the county jail to the prison to begin serving his sentence. Finally he decided, "I could either keep blaming her and suffer and be miserable the whole time, or I could accept responsibility and try to do something good for myself while I'm here." Even his own family resisted this shift in perspective, and he had to confront his mother about it. "I said, 'Look, Mom, I'm the one that pulled the trigger.' Once I did that I felt a lot better."

Introduction to Dialogue and Reasons for Participating

Several years into Mike's sentence, the victim coordinator at his prison came to tell him his victim had requested a meeting and ask if he would like to participate. "I was excited. I said yes — how could I refuse? I felt I owed it to her if she was requesting it." He felt at the very least it was a way for him to accept responsibility directly, and he hoped for some level of closure and perhaps acceptance or even forgiveness. He didn't feel he would incur any risks; he had just been given another 10 years until parole eligibility so didn't foresee any possible negative impact in that regard. However he did expect to be yelled at, "for as long as she felt like yelling." He thought Melissa would want to get her frustration out.

Preparation

Mike had two one-hour meetings with his facilitators in preparation for his meeting with Melissa. He felt since he was already expecting the worst, there wasn't much they could do to convince him otherwise. He appreciated that they were able to take questions back and forth between him and Melissa. He felt adequately prepared and wouldn't have wanted the preparation to last any longer because he was anxious to go ahead with the meeting.

Mike's facilitators had assured him of their neutrality, but at first he was dubious. He knew their initial contact had come from Melissa. "They kept saying they were neutral, but I know where I'm at, I didn't know them from Adam." But gradually they made it clear if his victim became verbally abusive they would stop it, so he relaxed somewhat. He elected to bring a support person with him to the meeting and chose the leader of one of his counseling groups because "he knew my case, my character, my personality."

The Mediation/Dialogue Session

Mike was "very anxious" immediately before his meeting. He had spoken with his whole counseling group and received their support. "They all wished me the best, and hoped it would be the start of something for somebody else, too." He chose not to have the session videotaped because he was afraid of how it might be used, but later had regrets: "Had I known it was gonna go so wonderful, I would have wanted the world to see it." Melissa chose not to bring any support person, because, as she told Mike, "It was just between me and you." Present were Mike, Mike's counselor, Melissa, and the two facilitators. The session lasted for about three hours.

Even upon first seeing Melissa, Mike remained quite nervous. "She looked at me and said, 'Mike, it's all right, calm down.' Just those couple words from her had a soothing effect on me and I was able to relax." The facilitators opened the session and went over ground rules but then mostly stayed in the background. "We went back and forth about what happened. I told her I'm so sorry. She said there was nothing to forgive, she didn't think I was a monster." Mike learned that Melissa's wound had healed fairly quickly because he hadn't hit any bones or arteries, which was a great relief for him. Melissa made it clear she didn't think he had planned to harm her. She also said she had gone on with her life and wasn't living in fear, and Mike assured her she had nothing to fear from him. After that "we just caught up — we spent three hours catching up on all those years." It was important to Mike to learn that Melissa hadn't let the incident stop her life: she had completed her education and had gotten married.

Outcome and Evaluation

Immediately after the meeting was over, Mike was "on top of the world, floating on a cloud." It felt good to be able to tell her he was sorry "and to see in her eyes that she truly did believe that or accept that. There's nothing else like that." The meeting far exceeded his expectations, which were chiefly expecting to be yelled at. He also received a great deal of information that he found to be very helpful. "I learned stuff about that day that I didn't even know — I was in such shock that I didn't remember." Not only had he lost track of time; "I didn't know truly how scared she was, what her actual feelings were. That affected me a lot, to know she was scared for her life." And he learned that from the very beginning Melissa had wanted to contact him but had been prevented from doing so. "That just meant so much to me."

The most helpful thing the facilitators did during the session was "just sit there and be quiet. We had such a flow going, if they would have interrupted and tried to steer the conversation any other way, I think that would have been a hindrance."

Advice to Others

Mike felt the major potential advantage for other offenders would be closure and forgiveness. A close second was information. He hoped other members of his prison counseling group would have similar opportunities.

Case Study Five: Incest — Offender Perspective

The Experience of the Event

Johnny Maxwell did not want to go into detail describing his crime, but simply stated what he had done in a straightforward manner: "I committed incest with my stepdaughter three times." His victim had fairly quickly informed her mother, who sought intervention from authorities and eventually divorced him. When officials came to question him he admitted to what he'd done and turned himself in. At first he thought "well, they can't put me in jail — I've got enough money to keep myself out." But ultimately he received a 20-year sentence.

Introduction to Dialogue and Reasons for Participating

More than halfway through his sentence, Johnny was approached by the caseworker from his penal institution, who told him his stepdaughter, now a grown woman, was interested in meeting with him. His immediate reaction was positive, for many reasons. He'd known the caseworker for a long time and felt she would only suggest it if she thought it would be good for him. He also felt that the meeting would be good for his stepdaughter, Susie: "I wanted to do what I could do, my responsibility, I just thought it was the least I could do." He hoped it would help her put what happened behind her and continue to heal. He added that he himself had been similarly victimized, although his experience had been a violent one. This made him all the more impressed that Susie would be willing to talk with him: "I know the person who was involved in my case, if I ever saw him, like in the shopping center or somewhere, I'd probably run over him with my car."

Preparation

The facilitator came twice to the prison to meet with Johnny in person, for an hour each time. Johnny felt adequately prepared. It was especially helpful for him that the facilitator had been meeting with Susie and could brief him on her feelings, her attitude about the meeting and the things she wanted to discuss. He was surprised and saddened to learn that Susie was still scared of him, and hoped that his meeting with her would help allay these fears. He suspected that his ex-wife, Susie's mother, might have been contributing to Susie's negative attitude, and he was looking forward to giving Susie an opportunity to decide about him for herself through their direct encounter.

Johnny also found it helpful that the facilitator spent time with him going over Johnny's feelings and helped him bring to the surface the things he would want to say. "If I had just gone in and sat down, after it was over with, I would have wished I had thought of this or that. This way, I knew ahead of time." The facilitator made him feel very comfortable, which he felt also helped him relax on the day of the mediation.

The Mediation/Dialogue Session

Johnny was "on pins and needles" the day of the dialogue, mostly worried that he might say something wrong, or that Susie might take something the wrong way and be somehow harmed by the meeting. He also was somewhat nervous about facing "someone you know is scared to death of you and probably hates the ground that you walk on."

Present at the meeting were his caseworker, a female guard, the facilitator, Susie and Johnny. The meeting lasted for about an hour and a half. Johnny had been offered the chance to speak first and felt he would like to do so. "So I talked for maybe five minutes, to tell her I had no hard feelings against her." He was troubled to learn that in addition to remaining scared of him, Susie was worried he would harm her or her children once he got out of prison. She also described how his abuse had affected her life. "It made me feel bad because I had no idea this was affecting her this long. I wish maybe we could have done this a lot sooner, she's been living in hell all these years." He thought he might have been ready to meet with her five or six years into his prison term.

Outcome and Evaluation

When it was over, Johnny felt "like someone took an anvil off of me, lifted a lot of weight." This did not mean it had been an easy thing to do: "I'd say this is probably the worst thing I've had to do since I've been in prison, having to come to grips with myself, to admit how wrong I was." He received a great deal of new information from Susie about her life. He hadn't known she was married or that she had children. He was very impressed with her: "My feeling was that she grew up to be a pretty good person, I can see that."

Johnny was grateful the facilitator set the stage with ground rules and then mostly stayed in the background, leaving the process up to him and Susie. He liked his facilitator's "soft spoken" style and also the fact that she had "done her homework" and knew what to bring up on the few occasions where their process slowed down.

Advice to Others

Johnny thought the major advantage for other inmates in his situation to participate in a similar dialogue would be "just the relief," not only for themselves, but for their victims, too.

CHAPTER 8.
OHIO VICTIM OFFENDER DIALOGUE PROGRAM: A STAFF AND VOLUNTEER PERSPECTIVE

The Ohio Victim Offender Dialogue Program in the Office of Victim Services of the Ohio Department of Rehabilitation and Correction (DRC) represents the incorporation of a progressive restorative/community justice intervention within what most observers would expect to be a traditionally entrenched corrections establishment. We were told that in many ways Ohio correctional institutions look, feel and smell like those in sister states. As in other jurisdictions, security is the number one objective in the system, for little else can happen unless and until the correctional environment is relatively safe for both staff and inmates.

Yet within this institutional context has emerged a growing concern for what staff call "community justice," which resembles in principle the notions of restorative justice. Ohio staff prefer to emphasize *community* not only by involving the outside community in an institution, but also in viewing the life shared between staff and inmates on the inside as an ongoing human community. While this idea of the prison as community is old, going back at least to Donald Clemmer's work *The Prison Community* in 1940, the Ohio DRC is placing a different twist on it. Under its community justice initiative, which is coordinated by a full-time staff person, inmates and staff who are victimized within the prison setting may seek resolution just as they might do if they were on the outside. As a result, a wide array of personal consequences for inmate violations are being employed other than traditional lock up or adding time to length of stay. Such consequences underscore the human nature of violations occurring within the prison community. Thus, within the institutional context in which the Victim Offender Dialogue Program functions is lodged, there exists a climate of administrative support for involving community members, especially victims, in the justice process.

In 1995, the Office of Victim Services was established by legislation. Unlike many such offices around the country, the Ohio office is housed within the Department of Rehabilitation and Corrections. While some detractors have criticized this arrangement, believing that the office would be in a better advocacy position if it were not administratively under DRC, others regard this arrangement as beneficial because it ties victims' interests directly into mainline corrections. A small central administrative office directs the activities of victim services; some of these staff are also involved in direct victim crisis intervention, education and referral. Each correctional institution has a position, sometimes part time and sometimes full time, called "Victim Coordinator." The person filling this position is responsible for answering the questions of victims about the progress of particular inmates, informing appropriate persons of hearings and inmate transfers, dealing with inmate questions about victims, and often for offering victim-sensitive programs to inmates. The victim coordinator often plays a key role for victim offender facilitators in setting up dialogues, and the coordinators' existence and role within the institutions also help provide a climate in which victim offender dialogue may favorably be received.

Karin Ho joined the department as Director of the Office of Victims Services (OVS) in 1995, and was still in place in May, 2003, when the present volume was written. A survivor of violent crime herself, Ho came to the department with extensive experience in the victim's movement and helped shape an office that is driven to meet the needs of victims. As with many such offices, OVS initially offered crisis intervention, education, notifications regarding hearings with inmates, and working with crime victims; services were provided by staff employed by the department.

Within a month of Ho's arrival at the department there was a request by a victim/survivor of a violent crime to meet with an offender. Within six months, there were 14 more such requests. Clearly, victims/survivors of severe violence were expressing a desire and a need to meet with the offender who had violated them.

One approach for meeting that need, with which Ho and others were intrigued, was Victim Offender Dialogue (VOD). Although it was toward the bottom of her initial planning list of programs to develop, it soon emerged as an idea and an approach that she and her planning committee wanted to pursue. In order to broaden the potential base for such a program for victims of severe violence, Ho made certain that skeptics and critics were on the planning committee along with proponents and supporters. If Ohio was to adapt some form of Victim Offender Dialogue, it had to be able to function within DRC institutions. Thus the 20-member committee included "mental health staff, community victim advocates, wardens, regional and legal correctional representatives." There was no doubt, Ho claimed, that the widespread representation on the committee had a lot to do with the acceptance of or at the least willingness to give VOD a chance.

Ho and others participated in training conducted by Mark Umbreit at the University of Minnesota, and visited other states, such as Texas, where victim offender mediation for serious and violent crime was either being done or being considered. In May of 1996, Karen Ho conducted the first violent crime victim offender dialogue in Ohio. A few more dialogues were completed over the next two years or so, some by Ho and some by contracted private providers.

A critical decision was made by the planning committee to use volunteers from inside as well as outside the DRC to conduct the dialogues. The current configuration of volunteers includes both. Two years were spent gaining experience within Ohio and collecting more information from others outside the state to develop a training program for volunteers. In March of 1999, 33 volunteers went through an intensive five-day training session to become victim offender dialogue facilitators.

In the Ohio program, two volunteers called co-facilitators share responsibility for preparing and bringing victim and offender together for a joint dialogue. In most instances, one volunteer co-facilitator is employed by the DRC and one is from the outside community-at-large. It should be very clear that each of these facilitators is a volunteer. Facilitating dialogues between victims and offenders is not part of their job descriptions, nor are they paid to do them.

The remainder of this chapter will consider the program's guiding philosophy and purpose, selection of volunteers, training, preparation, meeting, follow-up, supervision and accountability, forgiveness and self-care. This information was gathered through extensive staff and volunteer interviews and review of program documents during a site visit conducted in October of 1999.

PHILOSOPHY AND PURPOSE

The underlying premise of the Ohio program is that victims and offenders define their own needs regarding meeting one another and that the program exists to facilitate that meeting in a manner that is safe for all involved. There may be a wide range of needs and questions to be answered and stories to be shared, or that range might be quite narrow, centered on one or two specific questions. Thus, the amount of time spent in preparation and the length of meetings vary quite a bit, depending upon the articulated needs of the participants.

The facilitator functions, in part, to help the victims and offenders clarify their needs; it is not the task of the volunteer to try to expand or alter the participant's understanding of his or her need. The process is victim-driven, that is, it is initiated by the victim. Although the victim makes the initial request, the inmate is not coerced to participate. As Ho pointed out, "victim and offender should be viewed as equal participants by the facilitators." Another staff person stated it slightly differently: "there needs to be an equitable balance between victim and offender before the dialogue proceeds."

Not surprisingly, a number of volunteers echoed this important premise. "Whatever victims want to get out of the dialogue is of paramount importance." "Looking for a positive outcome for all parties is the goal. It's my hope that the offender, if nothing else, will get enough out of this that he does take advantage of the opportunity to make amends to whatever extent possible." "The key things that I want to make sure of are that we're having something that's going to be safe for both the offender and the victim, and in the end it's going to benefit both of them… much of our goal is to help them keep on track."

Occasionally, a volunteer expressed a hope that this dialogue will bring about "closure" for the victim. Ho remained doubtful whether closure is a realistic goal for the program. She understood that victims are involved in a "healing journey," and hopefully, participation in dialogue will contribute to that healing. But the healing process will continue for a long time after, if not for a lifetime. "We're just simply listening to their needs (at the moment) and trying to do the best we can to fulfill them," Ho said. "They will have several more steps or chapters to go through."

While Ho claimed that the participants, and not the facilitators, are in control, it is also true that the facilitator is not expected to meet unreasonable demands. Cases have been aborted if the inmate becomes overly manipulative, if the victim appears to be too volatile, or if the desire to meet is discovered to be merely a way to get around the department's rules against visitation between victims and inmates.

A word used by some and implied by many to describe what they do with dialogue participants is "empowerment." To help the victim and offender frame their questions, or make clear the pain of their loss, or to express sorrow and sadness about what they have done — these are actions which empower participants to be in charge of what they need at that moment, while recognizing the person across the table is a human being capable of tears and laughter.

The following comment by a volunteer facilitator may sum up this empowerment issue best: "I think that the great thing about it (victim-offender dialogue) is just the process is not ours, it's theirs. And all we're doing is feeding them information and debriefing them and that kind of thing. I don't think it would be good if we took ownership of that process. It's their process."

SELECTION OF FACILITATORS

As noted above, volunteer facilitators are selected from those who apply from within the DRC and from the community-at-large. It is believed desirable to have co-facilitators, ideally with a DRC staff person matched with an individual from outside the DRC. Volunteers are selected by a subcommittee of the planning group.

While it had been anticipated that 15 volunteers would be selected for the initial training to be held in March of 1999, 33 individuals were selected from the 77 who applied. The committee was amazed by the amount of interest and was hard pressed to make the best possible selections. Committee members were divided into teams of two, who then interviewed each candidate and ranked them. In addition to answering questions, the candidates viewed a videotape of a violent crime mediation and were invited to make comments about the challenges faced in working with the participants in that case and to share their feelings about what they had just witnessed.

Committee members articulated a fairly wide range of criteria used for selection purposes: "compassionate, tolerant, easy to talk to, good eye contact, fair, unbiased." While making selections was tough, final decisions often came down to "gut instinct," such as, "the person did not put me at ease, made me feel uncomfortable. Or the person didn't seem to want to understand both sides of victim offender issues."

"We were looking for a diverse group of people engaged in different kinds of professional experiences," said Ho. "We wanted persons from within corrections and parole and people from the broader community. Yet we knew we needed to look for the person rather than the profession."

When facilitators were asked about the type of person who should be selected for the next round of training, many of the same attributes were identified. Being a "good listener," "open," and "compassionate" were frequently listed as desirable characteristics. "Non-judgmental" was another trait repeatedly mentioned. As one volunteer put it, the facilitator "has to be somebody with a really open mind who is not quick to pass judgment because a lot of times you may not agree with what's happening, you may not agree with how the victim or inmate feels but it's not your process, it's their process."

Clearly, while there are specific characteristics that are sought in a volunteer facilitator, as Ho suggested, it boils down to "looking for the *right kind of heart*."

Training

Training curricula and format were in preparation for two years. Experiences garnered by talking with persons in other states, by participating in other training programs, and by conducting some pilot dialogues fed into the training of facilitators.

The initial training took place in March of 1999 and ran from Tuesday through Saturday, beginning at 8:30 and continuing on into the evening, totaling over 50 hours. Some of the evening time was used for informal bonding and some was used for presenting case studies. Most participants described the experience as "very intense," the "richest training" they had participated in, and "incredibly helpful." Some thought, "the days were too long." Others wanted more time set aside for training, but realized it would be difficult to accomplish due to work schedules.

Because volunteers came from outside as well as inside DRC, a fair amount of the content dealt with DRC procedures and policy. As with any correctional system, security was the number one concern. Within a safe setting, many different kinds of programs can be implemented, but all participants must first be aware of and sensitive to security issues. An example of a policy issue directly related to victim offender dialogue is visitation. It is against DRC policy for there to be contact between a victim and the person who violated them. Wardens may approve exceptions, but this is seldom done. A concern, then, is that neither the inmate nor the victim is entering the dialogue program to get around the visitation policy. Given this policy, it is surprising, when listening to facilitators describe their cases, to learn just how many inmates have actually had some unapproved contact, usually via mail, with their victims.

Other training components included victim sensitivity, inmate sensitivity, exploration of cultural differences, communication, self-care, spirituality and forgiveness, case studies, videos of actual dialogues, and mock scenarios. Just about every topic was highlighted by a volunteer as being crucial, even the material on departmental policy and procedures. Many of the volunteers we interviewed pointed to the sensitivity training, videos, and mock scenarios as most helpful. The mock scenarios involved bringing other DRC staff in as actors to play the parts of victims and offenders. This component received rave reviews. Some volunteers reported that they would like to have seen as much emphasis on portraying preparation and follow-up. Staff were considering spreading the mock scenarios out across the week rather than loading them up at the end. It was believed that this would better allow for illustrating how a case is actually developed over time.

Perhaps not too surprisingly, corrections staff frequently pointed to learning more about the victim experience as very important, and community volunteers — who often had a background in working with victims — reported that being provided with the opportunity to tour the prisons and hear directly from inmates was very revealing. One facilitator who worked within the DRC stated, "After a decade in the department of corrections you become very brash and matter of fact about things. Things don't shock you like they do other people. Can't be that way around victim survivors. Need to know what (we say) and how we say something may offend or upset them."

"It was wonderful training," responded a volunteer, " as far as how in depth it went… It was five days, it was very intense. We would start at eight o'clock in the morning and maybe go through till eight o'clock at night and then even after that we'd go to our rooms and everyone would gather and still talk about it into the night."

A number of facilitators pointed out that a significant long-term outcome of the training was the bonding that took place. As one stated, the training helped "in forming those bonds between fellow facilitators and later being able to pick up the phone and call them with a question or for support."

No matter how helpful facilitators felt the training was, they indicated a continuing need for more. Ho took that need very seriously. The facilitators were required to meet quarterly to go through more training and to have the opportunity to share their own case experiences and receive feedback.

Ho pointed out that it is human nature to forget. She pointed to instances where questions were raised later that were thoroughly handled in the initial training. For example, one facilitator reported being unaware that the victim and offender must sign a waiver indicating that their participation is of their own free will and that DRC's role is simply to facilitate. It is important for each participant to know that no one is "pushed" into meeting with the other. This simple waiver is testimony to empowerment. When the question about waivers was raised at a quarterly meeting, a number of facilitators reached into their briefcases and pulled out the waiver forms. As Ho claimed, "That validates my need every quarter to give a booster shot."

Preparation

The goal of preparation is to help the victim and offender clarify what they want to get out of the dialogue and to help each understand what the other wants from that dialogue experience. In preparing the participants, Ho stressed the desire "that there will be no major surprises" during the meeting either for the victim, the offender or the facilitator. "No surprises" became a refrain when listening to the facilitators speak about their cases.

How is this achieved? According to Ho, "you need a facilitator in the process to do what I call push their hot buttons, this is paramount." Facilitators need to probe and explore how the victim and inmate are feeling, not necessarily for the purpose of changing how they are feeling, but to be clear how each participant is defining needs and to what extent, if any, those needs or "hot buttons" threaten a safe environment for the dialogue.

One way to explore this mentioned by facilitators is getting the participant to talk about what they think will happen, what they hope will happen, and what the worst possible outcome they can imagine would be. As Ho pointed out, "if you don't get to their fears or worries about the meeting then you won't hit their anxiety, their hot button." If the victim is expecting to hear an apology, but the inmate is not prepared to make any such statement, then at the very least the victim needs to know that information in order to decide whether to proceed. Perhaps there are other bits of information that will be shared which still will cause the victim to move forward with the meeting. Or perhaps the victim will simply choose to abort any further consideration of a meeting.

Ho cited the following case as an illustration of a potential surprise for the inmate which might have been so unsettling as to cause more pain and hurt for the inmate than the inmate was prepared for. After a lot of pre-paratory work with the victim and offender, whereby each basically knew what kinds of questions and information would be shared, the victim decided that she wanted to share the picture of her murdered daughter in her coffin. Ho took that information to the inmate, who initially felt that she could not deal with the photo. Then the inmate said, "If she needs to share this with me, then I do need to see it." Still, she couldn't figure out how she could emotionally survive the experience. In that context, since the inmate wanted to proceed, Ho suggested that she might want to consider simply looking at the border of the picture. In the meeting, the survivor did share the photo and the inmate left with it in her possession. She now carries it in her Bible. The "no surprises" dictum probably turned a poten-tial disaster into positive experience.

The typical steps in the preparation process begin with the vic-tim/survivor initiating a request to meet with the offender. This request is often made to the central office, but occasionally is made to a victim coor-dinator working in one of the prisons. The next step is to determine if the inmate is willing to even consider the possibility of meeting with the vic-tim/survivor. The inmate may be approached initially by one of the as-signed facilitators or by the victim coordinator responsible for that institu-tion. While not all victim coordinators are facilitators, they have all been thoroughly informed about the dialogue program. A few facilitators ques-tioned this procedure, believing that the facilitator is in a better position to explain the program and the victim's interest.

Inmates frequently express surprise that the victim would want to see them. "He just really finds it amazing that she wants to meet with him," reported one facilitator. "I think he does see this as an opportunity to do some cleansing and to explain himself."

Once the inmate expresses interest, the facilitators typically meet first with the victim to develop a better understanding of why the vic-tim/survivor wants to meet as well as to look for those "hot buttons." Some victims are very focused, wanting something narrowly specific, such as to express loss, to learn some thing particular about what led up to the crime, to express forgiveness. Others are more interested in hearing the offender's story, however long that might take. Or they might want to share their own story or the victim's story, to be certain that the offender knows that what he or she did has continuing consequences for all involved.

As facilitators described it, this initial meeting frequently lasts from two to three hours. One or both facilitators then meets with the inmate to elicit why he/she is interested in meeting and what that person expects to get out of it. Inmates are told explicitly that participation will not affect parole hearings and release dates. They often participate because of strong feelings of guilt — that if the victim wants to meet them, then they should. Some want to apologize. Some want to try to explain what happened. Frequently, the victim and offender may have known each other and issues arise out of that prior relationship.

Typically, each participant is conferred with at least twice before a meeting occurs, and there are often a fair number of phone contacts with the victim. But distances and work schedules often dictate flexibility for this preparatory phase. As one facilitator stated, "We actually did not get to meet with her (victim) a second time because of her work schedule, her health problems and our own work schedules. But I talked to her on the phone probably a dozen times, if not more. We spoke at least once or twice a week." Her co-facilitator also spoke with the woman once a week. Because of location, the co-facilitator had more contact with the inmate.

It was frequently noted by facilitators that there would be an imbalance in their contacts with victim and offender. One facilitator tended to focus more on the victim or the offender than did the other. When asked whether this imbalance ever put them into positions of advocacy for the inmate or victim, the response was "no." Some suggested, however, that having a co-facilitator may have provided a check and balance if one facilitator identified too much with one participant or the other. The facilitators were in frequent contact with one another and this bond seems to have superseded any developing attachment with victim or inmate that might have led to a disruptive form of advocacy.

How do facilitators decide that the participants are ready to meet? Many factors feed into this decision. Some are fairly observable while others depend upon "gut instinct." Ho described two conditions of readiness: "When it looks like they're emotionally reasonably making for a safe environment...and when the victim and offender feel like they know what to expect and are prepared to deal with the other's questions."

In one instance, the victim did not want the offender to ask for forgiveness. The offender agreed to abide by that request, and the facilitators believed that he would honor his commitment. Both parties are informed that if things begin to deteriorate in the meeting — for example, in the above case if the offender went ahead and pressed for forgiveness — the facilitators would stop the dialogue. "We can stop the meeting at anytime," said a facilitator. "He (inmate) knows if he crosses the line we will stop it...he doesn't have control over it." This is equally true for victims and also underscores the limits on the goal of empowering victims and offenders. Empowerment does not mean giving one person the power to abuse another.

Another facilitator reported being initially uncertain about an offender's readiness. The inmate had to do a lot to convince her that he wasn't trying to gain by influencing his release date. Once she was clear that he wanted to participate, "for his own feeling that he needed this as well (as did the victim)," then the facilitator knew that "they were ready to do it."

In one murder case, the offender at the beginning of the preparatory work did not own his responsibility for causing the victim's death. Someone else had pulled the trigger. He was not ready to meet. By the time the preparatory work was finished "he owned his responsibility, making it more beneficial to meet with the victim."

Still another facilitator was concerned about the briefer than expected time frame needed for preparation. "I kept thinking it's too quick, it's too quick. But then I thought, you know, if they know what they want and if the offender is able to address what the victim wants and victim is ready to address what the offender wants, then I think they're ready... and once ready I don't want them getting frustrated by unnecessary delays."

This was a case that took only a month of preparation. Most will likely take three to four months. And others may require extended time periods before emotional pain and reactions have been dealt with enough to permit such a meeting to move forward. These variations underscore what many staff and volunteers were quick to point out — that each case is "unique, requiring flexibility." No one wanted to be part of a "cookie cutter operation."

In one case, the offender told the facilitator that the preparatory period "took forever." The delay was not accidental. The volunteer agreed that it did take a long time. "We wanted to be sure he wasn't obsessed with the victim. Our main goal was to make sure that it was a safe environment."

Clearly, not only are the victim and offender being prepared to meet; so are the facilitators being prepared to facilitate a dialogue between a specific set of participants. As one facilitator reflected, "The person (facilitator) prepares himself just as you're preparing the victim and offender. We need to prepare ourselves because we have to be sort of complacent throughout the dialogue, you know. We don't need to bring our own issues into it. I think that's very important. I had one victim who wanted to start the meeting with a quiet moment of prayer. I personally don't think that was appropriate. That this is not the appropriate place for it. But if the victim asked the offender, 'can we have a moment of silence or prayer?' and the offender said: 'yes,' then that's fine. But for the facilitator to suggest that, I think that would not be appropriate. And we do need, however, to be careful about victim and offender motives."

Other preparatory tasks may be more of a logistical nature. If possible, arranging a tour of the institution for the victim can be quite important to sensitize them to what they will see on the day of the dialogue, although some live a considerable distance from the institution and cannot afford to stay overnight to accommodate such a visit. The facilitators work with victim coordinators or other institutional staff to reserve and set up a room for the meeting. An inmate or a victim may want to see a picture of the other before the day of the meeting. A myriad of logistical matters may arise to be handled. Facilitators often expressed gratitude for being part of a team where these tasks can be shared.

The decision to move forward to a meeting rests in the hands of the facilitators. "If we don't see or sense that there's going to be a good outcome," said a volunteer, "for both (inmate and victim) then it (dialogue) doesn't happen." They would likely continue to work with the victim or inmate, if either so wished. The Office of Victim Services would stay involved with the victim and the victim coordinator and other institutional staff would work with the inmate.

Preparation involves a continuous assessment of victim and inmate readiness in order to assure a safe environment and an experience that is more helpful than hurtful. Facilitators continually evaluate the readiness of both parties to meet, any potential benefit of extending the time for preparation, or the desirability of stopping the process.

MEETING

At the time of our site visit in early October of 1999, 17 cases had reached the point of having the victim and offender come together for a focused dialogue.

Often on the day of the meeting, one of the facilitators is involved in providing transportation for the victim to and from the meeting. This provides an informal atmosphere for assessing the victim's readiness and gaining immediate responses afterward. The victim is usually shown the room where the meeting will be held and has a choice about how the seating arrangements will be arranged.

At the same time, the other facilitator is typically checking in with the inmate to determine how the offender is feeling about the meeting. The inmate as well as the victim can call off the meeting at any point, even on the day of the scheduled dialogue. Both seem to appreciate the understated encouragement and support they receive.

In Ohio, victims and offenders are encouraged to have a support person in the meeting with them. Some choose not to do this, but they appear to be the exceptions. Often the victim coordinator or a chaplain is chosen by the inmate as a support person. For victims, support persons are often a clergy person or a friend. Frequently, other family members and often friends fail to understand why the victim would ever want to meet the offender face to face. Many of these individuals have tried to discourage the victim from taking such a course of action and are unwilling to sit in the meeting as a support person.

Support persons are supposed to be present simply to lend support. Occasionally, some actually participate in the meeting. This has been a surprise in some instances. It remains unclear how much preparatory work is done with the support person by the facilitator. Most indicated that they tried to be in phone contact with that individual and made clear what the limits of the role were. Yet in at least a couple cases it was reported that support persons did speak up. One was a victim's fiancée, and this person's participation seemed to make sense to the facilitator. Another involved a clergy person talking about forgiveness. The victims wanted the meeting in order to express their forgiveness to an inmate who had murdered a family member, and the pastor was asked by one of the victims to explain what they meant by forgiveness. Over all, there remained some concern on the part of staff and volunteers about the potential unknowns that support persons may bring to the table if they begin to play an active role.

The dialogue meetings do not follow a rigid format. In one instance, a facilitator reported, "We started to introduce them and immediately, they started talking. She asked him her first question and from there on then it was them." Some victims or inmates want to begin by making a statement. The victim is given the opportunity to go first. Other victims want to begin by asking questions.

Typically meetings run two to four hours, with breaks when necessary. Facilitators indicated that the bulk of their work takes place in the preparatory phase. In the actual meeting, they may find themselves occasionally reminding a victim or offender of something they wanted to say or ask. One facilitator noted, "If you've done your job well, if you've prepared properly, then your job is pretty much done."

Another facilitator described the facilitator role in the meeting in this way: "Once they sat down we opened it up... with the ground rules. We told them, 'This is your meeting.' I think there were two or three times when I chimed in to mention something that slipped their minds, asking if they wanted to ask about it now."

A number of facilitators expressed surprise at witnessing victims and offenders identifying common ground. Because of their training they had expected this, but watching individuals suffering so much because of violence search for and seemingly find shared experiences and concerns was nonetheless wrenching.

In one case, the survivor wanted to know if the offender, who had killed five members of her family when he was driving drunk, had been "saved." While neither participant felt particularly "religious," both shared similar thoughts regarding a higher power. The offender brought several songs that he had written. The facilitators had alerted her to the songs beforehand, and she acknowledged an interest in seeing them. She brought "a whole photo album of pictures," but she only showed him a picture of her mother. On the ride home after the meeting, the victim indicated to the facilitator "that she felt that he did seem very remorseful and that he did answer her questions and that she didn't feel the need to torture him with photos of her family."

In an aggravated kidnap case, a facilitator said that she felt that she and her co-facilitator "were just observing. It was very personal space. It just seemed like a really sacred space... At one point, he (the inmate) started crying and she pushed the Kleenex across and handed it to him. It was pretty amazing."

"It was like being in a sacred place," admitted a facilitator working on homicide drunk driving case. "We started the meeting and laid out the ground rules and then it just moved on...Ultimately, this shy inmate was able to hold his head high and tears streamed down his face and say what he thought and felt and this family could say to him they wanted to forgive him and that they'd all made mistakes."

Follow-up

Immediately after the dialogue, facilitators meet with the victim and the offender separately to determine how the individuals felt about the meeting and whether there are significant remaining questions. One of the facilitators may also be involved in transporting the victim home.

Later that week follow-up calls will be made to the victim. One of the facilitators or the victim coordinator will remain in contact with the inmate. It is expected that cases will be closed within a month of the dialogue. Some facilitators were reporting having been in contact for two months, but all seemed quite clear that follow-up would require a limited amount of time and then the case would be closed. Theoretically, if at some later point the victim again desires to meet with the offender, that request needs to be made to the Office of Victim Services.

Over coffee immediately after the dialogue, one victim explained to the co-facilitators what she experienced. "She basically said, 'it's the best feeling in my life that I have ever got.' She said, 'I needed this more than anything else.' She spoke of those things that were most empowering for her. She felt like she could get on with her life without guarding her back."

Some facilitators felt some strain around the boundaries of the case at closing. "It'd be nice to pick up the phone and say how you doing? But this is a one-time thing and we're not there to encourage relationships and to continue to be a conduit between the two. Hopefully, everyone is up front about it at the beginning — this is a one time deal."

SUPERVISION AND ACCOUNTABILITY

Perhaps it is in this nebulous area of supervision and accountability that we best witness the dynamic tensions that undergird this program. While on the surface, because the scope of the dialogue is often narrower than it may be in other places, victim offender dialogue as practiced in Ohio may appear to be rather "cut and dried," it is anything but. Although there are frameworks for working a case and expectations about how to do that, the actual implementation requires a fair amount of give and take, a lot of flexibility. A significant part of that give and take, that dynamism, comes with the interaction between the central office and the facilitators. Some of this is explicit; much of it is subtle, matching the personality and style of the program's director, Karin Ho.

Ho nurtures, cajoles and leads the facilitators. She provides advice and intervenes, if necessary, to make a decision regarding a case. She may instruct a facilitator to slow the case down to give the victim or offender more time to deal with emotional baggage. She may pick up the phone and advocate for her facilitators, victims, or offenders with a recalcitrant warden. While deceptively mild mannered, Ho is a product of victim advocacy, and that desire and will to empower victims and offenders to seek what they feel they need is often seen in her ability to enlist the assistance of resistant individuals. From the beginning, she tried to give proponents and opponents of the victim offender dialogue concept some kind of stake in the resulting program. That care for program development paid off hugely as facilitators implemented the program.

As one facilitator addressed the question of supervision, he preferred to use the word "facilitate" or "mentor." "Karin's a master at asking you hard questions but somehow making you think that it was your idea. You know there's a trick to that. Have you checked? Have you considered this? Or you might want to consider that. There is just about the right amount of nurturing along the way. Certainly we felt ownership of the case, but we felt we had guidance."

Most facilitators reported that they stay in regular contact with Ho or her staff about the progress of cases and for support. "Any time I ever have a question, I've called up and if they don't know, they find out," said a volunteer. "They'll call me back. They're very supportive. I've gotten calls of encouragement before the dialogue and again afterwards."

Another facilitator noted: "Karin Ho, she's a remarkable person. All the people out of the office have been great. I've gotten nothing but support. If I call, I get responses back very quickly. It makes me want to be just as efficient, just as professional."

Still another: "Karin's a wonder woman. In terms of accountability she is very thorough with people and she'll check on them, make sure what's going on. And she'll even talk to the victims and the offenders to make sure if things are going the way they should go."

Much of this supervision and monitoring takes place informally. "I see Karin all the time," reported a facilitator. "We're in and out of the same places. We just kind of let her know about scheduling a meeting or complications."

The quarterly meetings provide an opportunity for facilitators to talk about their cases in the group and/or privately with Ho. Opinions of facilitators are solicited, which serves to enhance the bond among volunteers. In addition to seeking assistance from central staff, facilitators also telephone one another for support. Ho described the quarterly meetings as "an opportunity for going over the logistics of each case which is the staple of our environment. It's also a time to go over the philosophy of our office to make sure they're carrying that forward."

Actual paperwork on a given case is relatively light. A referral form is filled out identifying key participants and volunteers as well as whether a local victim advocate or a therapist is involved. This form contains a preparation checklist for the day of the dialogue. Date of dialogue completion, participants and additional comments complete this two-page form. A second form is the facilitator time sheet, which allows spaces for recording names of key participants, the date that the dialogue was completed or stopped, and contact dates. Each facilitator is to indicate whether contact was by phone or in person, purpose of contact, and length of contact. The facilitator is responsible for obtaining waiver forms for the inmate and for the victim.

Ho was very concerned about balancing the need for information with the amount of paperwork effort one can reasonably expect from people who are volunteering precious time. She expected the amount of paper accountability to increase somewhat, but not by much. And she was also sensitive about balancing supervision and support. "We ride that fine line," she said, "of looking over someone's shoulder but yet giving them autonomy to feel that they can make some choices in what they're doing. And I always strive to make sure they know they need to be flexible in each case; there's no one right answer."

It was also evident that some accountability is built into the structure of the system with the employment of co-facilitators. "I also have the accountability issue not only in our quarterly meetings — that's also raised between the facilitators. I think accountability is maintained," claimed Ho, "when you have co-facilitators who can trouble shoot and say, 'let's not forget this,' or 'let's do that.'"

In many ways, we saw reflected in Ho's supervision style the principles that she hoped the facilitators would build into their own way of handling a case. She tried to empower the volunteers to do the work of the dialogues. Yet she continued to ask questions, probe and if necessary slow things down until she felt that the case was ready to proceed. Just as with victims and offenders, there are parameters within which the facilitators function. If they go too far outside the boundaries, they will simply not receive another case.

In keeping with the desire to keep things fluid with a minimum of explicit controls being exercised by the central office staff, there were initially no formal policies about volunteers letting the office know how a case was moving through various checkpoints, such as victim and offender readiness to meet or the scheduling of a meeting. As a result, one case came to a dialogue without any notification to the central office. Other facilitators were flabbergasted that this had happened. Formal checkpoint procedures were being established in November of 1999 so that the office would be informed of any planned dialogues. As one facilitator put it, "I know definitely that if something goes wrong they're (office) ultimately accountable."

Forgiveness

Often when dealing with victims or survivors of violent crime, the notion of forgiveness seeps into the mindset of victims and offenders. Some offenders want forgiveness desperately; others feel themselves unworthy of forgiveness. Some victim survivors find the idea of forgiveness to be anathema. Others feel guilty because they believe they ought to be more forgiving. Still others are prompted by genuine religious commitments to forgive. And there are likely many variations among and between these possibilities.

Forgiveness is discussed during the training program. Initially, a number of the volunteers were surprised that the topic was included. Now some would like more training on spirituality and forgiveness as both are frequently recurring themes in their cases.

The notion of forgiving another person for extreme acts of violence or for a murderer to seek or expect forgiveness is an extremely personal matter. In Ohio, forgiveness will be dealt with only if the victim or offender brings it up. The facilitator will not initiate such a discussion. As one facilitator said, "Unless they bring up the word forgiveness, I won't address it with them. Because I think it's so much a personal thing…I will never push that on them. Never. I wouldn't."

This facilitator is reflecting the office's expectations regarding forgiveness. Ho noted that victims and offenders often have different understandings of what forgiveness means. For some victims, it is a process of letting go so they can get on with the rest of their life. On the other hand, "it's very offensive to victims to say, oh it's okay you raped me, it's okay you murdered my son. Those are the issues — that is such a hot button… If one or the other asks for forgiveness or shares that they'd like to forgive the offender then in the preparation it is woven in and we work with it from that point forward."

The desire for forgiveness may be lurking in the offender's motivation to participate in the dialogue. Ho believes it is important to smoke out that possibility so it does not come as a shock during the actual meeting. "If I think the offender is kind of insinuating that he or she would like to get forgiveness, I'll cold ask them right on the spot. Just to clarify for myself. I'd do the same with a victim, if necessary."

Another confounding problem arising with matters of forgiveness is that where there are multiple victims participating one may want to forgive and another may not. It is important to be able to interpret for the inmate what is happening. It must be okay, for example, for the mother to express her forgiveness while the father remains silent. And the offender in such a case should not be led to expect more than that. "It's important to respect everyone's feelings in that way," said Ho.

SELF-CARE

Preparing victims and offenders for dialogue and then being present for that meeting can be intense if not overwhelming. Facilitators must listen to the details of heinous crimes: bludgeoning, multiple stabbing, decapitation. They hear and feel the pain of loss and witness the valiant struggle of survivors to continue on. They must witness an offender's horror as he or she takes responsibility for unimaginable actions. And they must see the callousness of those inmates who still try to manipulate everyone, including the facilitator, while denying their own behaviors and emotions.

The following are a series of facilitator comments reflecting upon their own humanity in this very human process:

> She showed us pictures and newspaper clippings she had saved and things like that, some of which were quite heart wrenching.

> We don't have to be a cardboard figure...I sobbed some (during the meeting). I felt fine about it, but really I thought it doesn't matter. I'm a human being. I'm here, this is how I feel. Plus nobody was paying attention to me.

> Is it such a bad thing to let a tear come down and for them to see it? Are we to appear cold hearted? We talk so much about neutrality and being unbiased and being balanced — if I'm allowed to cry for her (victim), why can't I cry for him (inmate)?

Part of the function of the quarterly meeting is to provide support to facilitators and to help them bond with one another. Facilitators were quick to point out that they often find their co-facilitator to be their best support person and that this is a huge advantage of being part of a team. As one volunteer put it, "I had a lot of really supportive friends and family that I feel comfortable talking to. And my co-facilitator is an invaluable support. Because we have so much in common."

Another facilitator pointed back to the training as sensitizing her to the need for self-care when working in this kind of program. "The biggest thing is having somebody that you just can vent to when you need to talk."

This same volunteer indicated that part of self-care begins when working with the office staff to choose an appropriate case. "If there's a case you cannot do, if it maybe happened to you once, just pass it on." This self-awareness of the kinds of cases one cannot work on, and the importance of it being okay to pass, are dealt with in training. A couple of facilitators said that they would not take cases where children were victims of intentional violence. Ho and other staff made a point that rejecting a case "is not a sign of weakness; it is a sign of strength, of knowing yourself."

Exercise and hobbies were cited by some volunteers as ways of taking care of themselves. And one mother of young children said that she did not live and breathe her work or her volunteer effort; "my kids won't allow that to happen!"

Many volunteers emphasized the importance of using members of the training group as support persons. And most looked to Ho as someone who would be there for them during and after the process. Apparently she was as concerned about the emotional well being of her facilitators as she was involved with the cases themselves. Facilitators indicated that they expected that hardly an evening went by without Ho on the phone supporting somebody in the field facing a challenge. As one volunteer put it, "she works herself to death being available for us." Some seemed to be suggesting that while Ho is a tremendous role model, she might want to think more about how to model self-care.

CONCLUSION

Victim Offender Dialogue as practiced in Ohio is an intensive effort carried out primarily by volunteers to provide an opportunity for violent crime victims and survivors to come together in a relatively safe environment with offenders to have a focused conversation about specific questions and concerns. Explicitly and implicitly, the program seeks to empower individuals as they make crucial decisions that impact their own lives so they can take one more incremental step in dealing with what has already likely been the most horrific experience of their lives. Some find the preparation and dialogue relieving. Others say it is life altering.

Facilitators are aware that they are participating in an experiment that is unique in the justice system. As one stated, "The most unique thing is the fact that you have a victim and an offender coming together. I know the first time I mentioned to someone what I was doing they thought it was crazy. Yet when the victim and offender do come together that space is so sacred."

And another facilitator summed up a case in this way: "It was a journey of the heart for assisting people to get on with the rest of their lives. I felt we accomplished that; you could see it on their faces."

Karin Ho reminded us again of the focus of the Ohio Victim Offender Dialogue:

> The program is victim initiated. Yet the facilitators are concerned for the well being of the inmate or offender under supervision as much as the victim. They probe with the victim and offender to make sure that all explicit needs are met that can be. It's not simply victim driven to the point that victims say this is what the victim wants and put a period at the end of the sentence. We focus on the needs of both and what they want to get out of the process.

CHAPTER 9.
OHIO VICTIMS: EXPERIENCE AND IMPACT

This chapter and the next present results from 40 interviews with persons who participated in 25 mediation/dialogue sessions facilitated by the Ohio program. A total of 20 victims or victim family members and 20 convicted offenders were located and agreed to be interviewed for the participant component of the Ohio study. Two of the authors completed the 40 in-person interviews between December 1998 and February 2001.

Because these interviews were begun after several Texas pilot interviews had been completed, they had the benefit of a more developed and stable interview schedule, and there is more consistency across the data set in questions asked than in the Texas interviews. Nonetheless, in reporting results in these two chapters, every effort has been made to clarify whether participants are making spontaneous comments or responding to specific questions.

OHIO RESEARCH SAMPLE DESCRIPTION

The present chapter opens with introductory information about all participants in the 25 mediation/dialogue sessions and the 24 crimes about which they met. The remainder of this chapter focuses on the experiences and perspectives of the 20 victim/family member participants who were interviewed. Ohio offender accounts will be taken up in the following chapter.

Descriptive information for the cases covered in these mediation/dialogue sessions is provided in Table 9.1 and Table 9.2 below. The 25 sessions were held between June 1997 and November 2000, and they involved 24 offenders and 28 victims or victim family members who met in dialogue regarding a total of 24 crimes. Of these, a total of 20 offenders and 20 victims participated in research interviews. There were 13 crimes for which both offenders (13) and victims (16) were interviewed, 7 crimes for which only the offender was interviewed, and 4 crimes for which only the victim was interviewed.

The 24 crimes included 10 instances of murder or manslaughter, 5 vehicular homicide cases involving alcohol, 5 felony assaults, 3 parent/child sexual assaults, and 1 theft. In 10 of the crimes, the victim did not die as a result of the crime; nine of these victims met with their offender. In the remaining such crime, the victim had since died of natural causes, and her stepson met with the offender. All remaining instances of victims' relatives meeting with offenders took place in crimes in which the actual victim died as a result of the crime; these totaled 17 victims in 15 crimes and included 8 mothers, 1 father, 4 sisters, 1 brother, 1 husband, and 2 daughters.

Table 9.1: Ohio Research Sample — Summary by Crime Type

CRIME	RESEARCH INTERVIEWS			
	Both Victim and Offender	Victim only	Offender only	Total
Murder/manslaughter	4	4	2	10
Vehicular homicide (all involving drunk driving)	4		1	5
Felony assault and attempted murder	3	1	1	5
Sexual assault	2	1		3
Theft	0	1		1
TOTALS	13	7	4	24

Characteristics of Victims/Family Members and Crimes

The 20 victim participants who were interviewed were victims of 17 crimes, including six murder/manslaughter cases (6 victims), 5 vehicular manslaughter cases (7 victims), four assaults (4 victims), and two sexual

Table 9.2: Ohio Research Sample — All Victims and Offenders

Case	Crime	Victim Died?	Relationship of Dialogue Participant to Victim	Research Interviews[a]	
				O	V
1	Robbery felony assault	N	Victim	1	1
2	Murder	Y	Mother	1	1
3	Rape, 2 counts	N	Victim	1	0
4	Aggravated vehicular homicide, 3 counts	Y	Husband	1	1
5	Sexual battery	N	Victim, victim	1	2
6	Felony assault, Aggravated robbery	N	Victim (2 sessions)	1	1
7	Kidnapping, Aggravated murder	Y	Parents	1	1
8	Involuntary manslaughter, Aggravated robbery	Y	Mother	1	1
9	Aggravated vehicular assault & homicide	Y	Parents, Brother	1	3
10	Involuntary manslaughter, Aggravated veh. homicide	Y	Daughter	1	1
11	Aggravated vehicular homicide	Y	Daughter	1	1
12	Rape, 4 counts	N	Victim	1	1
13	Aggravated manslaughter, Intimidation	Y	Sister	1	1
14	Grand theft, Voluntary manslaughter	Y	Sister	1	0
15	Felony assault, Kidnapping	N	Victim	1	0
16	Murder	Y	Mother	1	0
17	Involuntary manslaughter	Y	Sister	1	0

continued

Case	Crime	Victim Died?	Relationship of Dialogue Participant to Victim	Research Interviews[a]	
				O	V
18	Theft	N	Stepson	1	0
19	Voluntary manslaughter	Y	Mother	1	0
20	Attempted murder, Abduction	N	Victim	1	1
21	Aggravated assault & murder	Y	Mother	0	1
22	Felonious assault	N	Victim	0	1
23	Aggravated vehicular homicide	Y	Mother	0	1
24	Involuntary manslaughter, Kidnapping	Y	Sister	0	1
			Total	20	20

a) O = offender; V = victim.

assault cases (3 victims). The sample included 7 surviving victims of the 6 assault/sexual assault cases and 13 family members of the 11 deceased victims. Family members included 6 mothers, 1 father, 1 husband, 2 daughters, 2 sisters, and 1 brother. The participants' average age at the time of the dialogue was 41, with a range of 19 to 56. The 20 participants included 6 men and 14 women.

Six participants knew the offenders prior to the crime. This included the three sexual assault victims, one physical assault victim, and two family members of murder victims. One of these offenders was a fellow employee of his murder victim and was casually known by her family. The other was a brother in law to the murder victim and a former friend of his victim's sister. The remaining 14 crimes took place between strangers, and none of these offenders was known to either the actual victim or the family member who participated.

EXPERIENCE OF THE CRIME

Both the family members and the victims described their experience of the crime, including, for family members, how they first leaned about it, and for all interviewees, their experience with the justice system.

Learning of the Event

In the seven assault/sexual assault cases, the interviewees were themselves the direct victims of the crime and had no need to be informed. Additionally, of the 13 participants whose family members died in the crime, two were present during the crime. One was the husband of a vehicular homicide victim; he was the only survivor of the four persons in the car. The other was the sister of a murder victim, who was only six years old when the offender abducted her and her three year old brother; the brother was murdered after the sister had been set free to return home.

Ten of the 11 family members who were not present during the actual crime described how they first learned of their family member's death. Two were informed by other relatives, who had been called by authorities. Three received word from hospitals that their family member had been injured. In one instance, the parents of a vehicular homicide victim first received a call by mistake from the hospital where their daughter's fiancée (also killed as a result of the accident) had been taken. Within minutes the hospital providing care for their daughter called them and they rushed to the emergency room, where they were not permitted to see their daughter in her final moments. These parents understood the need for this decision but felt its pain:

> While that was probably best that was hard to not be able to — whether she knew it or not, to know that we were there....They told us that we would be in the way. At that point we would have been in the way. They were so desperately trying to figure out why she wasn't responding. They did say they would tell her we were there.

A mother of a murder victim was working the night shift when she received the call from the hospital that her daughter was injured. She said as she left work she "just knew," and told the guard, "my daughter's dead."

Five family members were informed by justice system staff. Learning a family member has been injured or killed is always shocking and often awkward at best. One mother of a murder victim reported the following:

> I got a telephone call from (the police sergeant) and it was the most awkward phone call. It ended up that I felt really bad for him. He was in a real difficult situation and I guessed what he had called me about. And he and his squad were actually at the morgue waiting for me to come.

A single mother of a murder victim reported that a county sheriff, a local policeman and a city policeman arrived together at 5:00 a.m. and handed her a slip of paper with a phone number to call. The first two times she dialed, she reached a recording; when she finally connected with the hospital, the staff wouldn't tell her the condition of her son. She exploded and said the police had told her to call this number, so hospital staff asked to speak to the police and told them the victim was dead, and police informed the mother, who told them:

> I don't care if my son was a drug dealer, I don't care if he was a mass murderer, but the way you walk into an individual's house and tell them about the death of their child is horrible.

A sister of a murder victim reported, "the cops came and told me they found my brother's body at the scene of a murder. We went to identify him."

Experience with the Justice System

Nine participants did not comment on the role of the justice system in responding to the crime. Two of these were themselves in some way connected with the system, one as a sheriff's deputy and one as an emergency medical system worker. Both of these participants were present during the crime, and their familiarity with the process enabled them to take appropriate action. "I got on the fire truck radio and called for help." "I called the sheriff's office, got on the line with the dispatcher and started telling her what was going on."

Of the remaining 11 participants, six reported having positive experiences, three described negative experiences, and two reported a mix. Among those with positive comments, four spoke of how quick, efficient or helpful the police were in solving the crime. One of these was a justice system employee, who was off duty at the time of the crime. "The response was immediate and swift. They arrested the offender, who had taken his girlfriend hostage." "The detective recovered this revolver in another robbery and asked me if it was the gun." "I'm lucky. Two women looking out the window had the license number, police went to the address where it was registered." Two reported positive personal experiences: "Our police are the best, taking care of us, protecting us. They sent an old friend of mine I grew up with." "At the funeral procession, police were at every corner, each officer standing at attention. I think that made us realize how badly they felt, that they had not gotten this guy into jail earlier."

The negative experiences included: "I am angry because every time I went to the trial, it was postponed. They had all the consideration for the offender, none for the victims." "The way the police, sheriff and everyone from the hospital handled it was ridiculous." "They weren't gonna do anything to him. I got an attorney and we started doing our own investigation."

The two mixed reports followed the same theme. One participant felt the response to the 911 call was extremely prompt, but that the conversation in which she was informed of the crime was "awkward." The second reported a shift over time. At first, "the cops couldn't find the car, so I found the car at the junkyard. They told me to go look through it to see if there was any mud or blood, and if there was they would go and check the car." However, by the time of the trial, "the detective came up every once in a while and checked on me."

Impact of the Crime

All 20 participants spoke of the impact the crime had upon their lives. Nineteen described a range of uncomfortable emotional reactions, 13 spoke of disconcerting changes in their lives, and seven mentioned specific actions they took in an effort to cope with these effects.

The troubling emotional experiences included feeling overwhelmed, afraid, sad, angry, shocked, lonely and guilty. Seven participants emphasized how enormous and far-reaching the impact was. "Oh wow, it was just total. My life was just turned upside down." "The worst in the world has befallen us." "My life's not the same." "It destroyed my life."

Fear, sadness and anger were all next on the list, mentioned specifically by six participants each. Fear reactions ranged from moderate to extreme. "I became overprotective of our son." "I looked over my shoulder a bit more often; I was frightened for my family because I'd lost my wallet and began getting these strange phone calls." "There for a while I carried a gun, started not sleeping at night, pointing the gun at the door every time it creaked, I literally tripped out." "I had PTSD." Similarly, sadness ranged from simply crying a lot and feeling emotional to reports of depression and suicidal ideation. "I cried, did anything I could do to kill myself." "I just wanted to die. I wanted my heart to stop at any time. At the hospital that night I tried to get it to stop but it wouldn't."

Six participants spoke of anger directed at the offender; two were so enraged they wanted to kill him. One of these spoke of how this anger protected her from fear: "People asked me if I was afraid when he comes out (of prison) — I said 'I'm not afraid — I've got a license to kill.'" Two participants used their anger to help hold the offender accountable in some way. "More than anything, it gave me a resolve that I'm going to do everything that I can that the people are held responsible for their actions." "I put everything I had into getting him convicted. I needed my anger to keep me going." One victim who was angry at the offender also spoke of anger at God: "I look back and think why God gave me a raw deal, why did he let this happen."

Three mothers commented on the initial shock of learning a child had died: "It was just so foreign, feeling so disoriented, like riding a wave or a roller coaster. Kind of going in and out of what's real and what isn't." "It was just total confusion." "I was still in a fog, basically. A numbness of sorts." Two participants focused on loneliness and isolation. "Going to bed at night is very lonely." "When my husband tried to help, I told him, 'you're not family. My family is gone.'" And both of the family members who were present at the time of the crime spoke of feelings of guilt. "I felt like it was my fault because I was the last one with my brother, I felt like I could have stopped him."

Of those participants who described more concrete life changes, the most frequent impact was lost time at work or school, mentioned by seven persons. For some this was relatively brief: "I took a week off." "I took some time off work, 'cause I knew the sheriff's department and everybody would be wanting to talk to me." For others this was more far reaching. "I tried to continue working; I found that I couldn't. I had to concentrate on healing." "I did take time off work. I was just not able, my heart and soul was trying to help ... it was months." "I went back to school but dropped out within a week."

Four spoke of having trouble sleeping. "I had nightmares for three to five years. I began working two years later and that helped during the day, but at nighttime, nothing helps you." "I had nightmares for years even after he was in prison, of this terrifying person just being larger than life."

Two who were victims as children reported being made to change homes as a result of the crime. One went to a foster home and ultimately a children's home; the other was sent to relatives during the immediate aftermath of the crime. One of these, and one other childhood victim spoke of experiencing behavior problems as children. "At the time, I kind of withdrew from everything." "The case details were in the local paper... my classmates ridiculed me and I developed behavior problems." A mother of a murdered son spoke of the impact on her identity: "One day I was a mother, buying special things, fixing lunch and dinner, the next day I was not a mom." A sexual assault victim spoke of how it changed her view of her father: "I thought my dad was the greatest guy in the entire world. And then when all this stuff happened, it really shattered that whole view." And one physical assault victim was severely injured: "I had surgery that night, four other operations. I'm lucky that I didn't have much permanent damage; I still don't enunciate clearly if I don't think about it."

Seven participants spoke explicitly of their various efforts to cope. Two turned to alcohol; one stated "my drinking escalated and shortly after the shooting is when I sought retirement." Two commented on just trying to stay busy with daily routines. Two made career changes, including, for one quoted above, an early retirement. One kept a journal because "I wanted to make sure I maintained the memory of what was said and who said it and when they said it and why, because memory doesn't work during stressful periods." And one assault victim described in Case Study One took charge of the situation from the moment the crime began. It should be noted that the time taken off work, listed above as a negative life impact, may also have been a purposeful coping device for some of the seven who reported it; this would bring the total who listed coping efforts to 10.

INTRODUCTION TO DIALOGUE AND FIRST REACTIONS

Fifteen of the participants spontaneously decided that they would like to meet with the offender who caused them harm. Six of these reported coming to this decision fairly early in the process. "At the time the man was arrested, I said that I wanted to meet with him." "I wanted to meet fairly soon, but felt some time needed to pass first." "I always thought that sooner or later the offender would get out of prison, and I just felt a need to sit down and spend a little time with him." "I contacted the system three years after the crime, in 1994, but it wasn't policy."

Nine reached this decision somewhat later in the process, for a variety of reasons. Four were responding to the possibility that the offender would soon be released. "They contacted me because they wanted to let him out. I told them in order for him to be let out I would have to talk to him. I wanted to meet him." "We kind of knew each other through high school. I wanted to go and see him before he got out." Two sexual assault victims saw the offender at a family event. As one reported, "I just all of a sudden felt like I need to do it, just talk to him." Two surviving family members had attended Mothers Against Drunk Driving

(MADD) training sessions, where they first learned about the program and decided they would like to meet the offender. And one victim attempted to visit the offender (her father) at the prison as a family member and was refused because "prison policy prohibits the victim from being registered on the visiting list."

Surprisingly, five of the interviewees (in three offenses) reported that the offender initiated the request to meet, in spite of both program and institution policies designed to prevent offender initiation. The offender in a vehicular homicide case sent an apology letter to his victim's family as part of his twelve step amends; neither the family nor the institution can explain how the letter slipped through their usual screening processes. "We didn't come up with any idea of (meeting him) until we heard from him, which in God's providence got through. (Program Staff) apologized and I said it's wonderful, we've been praying for something like this." Three research participants were members of this one family. In a murder case where the victim and his sister were relatives of the offender, the offender communicated his wish to meet through a friend who was also in prison and was known to the participant.

The last offender-initiated situation was perhaps the most coincidental. The assault victim had changed careers and worked in drug and alcohol treatment. Some 10 years after the crime, a client approached him and said, "Were you ever shot at on the highway?" When the victim said yes, the client revealed that the offender was his cousin. "He said, he's in prison still. He's changed his life. And would I be interested in talking to him, because he wanted to make amends."

Initial Program Response

Many of the participants interviewed in the present project were among the first victims and victim family members to participate in the newly formed Ohio program. Some of them had reached the decision to try to meet with their offender long before there was such a program in place. Seven early participants reported experiencing some sort of difficulty making arrangements with the program; all of these dialogues took place between June 1997 and July 1999. Four met with obstacles from the Office of Victim Services. The earliest of these described the program as "an impediment, initially. All I wanted to do is have a conversation. To me it seemed really simple." Another called the local victims' advocate office and reported the following: "She told me they didn't have anything like this in Ohio, but they were working on it, and I was number 13 on the list."

One of these, and one additional participant, tried going directly through the institution where the offender was being held. "I really ran into some problems with his case manager. He was rude to me. He wanted to interrogate me over the phone." "I contacted the institution, but they said, no, it was not policy." Two additional participants simply reported time delays. "It took quite a while for the office to contact us." "The first person who called never called back." All seven of these participants reported that once they were able to speak directly with the director of the new program, they were responded to with support and expediency.

Two additional participants had somewhat negative comments on the program's initial response to their request. One family member of a murder victim was dissatisfied with the first facilitator assigned to her case:

> After I made the trip to meet with her, she wrote down that it is not advisable for me to have this meeting because she does not feel that a reconciliation is advantageous to either one of us. I asked her, who in the world are you to judge me?

She was assigned a different facilitator and was able to arrange her meeting. Another remained uncertain until the day of the meeting whether the facilitators were for her or for the offender. Both these participants ultimately felt their concerns were appropriately handled by their respective facilitators.

Only one other participant commented at all about the initial response of the program. This family member was very grateful for the speed and responsiveness of program staff, who were able to arrange the meeting and complete the preparation in short order before the family support person, their pastor, left the state for another assignment.

REASONS FOR PARTICIPATING IN DIALOGUE

All 20 interviewees described their reasons for choosing to meet with the offender; most named several reasons. Only three participants spoke of crimes in which there was more than one offender; each described their reason for selecting whom to meet with. "I wanted the trigger man because he was the person that actually murdered him." A second participant who met with the driver of the get-away car had no interest in meeting the person who actually shot her son. "I don't know how that would be helpful to me. He's not eligible for parole for maybe 30 more years. I don't have anything I want to ask him or tell him." The third, who met with the driver in a vehicular homicide, commented: "I don't have any desire to talk with (the person who gave the offender the keys). He's in a state of denial. It wasn't his fault, that's his attitude."

The reasons interviewees gave for initially seeking dialogue fall into the following categories: to seek information (10 of 20), to seek closure or healing (8 of 20), to have a human, face-to-face encounter with the offender (8 of 20), to find out if the offender has remorse (7 of 20), out of concern for the offender (7 of 20), to show the offender the impact of the crime (6 of 20), because it seemed right (5 of 20), to share forgiveness (4 of 20), to work out their future relationship (4 of 20), to prevent further crime (3 of 20), to decide whether to fight or support release (3 of 20), to hear a Twelve Step amends (1 of 20), to hold the offender accountable (1 of 20), and to help other victims (1 of 20).

The most common theme among reasons participants gave for choosing to meet was seeking information or getting questions answered about the actual crime, named by 10 participants. "We had got to the point that we were tired of hearing second, third and fourth hand information." "I wanted to know why he hit him, why he kept going, did he ask for anybody." "To ask, you were so close, you could have shot me, nobody'd ever seen you. Why did you not do it then?" "I wanted to find out what really happened." Two of these commented that the urgency of this reason diminished over time: "After all those years passed, it didn't seem important any more."

Eight participants spoke of seeking closure, advancing their own healing, or finding a way to move on as a reason for seeking to meet: "I wanted to get some closure on this thing." "I guess it was just kind of like the final chapter. To do that sort of would be like the conclusion of everything." "I want to move on with my life. I needed to confront a demon." "To try to finally put to rest all of my fears." "To face my fears and see that I am stronger than (the offender.)"

Eight respondents used language emphasizing the human nature of the encounter in describing why they sought to meet: "I wanted to be able to sit across the table and look at him." "I wanted to understand who this person was, and what it was that made him who he was." "I wanted to go face to face with this individual."

Seven reported wishing to find out whether the offender felt remorse or was sorry. "I wanted to know if he was sorry." "I wanted to know if he felt remorse, because some people, if you look at them, you can tell that they're faking." "To see if he felt any regrets." For two of these, courtroom behavior had demonstrated just the opposite, and they sought to know if the offender had changed: "Because when we went to court, it was jokes and games to him." "I think basically just to hear him tell us himself that he was sorry, because in the courtroom during the sentencing he sort of sat and half smiled at us. It was like he didn't care."

Some degree of concern for the offender was mentioned as a reason by seven participants. "I wanted to see what plans he had for getting back into the community." "I wanted it for my benefit as well as his, because I knew he was hurting." "I had his heart in mind." "To let him know that we didn't hate him." One participant was concerned that the offender not feel pressured "about coming up with anything to make me feel better or to justify what happened that day. I didn't expect that of him."

Six participants spoke of how important it was to let the offender know the impact of the crime, on themselves or on the family member who had died. "To tell him that my five years have been living hell until I finally had worked through this." "I wanted him to know about my son and me and my family." "To finally get to show her that my daughter had somebody who cared, that she was a living being and not just a name. I wanted her to know what she's done to my family." "We are real people. My son is gone. My family still hurts because he's gone."

Five participants, all of whom also listed specific reasons, spoke of first having a strong feeling that they simply needed to meet the offender. Reasons apparently fell into place after they paid attention to the feeling. "Something just told me I had to meet him." "I didn't intellectualize it – it just came outta me that I wanted to do it." "I didn't have words. I just felt it was something I had to do." "I don't know. I just wanted to talk."

Four participants (including three from the same family) hoped to share their forgiveness with the offender. "To say that I was forgiven of my sins, so I need to forgive others." "To let him know the burden he was carrying, if he approached it in the right way, he could get forgiveness and relief from that burden through faith." "To let him know he could get forgiveness by asking. It's pretty hopeless to think that you can't be, and that's how I felt for 19 or 20 years, and I would hate for him to never know."

Four described in a variety of ways needing to figure out their future relationship with the offender. "I thought it was going to be a basis for any future contact." "I was hopeful that we could part amicably." "We had kind of known each other through high school. I wanted to go and see him before he got out."

Three hoped to make some kind of impact on the offender's future behavior. "To hopefully be a part of making a difference in his life, so that he won't hopefully come out and do this again or offend somebody again." "Hope that making that situation and all of us real to him would have some effect on him, make some impression on him for his actions in the future."

Three specifically sought to decide whether to fight or support release: "They contacted me because they wanted to let him out. I told them in order for him to be let out I would have to talk to him." "I thought I might be able to get a feel for him and perhaps do what we can to get him out of prison."

Three additional reasons were mentioned by one participant each. One wished to hold the offender accountable, one felt that seeking to meet and being able to accomplish it would be helpful to other victims in similar situations, and one sought to hear a Twelve Step amends.

Ten of the 20 participants reported involving family members in their process of deciding to meet with the offender. Three participants found family members to be chiefly supportive. "My Dad supported me, said if it's going to make me feel better, then do it." Four reported a mix of reactions. One participant whose daughter and niece accompanied her for support reported "My son had no desire to go. He thought it was a really stupid idea." Another participant was grateful for help from the facilitators in dealing with family members: "My mom was really worried, they took a lot of time, talking to (my family), letting them know this is going to be a controlled thing." One family was protective of their children, who expressed an interest. "I said maybe this is just something Daddy and I need to do. I thought if we get anything real positive, I would relate it. If it didn't come back positive, forget it. They don't need that."

Three participants reported a more negative response from family members: "I just told my husband, he wouldn't even drive me there." "My mom didn't want me to do it. I told her to step back." One participant purposefully told no one, not even her husband, what she was planning to do. And nine made no mention of sharing or consulting with others in making their decision.

Risks Considered

All 20 participants were asked if they felt there were any risks involved for them in meeting with the offender, or if they had considered risks. Nine simply reported that they didn't feel there were any risks and made no further comment. Two additional persons felt there was no risk because there was nothing to lose: "I figured I had lost everything anyhow. They had taken my soul, my child, my lifeline, that was my only child, no grandbabies, no daughter-in-law, no nothing." "The worst thing in the whole world that could ever happen to any person on earth already happened, there's nothing he could tell me that would be any worse."

Four participants mentioned potential concerns about offender behavior: being lied to, perhaps being called names, or attempts to cause physical harm. "We'd be sitting at a desk, there wouldn't be nothing separating us. My first theory was, he's going to come across the table at me." "I was scared he would wait till the last minute and let people know and a riot would break out."

Three participants were concerned about their own feelings. "Very nervous, just the fact of facing him and having to look at him." "I didn't know if I was prepared to see how he had aged." "I knew I probably had to re-live everything, I hadn't thought about it in quite a while."

Two mentioned concerns about the relationship between offender participation and parole hearings. One, who had reported no sense of risk on her own behalf, stated that her spouse worried that the offender's participation might help him with the parole board. And another who worried about physical harm from the offender also worried "was he just doing this to get parole, and I'd get nothing from it." This participant handled this concern by waiting to meet until the parole hearing had passed and then seeing if the offender still wished to participate.

The remaining two participants reported one risk apiece. For one, the major risk was family conflict: "My husband and I fought over it. As far as I was concerned it was non-negotiable." And one was "afraid I would betray my son," but later added that her son had been a very kind person who would be glad she didn't harbor anger toward the offender. Clearly, for all nine who reported any degree of risk, the benefits and need to meet outweighed potential risks. "She was my daughter, I feel it's something I have to do."

PREPARATION FOR THE DIALOGUE SESSIONS

All 20 participants received preparation from program facilitators. This included both face-to-face meetings, held with 19 participants, and telephone contacts, held with all 20 participants. The average total length of personal and telephone preparation combined was 4.8 hours, with a range of 30 minutes to 11 hours. Preparation took place for an average of four and a half months and ranged from one month to 15 months. The sexual assault and murder cases spent the longest time span in preparation, at about six months each. Assault victims averaged only three and a half months. Vehicular homicide family members averaged four and a half months, but this figure was inflated by the victim who was in the car where three other people died. His was the longest time span, at 15 months. The remaining four vehicular homicide cases (involving six participants) averaged 1.75 months in preparation.

Victim/Family Member Evaluation of the Preparation Process

Participants were asked to score their evaluation of the preparation on a Likert scale; these results are reported in Table 9.3 below. The single participant who reported being "somewhat satisfied" was a family member who wasn't present for most of the preparation the rest of his family members went through. Overall comments echoed one another: "I think she armed me with everything she could possibly give me." "He did everything he could." "I don't think there was anything she could have done to make it any easier."

– 237 –

Table 9.3: Victim/Family Member Satisfaction with Preparation for Dialogue

Very satisfied	19	(95%)
Somewhat satisfied	1	(5%)
Somewhat dissatisfied		
Very dissatisfied		
Total	20	(100%)

In the open-ended interviews, all 20 participants commented about the components of preparation which they found helpful. The elements they mentioned included explanations of what would happen, the facilitators' manner of relating, information they received about the offender, choices and opportunities for control, and help in clarifying expectations and goals.

Explaining what would happen topped the list of helpful preparation elements; 14 participants mentioned this in their evaluation, and seven of these listed it as among the "most helpful" part of preparation. All 14 offered comments about the specifics of dialogue procedures, such as: "He painted a very clear picture of what was going to happen, what the rules were, what the parameters were." "They told us everything about what to expect." "They even went so far as to say, the table is going to be here, the chair is going to be here, the glass of water is going to be there." "There were guidelines set up, no racial slurs or yell or scream or cuss."

Five of these participants mentioned in addition how helpful it was to have specific information about the prison environment itself; one of these listed this factor as among the "most helpful" elements. "What kinds of things to expect from guards, fences, those types of things." "What it's going to be like in there. I was in law enforcement, but I had never sat down in a prison before, so it's a good preparation." "We'll meet in the parking lot, you'll be checked for bombs, firearms, there won't be a screen — they really laid it out exactly so when we got there we weren't frightened."

Often a prison tour is offered as part of the preparation; however none of these participants reported taking a tour of the prison. A prison tour was irrelevant for one participant, whose offender was already out on parole, so that the meeting did not take place in a prison setting. Eight participants made no mention of a prison tour and had no further comments about preparation for the prison environment. An additional three participants felt already prepared because of previous experience in a prison environment, two as visitors of relatives, and one in a professional capacity. Two who were offered tours declined them. "I didn't want any of that. I just wanted to get in and get out." "They said, 'Would you like to see the building?' I said, 'We can handle the building.'" One additional participant found the environment less threatening than expected: "I expected guns and increased security like at the trial, but it didn't happen like that." The only participant who accepted the offer of a prison tour commented was ultimately unable to receive one: "That was one of the things that we did try to arrange, but I think it had to do with the warden not wanting me to get in."

Four participants reported that even the amount of information shared did not fully prepare them for the experience. "The only thing that my wife wasn't prepared for was walking through the gate and seeing the razor wire and things like that. That was kind of difficult for her." "I was a little nervous going into a hostile area. I had to take everything out of my pocket." Even the participant familiar in a professional capacity commented, "It was still a bold reminder of how stark, how I'm about to enter a different world from the gentle, pastoral countryside around it."

The next most frequent element of preparation named as helpful was the facilitators' manner of relating and overall concern for the victims, highlighted by 10 participants over all, and mentioned as "most helpful" by five of these. "Everyone cared." "They were sincere about what they were doing." "Feeling like she was on my side." "He has such a good way with people." "They came to our home; I didn't want to go to the corrections department again." "I always felt that they were working very hard at making this happen, helping me."

Nine participants reported that having the facilitators share information back and forth about the offender was helpful, and for seven of these it was among the "most helpful" elements. "She had a bunch of meetings between herself and him, and then me and her, so I knew pretty much what was going on." "Once they'd gone and talked with him, what he was like. 'Cause I had a fear of going to meet him, having him be real non-caring, and them assuring us that they didn't think that would happen was probably a little calming." "Providing me information about the offender's willingness."

Providing choices and control for participants was important to eight respondents, four of whom named it as a "most helpful" element of their preparation. Comments ranged from general assurances to specific issues about which participants had strong feelings. "This is your day, just do whatever, say what you gotta say, if you want to get up and walk away, tap or something and we're outta here." "She told me it was basically my ball game. It made me feel good. It gave me some sense, I hate to say, of control, but I had such a sense of losing control over all of this, from the moment I got word that he had been murdered." "They asked me would I feel safe, did I want a guard in there. I thought, well, if you have a guard in there and in a place like that if he goes and tells everybody, then (the offender) might not be as open about the whole thing."

The final element named as helpful was assisting participants in clarifying their expectations and goals for the meeting, named by six, one of whom listed it as the "most helpful" element. "What turned out to be the best was she said many people liked to write out how they'd been harmed by the person." "She asked us what we wanted to get out of it." "She really helped me form what I was going to do without telling me what to do."

Suggestions for Changes in the Preparation Process

There were no direct questions probing recommended changes in the preparation process, and most interviewees made no spontaneous mention of changes they wished to see. Participants were asked what they found least helpful in their preparation, and whether there was anything else they wished facilitators had done to help prepare them. Only five responses across these two questions have any implication for potential preparation changes.

Two family members raised objections to the notion of being screened or evaluated as to their readiness to participate. One interviewee felt the preparation phase had lasted too long: "I had all these things I wanted to ask him. When we finally got to sit down across the table from him a year later, I was like, okay, there was something that was really important — it was just, the length of time was a little much." One participant wished for more support with what he termed "theological issues" but felt this concern might not apply to most other people.

The fifth participant had extensive comments about information she wished she'd been given ahead of time:

> He was not chained or anything, that was what threw me. And it was a very, very small room, even though I lived through it, it was a little too close for comfort for me…I just didn't know what the whole set up was going to be. And I think she might have explained it.

Feelings Immediately Before the Dialogue

Only two participants did not describe any of their feelings immediately preceding the dialogue. Of the remaining 18, 13 reported some degree of nervousness, anxiety or fear. "I was a little nervous about what happens, since I thought I knew what the outcome was going to be, but you never know." "I didn't get nervous until we sat down at the table before he came in." "I felt anxious, but didn't think of not going." "I was nervous, pacing, trying to settle myself down, wanted to make sure I didn't forget anything." 'I was scared. I kept thinking, what's the big deal, then all of a sudden he walked in and it was just really scary at first." One family that got lost following bad directions and were quite late worried the prison would cancel the meeting: "Since it was so hard to get the warden to agree to it, I was really nervous, something worse than butterflies. I was sick, I felt like I wanted to run away."

The remaining five participants felt calmer. "I wasn't nervous. I was glad that I finally get to see her." "I trusted that it would be a productive session. I just had confidence in the way it had been handled." "I was really okay. I felt very comfortable."

THE DIALOGUE SESSIONS

According to program records, the 18 sessions ranged in length from one hour long to eight hours and averaged 2.5 hours, with a mode of 2 and a median of 2.5. All participants but one were asked how long the dialogue meetings lasted. Six were completely accurate, and another five were within 25% of the actual recorded time. The remaining eight, however, were off by margins of 33% to 400%, in both directions. Four thought it was longer than it actually was, and four thought it was shorter.

The number of persons included in the 17 dialogue sessions, excluding camera crews, averaged 5.6 and ranged from three to eight. Only a single dialogue was at the lower end of the range, attended by only the victim, the offender, and a facilitator. Similarly, only a single dialogue had as many as eight; this included three family members and their support person, the offender and his support person, and two staff. Only two sessions took place without the presence of any support person for either the victim or the offender. In five sessions (attended by seven interviewees) support persons were present for both offenders and victims. Six dialogues (with seven interviewees present) had support persons for the offender but not the victim; and four sessions, with four interviewees, had support persons for only the victim. Most often there were two facilitators present. Only in two instances were prison guards reported to be in the room; in one additional instance the participant reported that the guard was right outside the door.

Participants in nine dialogues reported that the total speaking time in the session was fairly evenly balanced between the victim and the offender. "It was pretty much equal." "It was kind of a mix, an open dialogue. No one really had any great speeches." In seven dialogues, involving 10 participants, the victim spent more time speaking. "I probably talked more cause I don't shut up." "I did, which is fairly typical. I'm very opinionated." In only a single dialogue was the offender reported to have spent more time talking than the victim. "I didn't have a problem with that, because I know that he had a lot to say."

Participants reported that, for the most part, the process of the meetings resembled a conversation, and that they and the offenders carried on the dialogue with very little input from the facilitators once the introductory material was finished. For ease in presenting the dialogue process, after information on the opening moments, the following discussion of the elements of the conversation is broken out into the components of what the victim or family member shared, how the offender responded to the victim's material, what the offender shared, and how the participant responded to the offender's material. However, it must be remembered that the actual process usually did not follow these categories in any orderly fashion, but more often flowed back and forth across them.

Opening Moments

Descriptions of the first contact and opening moments are sporadic and incomplete. Five participants described the initial awkwardness: "At first it was uncomfortable, no eye contact"; "I didn't even want to look at him." One of these commented on shaking the offender's hand at the beginning of the session: "It was weird. It's not comfortable, but it's not bad. If I can't touch him, then who's to say I can forgive him, and I don't know that he wouldn't think that."

Clearly participants had choices about who was in the room first; some chose to be seated and have the offender brought in, others to come in with their support persons after the offender had been seated in the room. Most sessions were held in the small conference rooms of the type often used for inmates to meet with their lawyers. Within the confines of the typically small space, victims had some choice about where to sit. "My husband wanted to sit far away from him. I said oh no, the challenge for me was to be able to sit there and look him in the face just like I do my own children when they tell lies."

Those who commented on the opening moments all concurred that the facilitators were the first to speak, handling introductions, describing what would happen, and setting ground rules. Victims then had a choice about whether to speak first or have the offender speak first. Only eight commented specifically about who went first; five reported that they had chosen to begin. "I had some things I wanted to say up front, and then (the offender) joined in very quickly with me. "I asked the questions and he answered them." Three reported that the offender went first. For two, this was unremarkable: "He started out doing most of the talking." "We let him do his thing first." The third commented, "I wanted to speak first, but as soon as we got there the facilitator asked if the offender could go first. And since the boy did agree to see me, I said yes. Because he had a right not to even see me, so I gave that to him."

Victim/Family Member Participation

One participant clarified that he did not give a statement because his purpose in meeting with the offender was to provide the offender the opportunity to make his Twelve-Step amends. Two additional participants did not offer any details about a statement; one of these spoke of asking questions but did not further elaborate on the content. The remaining 17 named a total of 23 themes that were part of their statements; three of these also mentioned asking questions.

The most often named component of the victim statement was sharing with the offender something of the impact of the crime, named by 10 participants. The six family members of victims who had died focused on both the details of their family member's life, and the impact of the loss on the rest of the family. "(The offender) knew my son when I left the room." "I took a small photo album of our daughter, and I gave it to him, I said I want you to see and touch what you've taken from us." "He did not realize anything that he did to my family, he thought he just took a child's life and that was it."

The four surviving victims described the changes in their own lives. "I told him that I was freaking out at night when it turned dark, that I couldn't go outside." "I really wanted him to be able to see that what happened was really bad, but that I had worked really hard and was very proud of where I was now."

Two participants reported that they chose not to focus their statements on the impact of the crime. One had planned to "dish out a little stuff" but changed her mind on seeing the offender because he was so much like her father. The other simply stated "I didn't focus on that as much."

Four interviewees had something to say about the offender's future behavior. "I told him I would be very, very disappointed if I ever hear of him hurting another person. I hope he has a productive life." "The meeting was to see if we were going to have any future contact." "We talked about our plans to do speeches about the accident, some activities prisoners can do."

Three reported that they gave the offender specific information about the crime; in all three instances, the offender had not fully admitted to elements of the crime. "We have the coroners report. I said there was no drugs or alcohol of any kind. I reviewed the facts. So the coroner goofed?" "So when I drew him a picture of where he was, and where I was, and where his companions were, he just couldn't come clean." "I told the offender, do you know what hung you? I didn't hang you, you hung yourself."

And two participants spoke with the offender about the punishment. "I said you have paid your debt according to what the law said you should have done, and I'm okay with that." "I told him I would fight the rest of my life to keep him incarcerated."

Offender Participation

Participants commented on six of the 17 offenders' responses to what the victim or family member presented. Participants in five dialogues felt the offender was moved by what they shared. "He was aware for the first time that he had killed an innocent person." "The tears just flowed and he looked down and just kept shaking his head, like, no, no." "He said 'The only thing I know is what I've read in newspaper articles.' So he was taking in this information. He didn't just cursorily go through it and try to escape the pain." "Just by the expression on his face when he was finally told some of the things that I've been going through, I think that he really thought about that." Only one reported an opposite experience. "He didn't seem really very interested to hear what we're doing in our lives at all."

Participants commented on what all 17 offenders had to say in making their statements. Offender expressions of remorse or regret topped the list; participants reported that 13 offenders apologized. "He told me how sorry he was he'd committed the crime." "He said he felt he owed me that, and that he was very sorry my Dad and Mom were deceased, 'cause they needed to know (the truth)." "He said, I didn't mean to shoot you."

Twelve offenders were reported to have given information or details about the crime. "We discussed it, and most of the evening to him was a blur. He knew he was drunk." "He knew Dad was in the back of the truck when he left, he didn't see him when he hit him." "When he saw my son was driving a brand new car, he thought he had the right man, because the kid must have spent the drug money." "He finally told us why he did what he did." "Yeah, he did tell me some of the things that were happening. He was at a party and he had been drinking all day."

Participants in 13 of the sessions spoke about the whether or not the offender fully admitted what he or she had done. Nine offenders were reported to have done so. "He did admit that he murdered my son." "He showed some insight into what he'd done." "I was really surprised and extremely unprepared to hear him say that he was sorry and to hear him admit that what he did was wrong."

Four offenders, however, were reported to have only partly admitted to their actions. "He says they weren't alone, there was another man." "He said to me, I want to know why you said I was the one who had the gun." "He shared his version and basically made excuses for his actions, blaming it on the circumstances and not him." "Oh, and the one that tore me up, that he didn't suffer. Even though he wants to tell the truth, he's not telling me all of that truth. He's giving me a different story."

Six offenders shared information about their own life history. "He told me about his childhood." "I learned a great deal about the offender and his family." "He even had a portfolio of pictures of his family that he wanted to show me." "All of a sudden he just went into all his family problems, talking about his mom."

Three offenders spoke some about future plans. "He was an auto mechanic. The car industry had sort of passed him up and he didn't know how he was going to make it any more." "He plans to discontinue drinking." "Towards the end he asked if I could leave with the mediator the name of the cemetery where my son was buried. He wanted to go there."

Two offenders were reported to have shared about how the crime had affected them. "There was a period of time when he wouldn't talk to his mom and dad because of what he did. His mom and dad believed up until then that he was innocent, that he was paying for a crime he did not commit." "He is still somewhat bitter and he looks at it as 'we screwed up his life.'"

Victim/Family Member Evaluation of Offender Participation

Two of the 20 participants did not comment on their reactions to what the offender shared during the meeting. Among the remaining 18, the most frequently mentioned component of participants' responses to the offender statements focused on the reaction to offender expressions of remorse, named by 17 participants in 13 dialogues. Eleven participants in eight dialogues felt that the offender expression of remorse was genuine. "Just his whole demeanor was very humble." "I knew he was sorry for what he had done, but to see the look on his face, to hear the words come out."

Six participants, in seven dialogues, doubted the sincerity of all or part of the offender's expression of remorse. "I don't care what she says down there or how much she says she's sorry or how much she cries, if I were in the situation, I'd do just about anything to get my hind end outta there, too." "He wasn't remorseful particularly about the incident. He was sorry for the trouble I went through."

Seven reported feeling some degree of anger or frustration at the offender. One was angry that the offender hadn't taken advantage of training programs to keep up in his technical skill; another was angry that technical training was available for free: "This is what irks me. If I wanted to get a cosmetology license, I gotta pay three or four thousand dollars, now I'm paying for her to get an education." "He talked about his family, which I thought was really selfish. ... I told him that's not what I am here for, I could care less about your family. This is about the person that you took away from me, that I'll never see." "It was very frustrating to me, these juxtapositions, with what my experience was and what he was telling me, almost to try to convince me that what I had experienced hadn't happened."

Five participants disbelieved parts of the offender's account of the events of the crime, and three of these reported directly challenging the offender. "You see, he made that decision to have that gun loaded, ... way before he robbed me, so he's just trying to minimize his role." "Every time I asked him what he did or certain things, he wouldn't look at me, and I knew he was lying, he was trying to cover up."

Four participants felt that the offender's account of the events of the crime had minimal impact on them. For one, this was because all the questions had already been asked and answered during the preparation phase. She reported that the day she first learned the information, she had to take the afternoon off from work. "It was shocking and I could not get it out of my mind. If the mediator had not told me those things, maybe during the meeting I don't know if I would have been able to stay as calm as I was." Two of these were participants who had chosen not to seek information about the crime. And the fourth simply said that what the offender shared "doesn't even matter any more." Two participants reported feeling some degree of sadness for the offender.

Victim/Family Member Surprises

Participants were asked if they were surprised by anything during their dialogue meetings. Five responded that nothing surprised them. Nine responded that they were surprised by the sincerity or level of remorse expressed by the offender; their comments have been included under the discussion of offender remorse, above. Three, including two who reported surprise over remorse, were surprised by the offender's negative attitude. "I guess he was a little more bitter than I thought he would be. I was not expecting the bad attitude." "The thing that I was surprised at was that he's still denying that he was the one who had the gun. He didn't move an inch off that."

Two more were surprised by other offender actions. One was surprised that, toward the end of the session, the offender started sharing material which the offender had specifically named during the preparation as off limits. "It kind of blew me away. I just sat there and just listened to what he had to say." One was surprised that the offender touched her. "I don't know why I let him do it, he reached out and put his arms around me."

Two were surprised by their own or family member actions. "The biggest surprise was that at the end I noticed I was feeling forgiving toward the offender." "That my husband brought a photo of our daughter and shared it with the offender, and that after he heard the offender's lies about what happened, he got up and left the meeting and waited outside the door." The final participant simply reported shock at information gleaned during the meeting: "I was alarmed to learn he would be eligible to receive his drivers license back within seven years of release."

Facilitator Role and Evaluation

Seventeen participants described the facilitator's main role as relatively quiet, and all 17 named this as one of the most helpful things the facilitator did during the session. "I appreciated that (the facilitator) did very little talking." "There was no need for them to do a lot of talking." "It wasn't their meeting — it was our meeting. And that's exactly how they dealt with it. It was great." "They sat back and didn't say nothing and didn't interfere with nothing."

Five participants felt reassured simply that the facilitator was there in the room with them in case a need should arise; for four of these, this was what was most helpful. "Had it gotten outta control, they would have stopped the meeting." "They were there to keep it in control if necessary." "And if things had gotten heated or whatever, they would have been there to step in or suggest a break." "Just being there if I needed them."

When facilitators did speak, the most common action described by participants was monitoring participant needs, named by seven interviewees and mentioned by five as among the most helpful actions. This included both victim needs and offender needs. "Breaking up the meeting when the offender got overwhelmed." "At the end they questioned us if we needed any more time, did we feel a need to say anything that hadn't been said." "Made sure that I was all right, asked if it would be a good time to take a break now."

Other facilitator actions included reminding participants of things and helping keep the meeting focused, both mentioned as helpful by three participants. "He kind of said, well, don't you want to ask him about this?" "Helped remind me things I wanted to talk about." "The only time was when the mediator found that (the offender) was rambling in circles and going nowhere." "To ask the questions that were essential when it was appropriate to keep the conversation going."

Two interviewees felt that the facilitators' neutrality was among the most helpful actions. "The mediator was a person that's not really on my side or on his side. That was kind of helpful." "I think that the mediator tried his best to be in impartial third party, to facilitate the conversation." One commented that the facilitator "had a gentle way about her and sets a nice tone."

In 14 of the research interviews, participants were asked what the facilitators did that was least helpful. Eleven could think of nothing the facilitator did that was "least" helpful. "There wasn't anything that I thought shouldn't have happened or that was said or done, nothing." "I don't know if there was anything that was not helpful." One of these joked "she didn't buy me no lunch or anything!"

The three who did comment on the least helpful facilitator actions referred not to actions during the session, but rather to previous actions.

Two of the earliest participants commented again on their initial difficulties getting arrangements made. "I can't think of anything other than making me worry so much about whether I was gonna have a meeting." The third commented on feeling unprepared for how structured the process was.

Feelings Immediately Afterwards

No information is available about the immediate reaction of one participant; a second reported merely that "it wasn't a huge thing to me." Of the remaining 18, 10 had exclusively positive immediate reactions, four reported both positive and negative reactions, and four had more negative immediate reactions.

The most frequently reported reaction was feeling good or happy, named by 11 participants. "I was euphoric." "At that time, total elation, freedom." "I made it to the outside, I felt great." "Like when you're scared and then it happens and you realize, gee, it wasn't so bad, I did that. It was kind of a good feeling."

Relief or release was the next most frequent experience, named by eight participants. "I think we both felt a real relaxation." "I was released from prison, my own prison, that day." "I felt like a lot has come off me, my shoulders."

Four were grateful. "I'm lucky that (the offender) is the person that he is. He didn't have to have this meeting." "It was just pretty much a gift from God." "Some gratitude that it had happened." Three spoke of some measure of closure. "He's out there now and my son isn't, and it was just another phase, a door that I closed behind me and felt good about it." "Closure. All my hurt and my loss came out." "The ride home was real quiet, this was kind of the ending of the ending for us."

The negative immediate reactions included feeling sad or disappointed, named by five, and simply being tired, named by three. The four who named only negative immediate reactions included three who were sad or disappointed and one who was tired. "It was more of a disappointment, he is going to live his whole life in prison under the assumption that the criminal justice system really did him wrong." "I was a little bit hurt and upset." "There was no joy. It was heaviness, it was sorrow, because my daughter isn't there." "Just tired. It was a pretty mentally and emotionally tired." The four with mixed reactions had comments like "really tired, really relieved, glad it was over with," "empty but content," and "confused …and kind of relieved, too."

LONGER-TERM OUTCOMES

A total of 12 participants spoke of major positive life changes that they attributed to their participation in the mediation/dialogue sessions, including changes in their general outlook on life for the better, (8), changes in their view of the offender for the better (10), personal growth and healing (10), and a positive impact on their spirituality (8). Two reported that their feelings about the offender changed for the worse. Participants also spoke about forgiveness (13) and raised the issue of future contact with offenders (13).

Changes in General Outlook on Life

Participants were asked both a closed-ended and an open-ended question about the impact of the dialogue on their general outlook on life. Results of the closed-ended question are summarized in Table 9.4 below.

Three additional participants commented that their outlook had already changed by the time they came to the dialogue. One felt the process of preparing had caused her change: "This whole process leading up to it does. Let go of the hate, taken a lot of pain out of my heart." Another felt the crime itself caused the changed outlook, and not for the better: "Oh yeah, the entire incident has. I'm still anxious when I go out at night, I don't trust people like I used to." For the third, time itself had brought about the change: "I had already moved past it."

Changes in View of Offender

Participants were asked whether their view of the offender changed as a result of the meeting, and if so, in what ways. Twelve reported that their view did change. Ten of these listed a total of 16 ways their view had changed for the better. Seven reported that they think the offender has changed. "He's suffered enough. He says he thinks about my nephew all the time." "In this case, I believe he is a better man." "I think he's changed a whole lot." Three who used to wish the offender dead no longer do so. Three reported that they moved from viewing the offender as less than human to seeing him as a human being. "He is not such a monster, I guess, as my view of him was that day in the courtroom. Seems to be more of a human being." "Before, I saw not the man, just the records." "He is not an animal, he is just a horrible person." Two reported that they have come to care about the offender and his future. "Now I care about him. I want him to have a good life." "Before, there was a disconnected, impersonal anger. Now, if there's anything, there's just hope that he will come out of the institution a better man than he went in." And one felt sorry for the offender.

Table 9.4: Has Your Overall Outlook on Life Changed Since Meeting the Offender?

No	12	60%
Yes	8	40%
Of those who answered yes:		
a. Definitely more positive and at peace with the circumstances I am faced with.	6	(30%)
b. Somewhat more positive and able to cope with my life.	2	(10%)
c. Somewhat more negative and less able to cope with my life.	0	
d. Definitely more negative and angry about the circumstances I am faced with.	0	
e. Other.	0	
None of the above.	0	

Two reported changes in their view that were not necessarily for the better; both of these were sexual abuse victims. One felt her view was now more realistic; and one reported that the offender had changed "a little bit, but it seems like he probably didn't change as much as I thought he would have changed."

Seven participants reported that their view of the offender did not change. "No, it's not any more favorable than it was." "From what I knew of her before this happened, (the offender) was a violent person to begin with." Among these were four participants who felt the offender was not telling the entire truth about the crime. "He didn't even feel any kind of impact of what he did." "He clearly portrayed himself as a victim." "We don't even care about him. All we cared about is that he would tell us the truth. That's all we wanted from him."

Personal Growth and Healing

A total of 10 interviewees named a variety of ways their healing and personal growth had benefited from their participation. Five spoke in general terms of greater closure and healing, though often clarifying complete closure was never to be expected. Three of the participants who reported being more "at peace" in the closed-ended question also spontaneously described themselves as being more at peace elsewhere in the interview. "Now I got peace that I didn't have." "I think most of all at peace about it." Three reported sleeping easier as a result of their meetings. "I woke up sometimes crying, screaming, two or three times a week, and I don't have them (the nightmares) now." "I had a hard time sleeping at night. After the meeting I felt relieved. It's had a major impact."

Four victims/family members reported that the dialogue helped reduce negative feelings, including anxiety or fear (2), anger (1), and hate (1). "It helped get rid of some anxiety." "It's like any kind of trauma, we tend to have a phobic avoidance. Facing the man, talking to him, dealing with him face to face was good therapy." "It healed anger stemming from even further back."

Impact on Spiritual Outlook

The spiritual impact of the dialogues was also addressed through both closed-ended and open-ended questions. These results are reported below in Table 9.5.

Table 9.5: Effect on Victim/Family Member Religious or Spiritual Life

Did the process of preparing to meet the victim and the actual meeting have any effect on your religious or spiritual life?		
No	12	60%
Yes	8	40%
Of those who answered yes:		
a. Greatly enriched my religious/spiritual perspective.	3	(15%)
b. Contributed to a deeper religious/spiritual perspective.	5	(25%)
c. Contributed to a weakening of my religious/spiritual perspective.		
d. Greatly weakened my religious/spiritual perspective.		
None of the above.		

Three of the eight who reported an impact on their spiritual life spoke of forgiveness issues and will be take up below. One of these further commented on the far reaching impact of this action: "It's had an impact on not only me, but the people I share this with …(one of them) made the statement, 'how can I hold a grudge or be mad at someone for something trivial, when you are able to forgive something of this magnitude?'"

Four of the remaining five reported a variety of changes. Two spoke of how it confirmed and increased their spirituality. "It made me trust that God was going to be in control of the whole situation." "It confirms a lot of things that the Lord truly changes you in the heart, cause I truly wanted to kill him, and now, I don't dislike him. He's no worse than me." One reported speaking to church groups more, and one stated, "I think our prayers are different, and I think we appreciate life."

The fifth participant who reported a spiritual impact did not elaborate further.

Only five of the participants who reported that their participation had no spiritual impact offered any further comments. Three stated that their spiritual life had already undergone significant change prior to their participation. Two of these felt that these changes were a result of the crime itself. "Right afterwards, I started going to church every Sunday. I thought, I've been given a second chance, I got to thank somebody." The third simply referred more vaguely to "a lot of other things" that were going on.

The remaining two participants commented that, in fact, it was their spirituality which affected their participation. "My husband has Crohn's disease, so my spiritual outlook on life changed when I was faced with the fact I might lose him. And that's one of the reasons why I was even able to have the meeting with (the offender)."

Forgiveness

Seven participants made no mention of forgiveness issues during the interviews. Of the remaining 13, nine participants reported that they had forgiven the offender. Six had already reached this decision prior to the actual meeting. "Meeting him was the right thing to do. To show him how to receive forgiveness from the Lord." "I had lost so many people and I did not know where to turn but to the church. And at that point was when I forgave him." Three more found that they forgave the offender during the dialogue process itself. "It was right after I saw him. Cause I got drunk drivers in my family, it could have been my family doing the same thing to his family. Why should I not forgive him?"

All nine reported that they shared their forgiveness with the offender during the session. For eight, this was very explicit and direct, although not always smooth and comfortable. "I told him that's why I was there, to forgive him." "I kind of had to gag the words out, I said, 'I didn't think I would ever be able to say this or wanna say this, but I forgive you.'" One felt it was more implied. "I don't think I ever did tell him I could forgive him. I think when we talked, it was more of a forgiving thing, it all had to deal with how comfortable we were with each other."

Three participants, all of them family members of murder victims, reported that they had not forgiven the offender. One had felt some pressure from the first facilitator who worked with her to forgive; this facilitator was replaced. She felt if she was forgiving it would interfere with her goal for the dialogue: "(The offender's) gonna have to face what she's done. I want her to see the anguish she put us through." The remaining two spoke of the difference between full forgiveness and simply not harboring hatred. "We're smart enough to know that when you have these feelings of hatred and bitterness, they only hurt you and the people all around you. We haven't forgiven him yet. I don't know that we can or that we ever will." "It's like I told him that day in prison, I don't hate you, it's not good to hate. But I will never forgive you."

The one remaining participant who mentioned forgiveness issues did not comment on whether he had forgiven his offender, but noted that in general, the dialogue "compels a person to deal with their own willingness to forgive. And maybe forgiveness for some has to be something down the road."

Further Contact with Offenders

Thirteen of the 20 participants made some mention of the potential for some kind of contact with the offender beyond the initial dialogue session. Nine victims, in cases involving six offenders, framed such contact in terms of a subsequent dialogue. For two participants, this had already happened. One assault victim sought a second meeting in the hopes that the offender would own what he had done; this meeting was shorter than the first, with no change in the offender story. Another assault victim, who had come to care about the offender, met with him a year later, after he was out on parole. No program facilitator was present at this meeting, attended by only the victim, the offender, his fiancée, and his parole officer.

Two of the sexual assault victims expressed a wish to have another dialogue meeting with their offender/father, but in each case the offender made it clear during the session he was not interested in further contact. Two family members of murder victims, in two different cases, stated they would be willing to meet again only if the offender changed his story and told what they felt to be the truth. Three family members in the vehicular homicide dialogue, that had been initiated by the offender's apology letter, reported that the offender had requested a second meeting but they had not yet reached a decision whether to meet.

Six participants, including two who mentioned further dialogue meetings, made other mention of potential future contact. A vehicular homicide family member felt she and the offender could be friends, though she worried what her family might think. Another vehicular homicide victim felt he wouldn't be friends, but felt he would acknowledge him if they were to meet by chance. Both these participants had spoken about the similarities they experienced between themselves and the offender. A third vehicular homicide victim had made plans during the dialogue session to make presentations on drunk driving jointly with the offender.

An assault victim knew that the offender, with whom he was previously acquainted, would return to the same neighborhood, and hoped they would be comfortable with one another. One assault victim thought he might write to the offender because he was concerned about him. And one sexual assault victim who had hoped for additional dialogue also wished for future informal contact.

VICTIM/FAMILY MEMBER EVALUATION OF THE EXPERIENCE

All participants were asked to rate their satisfaction with their involvement in the program and the helpfulness of the meeting on a four point Likert scale. These results are summarized on Table 9.6 and Table 9.7 below.

Table 9.6: Victim/Family Member Overall Satisfaction with Involvement in Victim Offender Dialogue Program

Very satisfied	20	(100%)
Somewhat satisfied	0	
Somewhat dissatisfied	0	
Very dissatisfied	0	
Total	20	(100%)

Table 9.7: Victim/Family Member Rating of the Helpfulness of the Meeting

Very helpful	14	(70%)
Somewhat helpful	6	(30%)
Not at all helpful	0	
Total	20	(100%)

All 20 also reported that they had "no regrets" about their participation. "No, I'm glad I was able to have the chance to talk to him, before he was released from parole." "No, I wish I'd done it sooner." "No, it helped ease me." "No. The first few weeks it raised a lot of questions that had stayed in the past for a long time. But now I'm glad I did it because it did help put things in a little bit more perspective." Only one who reported no regrets gave any indication of any other feeling: "I do regret seeing (the offender), knowing he is alive."

Over all, 17 of the 20 participants felt their expectations had been met, and three of these reported their expectations were exceeded. "I would say we came out of this thing pretty much getting everything that we had in our mind answered. We really got to say what we thought about for years." "Very much so. It was what I thought it would be." "Oh yes, actually, kind of exceeded." "More than, I think." Two of the remaining three reported that they really hadn't formed any expectations. Only one participant reported that expectations were not met: "No. I don't feel he told me the truth. I think there is more."

Recommendations for Other Victims and Family Members

Only one interviewee was directly asked about recommending participation to others: "Yes, I would. And I think that's another reason why I did this, because if I can get help from it, I want to be able to help other people." Four additional interviewees spontaneously offered that they would recommend it to others. "You should let more people do it, and the age criteria should just be that the person is alive. This is good for all people, even children who want questions answered." "Everyone has a right to see who has carried out the act ... every victim that wants to do it, their rights should not be violated." "I would like for (the other family members) to experience this, to talk with the offender."

All interviewees were asked what the advantages of participation can be. Seventeen offered reasons they thought others might benefit from participation, two responded with benefits they themselves had experienced, and only one did not list any advantage. This last participant felt it was hard to identify advantages because the offender didn't tell the truth.

Among the 17 who described advantages for others, eight included some precautionary concerns. Four pointed out that it's not for everyone. "It all depends on what the person is looking for. Some people are not ready for this type of program." "Everybody is different. Some people don't want to know any details." "I suspect there are some mediations that could go south and not be so favorable as what (the offender) and I had." Three felt participation would be advisable if anger has been dealt with. "If they're just saying 'I hate you,' cuss and carry on — you don't go anywhere to talk to somebody like that." "If they were going into it with a ton of hatred in their heart and just wanting to vent on the inmate, I don't know if I would suggest it or even recommend it. I don't think that clears anything up." And one emphasized timing issues: "It's something that needs to be addressed with extreme caution. Had someone (suggested it) to me in the courtroom, I would have probably thought it must be something I'm expected to do."

The advantages listed fell into three broad categories. Fifteen named the possibility of closure and/or healing for participants. "I think it can bring some healing." "There would be closure,...an emotional type of release that they don't even realize is there." "I think if they went into it with the right attitude it could help them to go on with their life." "It can give you control back in your life." Seven spoke of the possibility of having questions answered. "Finding out why it happened could be a benefit." "I think the main advantage is if you get some truth... all the questions you have, morbid or otherwise, are answered." "It's a lot easier to deal with what happened when you heard from the person that actually did it, instead of everybody else's stories and making up things in your head." And four felt an advantage is that offenders need to know the impact of what they've done. "To be able to tell (the offender) in a controlled environment what's been going on." "Making all this real to (the offender)."

Four participants had additional advice to offer other victims. Three advised coming to terms with hatred and anger before attempting to meet with the offender. "I don't know how one gets rid of anger but I think that it's not going to go away on its own, how to be strong and not be angry." "I think that in order for you to have peace in your mind, you have to forgive someone. You can't hate people. I'd just be as bad as he is if I hate." The fourth simply offered the following: "We can't be held hostage by these things, we have to face them directly."

Changes Recommended by Victims/Family Members

Toward the end of the interview, participants were asked if there were any comments they would like to make that had not been covered. Twelve of the 20 responded with a total of 17 suggestions for improvement: eight made suggestions specifically for the dialogue program, and nine recommended changes elsewhere in the system of responding to crimes.

Two interviewees felt the program should be made more available to others. The six remaining program-related suggestions were each offered by only a single participant. One wanted ongoing contact with the offender, who was already out of prison. "I wish there was some framework where we could have a periodic conversation." One felt there should be a better place for the meetings, "that wasn't inside the prison walls..." One recommended a quicker process "just that for people in similar situations in the future, that they be handled a little bit more expeditiously." One wished the meeting had lasted longer: "I was in there for about two hours; it felt like the mediator just thought, that was it, and she cut it off right there." It should be noted, however, that this interviewee in fact participated in the longest dialogue of the entire group, at eight hours.

One felt cultural issues had been a problem, with himself and the facilitator both being white males with a black male offender. "Perhaps he needed his own advocate. I mean, he was outnumbered. The very symbols of cultural power and powerlessness were right before him." And one recommended having someone trained in theological or spiritual issues on the staff "so that there's an understanding of how a Moslem, a

Catholic, an evangelical Christian, a Jew, an agnostic or an atheist would deal with these things...so you can better focus on the way they deal personally with their lives."

Among the eight participants who had suggestions for other changes in the community's response to crimes, three had specific needs or requests. One assault victim had been promised restitution for items stolen by another offender in the crime. "Don't say you're going to hold him responsible, then not." Another wished for access to a videotape of news clips of the crime that had been created by the offender's family. And a third pushed for more follow-through from the system so that she and the offender could carry out their plan to offer joint presentations on drunk driving. "People need to see what happens to the victim and the offender when they get out there and do this kind of stuff." She felt there would be a special impact from having the victim and offender present together.

The other six recommendations were more general. One wished for some mechanism to get information on how the offender was doing after release. One wanted more counseling resources to be provided to victims. One felt hospitals should treat offenders better. "They got a duty, whether that man killed one person or fifty persons, they should have treated him just as well as they treat me." One wanted the system to provide more timely notification if offenders were coming up for parole hearings. One incest victim wanted prisons to change regulations so that family members could be allowed to visit offenders even if they are that offender's victim. And one pushed for the entire system to better recognize victim needs and rights: "There are families that are left, and right now the system thinks, the hell with it, the case is closed, we've got the murderer and all that, but that's not where it stops."

CONCLUSION

All 20 of these victims/family members reported being satisfied with their involvement in the Ohio Victim Offender Dialogue Program. Not every question was answered, not every offender was forthcoming, and not all changes they experienced were for the better. Nonetheless, on balance they felt they had benefited from their participation, and most thought it would offer advantages for others in similar situations.

CHAPTER 10.
OHIO OFFENDERS: EXPERIENCE AND IMPACT

Twenty offenders who participated in the Ohio Victim Offender Dialogue Program for violent and serious offenses between June 1997 and November 2000 participated in in-person research interviews between December 1998 and December 2000. The interviews typically lasted about an hour, and consisted of a series of open-ended questions seeking the offenders' descriptions and perceptions, followed by a group of fixed-response questions. In the free-flowing open-ended segment of the interview, the research interviewers typically followed up with probes and additional questions to try to tap the specific concerns and insights of each offender. All research interviews were tape-recorded and transcribed. Data for the present summary of offender perspectives on their mediation/dialogue experience are taken from these transcriptions and from program records.

CHARACTERISTICS OF OFFENDERS AND CRIMES

Of the 20 offenders, one was female and 19 were male; 16 were Caucasian and four were African-American. At the time the crimes were committed, the offender ages ranged from 17 to 50, and averaged 27.8. Five offenders (25%) were under 21 when they committed their crimes. At the time of the victim-offender dialogues, the offender ages ranged from 19 to 64, and averaged 36.8.

The crimes committed by the 20 offenders are listed below in Table 10.1. Some offenders were convicted of more than one crime; where these involved multiple victims, the crime listed below is for the victim who participated in the dialogue. If a single victim was involved, the table reports the most serious crime for which the offender was convicted. The eight manslaughter/murder cases were further broken out into four murders, two cases of voluntary manslaughter, and two of involuntary manslaughter.

Table 10.1: Crimes by the Ohio Offenders

Crime	N	(%)
Murder/Manslaughter	8	(40%)
Vehicular homicide	4	(20%)
Kidnapping	1	(5%)
Assault	3	(15%)
Rape/Sexual assault	3	(15%)
Theft	1	(5%)
Total	20	(100%)

Twelve of the offenders reported that they knew their victim prior to the crime. These included all three sexual assault cases; each of the victims in these cases was either a daughter or stepdaughter of the offender. In addition, the offender and victim were acquainted in three of the four murder cases, three of the four manslaughter cases, one assault case, the theft, and the kidnapping case. None of the four vehicular homicide offenders were previously acquainted with any of their victims. For 15 of the 19 violent offenders, it was the first time they had been convicted of a violent crime. The offender in the theft case also had no previous conviction.

In the 12 cases where the actual crime victim died as a result of the crime, offenders met with family members of the victims, including six mothers, two fathers, one husband, three sisters, one brother, and two daughters. One of these daughters was also the sister and the aunt of additional passengers killed in her offender's vehicular homicide case. In seven of the eight cases where the actual victim was not killed, offenders met with the victim; in the theft case, the elderly victim had since died, and the offender met with her stepson, who had managed her estate.

Over all, the length of time between the date of the crime and the meeting of the victim and offender in dialogue ranged from 2 years to 16 years and averaged 9.0 years. Only the sexual assault cases were markedly different from the other categories, averaging 15 years to come to dialogue. Crimes in which the offender met with the actual victim took only slightly longer to come to the table (10.0 years) than crimes in which a victim's family participated instead (8.5 years).

At the time of the dialogues, 18 of the offenders were still incarcerated for their crimes, and their dialogue meetings were held at their respective institutions. Two offenders were out on parole and their meetings were held at their parole authority offices.

Offender Descriptions of the Crime Events and Reactions

The research interviews opened by asking the offenders to describe, in their own words, what happened at the time of the crime. Eleven offenders spontaneously mentioned alcohol or drugs or both in describing their crimes. In addition to the four vehicular homicides, these included all four manslaughter cases, two of the four murders, and one assault case. None of the sexual assault offenders made any mention of drugs or alcohol, nor did the offenders in the theft case or the kidnapping case.

There were differences in the level of ownership in the offender's descriptions of events. Twelve offenders took direct, explicit ownership of their offense: "I've taken three people's lives because I chose to drink and drive." "I struck and killed a pedestrian." "I sexually molested my daughter." "I murdered a friend." "I shot at somebody because I let things build up." Four used passive language to describe their own actions including: "There was racial slurs there, they got stabbed," "Next thing I knew, she was shot." "The act was sexual abuse." Two ascribed to others what they themselves had been convicted of: "My friend pulled a gun on him and took his wallet." Two reported having blacked out: "I don't remember the initial event. I woke up and found he was hurt," and "I heard the gun go off and I blacked out."

For all but two of the offenders, initial reactions to their crime involved strong negative emotions. Seven reported feeling scared, of such things as possibly being put on death row, knowing something bad was going to happen, or fearing having to go to prison. Other emotions included feeling devastated, ruined, betrayed, hopeless, ashamed, abandoned, and suicidal. Two who had negative feelings also reported some level of dissociation: "It was like a bad dream." "I was numb, it was almost like I was watching this happen to somebody else." One who reported feeling "pressure" also said his initial reaction was "they can't put me in jail, I've got enough money to keep myself out." Only two of-fenders did not report strong negative feelings as part of their initial re-actions. One said his initial reaction was, "Why are they doing this to me?" because it took him a long time to shift the blame from the victim (his ex-girlfriend) to himself. And the other simply reported that, "I ac-cepted my punishment, I knew whatever they gave me I deserved."

INTRODUCTION TO DIALOGUE AND FIRST REACTIONS

In all instances, the offenders reported that they initially learned about the potential for facilitated dialogue with their victim or victim's family member through a corrections staff member in their institution or parole authority. These included case managers, parole officers, institu-tional victim coordinators, training officers, psychological services staff, wardens, and chaplains. Typically offenders were called to an office where the staff member told them a victim wished to meet with them, explained the basics of the program, and asked if they would be willing.

The spontaneous reactions reported by 13 of the offenders were positive and included such comments as: "I was for it." "That was a lovely day for me." "My reply was spontaneous," and "I immediately said 'yes.'" Three of these 13 had already either hoped to meet or taken steps on their own to reach out to their victims. Six offenders had mixed initial reactions such as: "I was anxious to meet but I knew there would be restrictions." "I always felt like I should meet but I was sort of hop-ing it could be after I got let out. That way I wouldn't have a hidden agenda, there would be nothing to gain." "I wanted to give it more thought. I knew it was a good thing,…it's painful for everybody." Only one reported a negative initial reaction: "First thing that popped into my mind, they're about to mess with my parole."

Reasons for Participating in Dialogue

Offenders were asked why they chose to participate. Reasons in-cluded benefits to victims, benefits for themselves, and in one instance, benefits for other offenders.

All 20 offenders spontaneously reported at least some victim-centered reasons among the elements of their decision. Eight offenders offered general victim-related reasons, simply hoping victims could "get what they need," feeling "I owed it to them," "any way I could help," "whatever the victim wanted," and "it was the right thing to do (for them)." For eight offenders, a more specific reason was to apologize, reported in language such as "tell him I was sorry," "apologize to her," "express my regret." Helping victims or family members obtain some type of closure was also listed by eight offenders: "so they can move on," "for them to heal," to "bring peace to those who were harmed." Making some type of amends was mentioned by five offenders: "to rectify the bad, bring good to a situation;" "to try to make things right," "something that was wrong and I wanted to try to straighten it out."

Other victim-focused reasons were mentioned by fewer offenders. Three focused on the victim being able to "ask questions," "obtain an understanding," or "know what happened." Two spoke of reassuring the victims they had nothing to fear from the offenders; another two thought victims might need an opportunity to "lash out" at them or express "righteous indignation." And one offender anticipated moving back into the same community after release and wanted to "get the emotions out in the open before we meet each other on the outside." In total, 39 victim-related responses were reported, averaging 1.95 per offender.

In their spontaneous answers to the question of why they decided to participate, only three offenders mentioned any potential benefit to themselves. One was quite general: "I thought it would be good for her and for myself, also." One simply stated it was part of his treatment goals. And one wished to explain the truth about the incident and clear up misconceptions he felt the victim had.

One offender had an additional reason for participating. He was a member of a sex offenders group, and he hoped his session could be videotaped so he could bring it back to the group and possibly help group members see that this could be a positive step to take. He was disappointed that his victim chose not to allow the taping.

After offenders gave their spontaneous responses, they were asked whether they considered or hoped that there might be any benefit for themselves. Seven offenders hadn't thought of any. "I wasn't looking for anything from her, it was what I was trying to give her from me," "I didn't expect anything for myself." One listed only general results he hoped for both himself and the victim: "I thought it would be for both our benefits in the long run." The remaining 12 reported a total of 16 benefits they thought of for themselves in reaching their decision. Five spoke of some type of healing or closure for themselves: "Helping myself get rid or some of the guilt, stuff I've been holding on for the past nine years." "To stop having nightmares about the whole incident, what I could have done differently." "For me? I guess the healing." Five also wanted the victim to know something positive about themselves: "that I'm not a monster," "I'm not that type of person who doesn't care," and "I wanted the victim to know God had forgiven me."

Other benefits for themselves were mentioned by fewer offenders. Two hoped for forgiveness from the victim; one added, "that's the end result I wanted, but I realize it's not her obligation." One of these, and one additional offender, listed telling the victim they were sorry as something that would benefit themselves: "to help me, I wanted to let the victim know that I was sorry." One named a spiritual reason as a benefit for himself: "When I was in jail I read about Jesus. That's what gave me the initiative to keep going." And one wanted to tell his victim "the truth."

Only five of the offenders mentioned speaking with anyone else for support as part of their decision making process. Four spoke with family members, receiving mixed advice: "At first they was a little cautious, but they didn't know anything about it, so after I explained everything to them, after that they was all for it." "My sister, who still to this day doesn't want to forgive my children for some of the things that was done or said, she asked me to be very cautious and make sure there were going to be no repercussions as far as going back into prison." "I asked my mom. Naturally your mom is going to tell you to do what your heart tells you," and "My parents thought it was good, necessary, good for me." This last offender also spoke with a CO on his unit, whose own son had been killed. "He was talking about how this fellow was never charged. Here I am talking about that guy, and I so far haven't even said I was sorry to (my victim's mother)." One additional offender spoke with "just one" inmate, whose response was "that's good."

Risks Considered

Offenders were asked whether they considered any potential risks to themselves in their decision making process. Two stated they didn't think about any risks. The remaining 18 offered a total of 23 potential risks. Offenders feared potential anger, other negative feelings, verbal abuse, and even physical repercussions from their victims. This was a concern of 12 offenders, expressed through such phrases as, "I was wondering if one of those ladies was gonna jump across the table at me"; "as to physical, would there be any physical confrontations at all"; "not sure how the victim's mother would react"; and "I knew she hated me. I was scared she was going to lash out at me." Only one of the 12 added a concern for how he might respond if that happened: "I was about half scared, because I was afraid, (if) somebody swung on me, what I would do."

Six expressed concerns that participating could in some way negatively affect their case, including: "I'm in federal court right now fighting my case, and I had to consider that"; and "the victim could use my honesty against me with parole board." Three were concerned about the overall emotionality of the situation: "expecting the worst," "it's painful ...the revisiting of grief," "deep down inside, I didn't feel like some of the fear coming back." One simply stated that the unknown was intimidating, and one had concerns that the co-defendant, also incarcerated, might hear what he'd done and somehow strike back at him through prison connections.

PREPARATION FOR THE DIALOGUE SESSIONS

Data kept by the Ohio program indicate that mediators conducted 37 face-to-face offender preparation sessions for a total of 77.25 hours. They met face-to-face at least once with all 20 offenders. The number of sessions per offender averaged 1.85 and ranged from one to four; eight offenders had only one face-to-face preparation meeting. The amount of time spent in face-to-face preparation with offenders ranged from 45 minutes to 13 hours and averaged 3.86 hours per offender. Only three offenders received an hour or less of face-to-face preparation, and one of these received an additional hour of phone preparation spread over three phone calls. Clearly the emphasis was on conducting as much preparation as possible through face-to-face meetings; there were only a total of six preparatory phone calls recorded, lasting in total 2.83 hours.

Only one offender reported not having received any preparation, in spite of the hours documented in program records. It is not clear whether he misunderstood the question or simply forgot. "I believe it was something that I probably could have prepared better … it was a little awkward when we sat down … I had not actually sat down other than in my mind and worked out what do I want to accomplish with this meeting."

Offenders were asked to describe the preparation they remembered receiving. Not all offenders offered specific comments about the contents of their preparation; of the 15 who did, the element most often mentioned was providing information about what to expect during the session, highlighted by eight offenders: "She explained everything to me and what would probably take place." "Guidelines were set up about what was to be discussed. And that pretty much prepared me." "She just went over small points you know, how the room would be set up, people (the victim) would bring with her, which was her sister and her daughter."

Five offenders mentioned receiving more specific information about the victim, such as the questions they might have or their goals in seeking to meet. Five offenders offered positive comments on how the facilitator treated them during the preparation session: "In this environment you run into a lot of people who want to condemn you, you're just a felon, just an inmate. She was interested in my feelings, in calming my anxiety, I could sense that"; "They treated me like a human"; and "Encouraging. He had an air of expectation of good things." Three described receiving information about their own rights or possible needs during the session: "That at any time if I needed to take a break to just let her know and we would go ahead and take a break." "They told me that I can say anything and ask questions if I wanted to." "That I didn't have to answer questions I wasn't comfortable with."

In spite of the great concern offenders had about potential negative behavior toward themselves from victims, only two mentioned the element of being reassured about limits that would be set on victim behavior during the session: "she won't put up with any hollering or carrying on," and "that there really was to be no contact, things like that." And two offenders commented that facilitators clarified their neutrality as part of the preparation: "I know she was not just the victim's advocate, she was partially my advocate, too"; and "they went out of their way to let me know that they wasn't taking sides, they made me believe that they were neutral."

Offender Evaluation of the Preparation Process

The 19 offenders who reported receiving preparation were asked to rate their satisfaction with their preparation. Their responses are reported in Table 10.2.

Table 10.2: Offender Satisfaction with Preparation for Mediation/Dialogue

Very satisfied	16	(84%)
Somewhat satisfied	3	(16%)
Somewhat dissatisfied		
Very dissatisfied		
Total	19	(100%)

Those who were very satisfied had comments such as the following: "She did everything, she had me prepared." "I think they done a real good job, preparing me as much as you could be prepared for something like this....I really don't know of anything more they could have done." "I think the lady from the central office did a very good job, it seemed like she covered every little thing, she made you feel comfortable, she made it a lot easier for me to talk to (the victim)." Two of the three "somewhat satisfied" offenders offered comments focused on personal qualities of the facilitator who prepared them: "He's a good person." "He's a fine person to do this work."

Offenders were also asked what they found the most helpful in their preparation process. Four offenders (including the offender who stated he received no preparation) did not describe any specifics. The remaining 16 offered 22 elements that they found the most helpful. Six offenders listed bringing specific information about the victim as most helpful. "...The questions that the victim's mom might ask." "One thing, he told me that (the victim), it wasn't any hard feelings." Six also listed being treated with respect and having regard for their needs and feelings. "She went over my feelings and kind of brought things to the surface, helped bring the compassion to the front." "They were friendly, they didn't ridicule or anything, they didn't put me down." "It made a big impact that my feelings really mattered," and "they understood how hard it was to do this."

Five stated that the general information about what to expect had been most helpful: "She explained what the ground rules were going to be, that she would actually break the ice." Three focused on being reassured that any out of control behaviors by the victim would be stopped. "I was wondering if there was going to be screaming and yelling ...were there any kind of rules"; "to reassure me that they were not going to allow her to verbally abuse me, they would not just let me take abuse for three straight hours." And two felt that knowing the facilitators were neutral was most helpful: "they let me know that they weren't taking sides."

Suggestions for Changes in the Preparation Process

Offenders were asked what was least helpful in the preparation process, or whether there was anything else they wished the facilitators had done to prepare them. Seventeen had no negative feedback, and some were even befuddled by the question: "Oh man, I never thought about that." "I can't think of anything else they could have done." "I don't think so, I think they did a real good job." The three with changes to suggest included one who thought some of the questions used in preparation were too broad and didn't apply in his situation, one who simply felt the process took too long, and the offender who reported receiving no preparation and felt he should have had some. One offender who stated at this point in the interview that he could think of nothing else the facilitator could have done made a suggestion later on: "During our talks she would always make a list, write down the things I would say. What I felt she should have done, maybe, was compile all that together, like a little wish list, and maybe went back over it with me before the meeting."

Feelings Immediately Before the Dialogue

Sixteen offenders reported that they experienced anxious emotions immediately prior to their meetings. These ranged from merely "nervous" or "anxious," reported by 11 offenders, to "terrified" and "scared," named by five. "Like I was sitting on needles." "I was nervous, going over trying to imagine what it was going to be like." "I was so nervous that morning I don't think I can remember what I was thinking about." "Scared. The worst thing I could think of was having her jump across the table." "Terrified. I felt like I was being led to the electric chair. I was more nervous about that than being sentenced and going in front of the parole board combined. Because (those people), I didn't actually cause them pain, I didn't look right in the eyes of the person I caused pain to."

Four offenders, on the other hand, reported only neutral or positive feelings immediately before their meetings: "I was just curious, I'm one of those people, when I'm faced with the situation, I don't deal with it until it happens." "Quite happy and expectant." "At that point, I was ready to see her." One of these, however, reported that he nearly backed out of the meeting altogether when the warden asked him to change out of the personal shirt he had chosen to wear for the meeting back into an institutional shirt. In his words, "I want to be as comfortable as I can be, this is an intense situation. I am not wearing a shirt with a number on it." Ultimately he was permitted to wear his own shirt to the meeting.

THE DIALOGUE SESSIONS

Typically present at the dialogue sessions were one or two facilitators, the offender, the victim or family member, and support persons. Eleven victims brought one or more support persons; seven offenders likewise had a support person present. In three instances, security staff were present in the room; more often they were present just outside the room, affording more privacy for the participants. These combinations produced an average of 5.6 persons present per dialogue session, excluding camera personnel, who were mentioned in only a single case.

The length of the dialogue meetings ranged from half an hour to four and a half hours, though most fell between 1.5 and 2.5 hours. The average length was 2.1 hours.

Offenders were asked who did most of the talking in the session. The most frequent response, offered by 10 offenders, was that conversation was fairly evenly split between the offender and the victim or victims. Six offenders reported that the victim did most of the talking, and four felt they themselves had been the main talkers, usually because of the questions asked by the victim and the need to go into detail. One worried "knowing my character, I'd say I talk too much."

Even though both victims and offenders typically described events and may even have shared something that might be described as a "statement," in fact the dialogues appear to have unfolded more like a conversation than a series of statements. The following sections highlight particular elements of the conversations reported by the offenders.

Opening Moments

Facilitators in the Ohio program typically open the session with introductions and a review of the purpose and ground rules for the meeting. Offenders who commented on how the session began confirmed this pattern: "(the facilitator) broke the ice and set the ground rules." "(The facilitator) told me thanks for agreeing to this meeting, and some other stuff, and said, 'I'm gonna let her go first, is that okay with you?'" In working in violent and serious crimes, it is usually the practice to offer victims the chance to speak first after introductions, if they so wish. Only nine of the offenders who were interviewed commented on whether the victim or the offender spoke first; seven reported that it was the victim. Two indicated that they themselves went first: "She had asked me if I wanted to talk first and I asked her, if I can do that, it would be fine." Four offenders simply commented that the participants took over together after the introductions: "Then we just started talking." Then we just talked, like two hillbillies." The remaining seven did not comment on who spoke first.

Offender Descriptions of Victim/Family Member Participation

Whether as initial speakers or later in the dialogue, victims/family members are typically offered an opportunity to describe what happened to them and share the impact the crime has had in their lives. Three offenders were not certain the victim had offered this information. "I don't remember if (the victim) really said how it had affected him." "His feelings, those weren't really brought out." And "I think they had the opportunity to describe the impact, but I don't think they really did." Two of these reported that the victims spent more time telling them how well their lives were going in the present: "he's remarried, and has a six month old child, one of God's blessing," and, "she's getting along as well as I could ever hope she would and leading a normal life."

The remaining 17 reported that victims had shared how the crime affected them. From offenders who met with actual victims: "She went through all those surgeries," "she wouldn't even let her husband work third shift," and "the therapy she's had." From offenders who met with family members of deceased victims: "There's things that she would do every day that, at some point, she'd think about her son." "She told me her other daughter experienced feelings of guilt for not being home." "She told me about how she was involved with MADD mothers and what she's doing now as far as alcohol abuse." Three offenders, in two vehicular homicides and one murder case, added that their victims had brought photographs of the person who was killed.

Three reported that victims shared how they had felt about the offender, at the time or in the intervening years: "She told me I could have been off three years ago, and she was opposed to that cause she wanted me to do at least the minimum." "She said at the time she wanted to kill me." "She told me how scared of me she was." These victims included a vehicular homicide, a murder, and a sexual assault case.

Only six offenders mentioned whether or not their victims asked them questions during the dialogue sessions. Two did not further elaborate on what their victims asked about. Three reported that their victims asked for specifics about the crime: "(The victim) wanted to know what happened and why, the actual events that took place the night of the crime." "(The victim) wanted to hear from my mouth what had happened." And one stated "(the victim) asked me if I wanted to know what she thought happened."

Offender Response to Victim/Family Member Statements

Fourteen of the 17 offenders whose victims described the impact of the crime expressed how difficult it was listening to these accounts. Seven talked about how bad this made them feel: "God, it crushed my world." "Bad, it made me feel bad." "It really didn't feel good at the time." "It was tough." "It affected me deeply," and "That was probably the most difficult part of the dialogue." Four more talked about how hurt it made them feel: "It hurt me very deeply, like I hurt a friend." "It just hurt me on the inside to think about how hurt his family and he had to feel when this happened." And one used language describing sadness: "Just hearing those words, you know, I was really, really sad."

Empathy, putting themselves in the victim's shoes, and simply feeling the victim's pain were themes for 11 of these 14 offenders. Seven reported that even before the dialogue they had spent time thinking about this: "I already knew that it did a lot of damage, that their holidays were not the same any more." "It wasn't the first time it had hurt, because I was aware of all that she would have had to go through." "I understood part of it because I knew they still lived in the house where the crime took place." Four of these emphasized that they felt it much more intensely through he dialogue: "I guess it really got driven home when I was sitting there talking to her, how much it had affected her." "Regardless how often I've tried to picture myself in her shoes, it never came across until I actually sat and looked at her."

Four additional offenders who commented on experiencing the victim's pain either hadn't thought about it before, or didn't mention having previously spent time thinking about it. "It made me think, something that I didn't do before, I never thought of ... how hurt his family and he had to feel when that happened." "Seeing the pictures of her as a baby made me think of mine, spending time with them,...trying to imagine what it would be like if somebody took their life and they were just gone." "I had no idea it was affecting her this long."

The remaining three offenders whose victims did describe the impact of the crime had more neutral responses: "She had every right to feel that way, and I told her, I find no fault in you at all, I do not blame you for your feelings." "I was willing to sit and listen to this...it didn't really affect me personally, I was more focused on what she got out of it."

Offender Descriptions of Their Own Participation

Fourteen of the 20 offenders spoke at least some about what they shared in giving their own statement or account and/or in response to victims' questions. Six said that they shared specific information about the actual crime. "We talked about the night of the accident"; "I gave as much of a detailed description as I could without being graphic"; "apparently they didn't know the real story of what happened to their daughter...I told the truth." Five offenders shared comments that were more focused on their lives since the crime. "How it affected me with my present relationship." "How it has affected me, it hurts me to think that I was a young man before I left the streets." "I shared things that I went through and done while I was here, the loss of my mother, fears of returning to society, not being productive, not having the greatest support group." And five emphasized that they had been able to tell the victim they were sorry. " I just told her how I felt and how sorry I was." I did accomplish expressing to them my regret." "That's something I didn't get to do to the victims of my case before I left the county, so it kind of felt good to let him know I was sorry for what I had done."

Victim/Family Member Response to Offender Account

There was no routine question asking offenders how victims responded to their statements, but 10 offenders spontaneously offered information about their victims' reactions. Four said their victims spoke of forgiveness: "I think she told me she forgave me even before I told her how sorry I was." "She actually forgave me — we shook hands and everything. That was the best thing that happened."

Three spoke of their victims' emotions. "It always bothers me to see a woman cry, but especially her." "When she first started talking, you could hear the bitterness there. And at the end, you could hear it going away slowly." "The victim's mother wasn't sure she wanted to say anything; they told me she was still pretty bitter. But after the meeting went on for a little bit she started loosening up."

One reported that his victim's family member asked him to look her in the eyes when he made his apology; he stated this was the only time in their entire meeting that they had eye contact. And one reported the following experience: "I seen the revelation of Christ and I seen a glowing in his face, where man can sit and look at you right square in your face and not move an eye and not shed a tear and tell you straight from his heart that if it's God's will for (me) to take his wife's life in order for me to change my life, that's the blessing from it."

Offender Surprises

Offenders were asked if there was anything during the dialogue meeting that surprised them. Nine felt nothing had surprised them: "Not that I can think of." "I don't think so, though there's a lot that went on that I don't remember." "No, because I went over everything that could have happened in my head."

The remaining 11 offenders reported a wide range of surprises. Four were surprised at how well the meeting went, including the positive responses of their victims. "Actually the whole meeting (was a surprise), I just didn't expect it to go so peacefully. " "Just them being such good people, and their attitude. That surprised me, after what I done." "That she didn't think I was a monster, that made me feel really good, that she did understand me." Two were surprised that they themselves cried: "I think I came out for a break, and I broke down and cried outside the room, and I wasn't expecting to do that. It was the way she described all the pain, all the death and pain that had happened on both sides, it was just amazing because it wasn't just one sided all the time."

The remaining four surprises had nothing in common. One was surprised to learn of the rumors that had been circulating about his victim's death. One was surprised to learn how frightened his victim had been of him: "That she was scared to death that I would come and do something to her or her family...she felt I was gonna hold doing prison time against her." One was surprised that the victim didn't want to know about the crime: "I expected them to talk about my crimes and the why of it. To my surprise it was more a kind of closure type of thing, they wanted me to know what they had done in the past ten years." And one was surprised by how well the victim's life had turned out.

Nonverbal Communication

In describing their experience of both the preparation and their encounters with their victims, nine of the 20 offenders used phrases that underscored non-verbal elements of human communication. Eye contact was the most frequently mentioned aspect, named by seven offenders: "The ability to look at each other and have eye contact." I could see the pain in their eyes." "People can walk out the gates thinking they've paid their price but haven't looked in the eyes of the people they've harmed"; and "to see it in her eyes that she truly did believe (that I'm sorry) and accept that." One offender also spoke of eye contact in his choice of a corrections staff member as a support person to accompany him in the dialogue: "I picked him because my mother always said, if I can look into the eyes of someone and I could feel the warmth in my heart for them, to go with them."

Closely related, and perhaps conveying the same phenomenon, was reference to a person's face, mentioned by three offenders. "You can see it in their face, see what you did. It was almost like re-living it." "You don't see each other as faceless names. Bill Clinton can sit up there in the White House, fire missiles at Iraq, Kosovo, Yugoslavia, wherever the hell it is he's shooting at over there. And kill hundreds of thousands of people. That's easy to do. But to look a person in the face, to put a face with that."

Only five offenders mentioned physical contact. Three talked about shaking hands at some point. For one, this came at the most impactful moment of the dialogue: "She actually forgave me, we shook hands and everything. That was the best thing that happened, that she forgave me for what happened." For the other two the handshake came at the end of the dialogue, and was initiated by the victim. One offender, meeting with the former girlfriend who was his victim, stated: "we talked, we cried, we held hands." And one offender spoke of a hug, also in connecting with an impactful moment: I was telling her about that evening and when I got done she told me she forgave me and offered me a hug." (Interviewer: So did you hug her back?) "Yeah. It was quite a moment."

Facilitator Role and Evaluation

Offenders had three opportunities in the interviews to comment on what facilitators did during the sessions. They were asked to describe the facilitator role, they were asked what facilitator actions they found most helpful, and they were asked what they found least helpful.

Thirteen offenders offered comments simply describing what the facilitators did; most frequently mentioned was that they were quiet and stayed out of the way, reported by six offenders: "He really let us do it, I guess he thought we could handle it." "They stayed out of it." Two each mentioned that the facilitators helped remind them of things, that they made themselves available to the offender during the breaks, that they set the tone and made things comfortable, and that they started things off. One mentioned the facilitator's neutrality, and one spoke of encouragement.

Together the 20 offenders offered a total of 30 facilitator actions they had found "most helpful." Staying out of the way again topped the list, reported by eight offenders. "She was there but she wasn't," "I think basically she just let it run its course, so once the session started, it was between me and her." "Just being there and not interrupting." Five spoke of ways in which the facilitators made things comfortable and helped everyone feel at ease: "She's just got a pleasant way about her." "She says this is going to be a constructive meeting for all parties concerned." "She had water and tissues sitting there, which was nice." "Her personality, making the meeting less electric." Five also talked about ways in which facilitators steered the meeting, asked questions or offered reminders: "Her choice of questions, she's very, very good in her choice of questions." "Kept us talking, cause we stalled." "Steering our conversation from time to time." Three found the way the facilitators opened the meeting to be most helpful: "They laid down the ground rules, to freshen everything they had told us about." Three spoke of how the facilitators handled things when feelings became intense: "They interrupted a couple times for us to take a break." During the meeting things got a little emotional, and they'd stand and have us take a time out"; and "they let me leave when I was about to cry so the victim wouldn't see me cry."

The remaining "most helpful" facilitator actions were mentioned by one offender each: that they "weren't judgmental," that they "took their time and listened," that they were "encouraging," that they "asked if I was okay a couple times," and that they "reminded me this meeting was for me too."

When asked what was least helpful, 18 offenders could think of nothing, with comments such as "everything that he did was okay from where I see it," I can't think of anything more that they could have done," and "nothing comes to mind." One offender commented that the facilitators had "interrupted a few times." And the other one felt the meeting had ended too abruptly: "the least helpful thing was to wrap up the meeting, because we were talking real nice."

Feelings Immediately Afterwards

For the great majority of offenders, the feelings after the dialogue session was over were positive, in part or in whole. Eleven reported a range of only positive feelings; an additional five reported a mix of both positive and negative immediate reactions, and one did not describe any feelings. Among the positive were seven who simply felt better in some general way: "I came away thinking it was a good thing that had just happened." "Meeting her was like meeting an old friend. I felt a lot better afterward." Six spoke of feeling relieved: "I felt so relieved and warm inside"; "relief, like I had done what I could to understand the circumstances and clear my own conscience." Five described a weight being lifted: "about twenty pounds lighter, it was like a huge burden was lifted." "I felt that the world was lifted up off my shoulders." "Feel like someone took an anvil off of me, lifted a lot of weight." Two were glad it was over. Two reported feeling happy: "on top of the world, I was floating on a cloud," and "I was more happy that day after that meeting than I was the day I got parole." And two were "at peace."

Five offenders who reported the positive reactions outlined above also reported some degree of negative feelings: "When I left, my mind went blank. It's kind of like throwing too much at someone at one time. I was short circuited and I was just overwhelmed." "I remember that they left and then I left afterwards and I felt probably even worse than I did when I came in there." "At the same time, I felt heavy hearted, too." For each of these, while they experienced a mixed reaction, the negatives did not appear to outweigh the positives: "I was overwhelmed, I was at peace." "I was emotionally drained, relieved."

There were three offenders who described their immediate reactions in more uniformly negative terms. One, a father who met with the family member he had sexually abused, spoke of how sad it was for him when the visit was over and how emotionally drained he was "to hear her tell about all the hurt and the pain." One simply felt sorry for his victim, concerned about her, and said, "I feel like I didn't help her much." The third stated, "Immediately right after it was over, it was like going right back to the daily grind. It set me back. It took me way back and made me reanalyze things, review things, it made me understand things better, it just, it was difficult." Each of these three reported that with the passage of time, they felt better. "I went through different stages, I felt it was good."

In responding to this question, five inmates spoke of whether they felt the meeting had been helpful to their victim. Three were certain it had helped: "I'm glad I actually got the nerve to face them, and I felt like it helped them." "I was a little more at ease for the family, not for myself; I'll never be, I don't think." One hoped the victims "got out of it what they needed," and one was less certain: "I feel like I didn't help her much."

The positive reactions inmates experienced did not necessarily mean the experience hadn't been difficult. Three who described relief and one who spoke about a weight being lifted also made clear this was the most difficult thing they had done since being incarcerated: "It was more difficult to meet her than the stuff I went through when I was locked up. The punishment I got in there, I knew the consequences if I did anything." "Prison is no joke, but if you stay focused and just try to stay out of trouble it won't be that hard. Meeting with the victim's mom was hard because I was expecting the worst." "I'd say this is probably the worst thing I've had to do since I been in prison. Something you have to come to grips with…it's a hard thing to admit how wrong you are."

And there was one offender who responded to the question by talking about what he thought, rather than what he felt: "It just made me think. It made me think a lot about what we had did. Think once more, you know, why we couldn't just walk away, because it wouldn't have been that hard, to just walk away and just not do it."

OUTCOMES

Offenders were asked a series of questions about the outcome of the meeting and its impact on their lives.

Overall Outlook on Life

Offenders responded both to open-ended questions about the impact of their participation on their lives and to a fixed-response question which asked whether their overall outlook on life had changed since meeting the victim. Responses to the fixed question are reported on Table 10.3 below.

Only three offenders gave a negative response to the fixed question. One of these felt his crime had more impact than his participation: "The changes come within me. It's not because of programs. I was devastated by what I did, I couldn't believe that I did it, but I had to make a vow to myself not ever to raise my hand against another person again."

Table 10.3: Has Your Overall Outlook on Life Changed Since Meeting the Victim?

No	3	15%
Yes	17	85%
Of those who answered yes:		
a. Definitely more positive and at peace with the circumstances I am faced with.	13	(65%)
b. Somewhat more positive and able to cope with my life.	2	(10%)
c. Somewhat more negative and less able to cope with my life.	0	(0%)
d. Definitely more negative and angry about the circumstances I am faced with.	0	(0%)
e. Other.	1	(5%)
None of the above.	1	(5%)

One of the offenders who responded "no" on the fixed question, however, had much to say in the open-ended portion of the interview about how the meeting changed his life. Thus, a total of 18 Ohio offenders reported major life changes as a result of their participation.

Seventeen of these focused on changes in their personal growth and rehabilitation. "Back then (before the meeting) I didn't think about others." "I've got a stronger walk today." "By sharing with people that I have wronged and people that show a need for me to help them, I help myself." "It just reiterated to me how...I have to work desperately hard to be the individual that I want to be."

Three of these focused on helping other people. "Instead of hurtin' people, I think about helpin' people now. I do stuff I never woulda done. I already stopped to help a couple of people since I been home. If I never met her, I probably wouldn't have did it." "'Cause now I'm more geared towards helping others than I ever was. 'Cause maybe I can touch somebody the way she touched me."

Two simply said they feel better: "It made me feel better that they forgive me, not for the crime, but that they don't hate me"; and "I feel better. After it was over I talked to my mom. She said, 'I can hear it in your voice, you sound happy.'"

Four changes were mentioned by only one offender each. One spoke of his Twelve Step program and how he'd been able to give back "what little I could." One said he'd made peace with himself. One, who met with his daughter, was grateful to renew the relationship and felt "more drive to get back out on the street." And one felt more positive about people "because I'd have a lot of people who had helped me, but I hadn't had a chance to talk to anyone I'd really hurt."

Eight offenders offered some explanation of why the meeting had such an impact. For five, the main factor was an increased understanding of the other person. "That gave me an understanding of how it feels to be on the other side." "It really opened your eyes to the situation I was in, how many people was affected." Three spoke of spiritual changes: "I'm more at spiritual peace." "It's given me a better understanding that when I read verses in the Bible, that I actually understand what they are saying, instead of just reading it."

Changes in Offender View of the Victim/Family Member

Several questions tapped offender perceptions of the victim and/or the person with whom they met. Five offenders reported that their feelings toward the victim did not change. These included four who already knew their victims and had strong positive feelings for them, regardless of the meeting. Three of these were the offenders who met with family member they had sexually abused. The fourth was an offender who had murdered his ex-girlfriend; he responded, "No, I still miss her. I didn't kill her because I hated her. I still care for her and her family." The fifth person had never met the family member before. "I didn't know her, I couldn't have any negative or positive feelings, but I did hurt for her."

The remaining 15 all reported that their feelings had changed, offering a total of 17 changes. Eight said their feelings for the victim/family member they met with had changed for the better: "A great deal. When

I first met her (in court), it was fireworks. Now she's an angel." "I was just real surprised by them. I think they're wonderful people." Seven focused more on the fact that these previously unknown people were now known to them: "Yeah, I mean, she was still a victim, but it was more like I hurt a friend." "I didn't know where he stood, I didn't know the man's heart. Today I know his heart." "Before the meeting I didn't know her. I guess I felt like I had a friend," "I see her as a human being, not just a name, a faceless name." One reported that he felt sorry for the victim now and felt like he didn't help her much. And one was somewhat vague, stating, "Now that I have met her, I have to readjust my thinking and understanding of what happened."

A second question asked whether offenders thought the victim/family member's feelings toward them had changed. Four offenders either were not asked or did not really answer this question. Of the remaining 16, seven simply felt they didn't know if their victim's feelings had changed: "I don't know; I hope so," "I don't know what her feelings were, what her emotional state was," and "I'd really like to know that." Two of these conjectured that their victim's feelings might be positive: "I don't know. He did say 'the wrong guy's in prison'"; and "I don't know. They said they don't hate me. I appreciate that, cause that's been a thing on my mind." One who didn't know suspected his victim still felt bad about him: "I wondered about that. I can't imagine that she would ever feel good about me." All seven of these met with a family member of the victim who had died; five of them were not previously acquainted with this family member.

Six offenders reported that they felt the victims with whom they met feel better about them after meeting with them: "I think (her feelings toward me) were more positive, because I could tell the difference from when I first walked in"; "Really, from what he said, I think (their feelings) did change." "I think she cares about what happens to me." "Definitely. She's gotten to know me a lot better as a person, instead of must the monster that killed her son." Four of these, in three assault cases and one sexual assault case, had met with their actual victim.

Two offenders felt their victim's feelings probably hadn't changed; both of these were fathers who met with the family members they had sexually abused. And the offender in a manslaughter case was fairly convinced the feelings of his victim's sister had changed in a negative direction: "Probably, I wouldn't say for the better."

A third question tapped offenders' perceptions of similarities and differences between themselves and the victim or family member with whom they met. Four offenders gave no information about their perceived similarities or differences. Eight saw themselves as similar: "I think we'll always have a bond...we share things spiritually." "I don't see any difference at all. I was stupid and hard-headed, I truly believe that without drugs it would have been a lot better." "I don't think we're too much different. They seem like the type of people if we could have met under different circumstances, I think we could have been friends." Five more offenders described both similarities and differences: "I see similarities in the suffering we both are going through. The difference is, I feel I have a better understanding of hers, where she lacks the understanding of mine." "We're alike because we're both grieving for someone we love. The difference is that she is the mother, and I am the cause." "We share a lot of common thoughts; we are pretty much on the same level. But she's the victim, and I'm definitely the offender."

Three offenders saw themselves as primarily different from their victims: "He is really deep into the Bible and into church, and I am not into it like that." "I look at her and I see family, not the family that I have, but the family I would have wanted"; and "I would say I'm a little more introverted and she is a little more extroverted. She seems more in touch with her feelings than I am."

Changes in Offender Understanding of How the Crime Affected Others

Offenders were asked in a fixed-response three-point Likert format to what extent meeting with the victim changed their understanding of how the crime had affected others. Results are reported on Table 10.4 below.

Some also offered comments elaborating on their responses. Comments from those who reported "a great deal" included: "Basically, she went through way more than what I went through when I was locked up." "You can see when you're talking to them...bringing back what you felt before plus some on top of it cause you're actually seeing it, where before I was trying to avoid it." "I had not seen anybody or talked to anybody. I've never talked to nobody about this." "She was very articulate in expressing how much of an impact I have had on her and her family. It was making me understand that the impact I've had was much greater than I imagined."

Table 10.4: Extent to which the Meeting Changed Offender Understanding of How the Crime Affected Others

A great deal	14	(70%)
Somewhat	5	(25%)
Not at all	1	(5%)
Total	20	(100%)

Only three of the offenders who responded "somewhat" had comments. One focused on his work in counseling groups: "I had done extensive victim empathy stuff...during the meeting I realized that some of my fears were realities and others were not, that she had worked through these." Another simply said he was aware of the impact before the meeting. The third commented elsewhere "it definitely makes you aware of the impact of the crime." The one offender who felt it hadn't changed his understanding of the impact explained, "I truly feel that it had been healed, he had dealt with it, and I had dealt with it."

Impact on Spiritual Outlook

Offenders were asked about the impact of the meeting on their spiritual life in both open-ended and fixed-response questions. Offender responses to the fixed response question are presented in Table 10.5 below. The two questions were worded somewhat differently and there was some disparity between the two data sets. Two offenders who responded to the open-ended question by saying the meetings had not "affected their spiritual outlook on life" answered the fixed response question by saying that the meetings did have "an effect on their religious or spiritual life." An additional offender who responded "yes" to the open ended question answered "no" on the fixed response item.

Table 10.5: Effect on Offender Religious or Spiritual Life

Did the process of preparing to meet the victim and the actual meeting have any effect on your religious or spiritual life?	
No	8
Yes	12
Of those who answered yes:	
a. Greatly enriched my religious/spiritual perspective.	3
b. Contributed to a deeper religious/spiritual perspective.	8
c. Contributed to a weakening of my religious/ spiritual perspective.	0
d. Greatly weakened my religious/spiritual perspective.	0
None of the above.	1

Thus, across the two data sets, there were seven who consistently said it had no impact, and 13 who at some point said it did.

One offender who changed his answer from "no" in the open-ended section to "yes" on the fixed item did not elaborate; the other had the following comments: "No. My son had to grow up without a father, I'm going to die of old age in a penitentiary, and these people are dead. They ain't done nothing to nobody. They didn't deserve to die. Now you tell me there's a God out there? Nah, I lost my faith in God a long time ago. They can't tell me that there's a merciful God out there to let something like all this happen."

The seven who consistently said "no" were mixed in the extent of their spirituality. Four reported a fairly strong spiritual life that was not affected by their dialogue experience: "I have always believed in God." "Always had a strong faith." "My spiritual guides was always good." "Not really. I've been the same throughout — never lost faith!" Two did not offer comments, and one reported, "It reconfirmed my belief that there isn't a God."

Ten offenders consistently responded "yes" concerning the impact on their spirituality. Five spoke of how the meeting itself was spiritual. "Definitely. To be able to communicate with the mom, that right there was spiritual itself, because it ain't nothing but the works of God, and if I would have been the victim, I probably wouldn't have gone through with it." "I sat right here in this room, I seen Jesus Christ that day, because there was a glow over his head the whole time." "They're really strong in their religion, they just shine." "This is like redemption."

Seven offenders described changes in their beliefs or practice. Three spoke of increased awareness of their accountability: "Because He's our last judge, you know, if I die in here or on the street there's still one more person I gotta meet before it's all over with, one person I have to explain this to." "I feel guilty cause I didn't tell (about the murder). I don't know what I was after"; and "Yes, it made me understand that my life review is going to be a little bit more difficult than I had imagined." Two offenders reported changes in their beliefs: "Then after meeting with these people, I seen that God does exist, has to. And that even I can be forgiven, and that if nobody else, he knows the truth"; and "...I grasp a hold of this spiritual experience... the preciousness of life, how precious it is, and not the big things, the little things."

Three spoke of how spiritual changes make them want to be a better person: "It's just given me an encouragement to strive to be a better person, to treat life, you know, as a precious gift." "Seeing what they've got, it just makes you want what they've got. You can just look at them and see." One of these had become more active in church: "Since I got out I been going to church every Sunday. I knew that if I got back into the church and get back doing the things that the Lord wants me to do I can be more successful in society. I wanna be a model citizen." And one commented, "I guess I could say it took a burden off me, and in a sense too it has opened up a door for sharing my spirituality."

Forgiveness Issues

Forgiveness is not a goal of victim offender dialogue in violent and serious crimes. There was no specific question in the research interview guide focused on forgiveness. However, in some instances, depending on the direction of the conversations, the research interviewer did ask offenders questions about forgiveness. Thus, across their interviews, a total of 13 offenders made some mention of forgiveness issues, but these numbers are to some extent dependent on what questions were asked. One of these merely mentioned that his sister couldn't forgive his daughters for how they had treated him, but made no mention of forgiveness in relation to himself.

The remaining 12 offenders mentioned a total of 18 aspects of forgiveness. Four offenders spoke of hoping to receive forgiveness from their victim; this included the two who had named this as part of their reason for agreeing to participate, and two who still hoped for it after the meeting. "I have hopes maybe somewhere down the road she can put this behind her, say 'It was wrong but I understand him,' or 'I forgive him,' or 'I'll try to forgive him.'" "I remember a sense of regret that they didn't (forgive me). But I couldn't force that. I didn't feel like they had total animosity for me, but the words didn't come ... I also remember that I knew that while they didn't say 'we forgive you,' if I met them on the street I could say hi, how are you doing and greet them cordially." An additional offender simply said he hadn't sought forgiveness and didn't receive it.

Three offenders spoke spontaneously of receiving forgiveness from their victim during the dialogue session. One, who received a hug in the process, has already been presented above. Another commented, "Well, let me tell you the truth — I never expected her to forgive me, but when she did, it just made me feel so good. If she wouldn't have forgave me I don't know how I would have changed." The third had a different response: "She told me she forgave me and that's — there is no forgiveness. You can't forgive a person for doing what I done. She said, 'You haven't forgiven yourself.' And I said, No, and I never will."

Two additional offenders very nearly received forgiveness. One described his victim's response as follows: "She said 'there was nothing to forgive, it was just a mistake. I pray for you and wish you nothing but the best.'" And the other reported, "At that time she told me, that she had it in her to forgive me, but it was going to take a little time. She said she had it in her."

Two offenders spoke of their victim's positive responses to them in terms that suggested they felt it was close to forgiveness. One, who mentioned this experience as what surprised him, stated: "...he didn't have any hard feelings toward me, because I know if somebody sticks a gun in your face and takes something that you worked hard for, it don't seem like it would be that easy to forgive a person for something like that." The other commented, "They said they don't hate me...I guess it's some of that that makes me feel even worse, you know, here their daughter is gone, and they don't even hate my guts. It shows me how forgiving that they are."

Three spoke spontaneously about God's forgiveness. One, already described, sought to meet in part to let the victim to know God had forgiven him. The offender who spoke of coming to believe in God from his experience added, "What all of this has done is really help me to understand what Christ went through, what he must have felt, the pain. I mean for God to give up his only son so that sins of mine and other men can be forgiven." The third commented, "(Forgiveness) is something I don't expect, not by her. I have a need to be forgiven by God."

Two spoke of self-forgiveness. One is the offender cited above who stated he would never forgive himself. The second commented, "I believe in God with all my heart and soul, but I couldn't find that effort to forgive myself and find that peace within me (until the meeting)." And one offender, who was himself forgiven by his victim, spoke of how much other offenders hope for forgiveness: "A lot of them (inmates) said I was nuts for doing it. My best friend was happy he didn't have this type of victim to face. They would like the forgiveness but they don't want to take the chance of being spurned."

Further Contact with Victims/Family Members

Thirteen offenders made some mention of having additional contact with the victim or family member they had met with in mediation/dialogue. Five of these had already had further contact. Two met a second time at the victim's request. Two were exchanging letters, and one of these was also in telephone contact. The fifth one had made some restitution payments to replace funds he stole, but was not in further direct contact with his victim.

The most frequently mentioned reason for further contact was for victim needs or to be sure the victim was okay, named by five offenders: "I told her if she ever wanna see me again, my parole officer got my number, all you gotta do is call"; "I just want to basically know that she's all right, that she finds that peace within her"; and "I would like to hear from her if it would help her." Three offenders hoped to have further contact because there was more they wished to convey: "I'm kind of slow. There were some things I wanted to say to her that I didn't get to say because I didn't think about it until after I got back to the dorm"; and "there might be some things left to talk about. Everyone was nervous."

Three who had not previously known the victim or family member they met with felt a personal relationship and hoped it could continue. All three of these were already in contact. "It was nice seeing her again. I got a new fiancée now — I introduced her. I want to invite her to the wedding." "I wrote her again this week, she said she feels like she gained a brother." "I'm really glad she was willing to take things a step further. Because how else would I get to know her?"

Matters were more complex for the three fathers who met with family members they had sexually abused. One hoped the positive dialogue experience would lead authorities to permit his victim to visit him in prison "like other normal family members." Another was quite clear that as long as he was on parole no such contact would be allowed, so he clarified, "I have no thoughts to be with my victim, and then if I do it's going to have to be in a mutually agreed upon public place." But he noted his victim did wish to talk further. The third left it more open, up to what his victim might need in the future.

Two were unhappy with restrictions on letter writing between themselves and their victim. "I told her she could write if she wants. They said something about it wouldn't be allowed. I don't see how the hell they can stop a letter from coming — if she wants to write, she can write." The second had mixed feelings. The facilitator had told him he and the victim could exchange letters through the facilitator. On the one hand, he understood this because he knew of another situation in which a murderer had written his victim and "the victim got offended." But he still felt "the relationship between (the victim) and me is more personal, and now I feel offended if I was to transport it through the mediator."

OFFENDER EVALUATION OF THE EXPERIENCE

Offenders responded to a series of questions aimed at tapping their overall satisfaction with their dialogue experience. Tables 10.6 and 10.7 below reports offender responses to two fixed-response questions:

Table 10.6: Offender Overall Satisfaction with Involvement in Victim Offender Dialogue Program

Very satisfied	14	(70%)
Somewhat satisfied	5	(25%)
Somewhat dissatisfied	1	(5%)
Very dissatisfied	0	(0%)
Total	20	(100%)

Table 10.7: Offender Rating of the Helpfulness of the Meeting

Very helpful	18	(90%)
Somewhat helpful	2	(10%)
Not at all helpful	0	(0%)
Total	20	(100%)

Three offenders offered spontaneous positive comments about the program at this stage of the interviews: "I hope it would be seen by the state officials as a good thing. It's marvelous." "Hope it all works out because I think it's a wonderful program — everybody does benefit," and "You are in a ground breaking area. This is important."

Sixteen offenders stated unequivocally that their expectations had been met; most did not elaborate, but three reported that the meeting "more than met" their expectations. Only one of these reported in what way it exceeded what he hoped for: "being forgiven." The six who did elaborate reported a range of expectations: "I believe I expressed to her who I am: "I knew there was one person in this world that I needed to try and undo what I had done and somehow make the best out of a bad situation." "Its good because you can tell the victim how you really feel, now that you have had time to think about it." "There was no screaming and yelling, and I did get the opportunity to tell her I'm sorry." "She told me she felt bad about me being here."

Three were not as positive regarding whether their expectations had been met. One was simply uncertain: "If she got something out if it. It's not about me, it's about her." The other two were more negative. "Not really. I was a little disappointed... I'm not sure she believed everything I shared"; and "I'm always going to feel like I wished I could've done more. I think it might have helped them some, and I hope it did."

And one offender had initially stated he had no expectations, and re-iterated that in response to the question about whether they were met: "In order to have expectations, I would have had to be doing it for my-self, and that's not why I chose to participate."

In addition, offenders were asked if they had any regrets about their participation. Nineteen of the 20 offenders immediately responded that they had no regrets; four went on to say that the only thing they regret-ted was that it hadn't happened sooner: "I just feel bad because it's al-tered her whole life, and I wished it could have been taken care of be-fore now when she spent all these years living so uncomfortable, and she shouldn't." "I wish it woulda happened sooner. But I don't think I woulda been ready right after."

The one offender who had regrets was worried how it might impact his future: "Well, in a way I feel that it will probably be used against me in the long run. Ohio will find a way, the parole board will find a way."

Recommendations for Others

The interview schedule included a question about what advantages offenders felt could come from participation, and another about whether they would recommend it. Not all offenders were asked both questions. However, across these two questions and in their responses elsewhere in the interviews, all 20 offenders made comments that indicate they think other offenders should participate in dialogue meetings like theirs. Two reported that their participation motivated them to talk with others about it: "It's up to us to carry a message, spread the word, what we went through and how well it worked out." "Last week they asked me to talk at a victim's restoration, and I guess it made it a little easier, almost like I had a cause, something I cared about and I felt people needed to hear."

As a context for interpreting the results reported here, it should be understood that the focus of this portion of the interview was often on what the benefits or advantages might be specifically for offenders. Thus, across the questions about whether or not they would recommend it and why, 17 offenders listed various ways participation would benefit other offenders; 10 of these also spoke of ways it would benefit victims, while seven mentioned only offender-related reasons. Three offenders did not mention any offender-related reasons, focusing their description of the advantages only on how it might benefit victims.

The most frequent benefit listed for victims was "closure" or "healing," named as the primary victim benefit by seven offenders: "I think it's a necessary part of the healing process"; "Closure — you don't see each other as faceless names"; and "For the victim, closure and unanswered questions." Three felt that just having the interaction was beneficial for victims: "...they can benefit just by sharing their feelings and what they've been through ...the dialogue is sharing an experience, and that is always beneficial." One spoke of "relief" for the victim, one offered "for the victim to hear the truth," and one stated, "I don't know why you can't help somebody that you've hurt."

Seventeen offenders named specific benefits or advantages for offenders. The most frequent advantage named had to do with offender rehabilitation, listed by a total of 11 offenders. Responses were classified as "rehabilitation" if they focused on changes in the offender's behavior, healing or growth. "I think it's a necessary part of the healing process, not only for the victim but for the perpetrator as well. If either one of us are going to grow and lead a normal life, we've got to finally put this behind us... use it as a steppingstone for improvement." "If you have a chance to face your victim, it's going to soften you as far as getting past that stage of guilt ... You need to tell the victim that you are sorry... That will allow you to get on with your own rehabilitation." Offenders who spoke of such changes also mentioned that offenders would increase their understanding the impact of the crime on others (2), and gain self-esteem (1).

Many of the remaining benefits for offenders could be construed as contributing to offender rehabilitation; however, six of the offenders who listed them did not otherwise point to changes in offender behavior or growth as an advantage. These included closure, feeling better or relieved, and simply sharing feelings with the victim. Closure for offenders was the most frequent of these, mentioned by a total of eight offenders, including five who listed other rehabilitation advantages: "For those what care about what they've done, or care about maybe putting some closure not only for the family, but for themselves." "It helped me get a lot of things off my chest." "This happened for a reason. We can spread the word that both the offender and the victim will get some kind of closure on the situation."

Three offenders, including two who named rehabilitation advantages, felt that offenders will feel better if they participate: "Just relief, for her as well as for (the victim) as for the offender." "Because a lot of these women are in her for assault, and they can get ...that peace." "Self peace. For a person to go through this would only help them." And two, neither of whom mentioned other rehabilitation advantages, focused on sharing feelings as the main advantage for offenders. "They can benefit just by sharing their feelings and what they've bent through, the dialogue is sharing an experience, and that is always beneficial"; and "This gives you a chance to get those feelings out of the way."

Changes Recommended by Participants

Seven offenders had some sort of change or suggestion to recommend. Two felt that their participation, and what they perceived as its positive outcome, should count toward obtaining parole: "The system isn't looking at the right things. This needs to be taken into account." "The outcome should have an effect on the release." The latter offender felt that negative and positive experiences both should be considered at the offender's parole review.

Each of the other suggested changes was mentioned by only one offender. One commented that there should be someone available for the victim immediately after the session, for support. Another suggested a support group within the prisons for offenders who are considering dialogue or getting ready for it, to have someone to talk to. A third hoped offenders who have participated could be used to tell others about it: "I would like to see the Department of Corrections use someone like myself in further meetings, so that the perpetrator can talk to someone other than his parole officer or the people doing the questions, because then again there's a bond between offenders." He also felt it would be beneficial to have the offender's therapist sit in, and he encouraged having the dialogue take place while offenders were still on parole, as had happened in his situation.

One offender wished the room had been set up a little differently so that support persons could be seated beside the person they were supporting. One noted that when he went back over his notes and papers in preparing for the research interview, he realized that a lot of the questions he'd been told his victim had were not actually answered in the session. He felt that probably wasn't an issue for his victim, but suggested, "Maybe in (another) situation, maybe that would be something they would have to watch for."

CONCLUSION

All 20 of the Ohio offenders would recommend participation in the Dialogue Program to other offenders in similar situations, 18 of the 20 reported that their meeting had a major impact on their lives, and 17 had their expectations met or exceeded. In the words of a participant, "These meetings, I think that's something that's desperately needed so that not only victim but the offender can grow after incarceration."

SECTION III: RESULTS OF THE STUDY: ANALYSIS AND IMPLICATIONS

The three chapters in this section present what we have learned from our study. Chapter 11 provides an overview and summary of the experience of all 79 mediation/dialogue participants who were interviewed. In Chapter 12 we explore an emerging typology of victim offender mediation/dialogue approaches in cases of serious and violent crime, drawing on our staff and volunteer interviews in Texas and Ohio as well as interviews with several additional practitioners. Chapter 13 examines the implications of our findings.

CHAPTER 11.
SUMMARY OF FINDINGS FROM PARTICIPANT INTERVIEWS

This chapter presents the themes that emerged from our interviews with the 79 participants across Texas and Ohio. Following a description of the total study sample, the discussion below then turns to participants' evaluation of their experience, their reasons for seeking to participate, a description and evaluation of their preparation for the meetings, a description of their mediation/dialogue meetings, and participants' reports of the impact it has had on their lives.

STUDY PARTICIPANTS

The 79 individuals who were interviewed participated in 47 mediation/dialogue sessions regarding 46 serious and violent crimes. Exactly half of the crimes involved murder or manslaughter; the victim died as a result of 65% of these crimes, including both murder/manslaughter and vehicular homicide. For 30 of the 46 crimes, both the participating victim/family member(s) and the offender were interviewed. For the remaining 16 crimes, only a single participant was interviewed.

The sample consisted of 20 victims/family members each from Texas and Ohio, 19 offenders from Texas, and 20 offenders from Ohio. The distribution of the crimes for each set of interviewees is given in Tables 11.1 and 11.2.

The victim sample included both direct victims of the crimes and family members of direct victims (Table 11.3). In Texas, only 10% of the victim interviewees were direct victims; the remaining 90% were surviving family members of a victim who had died. In Ohio, 35% of the victim interviewees were the direct victims.

Table 11.1: Study Sample: Summary by Crime Type

Crime	Texas Research Interviews			Ohio Research Interviews			Total	
	Victim & Offender	Offender only	Victim only	Victim & Offender	Offender only	Victim only	N	(% of crimes)
Murder/manslaughter	12	1	0	4	4	2	23	(50%)
Vehicular homicide	1	0	1	4	0	1	7	(15%)
Felony assault & attempted murder	0	1	0	3	1	1	6	(13%)
Sexual assault	3	1	1	2	1	0	8	(17%)
Theft & burglary	1	0	0	0	1	0	2	(4%)
Total	17	3	2	13	7	4	46	

Table 11.2: Participants Interviewed by Crime Type

| Crime | Texas | | | | | | Ohio | | | | | |
| | Events | | Victims | | Offenders | | Events | | Victims | | Offenders | |
	N	(%)	N	(%)	N	(%)	N	(%)	N	(%)	N	(%)
Murder/Manslaughter	13	(59%)	12	(60%)	13	(68%)	10	(42%)	6	(30%)	8	(40%)
Vehicular homicide	2	(9%)	2	(10%)	1	(5%)	5	(21%)	7	(35%)	4	(20%)
Assault	1	(5%)	1	(5%)	0	(0%)	5	(21%)	4	(20%)	4	(20%)
Sexual assault	5	(23%)	4	(20%)	4	(21%)	3	(13%)	3	(15%)	3	(15%)
Theft/burglary	1	(5%)	1	(5%)	1	(5%)	1	(4%)	0	(0%)	1	(5%)
Total	22		20		19		24		20		20	

Table 11.3: Relationship of Interviewee to Direct Crime Victim

	Texas		Ohio		Total	
	N	(%)	N	(%)	N	(%)
Direct victim	2	(10%)	7	(35%)	9	(22.5%)
Family member	18	(90%)	13	(65%)	31	(77.5%)
Parent	12	(60%)	7	(35%)	19	(47.5%)
Sibling	2	(10%)	3	(15%)	5	(12.5%)
Spouse	2	(10%)	1	(5%)	3	(7.5%)
Child	1	(5%)	2	(10%)	3	(7.5%)
Grandchild	1	(5%)	0	(0%)	1	(2.5%)

PARTICIPANT EVALUATION OF THE EXPERIENCE

The participant perspectives on their experience with mediation/dialogue in cases of violent crime that are offered below have an important context: overwhelmingly, these are satisfied participants. All but one of the 78 participants who were asked reported that they were satisfied, with 71 selecting the highest rating, "very satisfied." In addition, 73 participants were asked how helpful they found the meeting to be; all 73 found it helpful, and 65 gave it the highest ranking, "very helpful" (Tables 11.4 and 11.5).

The single participant who reported being "somewhat dissatisfied" was an offender who offered several comments on his reasons for the rating. He felt his mediators brought the meeting to a close too quickly, and, perhaps as a result, he felt he had been unable to adequately convey the changes he had made in his own life to the family member of his murder victim. He also found the meeting quite difficult because it took him back to his experience of the crime. Yet even this offender found the meeting "very helpful," in particular because he gained a new understanding of himself and the events of his crime, and he strongly recommended that other offenders participate. He called the meeting a "stepping stone" in his personal growth.

Table 11.4: Satisfaction with Involvement in the Program

| | Texas | | | | Ohio | | | | Total | |
| | Victims | | Offenders | | Victims | | Offenders | | | |
	N	(%)	N	(%)	N	(%)	N	(%)	N	(%)
Very satisfied	19	(95%)	18	(100%)	20	(100%)	14	(70%)	71	(91%)
Somewhat satisfied	1	(5%)	0		0		5	(25%)	6	(8%)
Somewhat dissatisfied	0		0		0		1	(5%)	1	(1%)
Very dissatisfied	0		0		0		0		0	
Total	20		18[a]		20		20		78	

a) One Texas offender was not asked this question.

Table 11.5: Helpfulness of the Meeting

| | Texas | | | | Ohio | | | | Total | |
| | Victims | | Offenders | | Victims | | Offenders | | | |
	N	(%)	N	(%)	N	(%)	N	(%)	N	(%)
Very helpful	15	(100%)	18	(100%)	14	(70%)	18	(90%)	65	(89%)
Somewhat helpful	0		0		6	(30%)	2	(10%)	8	(11%)
Not at all helpful	0		0		0		0		0	
Total	15[a]		18[a]		20		20		73	

a) This question was not asked in the first five Texas victim interviews and one Texas offender interview.

Satisfaction ratings were so high across the board that there is no substantial difference in satisfaction between the two programs. It is important to recognize that these high ratings are not generalizable to violent crime victims or offenders who have *not* sought or agreed to meet with one another. In many instances, these satisfaction levels reflect the opinions of persons who have made great efforts over long periods of time simply to have the opportunity to meet; at the very least, these are the opinions of persons who have agreed to such a meeting.

PARTICIPANT REASONS FOR SEEKING TO MEET

As clarified in chapter 1, victim offender mediation originated in response to less serious crimes as a means of offering offenders an opportunity to repair some of the harm their actions had caused and to have questions answered and receive appropriate restitution or compensation for their losses. The impetus to apply the victim offender dialogue process in serious and violent crimes came from victims who felt it would meet their needs. In the violent crimes covered in the present study, there is no possible repayment for losses the victim has incurred; 30 of the victims were dead as a result of the crime, and most of the rest had suffered physical and emotional harm as a result of assault. An important question guiding the research was, in the absence of the need to develop a concrete restitution plan, what are the reasons victims and offenders in such cases seek or choose to meet with one another in dialogue?

Most frequently, victims/family members seek information or answers (see Table 11.6). Twenty-three of the 40 listed this as one reason for seeking to meet. Often family members are meeting with the last person to have seen their relative alive; they may have questions about actual events, about the offender's explanations, about what their relative said or experienced, and about how the victim was selected.

Showing offenders the human impact of their actions was the next most frequent reason, named by 17 victims/family members. They want to tell their own story, and they want offenders to know who the person was that was harmed. Having some form of human contact with the person responsible for the crime was the third most frequent reason, named by 16. And 14 spoke of seeking to meet to help themselves heal or move towards closure.

Table 11.6: Victim/Family Member Reasons for Seeking To Meet with Offenders

	Texas	Ohio	Total	
			N	(%)
Seek information/answers	13	10	23	(58%)
Show impact of the crime	11	6	17	(43%)
Have a human, face to face interaction	8	8	16	(40%)
Advance victim healing	6	8	14	(35%)
Share forgiveness	5	4	9	(23%)
Seemed right, needed to do it	2	5	7	(18%)
Hold offender accountable	6	1	7	(18%)
General concern for the offender	—	7	7	(18%)
Find out if offender has remorse	—	7	7	(18%)
Prevent further crime	3	3	6	(15%)
Work out future relationship	1	4	5	(13%)
Decide to fight or support release	—	3	3	(8%)
To hear a 12-step Amends	1	1	2	(5%)
To seek specific restitution	1	—	1	(3%)
Help other victims	—	1	1	(3%)

The remaining reasons listed by victims were mentioned by 10 or fewer, and included to share forgiveness (9), that it seemed right (7), to hold the offender accountable (7), to learn if the offender is remorseful (7), out of general concern for the offender (7), to prevent further crime (6), to work out a future relationship with the offender (5), to decide whether to fight or support release (3), to hear a Twelve-Step amends (2), to seek specific restitution (1), and to help other victims (1).

Why would offenders agree to meet? There is no direct benefit to offenders for participation; it does not earn them any rewards within the institution and is not taken into consideration for parole decisions. Yet 14 of the 39 offenders in the present study reported that they themselves had taken steps to try to meet with their victims or family members, and all 39 ultimately agreed to participate in dialogue.

Nearly all the offenders interviewed (37 of 39) focused first on benefits to victims in describing their reasons for seeking or agreeing to meet (see Table 11.7). They wished to apologize (15), to help victims heal (15), to simply do whatever would benefit the victim (10), to answer questions (8), to offer victims the chance to release their anger (5), to make amends (5), to ease victims' fears (5), to take responsibility for their actions (4), to listen to whatever the victim needed to say (3), and to prepare for meeting the victim in the community after release (1).

Table 11.7: Offender Reasons for Agreeing To Meet with Victims/Family Members

	Texas	Ohio	Total	
			N	(%)
General/because it's right	5	—	5	(13%)
Benefits to victim	17	20	37	(95%)
Apologize [to benefit victim]	7	8	15	(38%)
Help them heal	7	8	15	(38%)
General benefit to victim	2	8	10	(26%)
Answer questions	5	3	8	(21%)
Help them release anger	3	2	5	(13%)
Make amends	—	5	5	(13%)
Reassure nothing to fear from Offender	3	2	5	(13%)
Take responsibility	4	—	4	(10%)
Listen to victim	3	—	3	(8%)
Prepare for meeting on outside	—	1	1	(3%)
Benefits to self	16	13	29	(74%)
Rehabilitation, healing	8	5	13	(33%)
Give info re self /change victim view	3	5	8	(21%)
Spiritual reasons	6	1	7	(18%)
Seek forgiveness	4	2	6	(15%)
Explain the truth	3	1	4	(10%)
Learn who victim was, get story	3	—	3	(8%)
Apologize [to feel better]	—	2	2	(5%)

Offenders were asked more explicitly if they hoped for benefits to themselves, and 29 of the 39 responded positively. The most frequently identified potential benefit to themselves was their own rehabilitation and recovery, named by 13. This was followed by hoping to change the victim or family member's view or opinion of themselves (8), general spiritual reasons (7), hoping to receive forgiveness (6), wanting to explain what happened or change the family member's perception about the crime (4), wanting to learn who the victim was (3), and wishing to apologize because it would make them feel better (2) (see Table 11.7).

There is an important finding hidden in the above data: For any given reason, there were a significant number of participants who reported *not* having that reason. Among the 40 victims/family members, a total of 17 did not seek answers, and over half did not talk about hoping or planning to share the impact of the crime as a reason to meet. For example, both of the victims who wished to hear an "amends" were themselves Twelve-Step participants and simply wished to permit a fellow traveler to make an important step in his own journey. One of these sessions was the shortest meeting across the entire research sample, at under one hour.

Outside of the general hope that victims would benefit, offenders were even more scattered than victims in their range of motives for meeting, with fewer than half reporting any given reason. Contrary to the general VOM practice with lesser crimes, not all offenders had admitted to everything they had been charged with; some specifically hoped to change the victim's understanding of what had happened. This wide range of motives for seeking to meet means that programs need to be flexible and responsive to individual participant needs.

PARTICIPANT EXPERIENCE AND EVALUATION OF PREPARATION TO MEET

As described elsewhere, the length and extent of the preparation process is one of the distinguishing features differentiating the Texas program from that in Ohio. Texas preparation averaged 16 months and ranged from 2 months to 35 months. The Texas program did not report data on the number of face-to-face meetings held with participants, but according to both victim/family members and offenders there were numerous such meetings, often held monthly. Ohio preparation averaged 4.5 months and ranged from 1 to 15 months; contact hours were tracked (including both face to face and telephone contact) and averaged 4.8 hours for victims and 3.9 hours for offenders.

Participant satisfaction with the manner in which they were prepared for the dialogues was high in both programs: 35 Ohio participants and 36 Texas participants reported being "very satisfied," and another four Ohio and two Texas participants reported being "somewhat satisfied" with their preparation process. Only a single participant, a Texas victim, was "somewhat dissatisfied." This participant, one of the two who wished only to hear an "amends," felt that the preparation materials and the length of preparation required were much too involved and elaborate for that simple goal. Additionally, one Ohio participant reported having received no preparation, despite program records that documented otherwise. Thus, across the entire research sample, a total of 77 participants (97% of those interviewed) were satisfied with their preparation (Table 11.8).

Mediator relationship qualities topped the list of helpful preparation elements, named by 31 participants. Offenders in particular commented about being treated with respect and consideration. Bringing information back and forth about participants during the preparation phase (27 participants) and explaining procedures and what to expect (21 participants) were the two next most helpful components common to both programs. The Texas program preparation process involved an extensive packet of reading materials and questionnaires not used by the Ohio program. These materials, in general, received high marks from Texas participants, 24 of whom named them as helpful, and 12 of whom further specified that the materials helped uncover important feelings. Other components common to both programs and named as helpful by fewer than 10 participants included planning goals and what to say, offering choices, envisioning risks, assuring safety, and mediator neutrality. The Texas components of coaching, role-play and watching videos were also named as helpful. Two victims/family members and two offenders, all from the Texas program, added that the preparation alone had been instrumental in their healing process even if they had never gotten to have a meeting.

Table 11.8: Satisfaction with Preparation for the Meeting

	Texas				Ohio				Total	
	Victims		Offenders		Victims		Offenders			
	N	(%)	N	(%)	N	(%)	N	(%)	N	(%)
Very satisfied	17	(85%)	19	(100%)	19	(95%)	16	(84%)	71	(91%)
Somewhat satisfied	2	(10%)	0		1	(5%)	3	(16%)	6	(8%)
Somewhat dissatisfied	1	(5%)	0		0		0		1	(1%)
Very dissatisfied	0		0		0		0		0	
Total	20		19		20		19[a]		78	

a) One offender reported not having received preparation, so was not asked to evaluate it.

Consistent with the high satisfaction levels, few participants had changes to recommend. Changing the paperwork topped the list; seven participants, across both programs, suggested reducing its complexity and making it more flexible and responsive to individual situations. Providing more specifics about what to expect (5 participants), using photographs with participant permission to prepare for what one another looked like (3 participants), allowing participants to assess their own readiness (3 participants), and reducing the length of the preparation process (3 participants) were the remaining suggested changes.

PARTICIPANT DESCRIPTIONS OF THE EXPERIENCE

Because the application of mediation/dialogue in violent crimes is so new, one of the important goals of the present study was simply to develop a picture of its characteristics. Table 11.9 provides an overview of the basic characteristics across the two programs.

Table 11.9: Mediation/Dialogue Characteristics

	Texas		Ohio	
	Range	Average	Range	Average
Length of time, crime to dialogue	2.3 years to 27 years	9.5 years	2 years to 19 years	9.6 years
Length of dialogue meeting	3 hours to 8.5 hours	5.5 hours	1 hour to 8 hours	2.5 hours
Persons present for meeting (excluding camera personnel)	3 to 5 persons	3.4 persons	3 to 8 persons	5.6 persons

One important distinction between these cases and VOM in less serious cases is the relatively long period of time between the crime and the dialogue. Because these programs are so new, it is not possible to discern from the present data to what extent this finding represents what victims would ideally chose to do, and to what extent it is an artifact of the absence of such a service during the first several years after these crimes occurred. Among the 40 victims/family members interviewed, 13 (32.5%) experienced a wish to meet their offender relatively soon after the crime and/or the trial. However, all of these victims/family members who commented on the elapsed time felt it was a good thing that the meeting hadn't taken place right away. They felt it was important that they'd had the additional time to heal, and that their meetings were more productive than if they'd taken place immediately. The remaining 27 victims/family members did not develop a wish to meet their offenders until much longer after the crime, and many had never thought about the possibility until they heard about the program from other sources.

Across the board, victims/family members and offenders described the process of the meeting as a conversation. The interaction was respectful, for the most part voices were not raised, participants did not interrupt one another, and much of the time the conversation simply flowed back and forth among participants unaided by any mediator action. Offenders, in particular, were surprised by the lack of shouting or rageful behavior on the part of victims and family members.

During the course of the research interviews, 37 victims/family members and 32 offenders described what they themselves shared during the meetings (Tables 11.10 and 11.11). Because this question was not routinely asked in all interviews, what follows is offered not as a representation of everything that happened, but rather as a description of what stood out to participants enough that they spontaneously mentioned it.

For victims and family members, the major focus was the impact of the crime: on themselves, on the direct victim (if different), and on other family members and persons connected to the victim. Participants in Texas spoke in addition of telling the story of their own experience of the crime. In the Ohio victims/family members interviews it was not possible to distinguish "telling the impact" from "telling the experience of the crime." A smaller subset of victim/family member participants reported asking questions and focusing on the offender. In three Ohio cases where the offender had not taken full responsibility, participants reported that they gave detailed information about the crime.

Table 11.10: What Victims/Family Members Reported Sharing

	Texas	Ohio	Total
Impact on victim	14	10	24
Impact on family member	13	6	19
Experience of the crime	16		16
Information about victim's life	9	6	15
Asked questions	9	4	13
Expectations for offender's future behavior	8	4	12
Information about the crime		3	3
Opinion about offender's punishment		2	2

Among offenders, sharing information about the crime headed the list, followed by information about their life before the crime. Smaller numbers reported taking ownership, apologizing, sharing other information about themselves, and assuring the safety of the victim/family member.

Table 11.11: What Offenders Reported Sharing

	Texas	Ohio	Total
Information about the crime	11	6	17
Information about their life before the crime	7	5	12
Took ownership/were accountable	6		6
Apologized	1	5	6
Shared feelings	3		3
Assured victim/family member safety	1		1

When they were asked to describe the role of the mediator, many participants seemed surprised and appeared not to have thought about mediator activity. It was as if the mediator faded largely into the background and was, for the most part, unnoticed. All 64 participants who commented on the mediator role described it as relatively silent. Mediators were quiet and stayed out of the way. Offenders and victims/family members alike deeply appreciated this unobtrusiveness. The mediator's background role meant that the participants themselves could own the process and could be sure that no one else had pushed for certain things to be said or accomplished.

Participants were clear that this did not mean the mediators' presence was unnecessary. They felt reassured that mediators would intervene if things "got out of hand" and would ensure participants' safety. Offenders and victims/family members commented on feeling the support and encouragement of the mediator. They felt connected to the mediators, and it was important to them that the other participants also felt connected. Mediator "neutrality" was more than passively not taking sides. Rather, it involved forging a supportive and trustworthy relationship with each side.

There was broad agreement on what kinds of actions mediators did take on the few occasions when they got involved. They helped remind participants of topics they had wanted to bring up, they helped steer the conversation if it lagged or got stuck, they asked questions, they supported the expression of feelings, they monitored participant needs and suggested breaks when appropriate, and they challenged offender avoidance. Participants' comments made clear that they did all these things in a manner which left choices up to participants, rather than in the hands of the mediators.

PARTICIPANTS' DESCRIPTIONS OF THE IMPACT ON THEIR LIVES

Assessing the outcome of the mediation/dialogue meetings is one of the most important single domains of the present study. Statewide correction departments and their victim services units have invested considerable resources in attempting to meet the needs of victims and provide what they are seeking as part of an effort to assist their recovery from the trauma of violent crime. Therefore, in addition to ascertaining satisfaction levels, the study sought to discern what impact participants felt the meetings had made in their lives.

Overall life changes were assessed using both a closed-ended Likert scale question, asked of 73 participants, and open-ended questions probing changes in internal feelings, healing and well being, and spiritual outlook, asked of all 79 participants. A total of 63 interviewees, or 80%

Table 11.12: Participants' Report of Major Life Changes

	Texas		Ohio		Total
	Victims	Offenders	Victims	Offenders	
	11/15	13/18	8/20	17/20	49/73
Number who reported "yes" to the question: "Has your overall outlook on life changed since meeting the offender/victim?"					
"Definitely more positive and at peace with the circumstances I am faced with"	11	11	6	13	41
"Somewhat more positive and able to cope with my life"		1	2	2	5
"Other positive change in outlook"		1		2	3
Additional participants who listed positive life changes	7	2	4	1	14
Total number of participants reporting major life changes	18	15	12	18	63/79 80%

of the research participants, reported that their participation in the mediation/dialogue program had a profound effect on their lives. Victims/family members and offenders alike reported feeling more at peace and better able to cope with their lives (Table 11.12).

The types of life changes reported by the 30 victims/family members are summarized in Table 11.13 below. Letting go of hate, obtaining answers, placing the anger where it belongs, having a human encounter, and/or experiencing the offender's ownership and remorse were reported as important factors.

Issues of forgiveness are often a flashpoint of controversy among victim advocates and victim services staff. Both the Texas and the Ohio programs make quite clear that forgiveness of the offender is not a goal of the program and that such decisions are left entirely up to the victim. During the research interviews, 24 of the victims/family members (60%) spontaneously spoke of forgiveness issues. Of these, a total of 15 reported that they had come to forgive their offender, either prior to meeting with them (10 participants) or during the meeting itself (5 participants). Another eight reported that they had not forgiven the offender; five felt they never would, while three had moved towards forgiveness and left open the possibility that they might some day do so.

Table 11.13: Victim/Family Member Report of Types of Life Changes

Types of Life Changes	Texas	Ohio	Total Victims	
			N	(%)
Contributed to personal growth and healing	14	10	24	(60%)
Changed feelings about offender for the better	13	10	23	(58%)
Change in outlook for the better	11	8	19	(48%)
Changed or strengthened spirituality	9	8	17	(43%)

Types of life changes reported by the 33 offenders are summarized in Table 11.14. As with forgiveness, offender rehabilitation is not a goal of either the Texas program or the Ohio program. Both programs are victim-driven and are very careful not to put any pressure on victims to make a difference in offender lives. Thus, it is especially noteworthy that over 80% of the offenders who participated in our study reported that the meetings had, in fact, contributed to their own rehabilitation and personal growth.

Table 11.14: Offender Report of Types of Life Changes

Types of Life Changes	Texas	Ohio	Total Offenders	
			N	(%)
Contributed to rehab/personal growth and healing	15	17	32	(82%)
Change in outlook for the better	13	17	30	(77%)
Changed or strengthened spirituality	12	12	24	(62%)
Think victim feelings about them changed for the better	12	6	18	(46%)

In discussing reasons for these changes, offenders pointed to being accountable, seeing their victim as a person, understanding the impact of their actions, being able to give something back, and being more open to feelings. One of these domains was explored more fully in the structured component of the study interview schedule. Thirty-eight of the 40 offenders were asked to what extent their meeting with their victim/family member changed their understanding of how the crime impacted others. Responses are given in Table 11.15.

It is important in examining these results not to lose sight of the 20% of the study participants who did not report a life-changing outcome from their mediation/dialogue session. All of the 10 victims and six offenders who did not report any changes in their lives as a result of the mediation/dialogues were nonetheless satisfied with their experience in the program, with 15 of the 16 rating their satisfaction at the "very satisfied" level.

Table 11.15: Extent to which the Meeting Changed Offender Understanding of How the Crime Impacted Others

	Texas		Ohio		Total	
	N	(%)	N	(%)	N	(%)
A great deal	17	(94%)	14	(70%)	31	(82%)
Somewhat	1	(6%)	5	(25%)	6	(16%)
Not at all	0		1	(5%)	1	(2%)
Total	18	(100%)	20	(100%)	38	(100%)

All 10 of these victims offered comments on their life perspectives. Nine felt that they had already made significant changes before seeking mediation, including progress toward healing and closure from the harm caused by the crime. Their decisions to seek a meeting with their offender grew out of these changes, and they neither anticipated nor experienced significant further impact on their lives. The tenth victim who reported no change was one who simply wished to hear an amends.

Among the six offenders who did not report any life-changing impact from their meeting with their victim, three had no further comments about changes in their lives. Two reported that they had already changed their life outlook prior to agreeing to meet. And one reiterated that he had focused on what his victim needed and neither expected nor received any impact for himself.

One last component of measuring the impact of the mediation/dialogue on participants lives is to explore the question, "was anyone harmed by their participation?" Two domains were examined to help answer this question. The first was the extent to which interviewees reported having regrets about their participation. Across the 79 interviews, only a single participant reported having any regrets about participating in the mediation/dialogue. This was an offender who, despite his very high satisfaction with his participation and his positive assessment of its impact on his life, nonetheless feared that in some way the state might use his participation against him and negatively impact his case.

The second domain raised the question of whether as a result of their participation any interviewees may have received negative consequences that they would not otherwise have incurred. The only potential negative consequences which could be discerned from the information shared by both victims and offenders were outcomes affecting two offenders. For one offender, confidentiality regarding his case was breached when the victim's family member used real names in a presentation at which a reporter was present. For another offender (who was not interviewed), the participating victim reported that, as a result of the meeting, she would continue to fight the offender's parole. This latter case may in fact not be an instance of harm; the victim in this case already was in opposition to the offender's release, and simply did not change her position.

CONCLUSION

These 79 participants have provided us a window into the phenomenon of victim offender dialogue in serious and violent crime, offering us their reasons for seeking or agreeing to meet, their experience before and during the meeting, their descriptions of its impact on their lives, and their evaluation of their participation. All of these domains have important implications for the future delivery of mediation/dialogue services in cases of violent crime, which will be taken up in chapter 13.

CHAPTER 12.
AN EMERGING TYPOLOGY OF PROGRAMS

Data gathered from staff and volunteers in the Texas and Ohio programs fairly quickly made it clear that while the two programs offered the same essential service of providing a safe encounter for violent crime victims and their offenders, there were a number of differences between them in philosophy, emphasis, and operation. In order to provide a broader context for understanding these differences and moving toward developing program and policy recommendations, we interviewed mediators from three smaller-scale programs also offering mediated dialogue for victims of violent crime. These three programs are sufficiently similar to one another that we consider them to share a single approach, which we label for these purposes "the humanistic framework." A summary report from these interviews is provided in Appendix B, "Humanistic Dialogue: A Practitioner Perspective."

Information from these five sources led us to begin to develop a typology of approaches to mediated dialogue in serious and violent crime. By moving the analysis to typology construction, we hope to identify elements that make types and approaches somewhat distinct from one another. To the extent that we can tease out differences as well as recognize common ground, decision makers and practitioners should be in a better position to make informed decisions about what kinds of approaches best fit their own orientation, needs, and limited resources.

While the typology offered below is empirically informed, no doubt many more variations and combinations occur in practice than we have been able to discern in this limited study. Nonetheless, we believe it helpful to program development and practice to recognize commonalties and differences across approaches. There is no single way, and there is no best way of doing victim-sensitive dialogue with survivors of violent crime. There are different ways driven by the orientation of staff and possibly by the auspices under which a program functions.

Description of the Proposed Typology

A typology is an analytic construct that enables observers to identify and parse out characteristics and dimensions that shape and define an ideal type. Ideal types are abstractions that do not exist in their pure form. Rather, they are derived by making theoretical inferences based upon empirical observations.

All three of the approaches we sampled share in common the objectives of ensuring that the victim and offender freely choose to meet and of creating a safe environment in which face-to-face dialogue can occur. Three additional objectives were shared across the programs to a lesser extent: (1) assisting victims and offenders with healing and grief ("therapeutic" objective); (2) encouraging victims and offenders to own and share their own stories of the impact of violence and loss as a result of the crime ("narrative" objective); and (3) empowering particularly victims, but also offenders, to claim and obtain what they need by meeting face-to-face with one another ("empowerment" objective). These objectives need not be mutually exclusive. For example, telling one's story may also be a healing experience, and even partial healing may lead to empowerment. Yet in practice, the approaches we studied each tended to emphasize one objective more than others. It was this finding which led us to begin to think about developing a typology.

A typology often consists of a number of ideal types differentiated by underlying characteristics, dimensions and/or continua. The typology described here is constructed around three underlying dimensions related to the overarching objectives referred to above. We have labeled them "therapeutic," "narrative," and "empowerment." Each represents a focus of an approach in theory and practice. In our interviews with program staff and volunteers, these three foci were identified as pivotal to mediated dialogue in violent crime. The importance of any one of these in relation to the others had major implications for staffing, preparation, length of preparation, and the actual victim offender dialogue. We found that emphasis along these foci differed across the programs in Ohio, Texas, and those practicing within the humanistic framework. If we had studied a dozen approaches, we expect that these three foci would have remained significant; but possibly even more variations among them might have been discovered, and additional foci may have been identified as well.

In theory, one of these foci is dominant or primary in each approach. In the proposed typology each focus or dimension is rank-ordered first, second or third. If we consider these foci in their ideal form, we can begin to construct a typology of ideal types (see Table 12.1). For example, Type I would have therapeutic as the dominant focus. Narrative would be the dominant focus for Type II, and empowerment would be dominant in Type III. Within each type would exist the possibility of two sub-types, depending on the rank order of the remaining two foci. For example with Type I there would be the possibility of (1) therapeutic, (2) narrative, (3) empowerment; and, (1) therapeutic, (2) empowerment, (3) narrative. Other dimension combinations can be imagined if one allows for the possibility of tied rankings.

Table 12.1: Victim Offender Dialogue Typology in Crimes of Severe Violence

| | Ideal Types | | |
	Type I Therapeutic	**Type II** Narrative	**Type III** Empowerment
Rank-ordered foci	Therapeutic Narrative Empowerment	Narrative Empowerment Therapeutic	Empowerment Narrative Therapeutic
Approximate examples	VOM/D Texas	Humanistic Approach Minnesota, Iowa, Wisconsin	VOD Ohio

We define these foci as dimensions rather than continua largely because of "level of measurement" issues. At present the three objectives are ordinal-level variables, in that it can be discerned whether one program places more emphasis on a given objective than another program. In order to establish a continuum, we would have to be able to measure how *much* more, with interval- or ratio-level measures. For example, we would need to be able to determine that a particular program or approach scored, let us say, 70 on the narrative continuum compared to a score of 80 for another program. That level of measurement is not available to us, at least at this time. In part, the present effort to identify and describe ideal types is one component of the groundwork necessary to facilitate the potential for such specificity in the future if it is desired.

However, relying on the qualitative data generated by interviewing staff and mediators we are able to make judgments regarding whether a program places more weight, in general, on empowerment than on narrative or therapeutic. Thus we can rank order the foci within each program, providing us with an approximation of where a given program can fit within the typology. For example, if staff and mediators in Program A point to empowerment as the dominant focus of their work, then it would be placed under Type III. And we could determine further whether the remaining foci are ordered as narrative, therapeutic or therapeutic, narrative.

In the real world there will exist variations within programs. There may be differences in focus across staff and mediators. There also may be differences across cases. Yet, we submit that there will exist central tendencies within a given program across staff and mediators and across cases which will permit empirical assessment and classification vis-à-vis the typology.

ILLUSTRATIONS OF THE PROPOSED TYPOLOGY

To illustrate the use of the typology as a descriptive analytic tool we will classify the three program types we sampled and consider some of the differences across approaches. The reader must keep in mind that none of these programs/approaches are true ideal types. They are much more blurry than that. What we are suggesting is that each program/approach best approximates a particular type that underscores, again, the range, diversity and richness of victim offender dialogue practice in violent crime.

We will look at purpose, training of mediators, preparation of victim and offender and length of preparation, conduct of meeting and length of meeting, and follow-up and case closure across Texas, Ohio and the humanistic approach used in Minnesota, Iowa and Wisconsin. Based on interviews with staff and mediators we have classified the approaches in the following way: Texas — Type I — therapeutic, narrative, empowerment; Minnesota, Iowa and Wisconsin — Type II — narrative, empowerment, therapeutic; Ohio — Type III — empowerment, narrative, therapeutic. We are much more concerned, here, with the dominant or primary focus — that is, with which focus is ranked number one — than with the second and third rankings, which provide a picture of the sub-type. And it is important to stress that the rank-ordering we have provided is our own assessment based on the information shared with us by staff and volunteers, and may not reflect how programs would chose to present themselves.

The relative emphasis placed by programs on these three foci has implications for the program purpose, the training of mediators, the preparation of participants, the characteristics of the dialogue meetings, and the handling of case follow up and closure.

Purpose

In Texas, "the purpose of the process is healing," according to Doerfler. "While it is not therapy, it's very therapeutic." Victims continue to grieve the loss of loved ones and may be consumed by anger. Offenders suffer from feelings of guilt, rage, and hopelessness. It is hoped that by getting victims and offenders to look at themselves, to feel themselves — their strengths and fears, their joy and their pain — that they will be freed up to share their stories and thereby advance their own healing. A staff/volunteer notes, "We can't dictate when these things are going to happen to the people we work with…we give them lots of tools, but they are really the architects of their own healing." As we have shown in chapter 4, the Texas approach places much power in the mediator's hands to determine what a victim or offender should do before being ready to mediate. For many observers, vesting such power in the mediator means not empowering the victim or the offender. Doerfler countered: "We're not just facilitators — it's much more a therapeutic model. There is no doubt about that, but I think we're empowering people that much more." In other words, empowerment is understood to be a result of self-awareness and healing.

When we consider the purpose of the program, healing is at the center of the Texas approach: i.e., if individuals can become self-aware, own their feelings no matter how terrible, they will grow, be able to share their stories, and be further empowered. We therefore classify this approach as approximating Type I.

As we turn to the approach used by practitioners in Minnesota, Iowa and Wisconsin (see Appendix B), we see the dominance of the narrative objective of sharing the story. Wisconsin's Bruce Kittle stated, "To me the goal is to create a safe place for the storytelling to happen; all the other stuff grows out of that." Similarly, Minnesota's Umbreit commented, the objective is to "create a safe place, if not a sacred place, where people can tell their story. Where they can share the pain and have it acknowledged." For Iowa's Betty Brown, through telling their stories victims "find a voice." Offenders, too, may experience relief by "sharing a very hurtful experience."

There is the hope that by helping participants share their stories, they will be better able to integrate that horrific experience and better continue on with life. Mediators listen as individuals tell their stories. They may ask some questions to help elicit those stories, but there is much emphasis on listening to hear what the victim and the offender want out of meeting with the other. Each of the practitioners interviewed within this approach made it clear that they were not working with a therapeutic model, although the experience might be therapeutic for victim and offender.

Within the humanistic framework, story telling or narrative is at the center. Therefore we classify it as approximating Type II. Since we only interviewed three individuals using this approach, the sub-type may vary by individual. For example, it is quite likely that Brown would emphasize empowerment over the therapeutic sub-type. Kittle's attention to grief work may suggest that he would put the therapeutic over the empowerment sub-type. But, both use story as their primary focal point.

In Ohio, Karen Ho regarded her program primarily as attempting to "empower victims and offenders to meet immediate needs by meeting face-to-face in a safe environment." Facilitators help victims and offenders define their own needs and wants as they anticipate meeting the other. The facilitator will work to see that the meeting is safe for all involved. Victim or offender needs may be quite broad and may involve sharing stories of the impact of the crime, or they might be quite focused around a single question or two. It is for the victim and the offender to decide the scope of the meeting. "I think that the great thing about it," said a facilitator, "is just the process is not ours, it's theirs." Another indicated, "Much of our goal is to help (the victim and offender) keep on track."

Words such as healing and closure were seldom heard as we talked with staff and volunteers in the Ohio program. Karin Ho was doubtful that these are realistic goals for a short-term program. And both words raise suspicions among various victim advocacy groups. Victims are involved in a "healing journey" that is likely life-long. Ho hoped that her work contributes in some way to those journeys. But primarily she cautioned, "we're just simply listening to their needs (at the moment) and trying to do the best we can to fulfill them. They will have several more steps or chapters to go through."

We classify the Ohio approach as approximating Type III, empowerment, with the sub-types ranked as narrative first, and therapeutic second. Even the title "facilitator" was chosen over "mediator" to underscore this empowering theme in the Ohio program.

One might contend that statements regarding purpose are basically philosophical and may have little to do with actual practice. Based on interviews with staff and volunteers regarding practice, we believe there is a fairly strong relationship between purpose and how persons working within the various approaches go about implementing victim-sensitive offender dialogue.

Training

Training in Texas and Ohio was described as "intense" and "extremely helpful" by those respondents with whom we spoke. A primary focus in the Texas training is on stimulating volunteer self-awareness. As Doerfler stated, "we want each mediator to go through the preparation work as if a victim or an offender." Each mediator is interviewed twice before training and will write "their own life story and discuss what motivates them, what gives them strength, and where their spirituality lies." A staff member stated, "We force them to look at themselves." Volunteers complete the same grief inventory which victims and offenders are expected to work through.

This focus on feeling, "on the heart," helps trainees "work through baggage," freeing them up to focus on victim and offender issues and not be hooked into their own problems. The training experiences mirrored, in many respects, the ways of working with victim offender dialogue. That included learning to trust the process and to know that the work is ongoing. As one mediator stated, "there was day one (of training), but there hasn't been a last day yet." Such an explicit emphasis upon self-awareness and personal growth, we suggest, flows very naturally from an overarching therapeutic approach.

The Ohio five-day training experience was also described by participants as intense, useful and helpful. Yet the flavor of that training experience seems less personal and more focused specifically on what one needs to know about the system policies and procedures, victimization experiences, and inmate experiences in order to facilitate victim offender dialogue. Videos of actual dialogues and mock scenarios are used and well received by participants.

A number of corrections staff indicated that this training "was the richest" they had ever received. One mediator pointed out that having worked with offenders for years, very little is shocking. Yet with victim survivors there is a "need to know (that) what and how we say something may offend or upset them."

We expect that Ohio's training emphasizing practical "hows," "dos" and "don'ts" is a reflection of its empowerment focus. Mediators must know how best to work within the system, and with victims and offenders, to make it possible to provide choices for dialogue participants.

While training was not a major topic during our interviews with practitioners in Minnesota, Iowa and Wisconsin, we do know from brief discussions and our review of training manuals that the emphasis is upon helping potential mediators center themselves so they may listen deeply to the stories of victims and offenders and when needed to assist in eliciting those stories.

Preparation

When we look at the scope and length of preparation, it appears that the Texas model with its therapeutic emphasis requires more time and expects more work from both the victim and offender. Preparation at the time of our study usually required one to three years and was often seen as the most significant part of the overall process. The face-to-face meeting is but one point on a "continuum of care." Victims and offenders are provided with a vast array of tools, including grief inventories, exercises for exploring feelings, opportunities for journaling, readings on forgiveness and many more. The process involves numerous meetings with both parties giving them ample opportunity to explore feelings, to grieve and to grow.

A determination that victim and offender are ready to meet is certainly shared among the parties, but the mediator seems to exercise more power over this decision in Texas than in the other approaches. This would be consistent with a therapeutic approach that tries to maximize the growth potential of the process. Clearly, victims, eager to meet, can be put off by claiming that the offender is not yet ready to meet. One mediator, reflecting this therapeutic orientation, thought that a case was about ready to meet because "we're not going to get any farther. I'm getting into a place where I feel this one is ripe." Another indicated that "his goal" for the victim was to express her anger. Throughout preparation, according to Doerfler, one tries to move the participants to a next level, wherever that might be. "That goes back to that understanding of healing," he says, "(of) not trying to lock them in."

We do need to keep in mind that within this approach, in Doerfler's words, "the meeting is not necessarily the apex of the process." Other mediators echoed this theme as well. Doerfler explained further, "if you go in (throughout preparation) and you start asking questions, not giving them answers, but eliciting their stories, their feelings, they walk away and say 'Goll, this is the best thing that ever happened.' And it seems to me that's very significant."

Length of preparation among the practitioners from Minnesota, Iowa and Wisconsin ranges from six to 18 months. The longer waits are often caused by difficulties with system timetables and having the victims define what they need. Early stages of preparation focus on "storytelling and trying to get clear what happened." Brown, Kittle and Umbreit emphasized the importance of listening. According to Umbreit, to listen deeply is to "embrace the incredible healing power of storytelling" and helps the mediator "create a safe place, a real deep sense of safety where the involved parties can be vulnerable with each other."

Preparation will likely involve several meetings with the victim and at least a few with the inmate. Some of these latter may be phone contacts. The stories and the hopes of victim and offender are known and shared (with permission) with the other "so there is no secret what we are going to talk about."

Readiness to meet is determined by all the participants. As Umbreit noted, however, "Ultimately and honestly, you trust your gut. The reason multiple meetings are needed is not just for the parties, it is for you too. It is very important as the mediator or facilitator to feel comfortable and ready to go. You are part of the process." Kittle presses offenders, perhaps more than victims, to do the work, particularly around the impact of the crime. He indicated that while he has a time frame in his head, he continually checks in with the victim and offender regarding their self-evaluation of readiness. Cases with relatively brief preparatory periods that have worked out very well serve to remind him "to trust the process."

"No surprises," is the refrain among Ohio facilitators. The focus of preparation within this empowerment-oriented approach is to clarify with the victim and offender what they want to get out of the dialogue. That may be an opportunity to share their story surrounding the crime, or it may be getting a single question answered. A second component of this focus is to assure that the dialogue will occur in a safe environment where the victim will not be re-victimized nor the offender unduly accosted. Both components require the sense that there will be no surprises tossed out during the dialogue. Facilitators need to push the "hot buttons" of fear, anxiety or rage that may, if unacknowledged beforehand, disrupt the dialogue.

Each participant is typically seen at least twice before the dialogue takes place. Sometimes this is not possible because of travel distance, so phone contact is maintained. Victims often feel that they are ready to meet "right away." Karin Ho indicated that part of the choice to meet rests with the facilitator and in part that decision is a matter of "gut instinct." She elaborated that participants are ready "when it looks like they're reasonably emotionally ready making for a safe environment and when the victim and offender feel like they know what to expect and are prepared to deal with the other's questions."

Most cases in Ohio will likely take to three to four months of preparation. Each case is, however, unique. In a case that required only one month of preparation, the facilitator expressed an empowerment philosophy: "I kept thinking it's too quick, it's too quick. But then I thought, you know, if they know what they want and if the offender is able to address what the victim wants and the victim is ready to address what the offender wants, then I think they're ready, and once ready, I don't want them getting frustrated by unnecessary delays."

In a contrasting situation, a dialogue was delayed to assure that the offender was not "obsessed with the victim. Our main goal was to make sure that it was a safe environment."

Empowerment does not mean giving either the victim or the offender power to abuse the other. As one facilitator states, "If we don't see or sense that there's going to be a good outcome for both (victim and offender) then it (dialogue) doesn't happen."

The relatively brief preparatory period in Ohio, we believe, is a function of their empowerment oriented approach. Less time is required to discern what participants want and to assure a safe environment than if one were explicitly motivated by a more therapeutic oriented approach geared toward personal growth and healing. These may be welcomed by-products of the Ohio approach, but they are not its primary goal.

Characteristics of the Dialogue Meeting

As noted above, in Texas the mediation meeting is regarded as one point, albeit an important point, on a continuum of care. Even in those cases in which no meeting ever occurs, it is strongly believed that significant work often takes place. Said one mediator, "I don't think the focus is on the mediation. I think the focus is entirely on working with the people, helping them work through what happened. And if the mediation happens, that's wonderful. That's an incredible, wonderful by-product." Mediators and facilitators working within the two other frameworks would likely agree to a certain extent with this sentiment. Within a narrative approach, helping individuals claim and tell their story may be pivotal in and of itself. Within the empowerment approach, encouraging victims and survivors to make and own their choices will likely have some lasting impact. But none interviewed were as strongly convinced about the mediation being an important by-product of preparatory work as those in Texas.

The three approaches follow similar protocols for the actual meeting, beginning with the opening comments by the mediator/facilitator welcoming participants and reaffirming the guidelines for the meeting. That is usually followed by a statement by either the offender or victim, generally at the choice of the victim. An exchange or dialogue will then occur which may or may not evolve into some restorative steps ranging from an apology to whatever the participants agree upon. The flow is quite interactive within each approach. In Ohio, the victim may not want to make a statement, and may simply begin with the question or questions to which answers are sought.

Mediators/facilitators across the approaches employ a non-directive style during the meeting unless something out of the ordinary occurs, or a victim may have asked to be reminded about a point if it was forgotten, or if people become quite stuck (which seldom happens).

There is considerable variation among the approaches in terms of duration of the actual dialogue meeting. Two to three hours and one to three hours are the typical expectations in the humanistic and Ohio approaches, respectively. In contrast, meetings conducted in Texas range from three to eight hours, with five and a half hours being standard. We expect that this difference can also be attributed to the more well defined focus on healing within the Texas approach.

Follow-Up and Closure

Individuals within each of the three approaches struggle with the notion of follow-up and closing a case. De-briefing on the day of the meeting and some sort of follow-up within a week or a month or some set time frame are carried out by staff or volunteers regardless of their program type. As might be expected, the clearest closings occur in Ohio, where the defined purpose of the meeting is most narrowly circumscribed. The participants have been empowered to meet and deal with questions and issues related to the crime event. Within a month after the meeting, it is expected that the case will be closed. Follow-up contact, often by phone, will have been made with both the victim and the offender. A facilitator stated quite clearly the expectation regarding follow-up and closure: "It'd be nice to pick up the phone and say how you doing? But this is a one-time thing and we're not there to encourage relationships and to continue to be a conduit between the two. Hopefully, everyone is up front about it at the beginning; this is a one time deal." If at a later point, the victim desires additional assistance that individual would be referred to the appropriate component of the Office of Victim Services.

Within the narrative approach, follow-up and closure are a bit more fluid. It appears that while it is desirable for a case to be closed within a couple months after mediation, sporadic contact may occur as additional questions and issues arise. These contacts may result in referral to other community resources or even in a follow-up mediation. Such follow-up mediations are "victim-driven." This still remains a gray area. Brown, for example, is working with some victim/survivors who want to establish a continuing support group. And even though Kittle acknowledges that he must move on to other cases, he still remains open: "I am always there by phone, if they need me."

Follow-up and closure are much more of a wrenching dilemma within the Texas program. With its therapeutic emphasis, there is reluctance to close any case. To do so would be like walking away from people who still carry pain and harbor shame. The healing journey does not end with mediation. Volunteers and staff talk of the intense ties developed with victims and/or offenders that are long lasting. Doerfler said, "We don't know how to close a case yet." While another staff person declared, "Closed isn't a word we know!" Extensive follow-up often occurs with the victim and with the offender. For example, Doerfler was asked by offenders to be present at their executions. Such requests speak profoundly to very powerful, intimate relationships.

The agony is palpable as staff and volunteers consider how they might plausibly close a case. On the one hand is the desire, because of limited resources and the need to show "productivity" to outside sources, to move on and count a case as closed. On the other is the overpowering worry that maybe one more contact would have helped a person to the next level of healing.

By reexamining purpose, training, preparation, meeting, and follow-up and closure across the three approaches, we hope to have shown some of the commonalties as well as differences. We also believe that one can see fairly clearly the relationship between dominant focus — that is, therapeutic, narrative and empowerment — and actual practice. These descriptions allow us to classify these approaches in terms of the developing typology.

CONCLUSION

We have attempted, here, to elevate our analysis from pure descriptive case analysis to the construction of a typology of approaches to mediated dialogue in violent crime. We hope thereby to encourage others who are currently offering or hoping to offer such services to assess their own practice and conceptual framework. We believe sorting out where one fits within such a typology may help clarify purpose and practice as well as draw out implications regarding resources needed.

Again, we reiterate that this typology is in its nascent stage. To the extent it has utility for assessing practice and stimulating thought and discussion regarding mediated dialogue in violent crime, it should be considered. To the extent that it does not, it should be scrapped. Such is the nature of typologies. Given that they revolve around ideal constructs, the utility of any given typology may be brief. For example, we have dwelt upon three main types. If more research is done in this area, additional types will likely be found. This typology, at the moment, is seriously limited by having drawn upon so few cases/approaches.

We conclude with a cautionary note. It should be clear that none of the approaches studied here — in Texas, Ohio, or the humanistic framework — are pure types. They each approximate a particular type. While we believe each emphasizes a specific focus, and that each emphasis has implications for practice and resource utilization, each approach blends to lesser or greater extent the three foci identified. Further, nothing said here should be construed to suggest that one approach or one type, for that matter, is "better" than another. Each approximate type may be best suited for certain jurisdictions and individuals. There may, for example, be important differences across jurisdictions in the types of violent crime cases being handled, making one type more desirable than another. Each type will likely place varying demands on staff and volunteer time and on resource allocation within a given jurisdiction. We hope that this analysis may assist decision makers in determining the kind of approach that is best suited to their particular needs, goals, and resources.

CHAPTER 13.
CONCLUSIONS AND IMPLICATIONS

Our introductory chapter — and indeed, the very existence of victim offender dialogue services for victims of violent crime — began with victims. We would like to begin our concluding chapter with a composite of what we think they had to tell us about this important service.

Victims would like the service to be available for any violent crime victims who wish it, to be easily accessible, and not to be costly for them. They know that not every victim of violent crime wishes to meet the offender, and they believe participation should be not only voluntary for victims but in fact, exclusively victim-initiated. Most of them also believe that dialogue should be voluntary for offenders, though there were minority voices who felt it should be a victim's right to meet, regardless of offender wishes.

Victims would like to be in the hands of highly competent mediators who take time to get to know them, who listen profoundly, who validate their feelings and experience, who help them identify what they want to accomplish, and who then step out of the way during the actual dialogue, so that the participants themselves can own the process. They want certain safeguards in place: a physically safe meeting, with respectful conversation, no harm to themselves or the offenders, and no negative surprises. The victims we spoke with know that much of the safety they experienced grew out of the preparation process — both the preparatory work they themselves carried out with their mediators, and the extensive relationship building the mediators had engaged in with offenders. They want mediators not only who are impartial, but even more, who are able to connect deeply with both the victim and the offender, so that both parties feel safe and supported.

Victims in our study have great respect for the role of the passage of time: in their healing process in general, and in the process of creating a successful dialogue. Many who would never have considered such a meeting in the immediate aftermath of the crime changed their minds over the years. And some who experienced minor frustration with how long it took to reach the dialogue stage once they sought a meeting were grateful later. They felt the deliberateness of the preparation process permitted them to sort through and identify their needs and wishes in ways that would never have been possible in a vastly shortened time span.

We have begun with the victim composite because the service is victim driven. But our study examined in equal measure the voice of offender participants. A composite of what offenders told us would be identical on almost all points, although there were some offenders who wished the meeting could count towards parole, and some who wished they could initiate such meetings themselves. Even more than victims, offenders were struck with the quality of the relationship the mediators developed with them. The trust, respect, openness and caring they encountered was rare in the rest of their institutional experience, and for many, rare in their lives.

The offenders we spoke with would encourage other offenders to accept offers to meet with victims. First and foremost, they think this will help victims, and they see it as a way offenders can give something back, however small. But most also believe that such meetings will have a major impact on their drive to not reoffend, for a number of reasons. Accountability to a person rather than an institution, expanded personal and detailed recognition of the harm they have caused, and openness to both the victim's feelings and their own feelings were the major components they felt would make a difference. In addition, for some of them, the victim's investment in their future became an even more personal reason to change their behavior.

In the recommendations below we have attempted to tease out the policy and program implications of what we have learned. As restorative justice in general, and victim offender mediation and dialogue in particular, gain increasing acceptance around the globe, we believe it is crucial that these voices be heard.

As Howard Zehr (2002) points out, there are many unanswered questions and critical issues facing the field at this point in its history, precisely because of its growing acceptance. The service of victim offender dialogue was begun as a response to juvenile crime and has largely continued to be seen as appropriate in less serious cases. There is grave danger that continuing to focus only on its role in lighter cases will serve to further marginalize the restorative justice movement rather than to help it move into the mainstream. Responding to the requests of victims of severe violence to meet the offender clearly represents "deep" restorative justice practice that can be transformative for all involved. It moves far beyond what we refer to as "restorative justice lite" and its near-exclusive focus on low risk and quite minor offenses, many of which would have been ignored by the justice system and would have self-corrected on their own.

Victim offender dialogue in serious and violent crime is still largely uncharted territory and there remains much to be learned. We believe however that it is both possible and advisable to continue to develop and expand this important service. As additional states consider developing policies to provide opportunities for interested victims of severe violence to meet with the offender/inmate, we offer the following recommendations for consideration. These are not meant to be rigid recommendations that offer the final authoritative word on the subject. Rather, these recommendations are offered in a spirit of providing a framework for ongoing dialogue in the field toward shaping a process that minimizes unintended negative consequences and that can consistently be transformative for crime victims, offenders, family members and other support people in their search for meaning and healing.

We first present three policy recommendations that address broader issues facing the field as an increasing amount of restorative justice policy is being developed in states through out the country. Seven implications for practice are then offered. Together, these implications for policy and practice that grow out of our four-year research project are meant to be a starting point for framing the discussion, not an exhaustive and definitive list of recommendations.

Policy Implications

1. *Departments of corrections should consider developing specific procedures for responding to the requests of those victims who seek a mediation/dialogue session with the responsible inmate.*

The data that emerged from the present study, as well as an examination of the history of victims of severe violence seeking to meet their offenders, clearly indicate that far more individuals in American society are interested in meeting the person responsible for their trauma than had been initially envisioned. This is not to say that the majority of victims of severe violence would want to face their offender for the purpose of a dialogue. It is clear that most such victims of violence still remain uninterested in ever participating in a meeting with the offender, and this reality should be accepted and the choices of these individuals honored.

2. *Public funding should be appropriated to support the development and management of victim-sensitive offender dialogue services in crimes of severe violence.*

To date, very little public funding has supported program development and case service provision in this field. Small amounts of private funding and/or state or federal funding have helped cover the cost of program development, training, and coordinating volunteer mediators/facilitators. It has become clear that the demand for victim offender dialogue in crimes of severe violence is far greater than the supply of adequately trained facilitators and functioning programs. Crime is fundamentally an issue of community safety. Public policy must focus on providing the resources necessary to assist those citizens whose lives have been devastated by violent crime. This recommendation pertains to both victim assistance services in general and victim offender dialogue for those victims who request it specifically.

3. *Consideration should be given to amending current state crime victim compensation laws to allow reimbursement for the cost of victim-initiated mediation/dialogue services with the responsible inmate.*

We view such compensation as appropriate when such an encounter is clearly related to victims' healing process and when such services are provided only by mediators who can document that they have received advanced training in providing victim-sensitive offender dialogue services in crimes of severe violence. While there is naturally no fee charged to victims for the service, most victims incur considerable expense in the process of preparing to meet and actually meeting the offender. Mediators/facilitators are not always able to travel to the victim's location for preparation meetings, and dialogue sessions are held in whatever facility the offender is incarcerated in. Sometimes these sessions involve the expense of an overnight stay in addition to the extensive travel, and often the process requires taking substantial time off from work. Existing crime victim compensation laws allow for reimbursement for a range of services, including medical expenses and therapy. Victim offender dialogue services could be added to the list of reimbursable services.

Practice Implications

1. *Only persons who can document that they have received extensive advanced training in victim-sensitive offender dialogue in crimes of severe violence, and who are under the supervision and support of an appropriate mentor or supervisor, should be allowed to provide such services.*

The restorative justice field has grown extensively over the years, both in North America and abroad. Similarly, the field of alternative dispute resolution and mediation has grown extensively and is used in a wide range of conflicts, though primarily in civil court. There could be a temptation for some mediation practitioners to assume that their current level of training is quite sufficient for mediating any type of conflict. This may be particularly so among those who have experience with victim offender mediation in cases of property offenses and minor assaults.

There is a very real danger in applying a "one-size-fits-all" perspective of mediation. Each unique setting requires additional training to build upon the core training that all mediators receive. Victim offender mediation and dialogue in crimes of severe violence operates from an entirely different paradigm than most mediation practice. It is dialogue-driven and focused on healing the wounds left in the wake of severe criminal violence. While not psychotherapy, it does provide an opportunity for deep healing that is entirely client-driven. On the other hand, the dominant paradigm of mediation in Western culture is settlement-driven, with little patience for dealing with the emotional context of conflict. Applying settlement-driven models of mediation with little understanding of grief and or post-traumatic stress contains great potential for re-victimizing victims.

Staff and volunteer mediators in the Texas and Ohio programs participated in extensive training that has been described in chapters 4 and 8, respectively. The Texas program required 72 hours of group training followed by twice-monthly in-service training; and all mediators worked under close supervision. In Ohio, the initial training lasted for about 50 hours and was followed by quarterly training updates. Ohio facilitators were also closely supervised in their work. As an absolute minimum, we are recommending that mediators or facilitators planning to offer services to victims of violent crime undergo at least 40 hours of intensive training.

2. *When providing mediated dialogue services in cases of violent crime, a minimum of two in-person face-to-face preparation meetings with each party should be conducted.*

In many cases, it is more likely that four to six or more preparation meetings will be required. Early in the development of providing dialogue services in crimes of severe violence, even before the Texas program was initiated in 1993, it was assumed by many that numerous individual preparation meetings with the victim and offender were required in all cases. In some specific cases, eight to ten preparation meetings were held with each party, over an 18 to 24 month period. During these early years, the idea of victims of severe violence meeting face-to-face with the offender, who was most likely in prison, was totally taboo. Proceeding with great caution and lengthy preparation was clearly appropriate. The findings of this study, however, have made it clear that a far less intense and lengthy preparation process can also yield positive outcomes, though often not quite as extensive as those involved in a more lengthy process of victim offender mediation and dialogue. To avoid an insufficiently lengthy preparation process, a minimum of two individual face-to-face preparation meetings (in addition to several phone conversations) with each party is recommended in all cases of severe violence.

3. *The process of victim-sensitive offender dialogue in crimes of severe violence should be entirely voluntary for all parties.*

As the requests by victims of severe violence to meet the offender increase, and as correctional agencies and other justice officials become more supportive of this intervention, there will be a great temptation to order the offender to meet the victim. This has already occurred in two jurisdictions in which well-intentioned judges ordered the offender who killed a person while driving drunk to meet the victim who expressed a desire to do so. One of these cases was referred to a civil court-related mediation program that had never conducted a victim offender mediation in even a petty crime, and the model of mediation they used involved virtually no separate preparation meetings with the parties. In the second instance, during the course of a civil court case (following the criminal case), the judge suspended the formal proceedings and directed the victim whose husband was killed to talk with the offender in the conference room and work out a resolution that they could recommend to the court for approval. In an interview with this victim, she shared her story about how terrifying this encounter was and how it severely re-victimized her again. There was no facilitator or mediator present during this unfortunate encounter that was initiated by the judge. The importance of insuring that all participants are voluntarily involved in victim offender dialogue sessions in the context of violent crime cannot be overemphasized. Many in the field, including the authors of this book, believe this voluntary participation is also important in the more widely used victim offender mediation with property offenses and minor assaults.

4. *Victim-sensitive offender dialogue in crimes of severe violence should be victim-initiated.*

When inmates initiate the process through a letter of apology, their letter should be kept on file in case their victim(s) later request a mediation/dialogue session. The history and development of the victim offender mediation and dialogue process in crimes of severe violence is strongly grounded in the request, if not demand, of such victims who seek a meeting with the offender. The two programs examined in the present study had formal policies that required cases to be victim-initiated, although in our study sample there were four offenders who slipped through the restrictions and directly contacted their victims; the victims then approached their respective programs with a request to meet.

From a theoretical perspective it could be argued that limiting case initiation solely to victims is inappropriate, and that sincere offender/inmate requests to meet with victims should be responded to by contacting the victim. Not to do so is seen as prohibiting a potentially valuable service to their victim. On its face, there appears to be some validity in this position. On the other hand, until our systems of justice and corrections truly operate in a more victim-sensitive manner, the probability of re-victimizing victims through insensitive communication resulting from offender-initiated cases is too high.

A number of practitioners in various parts of the country who have worked with victims who received unsolicited apology letters from their offender report that most often this results in a high level of re-victimization and reopening of wounds, or a sense of trying to put a good spin on what happened by showing how the offender has now seen the light, perhaps even had a religious conversion. Even when practitioners thought the letter sounded reasonably sincere, through the eyes of the victim it appeared insincere and triggered anger and resentment.

On the other hand, the four offender-initiated cases in our present study resulted in a satisfactory outcome for both the participating victims and their offenders. It should be clarified that in these cases victims were not approached by practitioners and invited to participate. They received unsolicited apologies or requests from their offenders and followed up by seeking the contact themselves. It is not known how many other victims in Texas and Ohio may have received such communications and chose *not* to seek a meeting. Therefore, until we become more confident that the probability of re-victimization can be greatly reduced, it is our belief that we should err on the more cautious side.

5. *The planning, development and implementation of victim-sensitive offender dialogue services should be conducted with active involvement of victim services providers, correctional staff and other persons familiar with the process of providing dialogue services in cases of violent crime.*

Involving key stakeholders in the process of developing and operating new victim offender mediation and dialogue programs in crimes of severe violence is critical. This is particularly so when it comes to involvement of victim service providers. We hope that victim service providers will take the lead in advocating and developing such programs. Involvement of key correctional staff is also critical. Without their support and involvement it is unlikely that victims will be allowed to enter correctional facilities for the purpose of meeting the offender. As part of preparing to initiate a new service, we hope that both victim services and corrections staff members will seek and obtain advanced training in offering mediated dialogue with victims and offenders in violent crime. At the very least, consultation should be obtained from others with training and experience in providing the service.

6. *While programs will naturally develop protocols and procedures for efficiently handling their cases, they should maintain maximum flexibility and openness to meet the needs of their participants.*

Each victim who seeks to meet with the person who has harmed them in a violent crime has a unique profile in spite of the many features all such victims share in common. Reasons for seeking to meet vary greatly, as do the goals victims hope to accomplish. Even the most frequently named reason among the 40 victims interviewed in the present study — that of seeking information — was named by only 58%. Similarly, telling the offender the impact of his or her actions, the second most frequent reason, was named by less than half (43%.) Program procedures should allow for such variation; staff should remain flexible to discern what each participant is seeking and to provide an opportunity for participants to discover whether participating in a meeting will be the best way to meet their needs.

Such flexibility clearly has implications for the substance and amount of preparation required. Two victims in our sample, one from each program, wished only to hear an "amends"; both felt that the preparation they were required to complete was top heavy. Each commented that such preparation was probably appropriate in most of the program's cases, but not in their own.

Another common program policy in many mediation programs has been to pursue mediation or dialogue only in instances where the offender has clearly owned and admitted to the offense. Flexibility to provide what victims need would require that victims be given an opportunity to decide whether they wish to meet in instances where the offender may not have admitted to everything. In three of the cases in our present study, this opportunity was offered. The participating victims were satisfied with their participation in the program even though they felt the offenders in their cases were not telling the whole truth. Mediators are appropriately cautious to pursue a meeting under such circumstances; these are cases where careful individualized preparation is crucial, so that participants can be as well informed as possible about what they are getting into.

7. *In the context of the victim-centered focus of programs offering dialogue in cases of violent crime, it is important not to lose sight of the impact on offenders.*

None of the offenders interviewed in the present study felt that they had been harmed by meeting with their victims, and all concurred that they had no regrets about participating in the program. The one offender who was "somewhat dissatisfied" with his participation still reported that he found it helpful. Yet we feel it is important to ensure that programs not cause harm for the offenders who elect to participate.

In offering this recommendation, we do not wish to imply that victims should in any way be responsible for the well-being of the persons who harmed them. Rather, programs need to appropriately safeguard the offenders from potential harm. In the two programs studied here, this is largely accomplished through establishing supportive relationships with offenders during the preparation process and through providing them maximum information about what their victim is seeking and what may happen in the mediation. Offenders are thereby permitted to make an informed choice about their participation, and are assured that they can drop out at any point in the process if they make a different choice.

Our primary reasons for this recommendation are threefold: First, offenders in these cases have already been tried and sentenced for their crimes, and must be protected from double jeopardy. Second, most of the offenders in these cases will eventually be released back out into the community. As one of the victims in our study so astutely noted, "The more help (my offender) gets towards recovery, the safer the world is." Third, and most importantly, the programs are developed and offered as a component of restorative justice; it is imperative that restorative opportunity is provided for all participants and not just some.

CONCLUSION

It is clear that the principles of restorative justice can be applied in selected cases of severe violence, particularly through the practice of victim offender mediation and dialogue. A far more intense case development process is required in severe violence cases. Preliminary data indicate exceptionally high levels of client satisfaction with the process and outcome of victim offender mediation and dialogue in crimes of severe violence. This bodes well for the future development of this emerging restorative justice intervention.

However, there remain many unanswered questions. For whom, under what circumstances, and when is the use of victim offender mediation in crimes of severe violence most appropriate? How extensive should the case development process be? Is there significant variance in the degree and length of pre-mediation case preparation based on characteristics of individual cases? What types of crime victim and offender respond best to such an intervention? Can the process be adapted so that it is more respectful of diverse cultures, leading to more active engagement of diverse communities? How can victim offender mediation/dialogue services, in crimes of severe violence, be offered as a voluntary restorative justice intervention on a larger scale and in a cost-effective manner? How extensive should advanced training be? To what extent should families and other support persons be routinely involved in the process, at what points, and to what degree? Can state victim compensation laws cover the costs incurred by victims of severe violence who request this intervention? While nearly all cases to date are victim-initiated, is there a place for offender-initiated cases without triggering the unintended consequence of re-victimizing the victim? Can this intervention continue to be offered primarily through well-trained community volunteers?

In addition, there are many questions which can only be answered by extensive longitudinal studies. What is the strength and durability over time of the many participant benefits documented in this study? Has the healing that occurred led to physiological as well as emotional benefits? To what extent has the issue of forgiveness (either the need for it or the desire to avoid it) played a significant role in the victim offender mediation and dialogue process? Are there significant unintended negative consequences that only a longer-term assessment would find? These and many other important questions need further study.

At its core, the process of victim offender mediation and dialogue in crimes of severe violence is about engaging those most affected by the horror of violent crime in the process of holding the offender truly accountable, helping the victim(s) gain a greater sense of meaning (if not some degree of closure), and helping all parties to have a greater capacity to move on with their lives in a positive fashion. This emerging restorative justice practice certainly warrants further development and analysis, along with an attitude of cautious and informed support.

APPENDIX A.
ANALYSIS OF CAPITAL CASES

The Texas Victim Offender Mediation/Dialogue Program had only been in operation for two years when it was approached in the fall of 1997 by the mother of a murder victim who sought to meet with her daughter's death-row killer before his execution. No such meeting had ever previously been attempted with a death row inmate and no one knew whether it could be arranged, but program staff advocated for the victim's needs and received a green light to proceed a bare five months before the scheduled execution. This first death row mediation was followed by requests from three additional family members of capital murder victims during the data-gathering period of the present study. Thus, our final Texas interview sample of 20 victims/family members and 19 convicted offenders included four family members who met with three death row offenders. All three offenders were executed by the state of Texas not long after their mediation/dialogue sessions and their research interviews.

Material from these interviews has been integrated in the Texas program findings reported in chapters 5 and 6. However because of the special issues involved in these cases, this appendix is devoted to an in-depth analysis of the experience of these four family members and three offenders. Material from two of these cases was previously reported in Umbreit and Vos (2000).

There is inherent controversy in choosing to offer mediated dialogue in capital cases, and not all capital offense states have elected to do so. Of all the consequences an offender may incur for criminal behavior, capital punishment is clearly the most extreme. Some would argue that "restorative justice" programs have no place in such a context (Radelet and Borg, 2000). The Texas Victim Offender Mediation/Dialogue Program chose to act upon the requests of these four crime victims and obtained permission from the Texas Department of Criminal Justice for the dialogues to take place. The three offenders were offered the opportunity to participate or not, and each elected to do so, for reasons that will be presented below. The following analysis of what these seven participants had to say about their experiences is offered, in part, so that readers can reach their own conclusions about the impact of these meetings and the advisability of offering such a service in capital cases.

As with the other case studies reported in the present volume, names, identifying information and some details have been changed to protect the privacy of the participants.

CHARACTERISTICS OF THE EVENTS

The three participating offenders were convicted of a total of six counts of murder and two counts of attempted murder. Michael Henderson had been incarcerated for a previous violent crime and had been released early for good behavior. Not long after his release, he committed a series of violent crimes, four of which resulted in his conviction and death sentence: three counts of murder, two of which included abduction and rape, and one count of abduction, rape and attempted murder. Benjamin Graves had no previous history of arrest for violent crime, though he had served a one-year sentence for theft by check. He broke into a private home before dawn, murdered two of its occupants by stabbing, and attempted to murder the third, leading to his conviction and death sentence for two counts of murder and one of attempted murder. Paul Marshall was convicted and sentenced to die for a single brutal murder. With the aid of an accomplice, he entered a private home and killed the man who owned it with a medieval sword, dismembering the body.

All four family members who participated in the mediation/dialogue sessions with these three offenders were women. The first, Kelly Cartwright, was the granddaughter of an elderly woman who was abducted, raped and murdered by Michael Henderson. The second, Rachel Hollister, was the sister of another of Michael Henderson's victims, a young mother whom he murdered when she struggled during his attempted abduction. The third participant, Ellen Smithson, was the mother of one of the young women murdered by Benjamin Graves, and the fourth, Edwina Holmes, was the mother of the man murdered by Paul Marshall.

EXPERIENCE OF THE CRIMES

Family Member Perspectives

Kelly Cartwright was a high school senior at the time of her grandmother's murder. She was pulled from her classroom and told that her grandmother hadn't returned from her usual morning walk. The family drove 200 miles to the small town where her grandmother lived. There they waited together at the search headquarters that had been established in the church parking lot where her grandmother usually parked her car for her daily walk. Already there was a sense of dread; Kelly commented, "I think we all assumed the worst." But it was the evening of the second day before policemen on patrol some 14 miles away from town noticed fresh car tracks on a remote dirt road, investigated, and found her grandmother's body. The offender was apprehended in relation to a different crime; it was some two years before he confessed and stood trial for her grandmother's murder.

Rachel Hollister had a much shorter wait than Kelly Cartwright to learn what had happened to her sister, Michael Henderson's second victim. Rachel had spent the day with her sister and her five-year-old niece and had just gotten home when her brother-in-law called and asked her to meet him at the sheriff's station. There he told Rachel that her sister was dead. "That's really when the nightmare started, because my niece was there, and she was just covered in blood." Rachel assumed there had been some kind of car accident, and was horrified to learn instead that her sister had been murdered at a gas station while her daughter watched.

Ellen Smithson, the mother of Benjamin Graves' victim, had awakened with a strong feeling she should call her daughter at about 4:00 a.m. the morning of her daughter's birthday, but felt it was an unreasonable hour, so waited until 7:00. By then the phone line was busy, so Ellen left for work, where a truck backed into a telephone pole and knocked out all phone communication to and from work for the rest of the day. She did not learn of her daughter's death until late that evening, when her ex-husband's wife called her at home with the news. "The impact was just so devastating, I just literally died inside." Ellen later learned that her daughter's murder had occurred about the time she had awakened, and that when she had attempted her call later, the phone lines were busy with police making phone calls from the apartment.

Edwina Holmes, the mother of Paul Marshall's victim, was home washing dishes with her second husband, the victim's stepfather, when the phone call came. Her husband answered because her hands were wet and soapy. "When he got off the telephone he stood to face me with his hands on my shoulder and told me that my son had just been killed. I did not understand one word he said, it was like some kind of a garbled foreign language. I was in total denial." Ellen's denial only began to abate when they arrived at the funeral home. "Folks were upset, I had to believe something."

Offender Experience

In describing their own experience of the murders, all three offenders made links to their earlier life history and its impact on their crime. Beyond this similarity, there is little in common across the three accounts. Michael Henderson and Benjamin Graves both reported significant memory loss regarding the events themselves, and both asserted that the murders were not premeditated. Paul Marshall did not report any memory loss and was more vague about the level of premeditation.

Michael Henderson stated that from as far back as he could remember, he had developed a habit of burying emotions of any sort. "And of course this is a very explosive thing." He offered no further detail about what these emotions were or the events about which he came to harbor such explosive feelings. He reported that he did not use drugs or alcohol because his teenage experimentation had been unpleasant. All four of the crimes for which he was convicted followed a similar pattern. In each instance, he happened on a woman alone; he accosted her, abducted or attempted to abduct her, drove to a secluded area, raped her, and murdered or attempted to murder her. He reported that initially he found it difficult to remember the specifics of the crime. "I would suppress it so bad that even by the next day, I would almost have no memory."

Michael described his encounter with his elderly victim in vague, general terms. He gave somewhat more detail about the woman he murdered at the unattended gas station. He stated that he was filling his truck when he noticed the victim and her daughter filling their car at another pump island. He attempted to abduct the woman but she struggled. He remembered that he stabbed her multiple times and fled when it appeared other persons were approaching the gas station.

Benjamin Graves was more explicit about the links between his early history and his crimes. He reported that his childhood experience included flagrant physical and sexual abuse and early drug use. By the time of his crimes, he was a regular user of several drugs, and also a producer and dealer of amphetamines. Despondent over a failed marriage, he developed an idea that even he recognized as bizarre by the time of his interview: "I decided I would rape and make women love me, and if I could practice this and get real good at it, I could do it to my wife and then my personal life would be great again."

The two counts of murder and one count of attempted murder for which Benjamin was sentenced to die were the result of a single incident in which he reported that his intent was to carry out such a rape. But two factors intervened. By his own account, he was high on more drugs and alcohol than he had ever previously consumed. And, warned by her barking dog, his intended victim put up a struggle and screamed. Benjamin reported that he blacked out and flashed back to his early abuse. When he regained consciousness his victim was lying on the bed bleeding from multiple stab wounds. He heard more screaming and followed the sounds to encounter her roommate. Again, he reported blacking out during the actual murder. The second woman's boyfriend woke and attempted to pull the offender off his victim. In the struggle that ensued, the boyfriend also sustained multiple stab wounds, but ultimately survived. Benjamin escaped and reported having no memory of how he got home. He was apprehended within a week.

Paul Marshall described how he was picked on in elementary school to the point of becoming a "punching bag." In his account, his feelings simply came boiling over in the seventh grade and he lashed out. "From that day forward I was made a complete new person. I wasn't taking it no more." He was vague about the intervening years, reporting on the one hand that he was not involved in "the criminal element," yet on the other hand mentioning previous personal and property offenses. Finally, out of work, out of money and living in his car with his girlfriend, he reported that he agreed to her plan that they "knock somebody in the head and take their money."

Paul drove his girlfriend to a bar where she met the victim, apparently previously known to her, and persuaded the victim to take her home; he followed in his car. Growing tired of waiting, he approached the house to see what was happening and became enraged when he saw his girlfriend attempting to seduce their intended victim. "Picked a bad weapon for trying to knock him in the head. But it turned out a part of me really wanted to go in there and kill him…and that's what happened. And I mutilated the guy with a sword." Immediately Paul was nauseated by what he had done. "I wished I could have been able to pick him up and get him to a hospital and say, 'here, put this man back together,' but he was beyond putting back together."

REASONS FOR PARTICIPATING IN MEDIATION

Family Member Reasons for Seeking To Meet

The reasons volunteered by family members for seeking to meet with the offenders in mediation/dialogue are summarized in Table A.1. There is only one theme in common across all four family members: they sought a personal, human encounter.

I really needed to see this guy face-to-face. (Kelly Cartwright)

I needed to look him in the eye, just to see him, just to hear what he had to say. (Rachel Hollister)

I had to see his eyes, that he was a real person. (Ellen Smithson)

I wanted to look him in the eye. (Edwina Holmes)

Three family members sought information; only two of these wanted to know anything about why it happened. Two specifically sought to share their forgiveness. Two wanted to let the offenders know the impact of their actions. Two sought to hear him take responsibility. It should be noted that many of these themes turned up frequently in the benefits that family members said they reaped from the experience, regardless of whether they had listed the theme as a specific reason initially.

Table A.1: Family Member Reasons for Seeking To Meet

Reason	Capital Case One		Capital Case Two	Capital Case Three
	Kelly Cartwright (grand-daughter)	Rachel Hollister (sister)	Ellen Smithson (mother)	Edwina Holmes (mother)
Sit eye-to-eye, face-to-face	yes	yes	yes	yes
Seek details about the crime	yes	yes		yes
Seek to know why it happened		yes		yes
Share forgiveness			yes	yes
Advance their own healing in other ways			yes	
Show the offender the impact of the crime	yes	yes		
Make the offender take responsibility		yes	yes	

Three of the family members began to formulate their wish to meet with their offender during the trial proceedings. Though Kelly Cartwright was away in college during Michael Henderson's trial and unable to attend, she was in close touch with her family members who were present. She was distressed about the way in which the proceedings seemed more focused on protecting the offender than on protecting or supporting her grandmothers' family members. She felt the justice system caused separation and disconnection where there should be connection. A primary motivation for her was to let Michael know "how far reaching the impact is, and how time consuming, and how long it lasts, and what it does." She also sought detailed information about the actual crime, wanting to know such things as how her grandmother had been selected, whether she had said anything, whether she had been scared, and how he had gotten her in his truck.

Rachel Hollister attended Michael Henderson's trial and was active in asserting her rights as a victim from the very beginning: "I told them I wanted to be notified and called up on...every move Michael made." Initially she wanted to meet with him to rule out her suspicion that her sister's ex-husband might have had some involvement in the murder. Additionally, she hoped to find out why it happened and whether the offender knew her sister. She wanted him to know the impact of his action on her own life and the life of her sister's daughter, and she wanted to hear him take responsibility.

Ellen Smithson attended all of Benjamin Graves's pretrial hearings as well as the actual trial, a 16-month long process, and resolved before the trial ended that she would find a way to meet with him. "The man I saw in the courtroom was not human, he had no life in his eyes. For thirteen months I looked at his eyes and I saw absolutely nothing." The day after he was sentenced she went to the jail to try to meet with him but was unsuccessful. For the next 14 years she organized her work life so that she could always be immediately available to attend any new developments to try to prevent Benjamin's release, or to meet with him if he would consent. Her reasons for wishing to meet were vague at the time. She did not seek information, nor did she wish to know why. But she did wish to hold him accountable.

During the intervening years Ellen Smithson experienced a powerful event in which she came to forgive Benjamin, though not his actions. By the time it became possible for her to meet with him, she viewed sharing this as a potentially important part of her own healing. "I just knew this was something I needed for me to be able to go on with my life. And it was really important to me to let him know that he had been forgiven."

Edwina Holmes did not comment on how far back she had decided to try to meet with Paul Marshall. She simply stated that when she decided she wanted to do so, she spoke with the Victims Services workers who were already involved with her, and they put her in touch with the Texas Victim Offender Mediation/Dialogue Program. Her reasons were similar to Ellen Smithson's: "The main thing was that I wanted to look him in the eye and tell him I had forgiven him." She also had several details she wished to ask, including what her son's last words were and what the offender had done with some of the things he stole from her son's house. Her only worry was whether meeting with him or having forgiven him could in any way reduce his sentence; she was relieved to learn there was no way this could happen.

Offender Reasons for Participating in Mediation/Dialogue

The descriptions offenders gave of their reasons for participating are summarized in Table A.2. All three offenders stated that they had hoped in some way to be able to meet with family members of their victims before they were ever contacted by the Victim Services Division and invited to participate. And all three of them referred to their personal religious faith in discussing their reasons for participating. However, there were no specific reasons that were shared by all three offenders.

Table A.2: Offender Reasons for Participating

Reason	Capital Case One Michael Henderson	Capital Case Two Benjamin Graves	Capital Case Three Paul Marshall
Help the family member heal		yes	yes
Answer the family member's questions		yes	
Be accountable		yes	yes
To apologize	yes		yes
Felt they owed it to the family member		yes	
To ask for forgiveness	yes		
To relieve a burden	yes		
To feel better			yes
Felt they owed it to God		yes	

Michael Henderson reported that he had come to wish he could contact his victims' families to say he was sorry and ask for forgiveness. Some two years after this realization, Texas program staff contacted him to say there was a family member who wished to meet with him. "When he first contacted me, it was an answer to a prayer." He decided to participate in spite of the potential for risk to his case. "It got to the point where I really didn't care about that part of it."

Benjamin Graves's reasons were more focused on trying to help his victims heal, to offer something back for the wrong he had done. He remembered an interaction with his victim's mother in the courtroom at the end of his trial. He had looked at her and mouthed the words "I'm sorry," and she had responded, "It's not enough." He wanted to answer any questions she might have and to help her healing in any way possible, even if this meant experiencing her rage. He stated that he had wished to offer this to family members of his other victims as well, but no one else had accepted his offer. He also looked to his own history to explain what he hoped he could accomplish: "Because of my childhood, I understood that hate was a cancer." He hoped family members would be able to release some of their negative feelings and diminish the power of such intense feelings in their lives. And he felt it was a religious necessity: "I owed it to her and myself and God to do this."

Paul Marshall stated that he had "always wanted" to tell the mother of his victim that he was sorry, but hadn't known how to go about it. So he reported that when he was approached by the mediator, "I was all for it as soon as he opened his mouth." The only risk he considered was whether or not she might rage at him. He felt that if she did, he deserved it, and that it might help her to release her anger.

EXPERIENCE OF PREPARATION

All seven of these participants rated their preparation for the mediation/dialogue very highly. Five of the participants experienced a much shorter time frame for preparation than was usual for the Texas program, all at less than six months. Only one victim (Ellen Smithson) and one offender (Paul Marshall) had a more typical time frame; they were afforded nearly two years to prepare to meet.

All seven were very impressed with the questionnaires and written materials they were given to work with. Both Kelly Cartwright and Michael Henderson expressed surprise that such an elaborate set of materials was already prepared for them. All four family members felt that the preparation materials were helpful in their own healing process. Kelly Cartwright was also grateful for the way the questions helped her organize her thoughts and plan what she wanted to say. Rachel Hollister worked through the questions with another of her sisters. She found this to be very difficult work, but was impressed with how helpful it was for both of them. She later requested extra copies to share with her brothers and reported that this helped open up family communication about the loss of their sister in a way that had never happened since the murder. Ellen Smithson also commented that the work was difficult; yet she felt "it was totally necessary." She also was the only participant who referred to any type of conflict with the mediator during the preparation phase. "Even when I'd get mad at him and he'd push my buttons, it was still a very positive, positive experience, and it's one I wouldn't trade anything for."

Two of the offenders likened the preparation process to the twelve-step programs in which they participated. Michael Henderson felt, in addition, that it helped him open up and gave him tools to express his feelings. He used the materials to help him talk with his family members about his pending execution. He was grateful that after he began sharing with his family about his upcoming mediation, they began to visit more frequently and talk more about meaningful things in their visits.

Benjamin Graves felt the preparation materials actually pushed beyond the twelve-step program by helping him identify and understand both the cycle of abuse that had victimized him, and his own cycle of abuse and offense that had victimized others. Paul Marshall did not refer to twelve-step work, but felt the preparation helped teach him "how to talk to somebody you wronged...without bringing more pain to her."

All seven participants had high praise for the way in which their mediator conducted the preparation. Both Kelly Cartwright and Michael Henderson were particularly moved by how much the mediator cared. Edwina Holmes and Paul Marshall were each grateful to learn that the mediator shared their religion. Edwina commented, "When I discovered that the mediator was a Christian, I felt so good because I knew that he was going to see that everything was done properly, that I was going to be safe."

FEELINGS IMMEDIATELY BEFORE THE SESSION

There was some variation in the feelings that participants reported immediately prior to the sessions. Among family members, Kelly Cartwright was basically calm and reported that she experienced only momentary nervousness when the offender entered the room. Rachel Hollister was both excited and somewhat nervous, and Edwina Holmes reported feeling nervous and shaking. Ellen Smithson reported the highest degree of anxiety: "I was scared to death. It was a long walk, believe me!" She also was the only family member who identified any particular fear as a source of apprehension. She worried whether the anger and rage others had told her to anticipate might surface during the session and overwhelm her.

The three offenders were more uniformly apprehensive than were the family members. All three anticipated being on the receiving end of substantial rage; in Michael Henderson's words, "I really expected a lot more anger…This is something I could not blame them for if this was to take place." Benjamin Graves had similar expectations but tried to focus on staying calm and unexpressive in order not to re-victimize his victim's mother. Paul Marshall described a mix of sadness and fear, and added, "I felt like I was fixing to meet the most awful judgment I've ever faced."

THE MEDIATION PROCESS

All three mediation/dialogue sessions were held in the visiting room of the penal institution housing the death row offenders. The sessions were similar in several ways: each lasted approximately five to six hours, the mediator sat with the offender on the inmate's side of the glass partition, and the family member, with any support persons, sat on the other. The session with Michael Henderson departed in one important way from the usual Texas format. Due to the time constraints deriving from his scheduled execution date, he met simultaneously with the family members of two different victims in a single meeting: one victim's granddaughter, Kelly Cartwright, and another victim's sister, Rachel Hollister. Both this session and the mediation between Benjamin Graves and his victim's mother, Ellen Smithson, were videotaped; no recording was made of the third mediation/dialogue.

In general, the three sessions followed the usual format of the Texas Victim Offender Mediation/Dialogue Program. Michael Henderson had elected not to prepare a specific statement, so Kelly Cartwright and Rachel Hollister chose to begin by asking him to tell them about his life.

They had come with a list of questions about his history and the actions leading up to the crimes, and they had anticipated that it would be hard to get him to open up. But Kelly commented, "Actually, we didn't even ask him a question because he just went off and basically went from the very beginning of his life all the way up through the murders. It was very nice, actually." When he was finished, Kelly and Rachel traded off reading portions of their statements, using one another to take a break when emotions became overwhelming.

All participants in this session concurred that the total talk time was divided fairly evenly across the three of them. Kelly worried this might have created unfairness for Michael: "Because there were two victims and only one offender, I would say probably overall the victims had more talk time than the offender." In the second mediation, Benjamin Graves reported that his victim's mother probably had more total talk time than he did, but this was as he felt it should be. Both Paul Marshall and his victim's mother reported that overall talk time in their session was fairly evenly balanced between them, although during the first hour Paul spoke more.

Two of the four participating family members were in such an intense emotional state during the actual mediation session that they initially had very little memory of the details. Rachel Hollister was especially grateful for the video recording: "There was so much that I do not remember took place until I sat back and watched the video. It was like I was there, but I wasn't there." Ellen Smithson's language was similar. "I couldn't remember anything that we talked about, a fraction of what I said, or how I behaved." Much of the detail these two women gave in their research interviews was drawn from their review of the videotape. No such recording was made of the third session. However Edwina Holmes reported that in the days immediately following the session, she wrote a 10-page description of what happened so that she could share about it more easily with her remaining children. Kelly Cartwright did not report any difficulty remembering her session.

In general, the themes of the material shared by family members in all three sessions were very similar. They described their own experiences of the day or days surrounding the crime, they talked about its impact on themselves, and they shared its impact on others in their families. By all accounts, sessions one and two proceeded fairly calmly. Both Michael Henderson and Benjamin Graves reported that listening to the family member statements was highly impactful. Each had anticipated that the family members would be openly angry and attacking, and each was grateful this did not occur.

Session three produced a much more intense level of affect. Edwina Holmes had come to the session seeking detailed information about the crime, but found herself shocked and enraged when Paul Marshall answered her questions and described what he had done. Paul recounted the beginning of this exchange: "She covered a lot of areas that she wanted to know about...A lot of them were traumatic. She didn't ever see the body of her son, and when I talked to her about it, I could see the ripping inside of her." Edwina Holmes's description continues: "I found that I had some anger left inside of me that I didn't realize was there. I raised my voice to him, I began to cry, I was pretty much sobbing." She tried to stop herself because she's not normally "a person who screams and yells and raises my voice." But the mediator encouraged her to continue, "so that I could vent every bit of my anger. I believe that was really beneficial."

Both Kelly Cartwright and Rachel Hollister had developed a list of questions about the crimes for which they hoped to receive answers. As their session with Michael Henderson unfolded, the found that they did not in fact request many details. They became more interested in piecing together some kind of explanation through obtaining information about his life and history. And, as reported earlier, Ellen Smithson did not seek any details about either the events or the reasons surrounding her daughter's murder.

As described under reasons for seeking mediation, both of the mothers involved in these mediation/dialogue sessions reported they had forgiven their offenders prior to seeking to meet with them. Both were able to share this forgiveness during the mediations. Ellen Smithson felt this changed her perspective on her choice to witness Benjamin Graves's execution. "When I first decided I was going to witness, it's because I wanted my face to be the last thing that he saw, to be aware that he's where he is because of what he did to my daughter. And now I want him to see his victim's mother who has forgiven him." Benjamin was deeply moved by this aspect of their encounter. When asked what had surprised him most about the session, he responded "her compassion, her deep feeling for me. I met another face of God that night. The God

I know is a God of mercy, a God of love, a God of forgiveness, and that night I met all those things in her."

Edwina Holmes reported, "The most important thing was that I could tell him that I had forgiven him." She and Paul Marshall also spoke about his pending execution, but with a different flavor. Edwina had never wavered in her belief that he ought to be executed, even though she had forgiven him. As they discussed this, she asked Paul whether, if he were set free, he would commit murder again. "And he tossed this question around a bit...Then he said, "no, I'm sure, quite sure that I would." Paul confirmed this self-portrait in his statement to the interviewer: "If I was on the street I'd still be taken in...I would definitely kill again. Something would come on me where I would be placed in a high risk factor and I would kill somebody again. Once you kill once it's not hard to do it again."

The offenders did not give much detail in their interviews about the types of information they shared with family members during the mediation. Some differences in focus among the three were apparent, but these may have been more a consequence of the questions the family members chose to ask than of the offender's plan or intention. Michael Henderson shared his history: "I basically started with my childhood...and the things that led up to the crimes." Benjamin Graves tried to focus chiefly on understanding and responding to whatever his victim's mother shared. He reported that he tried hard to understand the feelings she had gone through but was also aware of his limited ability to do so. He was surprised to learn she had additional children. He reported that he had been deeply concerned that he had robbed her of any chance for grandchildren. He was relieved to learn this was not the case, but also stunned to realize how much devastation he had caused these additional two persons. Paul Marshall mostly focused on the details of the events, and on trying to reassure his victim's mother that he was sorry and didn't wish to add to her pain.

OUTCOME AND EVALUATION

The language used by all seven of these interviewees to describe how they felt immediately after finishing the meetings is remarkably similar: the experience was powerful and healing, and they were relieved and renewed.

When I walked out, it was like this load, some type of negative energy kind of was lifted out of me, and I was also exhausted. (Kelly Cartwright)

I felt a sense of relief. (Rachel Hollister)

There just aren't any words that would adequately express what I feel. I feel human for the first time in twelve years. (Ellen Smithson)

I was pretty much numb. I felt more relief the next day. It was so healing. (Edwina Holmes)

I think I'm more alive now than I ever have been at any one point in time. I'm actually living life now, instead of just existing. (Michael Henderson)

Very much at peace. I told the mediator I felt cleansed. I felt a great burden had been lifted off my shoulders. I felt joy. (Benjamin Graves)

Like a burden had been lifted off me, like something had been removed that was a thorn in my side for years. (Paul Marshall)

Thus, all seven participants experienced the mediation/dialogue as a very healing experience, even though not all of them explicitly named this as a goal initially, and not all of their reasons for seeking mediation were satisfied. The factors that led to this response naturally vary somewhat between the family members and the offenders.

Family Member Perspectives

For all four family members, an important component was hearing the offender take responsibility. Kelly Cartwright reported it this way: "I had heard that he had confessed — it was gratifying to hear it out of his mouth and not out of a reporter's mouth." Edwina Holmes echoed these sentiments: "He was extremely accountable for everything he did. He wanted me to understand that he was totally responsible for the murder of my son."

All four family members also reported that their negative feelings had greatly diminished, and all four mentioned a decrease in anger specifically. In the words of Rachel Hollister, "I'm not angry like I used to be." Rachel also reported a decrease in her bitterness and her fearfulness.

Three of the family members felt their respective offenders were sincere. Rachel Hollister had more doubts. During the session she told Michael Henderson that she didn't want him out on the street, and he assured her that he wouldn't do this again, but would admit himself to a hospital instead. She remained unimpressed: "I'd say that too, if I was on death row."

When asked if their opinions of their offenders had changed, all four family members responded affirmatively, in similar language:

> Before, he was just a murderer...After, he was a human being. (Kelly Cartwright)

> I pictured him as just an animal, but after meeting with him it was just so hard to. (Rachel Hollister)

> I saw a person and not just the man who murdered my daughter. (Ellen Smithson)

> I think I may have more compassion for him. I think I have more of an understanding. (Edwina Holmes)

In no way did this shift toward perceiving the offender as more human make the offender any less accountable. For Kelly Cartwright, it paradoxically made him even more so. "It's very easy in a crime as horrible as that one to not really be able to place blame anywhere...So for me it was important to establish some level or balance of accountability among everyone, and not no one and nothing." Rachel Hollister added, "After sitting and talking with him, he is a person, but he's not a person who needs to be returned to society."

The human qualities of the encounter were another crucial component for three of the family members, all of whom spoke of the importance of having met face-to-face and looking eye-to-eye. Ellen Smithson added, "Just being able to look at somebody and see that they smile with their eyes...It was very intimate, very spiritual and very personal." Kelly Cartwright felt just doing this much would have been sufficient: "Even if I had only gotten in the room and sat and done that for five minutes, I would have been happy."

As described above, receiving answers to her questions was a most powerful experience for Edwina Holmes. She attributed much of her healing to the opportunity this gave her to fully express and release her rage. The other two family members who had initially sought answers as part of their motivation for participating in fact received very few answers. Yet both of them found that this mattered less than they had anticipated. Kelly Cartwright commented, "It's funny how when you go through a process like that, the unknowns become much less important."

All four family members reported that their mediation experience enriched their spirituality. Ellen Smithson commented, "What I felt leave me that night, that was a gift that God gave me, he took that heaviness out of my heart." Edwina Holmes reported that Paul Marshall had been writing sermons and posting them on the Internet, and that he asked her if she would help disseminate them after he was gone. "Since I have committed to doing that, it is just unbelievable the way God is opening doors…The lives that I can reach out to try and do what he asked me to, it's almost like a burning desire within me now."

At the time of our interviews with family members, the executions of Michael Henderson and Benjamin Graves were still pending. Paul Marshall had already been executed, and Edwina Holmes had attended the execution. She reported what for her was a very moving experience, in which the offender made eye contact with her, nodded, and began to cry. "I personally felt like his tears were his last statement, and that he was saying to me again 'oh how sorry I am that I have hurt you.' I believe that he had repented for the sin, and I believe that Christ has forgiven him, and I think he's in heaven today."

The other three family members, all of whom were making plans to attend, reported some shift in their feelings about the death sentence and their offenders' pending executions. Both of the family members who met with Michael Henderson had initially been so enraged they wanted to kill him themselves: "For a very long time I would have put the needle in his arm" (Kelly Cartwright). "Before, I wanted to execute him myself. I think a lot of us did" (Rachel Hollister). Both Kelly and Rachel softened their positions after meeting with him, though they still experienced mixed feelings. Kelly added, "People have asked me if I want him to die,…and that is something I can't decide. I'm gonna leave that up to God." Ellen Smithson's changed perspective has been reported above, in her comments on sharing her forgiveness.

Offender Perspectives

All three offenders spontaneously described the healing that they felt had come to them through the mediation. Words in common to all three included relief, release, and the lifting of a burden. Benjamin Graves and Paul Marshall also described themselves as more at peace, and Benjamin added that he felt joy.

Restitution themes dominated their explanations of how such healing evolved. For all three, the most salient factor appeared to be the experience of doing something, however small, to try to make it better.

> That you've done something positive, that at least something positive will come out of this. (Michael Henderson)

> To take whatever darkness I could out of this world. I had already brought too much darkness into it. (Benjamin Graves)

> It felt good to be able to mend that broken spot in her life, though I can't ever replace what was lost. (Paul Marshall)

First and foremost was the impact of being able to offer something directly to the family members who participated with them in the mediation/dialogue sessions. All three offenders reported that they were grateful to have been able to help these family members begin to heal. Benjamin Graves commented, "For years I've paid for Ellen's peace, and I saw her possessing peace that night. That helped."

For all three, this impetus to "make it better" reached beyond the family members with whom they had met to include others in some way. Michael Henderson had left an open letter to be made available to any other family members of his victims. Both he and Benjamin Graves hoped that their participation and the videotapes of their sessions could help make it possible for more people to access the healing process of mediation. They felt this was as important for other offenders as it was for victims and their family members. Michael spoke further of his own efforts to reach out to other inmates on death row: "I can touch this person and say, 'Hey, I've done this, this is what I've learned, let me share this with you.'" Paul Marshall did not comment in his interview on his wish to reach out to others, but as described above, Edwina Holmes reported that he had been writing sermons and posting them on the Internet: "And he asked me if I would do everything I could to try to get those out, especially to young people who might be persuaded to avoid the road that he took and try to deter some of the violent crime that's going on. And I told him that I would do everything I could."

An additional factor in the offenders' positive response to the mediation derived from the humanizing nature of the encounter already reported on by the family members. When asked if they thought family members' perceptions of them had changed as a result of the mediation, all three offenders responded positively, and it is clear that they were quite moved by the compassion and understanding they felt they received. In their comments, two of the offenders conveyed a more personalized understanding of the relationship than was described by the family members. "I realized that all of a sudden, if I had met these people in other circumstances I probably could have been friends" (Michael Henderson); "Had I not killed her daughter, I think Ellen and I would have been best friends. I do see a lot of parallels to our problems" (Benjamin Graves). None of the three family members who met with Michael and Benjamin used the term "friend" in any of their descriptions of their own perceptions or relationship with the offenders.

All three offenders placed their positive responses to the mediation/dialogue sessions in the context of their upcoming executions. Each felt that having participated in the mediation made it easier to face his own impending death. Michael Henderson described it this way: "And it actually makes it a lot easier to face the execution...that you've done something positive, that at least something positive will come out of this." Even though one of his reasons for participating had been his hope to ask for forgiveness, he did not mention either asking for or receiving forgiveness in his discussion of the mediation process. But it is clear that for him, the actions of meeting with his victims' family members, facing what he had done, accepting responsibility and offering what he could to help all played a part in his own healing and readiness to face death.

For Benjamin Graves, Ellen Smithson's forgiveness was central: "She doesn't hate me, she hasn't forgiven the crime, but she's forgiven me. Now I know that when I'll be on that gurney, that a great burden has been taken away from me." Paul Marshall's comment was in response to the interviewer's question whether he had any regrets about his participation: "I would have regrets if I couldn't have done it and I was executed next Wednesday. That would be my regret, if I wasn't able to do it." He later commented on the difference between his victim's death and his own: "I took something from her, that she didn't get to say goodbye to him like my mama's doing now."

ROLE OF THE MEDIATOR

All seven participants were unanimous in their praise for the process and for their mediator. With one exception, to be discussed below, they concurred in their descriptions of his role during the session: after his introductory remarks setting the stage, he was relatively silent, and simply let the sessions flow freely. As Ellen Smithson noted, "He had tutored us both well, and he really didn't have to (talk) very much." Benjamin Graves, who met with her, found the mediator's respect for silence especially significant: "Those moments of silence were very precious at times because it was just a time to sit back and reflect momentarily on what we had said."

The exception to the mediator's typically silent, background role occurred during the mediation between Paul Marshall and Edwina Holmes, after she asked for and received details about her son's murder. Her comments about the mediator's role in helping her keep in touch with her intense feelings have been referred to earlier. In response to the interviewer's question "did the mediator talk much?" Paul Marshall gave a more extensive account of this departure from the more typical background role:

> He helped us see inside of emotion that was happening at that moment. She was having one emotion where it was angry and it turned into rage and then it turned into a void. And he walked her through it. And at the bottom of the void she was able to fill it with God. So he really guided her and me through the process. Without him it wouldn't have turned out near as well as it did with him...He really was a tool in helping the process come to an understanding where me and her could actually make a meaning of our hearts instead of just the flesh that was devastated.

All seven participants described the mediator's few interventions in similar terms. Clearly much of the mediators' role in these capital cases was not much different from their role in the rest of the Texas mediations described in chapters 3-6. Occasionally the mediator helped remind participants of topics they had wished to bring up, and the mediator consistently helped all participants stay in touch with feelings. There was less mention of redirecting the conversation or of keeping things going than in the non-capital mediations, suggesting that perhaps in these death row cases, there may have been even more space for silence and reflection than was typical in other mediations.

The family members commented on the mediator's sense of balance and his capacity to be fully present for both themselves and the offenders, a process they presumed was very difficult. Ellen Smithson commented, "It's hard to be fair in something like this …It would be hard, I think, to be fair to a murderer." Kelly Cartwright felt that without the mediator's intense preparation and his capacity to be present in his relationship with the offenders, Michael Henderson would never have participated so openly. "Michael had probably opened up more to the mediator than he had to anyone else, probably ever, about these crimes and about his life. I felt like he probably saw the mediator not just as a friend, but as someone he could go to and lean on a little."

ADVICE FOR OTHERS

All seven participants recommended that others in similar circumstances participate in mediation/dialogue. The family members clarified that they knew it's not for everyone, but they still felt strongly that family members should consider participating. Ellen Smithson was the most enthusiastic: "I think that if I could convince people to go through this program, not because they just need to sit with the offender, but just to do something for themselves, I would, because it's that good."

Edwina Holmes cautioned that mediation is difficult and advised, "Don't try it without God. It's a very stressful thing if you don't have something really solid to hold on to." Rachel Hollister felt the state should be more assertive in letting victims and family members know that the service is available. And Kelly Cartwright felt it was as much needed by offenders as by family members, to improve offender accountability.

As discussed above, two of the offenders hoped mediation would become more generally available for victims and for offenders. Michael Henderson was particularly concerned about the potential impact for offenders: "Maybe it can open up a lot more awareness as far as opening up and learning...that there actually can be attempts made at rehabilitation instead of just holding prisoners until their time is served." Benjamin Graves was more focused on helping victims heal, and offered the use of his interview and his videotaped session in any way "that you think would intensify the healing process." Both Michael and Benjamin also wished there was some way to alert family members if their specific offender wished to meet, without somehow implying that the family member ought to do so or in any way owed anything to the offender.

CONCLUSION

Both the family members and the death row offenders who participated in these three meetings were grateful they had the opportunity to do so and none of them had any regrets. All seven participants were moved beyond their expectations, all were relieved, and all reported significant impact on their healing. And all seven pointed to the same set of components to account for their response: careful, compassionate preparation, gentle and unobtrusive guidance during he session, and above all the opportunity for genuine, human face-to-face encounter which increased, rather than decreased, offender accountability and responsibility.

APPENDIX B.
HUMANISTIC DIALOGUE:
A PRACTITIONER PERSPECTIVE

In order to provide a context for understanding the range of approaches to mediated dialogue in serious and violent crimes, our study gathered data from additional practitioners not affiliated with either the Texas or the Ohio program. Project staff interviewed three individuals practicing in the Midwest: Betty Brown in Iowa, Bruce Kittle in Wisconsin, and Mark Umbreit in Minnesota. Betty Brown until very recently did her work almost "as an aside" while she worked with Polk County Victim Services. While on the faculty of the University of Wisconsin Law School, Bruce Kittle worked closely with the Wisconsin Department of Corrections offering victim offender dialogue in cases involving severe violence. He has since moved to Iowa, but our discussions with Kittle focused on his previous work in Wisconsin; it is important to note that Kittle is trained both in law and ministry. Mark Umbreit, on the faculty of the University of Minnesota School of Social Work, has worked for many years with cases involving violence in a number of states, including Minnesota. He has trained many hundreds of individuals in the process of victim offender mediation and dialogue in North America, Europe, and other parts of the world. Umbreit is the person responsible for developing the concept of a humanistic approach to mediation that is "dialogue driven" rather than "settlement driven" (Umbreit, 1997).

We pooled the data from the interviews of these three individuals because their philosophy about dialogue with victims and offenders as well as their practice is quite similar. This does not mean they are identical in their work, for they are definitely not. Yet what they shared permitted us to look at facilitated dialogue in violent crime through a lens somewhat different from the programs in Texas or Ohio, thereby expanding our understanding of the range of theory and practice. For discussion purposes, we have labeled this approach "Humanistic Dialogue," even though many practitioners refer to it as "humanistic mediation."

PHILOSOPHY AND PURPOSE

The purpose of Humanistic Dialogue with victims and perpetrators of violent crime is to bring the two parties together so they have the opportunity to tell their story of the crime event and its impact and to have questions answered. By the telling of the story, victims and even offenders, to some extent, may gain a feeling of empowerment, a sense of being more in control. And for both victim and offender, sharing their stories about the horrific event that so often shapes and defines their lives can be an important step on a lifelong healing journey.

Betty Brown became involved in this kind of work because "victims did not have a voice anywhere." Often the victim "just wants to know why." "They (the victim and offender) have been bonded whether they like it or not. This horrible, awful thing. They are bonded. What are they going to do about that?" Victims often want to know their loved one's "last words" or "did they die in pain...They have already thought the worst. They want to know no matter how awful it was...It is a matter of telling a shameful story. There is a lot of pain. A lot of shame."

Face-to-face conversations between the offender and the victim provide an opportunity for offenders "to get a very hurtful experience out into the open and it is such a relief for them to get it out into the open. I doubt that most of the inmates have ever told the story as truthfully."

Brown remained surprised at "the depth of information and pain that people need to share...As painful as some of this stuff is to hear, it is just so necessary, and the very worst thing has already happened. So, I don't have to worry about the damage because these victims already are in charge of that. And if we can be a conduit in a supportive way and not hesitate to seek out that which the victim needs and to ask those questions than no one else will ask, then we are doing the best that we can."

"A key is developing a level of trust with them (victim and offender)," said Bruce Kittle. "To me the goal is to create a safe place for the storytelling to happen; all the other stuff grows out of that." Questions of what and why underlie the story telling. It will take time for the victim to identify the questions; this is often done by sharing their story over and over with the mediator.

Work is done with offenders to deal with their fears regarding those questions as well as fears about sharing their stories. According to Kittle,

"We work a lot on storytelling: what happened. Realities of a lot of the offenders that I work with is that they are not able to express themselves, particularly their feelings...Sometimes they are afraid to talk about what actually happened. Sometimes they can't remember. So they tell me their stories. We go back and forth over them to work through the vulnerabilities around sharing emotional stuff."

Part of what happens in Humanistic Dialogue from Kittle's perspective is helping victims who have been shattered by violent crime to integrate and reconstruct reality so they can continue on. "I try to help them ask the difficult questions and give them some ideas. It's like the buoy is out there and you are sinking in this whole thing yet you can hang on to try to put those pieces back together." For victims who choose to participate in mediation, talking with and listening to the offender is one way to locate the pieces.

For Mark Umbreit, the objective of Humanistic Dialogue is to "create a safe place, if not a sacred place, where people can tell their story. Where they can share the pain and have it acknowledged." Listening to the victim's story and to the offender's story begins with initial contacts. "I emphasize really taking the time to listen deeply to the story of the person who is initiating this. The impact on their lives. Their personal contexts. Their network of support. How do their families feel about this? What do they want out of this? I don't get into a lot of questions. More often than not, they give me the information in their own time and their own way." While these words were used in the context of being with a victim, they also applied to being with an offender.

Umbreit described his approach as a mind/body/spirit approach. It involves "sensing the energy, literally — the energy I am feeling with this person and the energy I feel present." The approach integrates left-brain and right-brain functions. "There is left-brain stuff: case development, problem-solving, clearing the path." That which makes the dialogue "really powerful is what I call the peacemaking and spirituality dimension which is more right-brain. This is the more intuitive, the more circular; more comfortable with powerful emotions and even ambiguity. The mediator's role has far more to do with being than with doing. It requires deep, compassionate listening." Umbreit emphasizes "being fully present and supportive of the involved parties, being profoundly non-judgmental; honoring their strength and inner wisdom; respecting their needs and choices; and use of a very non-directive style of mediation;

and being mindful of not speaking too much while honoring the enormous healing power often found in silence."

This approach can make the mediator's role "deceptively simple." Mediators clear the path through the bureaucracy as well as through the baggage that each participant brings to the mediation. Preparation, as we will see, is extensive within the Humanistic Dialogue approach, requiring much listening and a fair amount of doing. Once the victim and offender come face-to-face, "our job," said Umbreit, "is to honor that safe place and to set the tone through the opening ritual and then to stay out of the way, which is one of the hardest things for any mediator or facilitator — to stay out of the way."

While each of these practitioners recognizes that going through the mediation process can be therapeutic for the victim and the offender, each makes it clear he/she is not doing therapy.

"This is not therapy," declared Umbreit. "It is incredibly therapeutic, as people report back, but it is not psychotherapy." While Kittle believes that therapy for victims and offenders is critical, that is not the focus of humanistic dialogue: "I've always encouraged other therapeutic contacts. I just don't feel like I'm one; I'm not trained enough. What I was there about was trying to set up a meeting for her to get what she wanted out of the face to face meeting." And Brown won't take a case if the victim has not worked with a therapist. "One of my rules," she said, "is that they've talked to a therapist, and they all have. I like that and I feel a relief by it; these folks are not in therapy with me."

While the Humanistic Dialogue approach to victim offender mediation attempts to balance the needs of victims with those of offenders, it is victim-driven. Each practitioner begins with the victim. "My approach is unequivocally victim-centered," stated Umbreit. "There is extra deference to the victim. You give the victim the first choice of what to do and when and then you negotiate with the offender if they are really upset with it."

MEDIATOR CHARACTERISTICS

We asked our interviewees what they would look for if they were hiring mediators or seeking volunteer mediators to work within this humanistic approach. Being "non-judgmental" was one characteristic identified. "They need to be open to hearing other people's stories and act in a way that is non-judgmental, not condemning." "Not judging them is pretty hard to do. It is very hard to do. But once you see them as human beings it is not so difficult."

Being self-aware was important. "You have to spend time searching yourself out: what pushes your buttons, what problems you have, and that kind of stuff." "Having gone through some therapy or counseling may be helpful, but that doesn't cut it by itself. One must be willing to ask for help." "You may have all the skill and all the understanding up in the head on trauma and recovery, but if you are not at peace with this stuff — if you are not able to be with suffering in a way that you do not run from it — then you cannot feel the pain."

Perhaps, not surprisingly for an approach that emphasizes telling the personal story of crime, capacity for deep listening is paramount to be an effective mediator. According to Umbreit, "To hear the story is to recognize and embrace the incredible healing power of storytelling — uninterrupted storytelling. Not active listening, not paraphrasing, but when you are fully present to listen from the heart. And time stops. Everything else is gone and you just listen." "More than tactical skills or conventional mediation skills, the nature of this work is about listening," said Kittle. "It is about listening in order to create a safe place, a real deep sense of safety that the people can be vulnerable with each other that allows them to reach that sense of empowerment and healing that they are looking fore, if that is what they are looking for." Brown agreed that "listening is critical. They have to be willing to hear lots of stuff."

Other qualifications identified by one or more of the participants were: willingness of mediators to develop a deep understanding of victimization; having a strong sense of intuition; being good communicators; having a sense of call or vocation; being able to collaborate with corrections staff; and possessing a sense of humility. Umbreit summarized the attributes of good humanistic mediators by simply saying, "They are people with a good heart and a good head."

PREPARATION

Within the Humanistic Dialogue approach, preparation is crucial and extensive, requiring a lot of contact and time. Betty Brown estimated that the average case requires six months to one year before the victim and offender meet face-to-face; most of the preparation time has to do with "the victims defining what it is they need." For Umbreit, that time frame was a year or more, often because of time required to work out logistics. And for Kittle the average preparation time was 18 months; Kittle also claimed that the length is determined by a number of factors, such as "their needs, my abilities, and sometimes a stuck system."

Brown described a case with an 11-year-old boy whose family was brutally killed while he was in the house. One of the offenders was credited with saving the young boy's life. The boy wanted to meet the offender who was involved in the killing of his family members but also wanted that offender's life to be spared. In that case, Brown met with the boy 10 or 12 times before a meeting with the offender was held. A co-worker also worked extensively with the boy and his remaining family, and the boy was seeing two therapists. As with most victims, the focus of preparation was on what the victim needed; in this case, the emphasis was on what he wanted to know. The boy developed his list of questions carefully. He did not want to go over the details of the murders. He wanted to know why: Why were others killed and he was not? And he wanted the "what ifs." If the offender had had a pager, would he have used it to page the police and possibly save somebody else? He agreed to have the session videotaped so he would have a record of what happened.

"Much of the preparation was done by my co-worker, an art therapist, who first met the boy. We wanted to know what he expected and if he understood the risks...We kept talking and talking. Each time he would come up with another question. Finally, there were several sessions when the list was set. We talked about what we do in a meeting."

We asked how Brown knew the boy was ready to meet. Her reply was: "A gut feeling (in addition to hearing no additional questions). His needs were no different than from an adult. He had to know what happened. He'd been through an extremely traumatic event and he needed others to acknowledge that."

Because of the particularly unusual characteristics of this case, Brown asked Umbreit to assist with some of the preparation work and to co-facilitate the actual meeting of the victim and offender. Typically, Brown reported that she would have several phone conversations with an offender while he is in prison. She wants to make the initial contact to explain the program and what typically happens, and what the victim needs. There is usually one face-to-face visit with the offender that is again followed by phone contacts. In Brown's experience, only one offender indicated that he had to think about whether to participate. While it is typical for victims to set boundaries during preparation about areas they do not want to discuss or hear about, this has not occurred in Brown's experience with offenders. "Basically, they go with the flow."

For victims and offenders, preparation may include showing videos of other mediations and the sharing of articles. Brown also shares information, with permission, from the preparation meetings with the other party. "So it is no secret what we are going to talk about. So they were really having a dialogue through me." Usually there are no surprises: "We talk enough and go over the day often enough and the impact of what's happened."

Brown tries to anticipate potential problems. For example, in the case referred to above, the young boy had some hearing problems and one of the participants was quite soft-spoken. The boy would raise a card with the picture of an ear on it if he was having difficulty hearing the speaker.

Preparation with the victim and with the offender for Umbreit begins with their story and being totally present to listen deeply. Through that heartfelt listening "you are witnessing their strength, their capacity to tell their story, what their needs are, what their expectations are…I only start imparting information after I have really tried to give them the opportunity, and it rarely isn't taken, to tell me their full story. And if things I need to know don't come out of their story, then I will go back and ask a little. But I don't probe or interrupt their storytelling."

One can "pick up all kinds of clues" during the storytelling. For example, Umbreit said, "You might hear that it was only through their priest or rabbi or shaman in their community of faith that they were able to deal with it (the victimization). That is a wonderful cue to ask if that person would want one or more of those people to be present."

Umbreit estimated that he meets an average of four to six times with each participant before the meeting between offender and victim occurs. And there are likely to be a number of phone contacts. Preparation typically includes a tour of the prison and meeting place a week or so in advance of the dialogue. Considerable time is spent on going over what to expect in the mediation in order to keep the expectations realistic. The guidelines or ground rules will be laid out. "Part of the preparation is making arrangements. I give the choice to the victim in particular but also try to include the offender." That will include choice of seating, who begins first after the opening, whether they would like support people or family members present, and in some cases, if requested, beginning the session with a prayer, a moment of silence, or the reading of a poem or a verse of scripture from their faith tradition. In some cultures, food would be expected as part of the dialogue or after the dialogue.

In response to a question about knowing when participants are ready to meet, Umbreit stressed the importance of the readiness of the mediator. "Ultimately and honestly, you trust your gut. The reason multiple meetings are needed is not just for the parties, it is for you too. It is very important as the mediator or facilitator to feel comfortable and ready to go. You are part of the process."

"The first two or three meetings with a victim revolve around explaining the process and helping them feel comfortable about making a decision whether they want to participate," explained Kittle. "I try not to go too far with them until the offender is contacted. The victim has told me some stories initially. It is really at their pace that we work."

Once the victim agrees to participate, a letter is sent to the offender seeking their willingness to meet. About 95% agree. After agreement, Kittle sets up a meeting with the offender and preparation begins to take a sharper focus. In his case, Kittle says it is very important to let the offender know that "I'm a lawyer, but I'm not your lawyer."

Early stages of preparation focus on "storytelling and trying to get clear what happened." Sometimes the victim and the offender differ regarding details. There will be situations where the offender will deny doing some things while taking responsibility for others. Such a denial will not come as a surprise if the preparation work has been carried out well. Often Kittle will have the victim and the offender write out their stories, particularly their impact statements. "I encourage them to work," stated Kittle. "I probably push it more with offenders to really recall the impact. With victims if they've written some stuff and they want to work with me on it and if it's helpful to them, we do that. But I've had victims who've never brought me the written part." Kittle uses worksheets similar to some used in the Texas program.

Determining readiness involves each of the participants including the mediator. "I'm always kind of checking with them throughout preparation," stated Kittle. He wants them to tell him when they are ready, but admits that he has a timeline in his head. He spoke of a victim who wanted to meet after only three months of preparation. "I was scared to death, but when I reviewed everything and looked at the parties there was nothing objectively that would indicate that they weren't ready. I felt real confident about her (the victim) and where she was coming from. We put it together and it was a very powerful meeting. It was a good lesson for me about kind of trusting the process."

Like Brown and Umbreit, Kittle will spend a fair amount of time going over expectations regarding the meeting, encouraging victims to tour the prison in advance, and making decisions regarding seating and speaking order.

Each of these three individuals also encourages victims and offenders to invite support persons to the mediation session. Kittle will try to meet with those persons individually. Sometimes it is not possible to meet in person, but each of the mediators tries to talk with support individuals before the face-to-face encounter. Support persons often provide transportation for the victim; it is not desirable for a victim to drive two or three hours afterward with out having someone to talk with. That support person will usually be with the victim after the meeting while the mediator does a quick check-in with the offender.

It is expected that the support persons will have non-speaking roles during the meeting, although occasionally they may be asked a question. Brown is most adamant about this: "I talk to them before the meeting to make sure they know their roles. So that I really am very clear that they are there for support only and they are not to open their mouth. I think people are so humbled by this experience that they wouldn't know what to say anyway." Depending upon the wishes of the victim, they may or may not sit at the table. Support persons for victims have included family members, friends, clergy, and therapists. Brown described a case where a sheriff came to the mediation, in part, because he had been so "traumatized" by the crime scene and in part to support the victim. In Brown's view, listening filled in a lot of gaps for him as well as being a "healing experience" for him. Brown suspects that we too often fail to realize that law enforcement and rescue personnel are frequently secondary victims of violent crime.

Most offenders do not have support persons; if they do, it usually is a prison counselor or chaplain.

MEETING

Each of the three mediators interviewed for this appendix handles face-to-face meetings in similar ways. Each will spend some time the day of the meeting being quiet, meditating, getting themselves centered, and prepared. Kittle stated, "It is really important for me, as I approach this, that I spend a lot of time, not just in the role of mediator but that I center myself in prayer and spirituality. I'm a firm believer that there is a power in the universe that connects us…and so part of my work for me is being able to feel, being in touch with that in a way that I can really hand the meeting off to that presence."

Each mediator will do a check-in with the victim and the offender before bringing them together "to go over immediate concerns or fears," "to review the ground rules," "affirm each person being there." Check-in may range from 15 minutes to an hour.

Some victims want to be seated first, while others prefer to have the offender in place before entering the room. Once seated, there may be a bit of silence just for folks to settle in. They know this will happen because the process has been reviewed "a dozen times," said Brown. Yet because the mediation setting is often so emotionally charged, she makes sure to remind them again before going into the room. Honoring the power of silence is central to humanistic dialogue, whether during preparation or during the actual face to face encounter.

Mediation sessions will usually last two to three hours. The mediator typically does a brief opening statement welcoming and thanks each person for being there. They are reminded that the conversation is to be between the two of them: "This is really meant to be a time for the two of you to tell your stories and there will be plenty of time for questions." The mediator will not do much talking. Either party can ask for a break at any time. The ground rules are "to listen respectfully and speak respectfully to each other; and that people won't do anything to intentionally hurt anyone." Umbreit described this opening ritual as "supremely important for creating that safe if not sacred place …It is less important what you say than how you say it. If you are nervous or sound like a stiff professional, that will not be conducive to people being vulnerable. I am much more focused on being fully present in the most comfortable way for them which is more conversational, natural and normalizing."

Increasingly, victims and offenders may work out in advance something they want to share as part of this opening ritual. It may be a poem, a candle, a piece of scripture, a prayer or anything that they requested and has been agreed before entering the room.

It will have been decided earlier who will speak first. Typically, the opportunity is given to the victim to speak first because he or she hasn't been able to do so in the criminal justice process. In any case, they have a choice to go first or not. From one mediator's experience the victim typically chose to go first; from another's experience victims wanted the offender to begin. In any case, "there are no surprises about who will speak first."

This is a pivotal moment when the mediator lets go of all the preparation and trusts what is about to unfold. Umbreit usually asks the following to the initial speaker: "Could you think back not just to how you are feeling now but when all of this began and the affect upon your life? Could you tell (the offender's name) what it was like?" And then, "I find myself often scooting my chair back and crossing my legs. With rare exception, those two or three minutes in which I gave the opening statement is 95% of all that I say. Typically in a three hour session I might also say a little transition thing and I'll always have a closing kind of ritual of just thanking parties for the work they have done and just kind of wrapping it up and pulling it together. We are not rephrasing or redirecting. We rarely need to. We are bearing witness to some of the most beautiful expressions of strength and compassion. And it is intense."

Like Umbreit, Brown and Kittle described their styles in the meeting as focused but non-directive. The bulk of their work has been done in preparation. Kittle noted that while the process "kind of follows the stages (what happened, impact, possible restorative steps) it also has its circular motion." He describes his role as helping with "transitions." He might ask for example, "We've talked a lot about what has happened, do you have any other questions or do you have anything you'd like to say abut what happened that you haven't already said?" Kittle described the victim's impact statement as an opportunity for the victim "to tell their personal story of how they were impacted by the offense...that is not a time where you get a lot of questions from the offender. It is usually a pretty humbling period." Again, after the victim has shared the impact, Kittle will check in to see if there is more from either party before moving on to what, if anything, can be done that is restorative. Sometimes all the victim wanted was the meeting and the answers. Sometimes a formal letter of apology is desired or perhaps asking the offender to do something for the larger community. Kittle will summarize this for the participants, but not ask them to sign anything. He will later send copies of his summary of the agreement to the victim and to the offender to be approved.

Betty Brown provided a window onto that initial interaction between offender and victim in the following way: "Usually at the beginning, after a couple of sentences, it seems like the victim bursts out crying. And I think that is just a relief of being there and it is a wonderful release. After that, they are back to telling their stories. It is almost like taking a deep breath and saying, well, let me tell you what has happened. Let me tell you about that day for me. The offenders have been so respectful and able to look the victim in the eyes. They really want this. They go through this trial where they are told, 'don't look at them, don't talk to them, you'll be in trouble.' Then I hear victims telling me, 'well that S.O.B. wouldn't even look at me in the courtroom and pled not guilty, can you believe that?' Well, yes I can because they have to. So it is profound, but they (offenders) are ready for this and terrified, you can almost see their hearts beating under their shirts, to have this connection."

Each mediator mentioned that often interaction spontaneously occurs after the mediation is completed, as individuals are preparing to leave the room. There are those "beautiful moments," according to Umbreit, when "these people walk up to each other or lean over across the table toward each other eight inches from each others face and just talk and share stuff they probably didn't even share in the session."

After the meeting, these mediators will do a check-in or debriefing with the victim and the offender. Brown explained: "It (check-in) seems like it's shorter with the inmate. They are really ready to go back and think. I always check with them though to make sure they are all right." Sometimes she encourages them to talk with their counselor. A couple she has known walked out "into the yard because that was a safe place to cry." Umbreit will also meet immediately afterwards to ask, "How did it go?" or whether there are any regrets. Kittle also checks in with both offender and victim to see if they are okay. "We just kind of talk about self-care during preparation," said Kittle. "We talk about how hard it is to go back to your regular life. We encourage them to take a day off from work."

FOLLOW-UP

Each of these mediators is open to some sort of follow-up with the victim and offender. In Kittle's approach that follow-up is a bit more structured than with the others. He will call to let the victim know that the summary and evaluation form is being sent in the mail, and will check on how the victim is doing at that time. A similar call will likely be made to the inmate's social worker. "At that point the case is kind of closed," said Kittle, "but then six months later I may get a call from a victim who just wants to talk. I don't have active contact and I work really hard (in advance) to let them know so they are not feeling let down or betrayed that while we are really, really close for all this time — and it is an intense relationship — due to the nature of the work, I must move on to the next one." He helps them find local support, "And I am always there for a phone call, if they need one." Kittle also sees a time in the future where more work will be done with the victim who has chosen to meet the offender and other victims from the same crime who have not. Often considerable conflict exists among family members. Frequently, victims will have family members who are vehemently opposed to the victim's meeting with the offender. One relative described by Brown, who did not attend the mediation, was furious after he watched the resulting video of the meeting. He complained, "I didn't want him to be a human being and look at that."

Another future possibility is working with members of the victim's family and with those of the offender's family. Often, particularly in small towns and rural communities, these families have known each other for years and their pain as a result of the crime "is probably more common and more similar than it is separate." And unless someone moves, these families will continue living together in the same community.

"There is follow-up ranging from a phone call a few weeks later to follow-up mediation sessions," reported Umbreit. These contacts are typically "victim-driven." Further contact is sometimes desired because the participants feel that the mediator has shared with them a very intense and powerful "altered state of consciousness, where time both moves quick and slowly." Occasionally, the victim or offender may have been overwhelmed and need to talk about that experience, perhaps even seeking clarification or confirmation of what was said.

Brown usually lets the participants sit with their experiences for a couple of months and then will check in by phone. "Each case is unique, but the sense of closure is phenomenal. They may just want to check one or two things out." She recounted the following interaction with a victim that underscores not only a victim's continued reaching out to the mediator but also continuing awareness of the offender: "She called me and said, 'I just read the inmate's mom just died. Could you check and see how he's doing? I wonder if he thought about me and my daughter.' He couldn't go to the funeral. So I am going to visit with him next month."

"About a half dozen victims have stayed in contact," said Brown. " I asked them individually if they would like to meet with other folks who have met the person who killed their loved ones." A date has been agreed upon. There is a continuing need that this group may meet. "There are issues that their friends and family do not want to hear about, and they want to know about. Maybe they just need to talk to each other."

As with other approaches, achieving closure is difficult. There remains a fine line between the usual follow-up regarding unanswered questions, recall of what actually happened during the mediation, and moving on with one's life on the one hand, versus the longer-run continuing care issues on the other.

FORGIVENESS

As we have discovered in Texas and Ohio, the notion of forgiveness is on the minds of many victims and offenders. Some victims are nauseated by the very notion of forgiving the person who claimed the life of a loved one. Some feel compelled, perhaps by their religious training, to somehow be able to forgive. Some offenders explicitly want to be forgiven. Others feel so shamed by their own actions that they would have a hard time accepting forgiveness. Into this human, emotional, spiritual morass mediators adapting a humanistic dialogue approach tread lightly.

"I do not verbally at any point in the preparation process use the R-word or the F-word, reconciliation or forgiveness," claimed Umbreit. "However, if they use the word, I view that as a wonderful opportunity to explore why this is important to them." If it is meant to happen, forgiveness will emerge spontaneously. Umbreit does not want to become "preachy" or feed into unrealistic expectations. He cautions the offender who seeks forgiveness not to do so in a mediation unless the victim raises the issue. There is a concern that an offender's need to be forgiven can revictimize the victim. "Victims have a right to the rage they have felt at different points along the way," commented Umbreit. If there is to be forgiveness, it must be genuine and freely given.

In Betty Brown's experience, the question of forgiveness has only come up in two or three cases. "If I heard an offender say that they wanted forgiveness, I would say that this is not what this is about," said Brown. Occasionally, forgiveness will come up during preparation with a victim who says, 'I'll never forgive him.' "Forgiveness is absolutely up to them," explained Brown. "I do not bring it up." She elaborated: "Very often victims of this very awful kind of crime leave their churches because they hear you have to forgive them (the offenders) and that there is more support for offenders in churches than for victims. So some come with a chip saying, 'I'm not going to forgive them.'"

Even Bruce Kittle, trained in theology and pastoral care as well as in law, is cautious about the place of forgiveness in victim offender dialogue. "I never encourage or force a victim to forgive, that is totally wrong," Kittle explained. "We talk about what forgiveness means; its role in this. Is it important to you? Do you want to talk about it? Should we explore that? But again, it's all abut victim choice and my job is just to be aware of it, to be thinking about it, and to encourage them to make intelligent choices about what they want out of the meeting and what is important to them."

Kittle is very concerned about what too often transpires within churches vis-à-vis victims of violent crimes. "They are revictimized by their faith communities," he said. "It's terrible because they go through terrible treatment by the system and then here they are trying to turn to their faith community and they are alienated and then they have a pastor telling them, 'Well, God requires you to forgive the person who killed your son.' Then they are done. They are out of that community and are totally alienated and what good is their faith then?" Kittle would like to see much more work being done with pastors around the issues of victimology.

So there are those, such as some clergy, who perhaps push prematurely for forgiveness, and there are victim advocates who "recoil against the idea of forgiveness so strongly that they don't create an environment where victims can work toward it if they want to." Kittle said, "I find victim advocates kind of speaking on behalf of victims when I feel like they prevent choice."

It is also critical from Kittle's perspective to be open to the offender's questions and concerns about forgiveness. This is part of the preparation before going to a meeting. "It is really important work," explained Kittle, "because their soul in this offense, voluntary or involuntary, is often really just ripped apart."

Still, forgiveness resides with the victim and there is no pressure to forgive prematurely. Kittle informs the victims he works with: "You are the one that suffered in this and forgiveness is a piece that you can deal with in your own time."

MEDIATOR SELF-CARE

"I am usually whipped then, absolutely whipped," said Betty Brown speaking about her own feelings immediately after sitting through a mediation.

There is little doubt for any of these mediators that self-care is a top priority enabling them to sit through the stories of pain, grief and shattered dreams that victims and offenders share. Brown felt she had an advantage working for victim services because others there knew what it was like to work with victims of violent crime and were a "wonderful support" for her. She also works out in a gym, eats reasonably well, does a lot of reading. The awe with which she holds the people she works with — the victims and the offenders — is expressed during alone time in her journaling. In that way, she keeps and honors her own ongoing story.

"The connection to this work for me is very spiritual," said Kittle. "So a regular routine for me includes daily devotions and daily prayer. The closer I get to the meeting the longer these periods of prayer are through a kind of centering." Another release of anxiety and stress for Kittle is found in physical exercise. He lifts weights, runs, swims and bikes. Also useful is debriefing with a co-facilitator, if there was another one.

Although this work is intense, Kittle finds it also advancing his own self-care. "Because I work with crime victims and the pain of offenders, the humanness and the pain of those realities are just really close to my heart. I feel it much easier to express my own emotions and letting them come out." He also spoke to a kind of self-care with which many in the field struggle: "I think keeping it all in perspective is important. I don't carry the need on my shoulders to fix victims, or to fix offenders. I feel like we are creating opportunities for them to grow and to heal themselves."

Like the others, Umbreit too sees the necessity of devoting considerable time to self-care. "I daily spend a significant period of time in meditation and prayer. Prior to preparation meetings and the actual mediation session, I also try to become more centered and focused through taking several deep breaths and spending a few moments in meditation with eyes closed unless circumstances do not allow for this." He also routinely does physical exercise including brisk walking and jogging, as well as reading both inspirational books and great novels.

CONCLUSION

While these three practitioners and spokespersons for Humanistic Dialogue offer differing viewpoints at times and implement the humanistic approach somewhat differently, they do share an overarching philosophy and commitment that emphasizes bringing victim and offender together in face-to-face encounter wherein each person's story regarding the crime and its impact may be shared.

Through the telling of the stories, anger, pain, shame, compassion and perhaps seeds of renewed hope are expressed. The humanity of each participant is lifted up and heard. Through the honoring of the story, those who feel powerless experience the power of their own story as well as that of the other. Through the honoring of story, the potential for healing, for letting go, for integrating the horrors caused by one person against another may be enhanced.

REFERENCES

American Bar Association (1994). "Criminal Justice Policy on Victim-Offender Mediation/Dialogue." Approved August 1994.

Austin, J. and B. Krisberg (1981). "Wider, Stronger, and Different Nets: The Dialectics of Criminal Justice Reform." *Journal of Research in Crime and Delinquency* 18:165-196.

Babbie. E.R. (2001). *The Practice of Social Research* (9th ed.). Belmont, CA: Wadsworth.

Bazemore, G. and M.S. Umbreit (1995). "Rethinking the Sanctioning Function in Juvenile Court: Retributive or Restorative Responses to Youth Crime." *Crime & Delinquency* 41(3):296-316.

―― and L. Walgrave (1999). "Introduction: Restorative Justice and the International Juvenile Justice Crisis." In: G. Bazemore and L. Walgrave (eds.), *Restorative Juvenile Justice: Repairing the Harm of Youth Crime*. Monsey, NY: Criminal Justice Press.

Binder, A. and G. Geis (1984). "Ad Populum Argumentation in Criminology: Juvenile Diversion as Rhetoric." *Crime & Delinquency* 30:624-247.

Bradshaw, W. and M.S. Umbreit (1998). "Crime Victims Meet Juvenile Offenders: Contributing Factors to Victim Satisfaction With Mediated Dialogue." *Juvenile and Family Court Journal* 49(3):17-25.

Braithwaite, J. (1989). *Crime, Shame and Reintegration*. Cambridge, UK: Cambridge University Press.

Bush, R.A.B. and J.P. Folger (1994). *The Promise of Mediation*. San Francisco, CA: Jossey-Bass.

Carr, C. (1998). *VORS Program Evaluation Report*. Inglewood, CA: Centenela Valley Juvenile Diversion Project.

Clarke, S., E. Valente and R. Mace (1992). *Mediation of Interpersonal Disputes: An Evaluation of North Carolina's Programs*. Chapel Hill, NC: Institute of Government, University of North Carolina.

Coates, R.B., A.D. Miller and L.E. Ohlin (1978). *Diversity in a Youth Correctional System: Handling Delinquents in Massachusetts*. Cambridge, MA: Ballinger.

―― and J. Gehm (1985). *Victim Meets Offender: An Evaluation of Victim-Offender Reconciliation Programs*. Valparaiso, IN: PACT Institute of Justice.

—— and J. Gehm (1989). "An Empirical Assessment." In: M. Wright and B. Galaway (eds.), *Mediation and Criminal Justice*. London, UK: Sage.

—— M.S. Umbreit and B. Vos (2000). *Restorative Justice Circles in South Saint Paul, Minnesota*. St. Paul, MN: Center for Restorative Justice & Peacemaking.

—— H. Burns and M.S. Umbreit (2002). *Victim Participation in Victim Offender Conferencing: Washington County, Minnesota Community Justice Program*. St. Paul, MN: Center for Restorative Justice & Peacemaking.

Collins, J.P. (1984). *Final Evaluation Report on the Grande Prairie Community Reconciliation Project For Young Offenders*. Ottawa, CAN: Ministry of the Solicitor General of Canada, Consultation Centre (Prairies).

Council of Europe, Committee of Ministers (1999). "Mediation in Penal Matters." Recommendation No. R(99)19 Adopted 15 September 1999.

Davis, R., M. Tichane and D. Grayson (1980). *Mediation and Arbitration as Alternatives to Prosecution in Felony Arrest Cases. An Evaluation of the Brooklyn Dispute Resolution Center*. New York, NY: Vera Institute of Justice.

Dignan, J. (1990). *Repairing the Damage: An Evaluation of an Experimental Adult Reparation Scheme in Kettering, Northamptonshire*. Sheffield, UK: Centre for Criminological Legal Research, Faculty of Law, University of Sheffield.

Evje, A. and R. Cushman (2000). *A Summary of the Evaluations of Six California Victim Offender Reconciliation Programs*. San Francisco, CA: Judicial Council of California, Administrative Office of the Courts.

Fercello, C. and M.S. Umbreit (1999). *Client Satisfaction with Victim Offender Conferences in Dakota County, Minnesota*. St. Paul, MN: Center for Restorative Justice & Peacemaking.

Flaten, C. (1996). "Victim Offender Mediation: Application with Serious Offences Committed by Juveniles." In: B. Galaway and J. Hudson (eds.), *Restorative Justice: International Perspectives*. Monsey, NY: Criminal Justice Press.

Galaway, B. (1989). "Informal Justice: Mediation between Offenders and Victims." In: P. Albrecht and O. Backes (eds.), *Crime Prevention and Intervention: Legal and Ethical Problems*. New York, NY: Walter de Gruyter.

—— (1995). "Victim-Offender Mediation by New Zealand Probation Officers: The Possibilities and the Reality." *Mediation Quarterly* 12:249-262.

Gehm, J. (1990). "Mediated Victim-Offender Restitution Agreements: An Exploratory Analysis of Factors Related to Victim Participation." In: B. Galaway and J. Hudson (eds.), *Criminal Justice, Restitution, and Reconciliation*. Monsey, NY: Criminal Justice Press.

Gustafson, D.L. and H. Smidstra (1989). *Victim Offender Reconciliation in Serious Crime: A Report on the Feasibility Study Undertaken for the Ministry of the Solicitor General (Canada).* Langley, BC: Fraser Region Community Justice Initiatives Association.

Hughes, S. and A. Schneider (1990). *Victim-Offender Mediation in the Juvenile Justice System.* Washington, DC: U.S. Office of Juvenile Justice and Delinquency Prevention.

Latimer, J., C. Dowden and D. Muise (2001). *The Effectiveness of Restorative Practice: A Meta-analysis.* Ottawa, CAN: Department of Justice, Research and Statistics Division Methodological Series.

Marshall, T. (1990). "Results of Research from British Experiments in Restorative Justice." In: B. Galaway and J. Hudson (eds.), *Criminal Justice, Restitution, and Reconciliation.* Monsey, NY: Criminal Justice Press.

McCold, P. and B. Wachtel (1998). *Restorative Policing Experiment: The Bethlehem Pennsylvania Police Family Group Conferencing Project.* Pipersville, PA: Community Service Foundation.

Miers, D., M. Maguire, S. Goldie, K. Sharpe, C. Hale, A. Netten, S. Uglow, K. Doolin, A. Hallam, J. Enterkin, and T. Newburn (2001). *An Exploratory Evaluation of Restorative Justice Schemes. Executive Summary.* (Crime Reduction Research Series Paper 9.) London, UK: Home Office.

Minnesota Department of Public Safety (1996). *Survey of Minnesota Victim Service Providers.* Minneapolis, MN: Department of Public Safety.

Nelson, S. (2000). *Evaluation of the Restorative Justice Program.* Eugene, OR: Lane County Department of Youth Services.

Niemeyer, M. and D. Shichor (1996). "A Preliminary Study of a Large Victim/Offender Reconciliation Program." *Federal Probation* 60(3):30-34.

Nugent, W.R. and J.B. Paddock (1995). "The Effect of Victim-Offender Mediation on Severity of Reoffense." *Mediation Quarterly* 12:353-367.

—— M.S. Umbreit, L. Wiinamaki and J. Paddock (1999). "Participation in Victim-Offender Mediation and Severity of Subsequent Delinquent Behavior: Successful Replications?" *Journal of Research in Social Work Practice* 11(1):5-23.

—— M. Williams and M.S. Umbreit (forthcoming) "Participation in Victim-Offender Mediation and the Prevalence and Severity of Subsequent Behavior." *Utah Law Review.*

Office for Victims of Crime (2000). "The Restorative Justice and Mediation Collection: Executive Summary." *OVC Bulletin,* July. Washington, DC: U.S. Department of Justice.

Peachey, D.E. (1989). "The Kitchener Experiment." In: M. Wright and B. Galaway (eds.), *Mediation and Criminal Justice*. London, UK: Sage

Perry, L., T. Lajeunesse and A. Woods (1987). *Mediation Services: An Evaluation*. Manitoba, CAN: Manitoba Attorney General: Research, Planning and Evaluation.

Pranis K. and M.S. Umbreit (1992). *Public Opinion Research Challenges Perception of Widespread Public Demand for Harsher Punishment*. Minneapolis, MN: Citizens Council.

Radelet, M. and M. Borg (2000). "Comment on Umbreit and Vos." *Homicide Studies* 4:1:88-92

Roberts, L. (1998). "Victim Offender Mediation: An Evaluation of the Pima County Juvenile Court Center's Victim Offender Mediation Program (VOMP)." Masters thesis, University of Arizona Department of Communications, Tucson, AZ.

Roberts, T. (1995). *Evaluation of the Victim Offender Mediation Project, Langley, BC: Final Report*. Victoria, BC: Focus Consultants.

Roy, S. (1993). "Two Types of Juvenile Restitution Programs in Two Midwestern Counties: A Comparative Study." *Federal Probation* 57(4):48-53.

Schiff, M. (1999). "The Impact of Restorative Interventions on Juvenile Offenders." In: G. Bazemore and L. Walgrave (eds.), *Restorative Juvenile Justice: Repairing the Harm of Youth Crime*. Monsey, NY: Criminal Justice Press.

Schneider, A. (1986). "Restitution and Recidivism Rates of Juvenile Offenders: Results from Four Experimental Studies." *Criminology* 24:533-552.

Stone, K. (2000). "An Evaluation of Recidivism Rates for Resolutions Northwest's Victim-Offender Mediation Program." Masters Thesis, Portland State University, Portland, OR.

Stone, S., W. Helms and P. Edgeworth (1998). *Cobb County (Georgia) Juvenile Court Mediation Program Evaluation*. Carrolton, GA: State University of West Georgia.

Strode, E. (1997). "Victims of Property Crime Meet Their Juvenile Offenders: Victim Participants' Evaluation of the Dakota County (MN) Community Corrections Victim Offender Meeting Program." Masters Thesis, Smith College of Social Work, Northampton, MA.

Umbreit, M.S. (1988). "Mediation of Victim Offender Conflict." *Journal of Dispute Resolution* 1988:85-105.

—— (1989a). "Crime Victims Seeking Fairness, Not Revenge: Toward Restorative Justice." *Federal Probation* 53(3): 52-57.

—— (1989b). "Violent Offenders and Their Victims." In: M. Wright and B. Galaway (eds.), *Mediation and Criminal Justice*. London, UK: Sage.

—— (1991). "Minnesota Mediation Center Produces Positive Results." *Corrections Today* (August):194-197.

—— (1992). "Victims of Violence Confront the Offender" (Editorial). *National Victim Center Newsletter* 7(1):6.

—— (1994). *Victim Meets Offender: The Impact of Restorative Justice and Mediation*. Monsey, NY: Criminal Justice Press.

—— (1995). *Mediation of Criminal Conflict: An Assessment of Programs in Four Canadian Provinces*. St. Paul, MN: Center for Restorative Justice & Peacemaking.

—— (1996). "Restorative Justice Through Mediation: The Impact of Programs in Four Canadian Provinces." In: B. Galaway and J. Hudson (eds.), *Restorative Justice: International Perspectives*. Monsey, NY: Criminal Justice Press

—— (1997). "Humanistic Mediation: A Transformative Journey of Peacemaking." *Mediation Quarterly* 14:201-213.

—— (2001). *The Handbook of Victim Offender Mediation: An Essential Guide to Practice and Research*. San Francisco, CA: Jossey-Bass.

—— and R.B. Coates (1992). *Victim Offender Mediation: An Analysis of Programs in Four States of the US*. St. Paul, MN: Center for Restorative Justice & Peacemaking.

—— and A.W. Roberts (1996). *Mediation of Criminal Conflict in England: An Assessment of Services in Coventry and Leeds*. St. Paul, MN: Center for Restorative Justice & Peacemaking.

—— and W. Bradshaw (1997). "Victim Experience of Meeting Adult vs. Juvenile Offenders: A Cross-National Comparison." *Federal Probation* 61(4):33-39.

—— R.B. Coates and A.W. Roberts (1998). "Impact of Victim-Offender Mediation in Canada, England and the United States." *The Crime Victim Report* (January/February):20-92.

—— and W. Bradshaw (1999). "Factors that Contribute to Victim Satisfaction with Mediated Offender Dialogue in Winnipeg: An Emerging Area of Social Work Practice." *Journal of Law and Social Work* 9(2):35-51.

—— W. Bradshaw and R.B. Coates (1999). "Victims of Severe Violence Meet the Offender: Restorative Justice Through Dialogue." *International Review of Victimology* 6(4):321-344.

—— and K. Brown (1999). "Victims of Severe Violence Meet the Offender in Ohio." *The Crime Victim Report* 3(3):35-36.

—— and J. Greenwood (1999). "National Survey of Victim Offender Mediation Programs in the US." *Mediation Quarterly* 16:235-251.

—— and W. Bradshaw (2000). *Assessing Victim Satisfaction with Victim Offender Mediation and Dialogue Services: The Development and Use of the Victim Satisfaction with Offender Meeting Scale (VSOM).* Washington, DC: U.S. Department of Justice, Office for Victims of Crime.

—— and B. Vos (2000). "Homicide Survivors Meet the Offender Prior to Execution: Restorative Justice Through Dialogue." *Homicide Studies* 4(1):63-87.

—— R.B. Coates and B. Vos (2001) *Juvenile Victim Offender Mediation in Six Oregon Counties.* Salem, OR: Oregon Dispute Resolution Commission.

—— R.B. Coates and B. Vos (2002). "The Impact of Restorative Justice Conferencing: A Multi-national Perspective." *British Journal of Community Justice* 1(2):21-48.

—— J. Greenwood, J. Umbreit and C. Fercello (2003). *Directory of Victim Offender Mediation Programs in the U.S.* St. Paul, MN: Center for Restorative Justice & Peacemaking.

United Nations (2000). "Basic Principles on the Use of Restorative Justice Programmes in Criminal Matters." ECOSOC Res. 2000/14. Adopted 27 July 2000.

Van Ness, D., A. Morris and G. Maxwell (2001). "Introducing Restorative Justice." In: A. Morris and G. Maxwell (eds.), *Restorative Justice for Juveniles: Conferencing, Mediation and Circles.* Portland, OR: Hart.

—— and K. Heetderks (2002). *Restoring Justice* (2nd ed.). Cincinnati, OH: Anderson Publishing Company.

Warner, S. (1992). *Making Amends: Justice for Victims and Offenders.* Aldershot, UK: Avebury.

Wiinamaki, L. (1997). "Victim-Offender Reconciliation Programs: Juvenile Property Offender Recidivism and Severity of Reoffense in Three Tennessee Counties." Doctoral dissertation, School of Social Work, University of Tennessee, Knoxville, TN.

Wright, M. (1996). *Justice for Victims and Offenders: A Restorative Response to Crime* (2nd ed.). Winchester, UK: Waterside Press.

Wynne, J. (1996). "Leeds Mediation and Reparation Service: Ten Years Experience of Victim-Offender Mediation." In: B. Galaway and J. Hudson (eds.), *Restorative Justice: International Perspectives.* Monsey, NY: Criminal Justice Press.

—— and I. Brown (1998). "Can Mediation Cut Reoffending?" *Probation Journal* 45: 21-26.

Wyrick, P. and M. Costanzo (1999). "Predictors of Client Participation in Victim-Offender Mediation." *Mediation Quarterly* 16:253-257.

Zehr, H. (1990). *Changing Lenses: A New Focus For Crime and Justice.* Scottsdale, PA: Herald Press.

—— (2002). *The Little Book of Restorative Justice.* Intercourse, PA: Good Books.